Visual QuickStart Guide

Illustrator 9

for Windows and Macintosh

Elaine Weinmann
Peter Lourekas

Peachpit Press

For Simona

Visual QuickStart Guide
Illustrator 9 for Windows and Macintosh
Elaine Weinmann and Peter Lourekas

Peachpit Press
1249 Eighth Street
Berkeley, CA 94710
510/524-2178
800/283-9444
510/524-2221 (fax)

Find us on the World Wide Web at: http://www.peachpit.com

Visual QuickStart Guide is a trademark of Peachpit Press, a
division of Addison Wesley Longman

Cover design: The Visual Group
Interior design: Elaine Weinmann
Production: Elaine Weinmann and Peter Lourekas
Illustrations: Elaine Weinmann and Peter Lourekas,
except as noted

Colophon
This book was created with QuarkXPress 4.0 on a Macintosh
G3 and a G4. The fonts used are Sabon, Gill Sans, and
CaflischScript from Adobe Systems Inc.

ISBN 0-201-70898-1
9 8 7 6 5 4 3 2 1

Printed and bound in the United States of America

Chris Spollen

Special thanks to

All the incredibly creative—and skilled—*artists* listed on the next page, whose illustrations appear in the color insert. In order to show Illustrator's range, we chose artists whose work represents a wide variety of styles and venues: maps, book covers, magazine covers, greeting cards, advertisements, medical illustrations, editorial illustrations, self-promos, logos, and more. Their work will provide an invaluable source of inspiration to our readers.

Nancy Aldrich-Ruenzel, Publisher, Peachpit Press; *Marjorie Baer,* Executive Editor; *Cary Norsworthy,* our Editor; *Kate Reber,* Production Coordinator; *Mimi Heft,* for her beautiful cover design; *Gary-Paul Prince,* Publicist; *Keasley Jones,* Associate Publisher; and the rest of the gang at Peachpit Press. They are really and truly a pleasure to work with.

Victor Gavenda, sharp Technical Editor at Peachpit Press, for his thorough and meticulous testing.

Frith Breitzer, freelance writer, for revising the Output/Export and Web chapters.

Jane Taylor Starwood and *Leona Benten* for proofreading and copy editing.

Emily Glossbrenner, of FireCrystal Communications, for indexing.

Mies Hora of Ultimate Symbol, for the extremely useful Design Elements CD. Contact Ultimate Symbol at www.ultimatesymbol.com.

Ted Alspach, Paul Asente, Paul George, Asako Yoshimura, and *Marcus Chang* at Adobe Systems, Inc., for their assistance.

The Artists

The Artists

Peter Fahrni
Voice 212-472-7126
fahrni@infohouse.com
www.fahrnidesign.com
192, 193

Barbara Friedman
Voice 212-533-9535
BatBF@aol.com
barbstudio@hotmail.com
www.theispot.com/artist/
friedman
color section

Yoshinori Kaizu
2-14-4, Kugahara
Ohta-ku, Tokyo 146-0085
Japan
Voice +81 3-3755-8704
Fax +81 3-3755-2186
y@kaizu.com
www.kaizu.com
color section

Diane Margolin
41 Perry Street
New York, NY 10014
Voice 212-691-9537
dimargolin@erols.com
*53, 67, 68, 95, 114, 122, 148,
154, 250, 251, 254, 262, 263,
288, 337, 339, 356*

Led Pants
led@ledpants.com
www.ledpants.com
color section

Chris Spollen

Daniel Pelavin
80 Varick Street
New York, NY 10013
Voice 212-941-7418
Fax 212-431-7138
daniel@pelavin.com
www.pelavin.com
*iii, v, vii, viii, xi, xiii, xiv, 59, 60,
61, 155, 315, 469, color section*

Marti Shohet
32 West 83rd Street, #6
New York, NY 10024
Voice/Fax 212-362-9082
mshohet@mindspring.com
www.theispot.com/artist/mshohet
color section

Jim Spiece
Spiece Graphics
6636 Quail Ridge Lane
Ft. Wayne, IN 46804-2876
Voice/Fax 219-436-9549
sggraphics@earthlink.net
www.theispot.com/artist/jspiece
color section

Chris Spollen
Moonlight Press Studio
362 Cromwell Avenue
Ocean Breeze, NY 10305-2304
Voice 718-979-9695
Fax 718-979-8919
cspollen@inch.com
www.spollen.com
*iii, iv, 61, 125, 275, 429 color
section*

Nancy Stahl
470 West End Avenue, 8G
New York, NY 10024
Voice 212-362-8779
Fax 212-362-7511
nancy@nancystahl.com
www.nancystahl.com
391, color section

Mark Stein
Mark Stein Studios
73-01 Juniper Valley Road
Middle Village NY 11379
Voice 718-326-4839
steinstudios@worldnet.att.net
www.theispot.com/artist/mstein
xxiv, 235, color section

Bart Vallecoccia,
medical illustrator
164 Manitoba Street
Toronto, ON, M8Y 1E3
Canada
Voice 416-255-7499
bartv@interlog.com
bartv@sympatico.ca
www.interlog.com/~bartv
color section

TABLE OF CONTENTS

Illustrator 9: New or substantially changed features are listed in **boldface**.

Chapter 2: **How Illustrator Works**

Chapter 3: **Startup**

Daniel Pelavin

Chapter 4: **Views**

Chapter 5: **Objects Basics**

Table of Contents

Daniel Pelavin

Daniel Pelavin

Table of Contents

Daniel Pelavin

Table of Contents

Daniel Pelavin

Table of Contents

Daniel Pelavin

Table of Contents

Table of Contents

Chapter 19: **Masks/Transparency**

Chapter 20: Filters

Chapter 21: Precision Tools

Table of Contents

Chapter 25: Separations

Chapter 26: Web

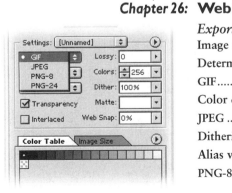

Table of Contents

©Mark Stein, Mark Stein Studios

Table of Contents

ILLUSTRATOR INTERFACE

This chapter is an introduction to Illustrator's tools, menus, palettes, and measurement systems.

Note: *If you'd like to glance on screen at the features discussed in this chapter as you read, launch Illustrator and create a new document (see pages 37–41).*

Chris Spollen

Pick your own *new*

To assign your own shortcuts for tools or commands, check out the new **Keyboard Shortcuts** dialog box (see pages 467–468).

Hide/show

Tab	Hide/show all currently open palettes, including the Toolbox
Shift-Tab	Hide/show all currently open palettes except the Toolbox

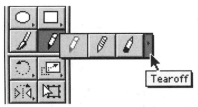

1 *Drag a pop-out menu away from the Toolbox by choosing the tearoff bar.*

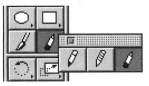

2 *A tearoff toolbar is created.*

Tools
Using the Toolbox

The Toolbox contains 53 tools that are used for object creation and modification. If the Toolbox is hidden, choose Window menu > Show Tools to display it. Drag the top bar to move the Toolbox. Click once on a visible tool to select it. Press on a tool with a little triangle to choose a related tool from a pop-out menu. Double-clicking some tools will open an options dialog box for that tool.

To **separate** a pop-out menu from the Toolbox **1**–**2**, release the mouse when it's over the vertical tearoff bar on the far right side of the menu. Move a tearoff toolbar by dragging its top bar. To restore a tearoff toolbar to the Toolbox, click its close box.

To access a tool quickly, use its letter **shortcut** (see the boldface letters on the next two pages). Some tools can be accessed using a toggle key (e.g., press Command/Ctrl to access the Selection when the Pen tool is chosen). We'll teach you the toggles later.

To turn tool pointers into a **crosshair** for precise positioning, check the Use Precise Cursors box in Edit menu > Preferences > General. Or press Caps Lock to turn a tool pointer into a crosshair temporarily.

➤ You'll probably want to leave the Disable Warnings box unchecked in Edit menu > Preferences > General. With this option unchecked, an alert prompt will appear when a tool is being used incorrectly.

The Toolbox

*Note: Many of the shortcuts are changed. You can no longer cycle through related tools using Shift. To **assign your own shortcuts** for tools, see page 467.*

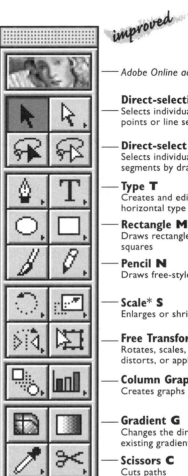

improved

— Adobe Online access

Direct-selection A
Selects individual anchor points or line segments

V Selection
Selects entire objects

new

Y Lasso
Selects entire objects by dragging

Direct-select Lasso Q
Selects individual points or segments by dragging

new

P Pen
Draws curved and straight line segments

Type T
Creates and edits horizontal type

L Ellipse
Draws ovals and circles

Rectangle M
Draws rectangles and squares

B Paintbrush
Creates calligraphic, scatter, art, or pattern brushstrokes

Pencil N
Draws free-style lines

R Rotate*
Rotates objects

Scale* S
Enlarges or shrinks objects

O Reflect*
Creates a mirror image of an object

Free Transform* E
Rotates, scales, reflects, shears, distorts, or applies perspective

W Blend*
Creates shape and color blends between objects

Column Graph J
Creates graphs

U Gradient Mesh
Creates and edits multicolored gradient objects

Gradient G
Changes the direction of existing gradients

I Eyedropper
Samples paint or type attributes

Scissors C
Cuts paths

H Hand
Moves the artboard in the document window

Zoom Z
Magnifies or reduces the view size of an illustration

X Fill
Color that is applied inside a path

Swap fill/stroke (Shift-X)

D Default fill and stroke colors

Stroke X
Color that is applied to the edge of a path

> Gradient

< Color

None /

F Standard screen mode

Full screen mode F

Full screen mode with menu bar F

*Transformation tools

The tool pop-out menus

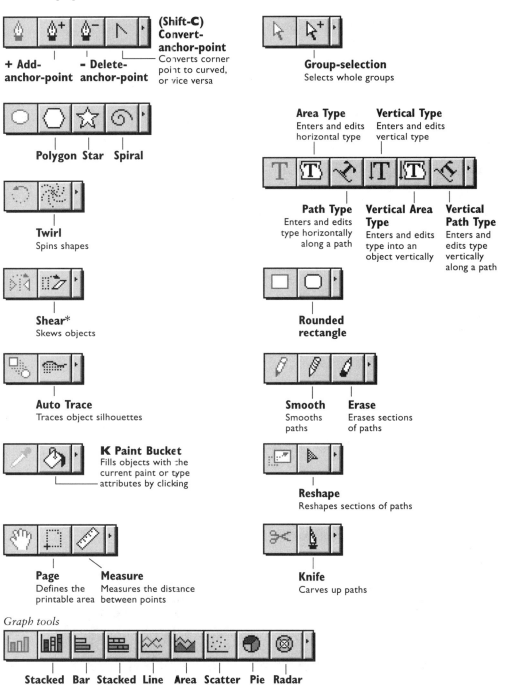

**(Shift-C)
Convert-
anchor-point**
Converts corner
point to curved,
or vice versa

**+ Add-
anchor-point**

**– Delete-
anchor-point**

Group-selection
Selects whole groups

Polygon Star Spiral

Area Type
Enters and edits
horizontal type

Vertical Type
Enters and edits
vertical type

Twirl
Spins shapes

Path Type
Enters and edits
type horizontally
along a path

**Vertical Area
Type**
Enters and edits
type into an
object vertically

**Vertical
Path Type**
Enters and
edits type
vertically
along a path

Shear*
Skews objects

**Rounded
rectangle**

Auto Trace
Traces object silhouettes

Smooth
Smooths
paths

Erase
Erases sections
of paths

K Paint Bucket
Fills objects with the
current paint or type
attributes by clicking

Reshape
Reshapes sections of paths

Page
Defines the
printable area

Measure
Measures the distance
between points

Knife
Carves up paths

Graph tools

**Stacked
Column**

Bar

**Stacked
Bar**

Line

Area

Scatter

Pie

Radar

Toolbox

3

On the screen

The Illustrator screen: Mac OS

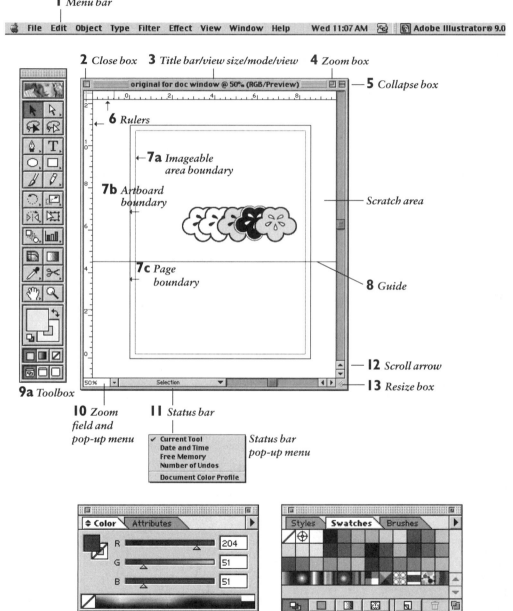

1 *Menu bar*

2 *Close box* **3** *Title bar/view size/mode/view* **4** *Zoom box*

5 *Collapse box*

6 *Rulers*

7a *Imageable area boundary*

7b *Artboard boundary*

Scratch area

7c *Page boundary*

8 *Guide*

12 *Scroll arrow*

13 *Resize box*

9a *Toolbox*

10 *Zoom field and pop-up menu*

11 *Status bar*

Status bar pop-up menu

9b *Color palette*

9c *Swatches palette*

Key to the *Illustrator screen: Mac OS*

1 *Menu bar*
Press a menu heading to access dialog boxes, submenus, and commands.

2 *Close box*
To close a document or a palette, click its close box.

3 *Title bar/view size/mode/view*
Displays the illustration's title, current view percentage, mode (CMYK or RGB), and view (Preview, Outline, Pixel Preview, or Overprint Preview).

4 *Zoom box*
Click a document window zoom box to enlarge the window. Click again to restore the window to its previous size. (Click a palette zoom box to shrink the palette or restore it to its previous size.)

5 *Collapse box*
Click the collapse box to shrink the document window to just the title bar. Click the collapse box again to restore the document window to its previous size.

6 *Rulers*
The current position of the pointer is indicated by a marker on the horizontal and vertical rulers. Ruler increments can be displayed in a choice of seven different measurement units.

7a–c *Imageable area, artboard boundary, and page boundary*
The imageable area within the margin guides is the area that will print on the paper size currently selected in File menu > Page Setup. The artboard is the user-defined work area and the largest possible printable area. The non-printing page boundary matches the current paper size. Objects located in the area beyond the artboard will save with the file, but they won't print.

8 *Guide*
Drag from either ruler to create guides to help you align objects. Guides don't print.

9a–c *Palettes*
Color/Attributes and Styles/Swatches/Brushes are five of 24 moveable palettes that open from the Window and Type menus. The Toolbox contains 53 drawing and editing tools and various color controls and screen view mode buttons.

10 *Zoom field*
Enter a new zoom percentage in this field or choose a preset zoom percentage from the zoom pop-up menu.

11 *Status bar*
Depending on which category you select from the pop-up menu, the Status bar displays the name of the Current Tool, the current Date and Time from the Mac OS Control Panel, the amount of Free Memory (RAM) available for the currently open file, the Number of available Undos/Redos, or the Document Color Profile (RGB or CMYK). Option-press on the Status bar pop-up menu to learn the Moon Phase, Shopping Days 'til Christmas, and other vital statistics.

12 *Scroll arrow*
Click the downward-pointing scroll arrow to move the illustration upward in the document window. Click the upward-pointing scroll arrow to move the illustration downward in the document window.

13 *Resize box*
To resize a document window, drag its resize box diagonally or drag any side of the window inward or outward.

Illustrrator Screen (Mac OS)

The Illustrator screen: Windows

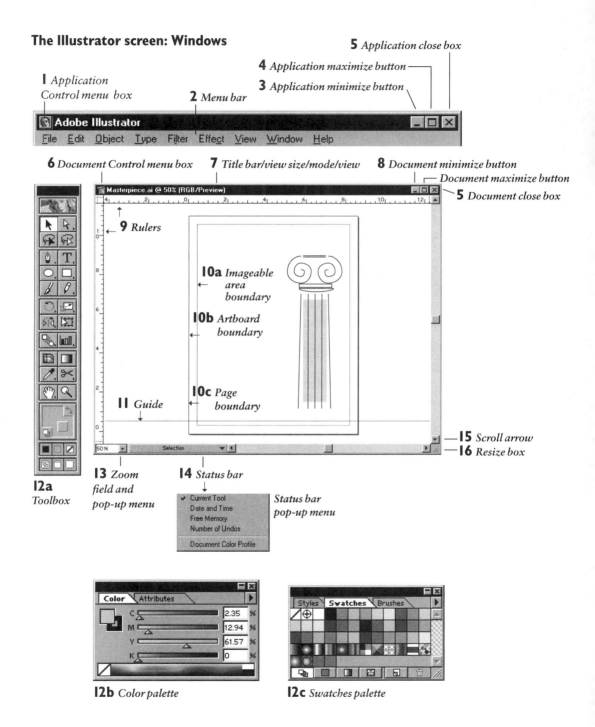

1 *Application Control menu box*

2 *Menu bar*

3 *Application minimize button*

4 *Application maximize button*

5 *Application close box*

6 *Document Control menu box*

7 *Title bar/view size/mode/view*

8 *Document minimize button*

Document maximize button

5 *Document close box*

9 *Rulers*

10a *Imageable area boundary*

10b *Artboard boundary*

10c *Page boundary*

11 *Guide*

15 *Scroll arrow*

16 *Resize box*

12a *Toolbox*

13 *Zoom field and pop-up menu*

14 *Status bar*

Status bar pop-up menu

12b *Color palette*

12c *Swatches palette*

Key to the *Illustrator screen: Windows*

1 *Application Control menu box*
The Application Control menu box commands are Restore, Move, Size, Minimize, Maximize, and Close.

2 *Menu bar*
Press a menu heading to access dialog boxes, submenus, and commands.

3 *Application minimize button*
Click the Application minimize button to shrink the application to an icon in the Taskbar. Click the icon on the Taskbar to restore the application window to its previous size.

4 *Application (or Document) maximize/ restore button*
Click the Application or Document Restore button to restore that window to its previous size. When a window is at the restored size, the Restore button turns into the Maximize button. Click the Maximize button to enlarge the window.

5 *Close box*
To close a document or a palette, click its close box.

6 *Document Control menu box*
The Document Control menu box commands are Restore, Move, Size, Minimize, Maximize, Close, and Next.

7 *Title bar/view size/mode/view*
Displays the illustration's title, current view percentage, mode (CMYK or RGB), and view (Preview, Outline, Pixel Preview, or Overprint Preview).

8 *Document minimize button*
Click the Document minimize button to shrink the document to an icon at the bottom left corner of the application window. To restore the document to its previous size, double-click the icon or click the Restore icon.

9 *Rulers*
The current position of the pointer is indicated by a marker on the horizontal and vertical rulers. Ruler increments can be displayed in a choice of seven different measurement units.

10a–c *Imageable area, artboard boundary, and page boundary*
The imageable area within the margin guides is the area that will print on the paper size currently selected in File menu > Page Setup. The artboard is the user-defined work area and the largest possible printable area. The non-printing page boundary matches the current paper size. Objects outside the artboard save with the file, but don't print.

11 *Guide*
Drag from either ruler to create guides to help you align objects. Guides don't print.

12a–c *Palettes*
Color/Attributes and Styles/Swatches/Brushes are five of 24 moveable palettes that open from the Window and Type menus. The Toolbox contains 53 drawing and editing tools and various color controls and screen view mode buttons.

13 *Zoom field*
Enter a new zoom percentage in this field or choose a preset zoom percentage from the pop-up menu.

14 *Status bar*
Depending on which category you select from the pop-up menu, the Status bar displays the name of the Current Tool, the current Date and Time from the computer's internal clock, the amount of virtual memory (RAM) available for the currently open file, the Number of available Undos/Redos, or the Document Color Profile (RGB or CMYK). Alt-press on the Status bar pop-up menu to learn the Moon Phase, Shopping Days 'til Christmas, and other vital statistics.

15 *Scroll arrow*
Click the downward-pointing scroll arrow to move the illustration upward in the document window. Click the upward-pointing scroll arrow to move the illustration downward in the document window.

16 *Resize box*
To resize a window, press and drag its resize box diagonally.

Illustrator Screen (Windows)

Mini-Glossary

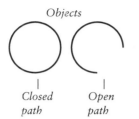

Objects

Closed path   *Open path*

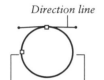

Direction line

Anchor point   *Curve segment*

Straight segment

Selected object

Selected anchor point

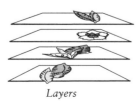

Layers

Path   (Or "object") Any individual shape that is created in Illustrator. A path can be open (a line) or closed. Paths are composed of smooth and/or corner anchor points. Smooth anchor points have direction lines. Anchor points and segments can be modified to reshape any path.

Anchor point   A corner point or smooth point that joins two segments of a path.

Curve segment   The segment between two smooth points or between a corner point and a smooth point.

Straight segment   The segment between two corner points.

Direction line   Each smooth point has a pair of direction lines. To reshape a curved segment, rotate, lengthen, or shorten a direction line.

Select   Only selected objects can be modified. When a whole object is selected, its anchor points are solid (not hollow). The Selection tool is used to select whole objects or groups; the Group-selection tool is used to select nested groups. Use the Direct-selection tool to select individual anchor points or segments.

Layer   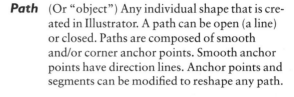 The positioning of a stack of objects relative to other stacks of objects. An illustration can contain multiple top-level layers and sublayers, which themselves can be restacked. The most recently created object is automatically placed at the top of its stack within the currently active layer. Multiple objects can be united as a group so they can be moved or modified in unison. When objects are grouped, they are nested within a group, which in turn is nested within the layer of the topmost object in the group. On the Layers palette, each level of nesting is depicted as an indent from the left edge of the palette.

improved

Fill

Stroke

Stroke The color that's applied to the edge (path) of an object.

Fill A color, pattern, or gradient that's applied to the inside of an object.

Scatter brushstroke

Brushstroke A calligraphic, art, scatter, or pattern brushstroke that is drawn using the Paintbrush tool or is applied to an existing path.

Gradient fill A graduated blend between two or more colors. A gradient fill can be linear (side to side) or radial (radiating outward from a center point).

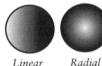

Linear gradient   *Radial gradient*

Gradient mesh An editable object fill, composed of multicolored gradients along mesh lines, that is created with the Gradient Mesh tool or the Gradient Mesh command.

Compound path Two or more objects that are combined into a single object. Areas where the original objects overlapped become transparent.

Gradient mesh

Clipping mask An object that trims (clips) away parts of other objects that extend beyond its border while the mask is in effect. Only parts of objects that are within the confines of a clipping mask object will display and print.

Transparent

Original objects   *Compound path*

Appearances Attributes that determine the appearance of an object, such as multiple fill and stroke effects, transparency, blending modes, patterns, and brushstrokes.

new

Effects Vector commands on the Effects menu that modify the appearance of an object without actually changing the object's path. Effects can be edited or removed at any time.

new

Original objects   *Mask (Preview view)*   *Mask (Outline view)*

The Illustrator menus

File menu

```
File
New...                    ⌘N
Open...                   ⌘O
Open Recent Files           ▶
Revert
Close                     ⌘W
Save                      ⌘S
Save As...              ⇧⌘S
Save a Copy...          ⌥⌘S
Save for Web...       ⌥⇧⌘S
Place...
Export...
Document Info...
Document Setup...       ⌥⌘P
Document Color Mode        ▶
Separation Setup...
Page Setup...           ⇧⌘P
Print...                  ⌘P
Quit                      ⌘Q
```

Edit menu

```
Edit
Undo Gradient             ⌘Z
Redo Move               ⇧⌘Z
Cut                       ⌘X
Copy                      ⌘C
Paste                     ⌘V
Paste In Front            ⌘F
Paste In Back             ⌘B
Clear
Select All                ⌘A
Deselect All            ⇧⌘A
Select                      ▶
Define Pattern...
Edit Original
Assign Profile...
Color Settings...
Keyboard Shortcuts...  ⌥⇧⌘K
Preferences                 ▶
```

Object menu

```
Object
Transform                   ▶
Arrange                     ▶
Group                     ⌘G
Ungroup                 ⇧⌘G
Lock                      ⌘2
Unlock All              ⌥⌘2
Hide Selection            ⌘3
Show All                ⌥⌘3
Expand...
Expand Appearance
Flatten Transparency...
Rasterize...
Create Gradient Mesh...
Path                        ▶
Blend                       ▶
Clipping Mask               ▶
Compound Path               ▶
Crop Marks                  ▶
Graph                       ▶
```

Type menu

```
Type
Font                        ▶
Size                        ▶
Character...              ⌘T
Paragraph...             ⌘M
MM Design...
Tab Ruler...            ⇧⌘T
Blocks                      ▶
Wrap                        ▶
Fit Headline
Create Outlines         ⇧⌘O
Find/Change...
Find Font...
Check Spelling...
Change Case...
Smart Punctuation...
Rows & Columns...
Show Hidden Characters
Type Orientation            ▶
Glyph Options               ▶
```

Glyph Options is not available in Windows.

The Menus

Filter menu

Filter

Apply Last Filter	⌘E
Last Filter	⌥⌘E
Colors	▶
Create	▶
Distort	▶
Pen and Ink	▶
Stylize	▶
Artistic	▶
Blur	▶
Brush Strokes	▶
Distort	▶
Pixelate	▶
Sharpen	▶
Sketch	▶
Stylize	▶
Texture	▶
Video	▶

Effect menu

Effect

Apply Drop Shadow	⇧⌘E
Drop Shadow...	⌥⇧⌘E
Convert to Shape	▶
Distort & Transform	▶
Path	▶
Pathfinder	▶
Rasterize	▶
Stylize	▶
Artistic	▶
Blur	▶
Brush Strokes	▶
Distort	▶
Pixelate	▶
Sharpen	▶
Sketch	▶
Stylize	▶
Texture	▶
Video	▶

View menu

View

Outline	⌘Y
Overprint Preview	⌥⇧⌘Y
Pixel Preview	⌥⌘Y
Proof Setup	▶
Proof Colors	
Zoom In	⌘+
Zoom Out	⌘-
Fit In Window	⌘0
Actual Size	⌘1
Hide Edges	⌘H
Hide Artboard	
Hide Page Tiling	
Hide Template	⇧⌘W
Show Rulers	⌘R
Hide Bounding Box	⇧⌘B
Show Transparency Grid	⇧⌘D
Guides	▶
✓ Smart Guides	⌘U
Show Grid	⌘"
Snap To Grid	⇧⌘"
✓ Snap To Point	⌥⌘"
New View...	
Edit Views...	

Window menu

Window

New Window
Hide Tools
Hide Appearance
Show Navigator
Show Info
Hide Color
Show Attributes
Show Transparency
Show Stroke
Hide Gradient
Hide Styles
Style Libraries ▶
Show Brushes
Brush Libraries ▶
Show Swatches
Swatch Libraries ▶
Hide Layers
Show Actions
Show Links
Show SVG Interactivity
Show Transform
Show Align
Hide Pathfinder
✓ flower.ai @ 66.67% (RGB/Preview)

Help menu

Help

About Balloon Help...	
Show Balloons	
Illustrator Help...	
Top Issues...	
Downloadables...	
Corporate News...	
Registration...	
Adobe Links	▶
Illustrator Links	▶
Adobe Online...	

Help menu > About Illustrator and About Plugins are available only in Windows. Balloon Help is not available in Windows.

Window menu > Cascade, Tile, and Arrange Icons are available only in Windows.

The Menus

Using dialog boxes

Dialog boxes are like fill-in forms with multiple choices. They are opened from the menu bar or via shortcuts.

Windows: To activate a menu, type Alt-[underlined letter], then release Alt and type the underlined letter on the submenu.

Some modifications are made by entering a number in an entry field. Press **Tab** to highlight the next field in a dialog box. Hold down **Shift** and press **Tab** to highlight the previous field. Press on a drop-down menu to choose from more options.

Click **OK** or press **Return/Enter** to accept modifications and exit a dialog box. To cancel a dialog box, click Cancel or press Esc.

Many Illustrator dialog boxes have a **Preview** option that when checked will apply the effect while the dialog box is open. Take advantage of this great time-saver.

Illustrator dialog boxes, like all the other features in the program, function the same way in Mac OS and Windows. The differences in appearance are due to the graphic interface of each operating system.

In Windows, you can type an underlined letter to activate that field (i.e., "U" for "Uniform"). If a field is already highlighted, type Alt plus the underlined letter.

*A **Windows** dialog box.*

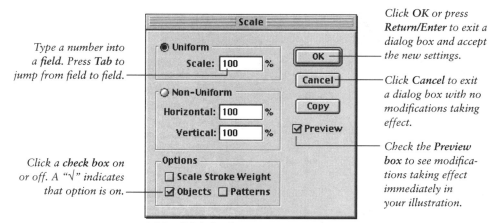

*Type a number into a field. Press **Tab** to jump from field to field.*

*Click a **check box** on or off. A "√" indicates that option is on.*

*Click **OK** or press **Return/Enter** to exit a dialog box and accept the new settings.*

*Click **Cancel** to exit a dialog box with no modifications taking effect.*

*Check the **Preview** box to see modifications taking effect immediately in your illustration.*

*A **Mac OS** dialog box.*

Using the palettes

There are 24 moveable palettes that are used for creating artwork. To save screen space, the palettes are joined into these default **groups**: Appearance/Navigator/Info; Color/Attributes; Transparency/Stroke/Gradient; Document Info; Styles/Swatches/Brushes; Layers/Actions/Links; Character/Paragraph; MM Design; Transform/Align/Pathfinder; Tab Ruler; SVG Interactivity; and Toolbox, but you can compose your own groups.

To **separate** a palette from its group, drag its tab (palette name) away from the group **1**–**2**. To **add** a palette to any group, drag the tab over the group. If you want to gather more palettes together, use as your home base one of the palette group windows that can be resized so the tabs (palette names) will be readable across the top.

To **dock** (hook up) a palette to the bottom of another palette or palette group, drag the tab to the bottom of another palette, and release the mouse when the thick black line appears **3**. To un-dock, drag the palette tab away from the dock group.

Open the Character, Paragraph, MM Design, or Tab Ruler palette from the Type menu. Open all the other palettes from the Window menu. The palette name you choose will appear in front in its group.

To **display** an open palette at the front of its group, click its tab. Palettes with an up/down arrow icon on the tab have two or more **panels**. Click the up/down arrow or the tab name to cycle through the palette configurations: tab only, two option panels, or one option panel. Or to display the full palette, choose Show Options from the palette menu. To shrink a palette to just the tabs, click the palette zoom box (Mac OS) or the minimize/maximize box (Windows) in the upper right corner. Click again to restore the palette's previous size.

Press Tab to **hide/show all** currently open palettes, including the Toolbox. Press Shift-Tab to hide/show all open palettes except the Toolbox. Palettes that are open when you quit/exit Illustrator will appear in their same location when you re-launch.

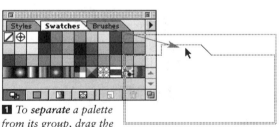

1 To *separate* a palette from its group, drag the tab (palette name) away from the palette group.

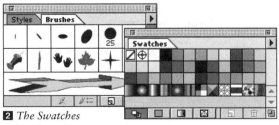

2 The Swatches palette is on its own.

3 To *dock* palettes together, drag the tab name of one palette to the bottom of another palette, and release the mouse when the thick black line appears.

The color controls

The current fill and stroke colors display in color squares on the Toolbox **1** and on the Color palette **2**. The Color palette displays the color model and breakdown of the fill or stroke in the currently selected object or objects, and it's used to mix Web-safe colors or process colors or adjust global process or spot color tints. The Stroke palette displays the weight and style of the stroke in the currently selected object or objects, and is also used to change those attributes. If no object is selected, then changes made on the Color or Stroke palette will apply to any subsequently drawn objects.

Color palette

The Color palette is used for mixing, choosing, and switching between the fill and stroke colors. Choose a color model for the palette from the palette menu. Quick-select a color, black, white, or None from the color bar on the bottom of the palette. Click the Last Color button if you've clicked None and want to return to the last chosen color.

Whichever box (Fill or Stroke) is currently active (is on top on the Color palette or the Toolbox) will be affected by changes on the Color palette.

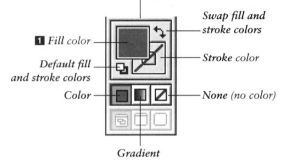

1 *Fill color*

Default fill and stroke colors

Color

Swap fill and stroke colors

Stroke color

None (no color)

Gradient

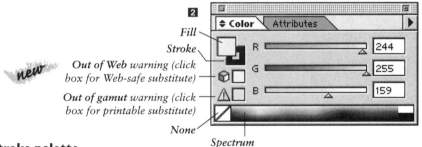

2

Fill

Stroke

new

Out of Web warning (click box for Web-safe substitute)

Out of gamut warning (click box for printable substitute)

None

Spectrum

Stroke palette

The Stroke palette is used for editing the stroke weight and style on the currently selected object, and for creating dashed lines.

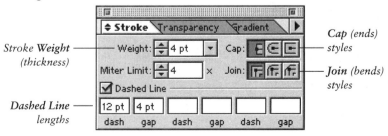

Stroke Weight (thickness)

Dashed Line lengths

Cap (ends) styles

Join (bends) styles

Swatches palette

Click on a swatch to make that color the current fill or stroke color, depending on which of those color boxes is currently active on the Toolbox or the Color palette. Drag from the current Fill or Stroke color box on the Toolbox or the Color palette to the Swatches palette to save a swatch of that color in the current file. Merge swatches or perform other color-related tasks via the palette menu.

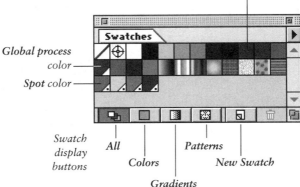

Non-global process color

Global process color

Spot color

Swatch display buttons

All

Colors

Gradients

Patterns

New Swatch

Gradient palette

Use the Gradient palette to edit an existing gradient or create a new gradient. Move a color by dragging its square, or click a square and use the Color palette to choose a different color, or click below the Gradient slider to add a new color.

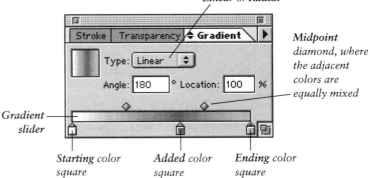

The gradient Type: Linear or Radial

Midpoint diamond, where the adjacent colors are equally mixed

Gradient slider

Starting color square

Added color square

Ending color square

Character palette

The Character palette is used to apply type attributes: font, size, leading, baseline shift, vertical scale, horizontal scale, kerning, and tracking. To apply an attribute to currently highlighted text, choose a value from the drop-down menu, or click the up or down arrow, or enter a value in the field and press Return/Enter. The palette is also used for choosing foreign language options.

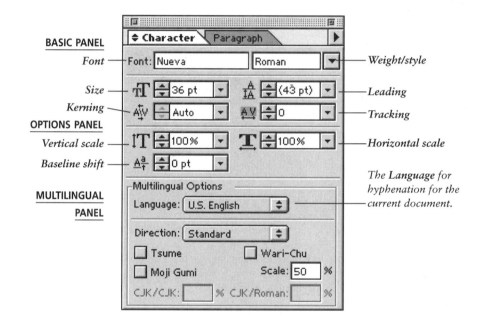

Multiple Masters Design palette

The Multiple Masters Design palette is used to edit the Weight and Width of a multiple master font. Each edited multiple master font is called an instance. Instances are saved with the document for which they are created.

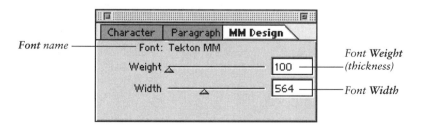

Character Palette; Multiple Masters Design Palette

Paragraph palette

The Paragraph palette is used to apply specifications to entire paragraphs, including horizontal alignment, indentation, space before paragraph, word spacing, letter spacing, hyphenation, and hanging punctuation.

Horizontal Alignment buttons

Left   Center   Right   Justify   Justify Last line

UPPER PANEL

Access the **Hyphenation** *Options dialog box via the palette menu.*

Left Indent ———

First line Indent ———

Right Indent

Space before *paragraph*

*Spacing between words. All the **Word Spacing** fields are available for justified paragraphs.*

Spacing *between* **characters.** *All the Letter Spacing fields are available for justified paragraphs. 0% uses the default (built-in) character spacing for a font.*

LOWER PANEL

Auto hyphenation ———

Hanging punctuation ———

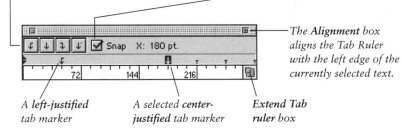

Tab Ruler palette

The Tab Ruler palette is used to insert or move custom tab markers, which are used to align columns of text.

*The **Snap** function makes a tab marker snap to the nearest ruler tick mark as you insert or drag it. Ruler increments display in the currently chosen ruler units (Document Setup or Preferences).*

Left-, Center-, Right-, and Decimal-Justified buttons

*The **Alignment** box aligns the Tab Ruler with the left edge of the currently selected text.*

*A **left-justified** tab marker*

*A selected **center-justified** tab marker*

Extend Tab ruler box

Paragraph Palette; Tab Ruler Palette

Layers palette *improved*

The Illustrator 9 Layers palette is so different, it's like a brand new feature. First of all, it's used to add or delete layers or sublayers. The palette can also be used to select; restack; hide/show; lock/unlock; change the view for; create a clipping mask for; target for appearances; or dim (for tracing) an individual layer, sublayer, group, or individual object. When your illustration is finished, it can be flattened into one layer, or the objects can be released to individual layers for use in an animation program.

Layers Palette; Info Palette

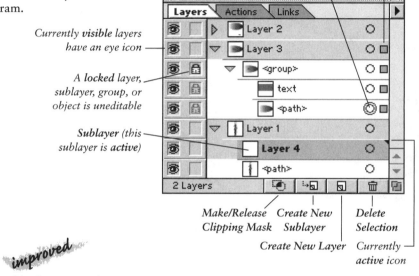

Selection square

*Click icon to **target** an object or group to edit its appearances; drag icon to **move** the object's appearance.*

*Currently **visible** layers have an eye icon*

*A **locked** layer, sublayer, group, or object is uneditable*

Sublayer (this sublayer is active)

Make/Release Clipping Mask *Create New Sublayer* *Delete Selection*

Create New Layer *Currently active icon*

Info palette *improved*

If no object is selected in the current document, the Info palette shows the horizontal and vertical location of the pointer on the illustration, as in the palette pictured at right. If an object is selected, the palette displays the location of the object on the page and the object's width and height. If a type tool and type object are selected, the palette displays type specifications. The Info palette automatically opens when the Measure tool is used, and displays the distance and angle calculated by that tool.

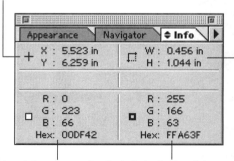

*Horizontal (X) and **Vertical** (Y) position of the pointer* *Object **Width** (W) and **Height** (H)*

*Fill **info** (color breakdown or pattern or gradient name and Hexadecimal equivalent)* *Stroke **info** (color breakdown or pattern or gradient name and Hexadecimal equivalent)*

Align palette

The Align palette is used to align or distribute two or more objects along their centers or along their top, left, or bottom edges, or to equalize (distribute) the space between three or more objects.

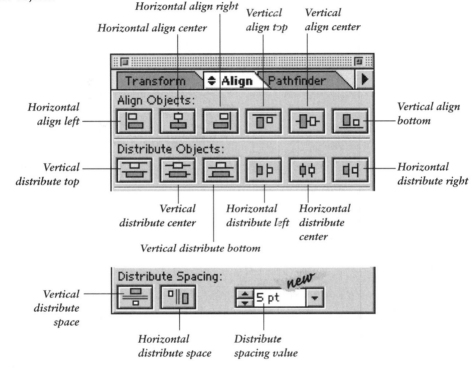

Horizontal align right

Vertical align top

Vertical align center

Horizontal align center

Horizontal align left

Vertical align bottom

Vertical distribute top

Horizontal distribute right

Vertical distribute center

Horizontal distribute left

Horizontal distribute center

Vertical distribute bottom

new

Vertical distribute space

Horizontal distribute space

Distribute spacing value

Transform palette

The Transform palette displays location, width, and height information for a selected object. The palette is also used to move, resize, rotate, or shear a selected object or objects.

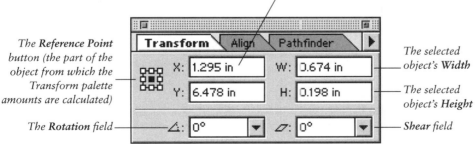

The x and y axes location of the currently selected object. Enter new values to move the object.

The Reference Point button (the part of the object from which the Transform palette amounts are calculated)

The selected object's Width

The selected object's Height

The Rotation field

Shear field

Actions palette

The Actions palette is an automation tool. You record a series of commands or steps as you create or edit an illustration, and then replay those commands on any file to create or edit objects. The Actions palette can also be used to create and access shortcuts.

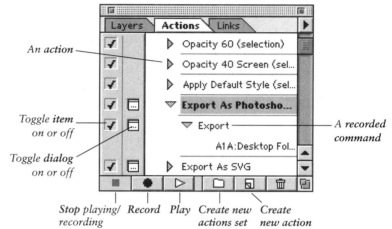

An action

*Toggle **item** on or off*

*Toggle **dialog** on or off*

A recorded command

Stop playing/ recording *Record* *Play* *Create new actions set* *Create new action*

Navigator palette

The Navigator palette is used for moving an illustration in its window or for changing an illustration's view size.

Artboard *View box*

*Drag the **view box** to move the illustration in the document window or **click** on the illustration **thumbnail** to display that area of the illustration.*

*Choose **View Artboard Only** and other palette options from the palette menu.*

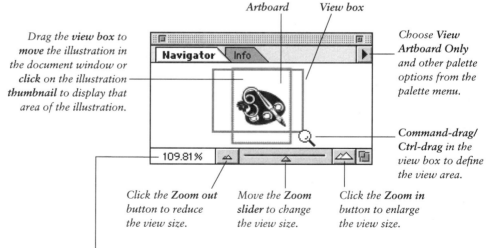

***Command-drag/ Ctrl-drag** in the view box to define the view area.*

*Click the **Zoom out** button to reduce the view size.*

*Move the **Zoom slider** to change the view size.*

*Click the **Zoom in** button to enlarge the view size.*

*Enter the desired **zoom percentage** between 3.13% and 6400%, then press Return/Enter. To zoom to a percentage and keep the field highlighted, press Shift-Return/Shift-Enter.*

Links palette

A linked image is an image that is placed into an Illustrator file from another application without being embedded into that file. The Links palette lets you keep track of and update linked images, modify a linked image in its original appli-cation, and convert a linked image to an embedded image.

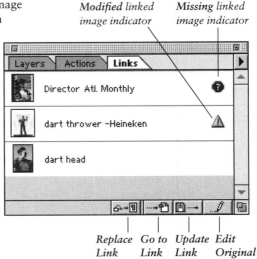

Modified linked image indicator   *Missing linked image indicator*

Replace Link   *Go to Link*   *Update Link*   *Edit Original*

Pathfinder palette

The Pathfinder palette is used for executing the Pathfinder commands, which combine two or more objects into either a new closed object or a compound path. (The Pathfinders were accessed via the Object menu in Illustrator version 7).

Unite   *Intersect*   *Exclude*   *Minus Front*   *Minus Back*

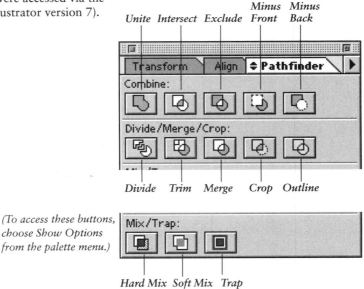

Divide   *Trim*   *Merge*   *Crop*   *Outline*

(To access these buttons, choose Show Options from the palette menu.)

Hard Mix   *Soft Mix*   *Trap*

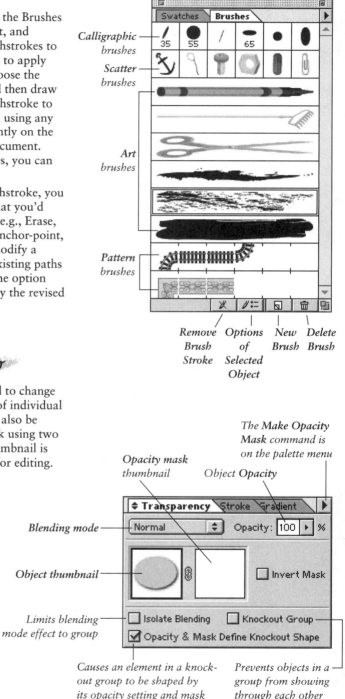

Brushes palette

The four varieties of brushes on the Brushes palette—calligraphic, scatter, art, and pattern—are used to apply brushstrokes to paths. There are two basic ways to apply brushstrokes. You can either choose the Paintbrush tool and a brush and then draw a shape, or you can apply a brushstroke to an existing path that was drawn using any tool. The brushes that are currently on the Brushes palette save with the document. To personalize your brushstrokes, you can create your own brushes.

To change the contour of a brushstroke, you can use any tool or command that you'd normally use to reshape a path (e.g., Erase, Reshape, Pencil, Smooth, Add-anchor-point, Convert-anchor-point). If you modify a brush that was applied to any existing paths in a document, you'll be given the option via an alert dialog box to reapply the revised brush to those paths.

Calligraphic brushes

Scatter brushes

Art brushes

Pattern brushes

Remove Brush Stroke

Options of Selected Object

New Brush

Delete Brush

Transparency palette *new*

The Transparency palette is used to change the blending mode and opacity of individual layers, groups, or objects. It can also be used to generate an opacity mask using two selected objects. The opacity thumbnail is used to select the opacity mask for editing.

The Make Opacity Mask command is on the palette menu

Opacity mask thumbnail

Object Opacity

Blending mode

Object thumbnail

Limits blending mode effect to group

Causes an element in a knock-out group to be shaped by its opacity setting and mask

Prevents objects in a group from showing through each other

Style thumbnails and names / *New Style* *Delete Style*

Break Link to Style

Styles palette *new*

In Illustrator, styles are pre-defined sets of object attributes that are used to change the appearance of objects. Among the attributes that a style can apply are color fill, pattern fill, stroke, transparency, blending mode, brushstrokes, overprint, and effects. Styles help to standardize the appearance of objects and streamline production.

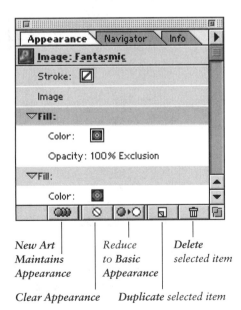

New Art Maintains Appearance   *Reduce to Basic Appearance*   *Delete selected item*

Clear Appearance   *Duplicate selected item*

Appearance palette *new*

The Appearance palette lists in minute detail the individual attributes that are applied to the currently selected layer(s), group(s), or object(s). It's used for editing, adding, or removing these attributes and for editing the attributes of a style in conjunction with the Styles palette. The palette is also used to apply multiple fill and/or strokes to a layer, group, or object, and to quickly access the palettes and dialog boxes that were used to create those attributes.

Styles Palette; Appearance Palette

SVG Interactivity palette *new*

The SVG Interactivity palette is used to attach interactivity to an Illustrator object for viewing in a Web browser. First you choose from a list of common JavaScript events on the Event pop-up menu. Then you add or enter a JavaScript command that will act on the object when the chosen event occurs in the browser.

Attributes palette

The Attributes palette is used to specify overprint options for an object, show or hide an object's center point, reverse the fill of an object in a compound path, or change an object's output resolution. You can choose a shape for the image map area from the Image Map menu. In the URL field, you can enter a Web address for an object to designate it as a hot point on an image map. Click Browser to launch an installed Web browser.

Reverse Path Direction Off and Reverse Path Direction On buttons switch a shape's fill between color and transparency in a compound path.

Don't Show Center

Show Center

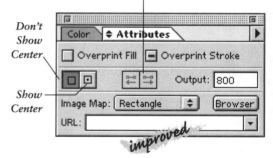

improved

Document Info palette

Like the Info palette, the Document Info palette isn't interactive. It's used solely for reading information about a Document, or individual Objects, Styles, Brushes, etc.

improved

Document Info

Objects:

Paths: 1 (4 points)
Clipping Masks: NONE
Compounds: NONE
Opacity Masks: NONE
Transparent Groups: NONE
Transparent Objects: NONE
Styled Objects: NONE
Gradient Meshes: NONE
Brushed Objects: NONE

✓ **Selection Only**

Document
✓ **Objects**
Styles
Brushes
Spot Color Objects
Pattern Objects
Gradient Objects
Fonts
Linked Images
Embedded Images
Font Details

Save...

Division the easy way

Let's say you want to reduce an object's width by 25%. Select the object, highlight the **entire** W field on the Transform palette, type "75%", then press Return/Enter. The width will be reduced to three-quarters of its current value (i.e., 4p becomes 3p). You could also click to the right of the current entry, type an asterisk (*), type a percentage, and press Return/Enter.

Symbols you can use

Unit	Symbol
Picas	**p**
Points	**pt**
Inches	**"** or **in**
Millimeters	**mm**
Centimeters	**cm**
Q (a type unit)	**q**
Pixels	**px** *new*

Points 'n' picas

12 pts = 1 pica

6 picas = 1 inch

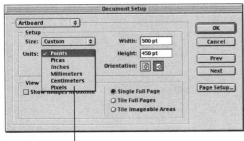

1 *Choose Units via a context menu...*

2 *...or choose Units in the Document Setup dialog.*

Measuring up

The current ruler units are used in most palettes and dialog box entry fields, and of course on the rulers. You can choose a unit of measure for an individual document (instructions below) that differs from the default unit of measure that is currently chosen for the application in Edit menu > Preferences > Units & Undo.

You can enter numbers in dialog boxes or on palettes in any of the units of measure used in Illustrator, regardless of the default general units. If you enter a number in a unit of measure other than the default units, the number will be translated into the default units when you press Tab or Return/Enter. If you enter the symbol for subtraction (-), addition (+), multiplication (*), division (/), or percent (%) after the current value in any field, Illustrator will do the math for you.

➤ To enter a combination of picas and points, separate the two numbers by a "p". For example, 4p2 equals four picas plus 2 points, or 50 pt. Be sure to highlight the entire entry field first.

Follow the instructions below to change the ruler units for the current document only. Choose a unit of measure for the **current** and **future** documents in Edit menu > Preferences > Units & Undo.

To change the units for the current document:

Control-click/Right-click on either ruler in the illustration window and choose a unit from the context menu **1**.

or

Choose File menu > Document Setup (Command-Option-P/Ctrl-Alt-P); choose Artboard from the pop-up menu; choose Units: **Points, Picas, Inches, Millimeters, Centimeters,** or **Pixels 2**; then click OK.

➤ The larger the view size, the finer the ruler increments. The current location of the pointer is indicated by a dotted line on both rulers.

Multiple undos

To undo an operation, choose Edit menu > Undo (Command-Z/Ctrl-Z). To undo the second-to-last operation, choose Edit menu > Undo again, and so on. To reverse an undo, choose Edit > Redo (Command-Shift-Z/ Ctrl-Shift-Z). Or Control-click/Right-click on the artboard and choose either command from the context menu. You can undo or redo after saving your document, but not after you close and reopen it.

You can undo up to 200 operations, depending on currently available memory. If Illustrator requires additional RAM to perform illustration edits, the number of available undos will be reduced to the value entered in the Minimum Undo Levels field in Edit menu > Preferences > Units & Undo.

Context-sensitive menus

Context-sensitive menus make for faster work. They allow you to choose a command from an on-screen menu without having to mouse to the menu bar or even to a palette. To open a context menu, Control-click (Mac OS) or Right-click (Windows) on the artboard.

Context menu offerings change depending on which tool is selected and whether any objects are selected in your illustration **1**–**3**. Not all of the commands that appear on a context menu may be applicable to or available for the currently selected objects.

Windows: To get context-sensitive help: Shift-F1, then click a tool, click in a palette, or choose a command.

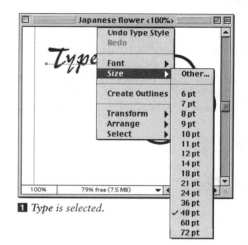

1 *Type is selected.*

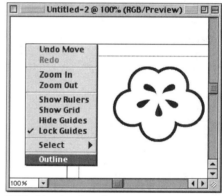

2 *Nothing is selected.*

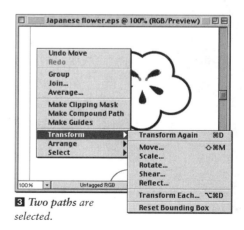

3 *Two paths are selected.*

In this chapter you will learn the basic differences between object-oriented and bitmap applications and you'll get a broad overview of how objects are created and modified in Illustrator.

1 *Object-oriented graphics are sharp and crisp.*

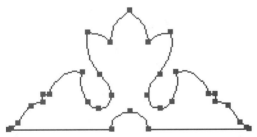

2 *Objects in an object-oriented program are mathematically defined paths (this object is selected).*

Vectors and rasters

There are two main types of picture-making applications: bitmap (or "raster") and object-oriented (or "vector"), and it's important to know their strengths and weaknesses. Bitmap programs are ideal for creating soft, painterly effects; object-oriented programs are ideal for creating sharp, smooth-edged layered images, like logos, and for creating typographic designs.

Some bitmap applications have some built-in vector capabilities. In Illustrator, you can **rasterize** a vector image—convert an object-oriented image into a bitmap image. And you can also place or open a bitmap image into an Illustrator document.

Drawings created in an **object-oriented** program like Adobe Illustrator or Macromedia FreeHand are composed of separate, distinct objects or groups of objects that are positioned on one or more **layers**. Objects are drawn using free-style or precise drawing tools, and are mathematically defined. An object drawn in Illustrator can be recolored, resized, and reshaped without diminishing its sharpness or smoothness, and it can be moved easily without disturbing any other objects. An object in an object-oriented drawing will look smooth and sharp regardless of the size at which it is displayed or printed **1**–**2**.

Object-oriented files are usually relatively small in storage size, so you can save multiple versions of a file without filling up valuable hard drive space. And object-oriented drawings are resolution independent, which means the higher the resolution of the printer, the sharper and finer the printed image will be.

An image created in a **bitmap** program, like Photoshop, on the other hand, is composed of one or more layers of tiny squares on a grid, called pixels. One pixel layer can be arranged above or below another pixel layer. If you paint on a bitmap image, you'll recolor just that area of pixels, not whole, independent objects. If you zoom way in on a bitmap image, you'll see a checkerboard of tiny squares **1**–**2**. Bitmap files tend to be quite large, and the printout quality of a bitmap image is dependent on the resolution of the image. On the other hand, bitmap programs are ideal for creating subtle color gradations, digital paintings, montages, or photorealistic images, and for editing photographs.

Though your Illustrator images will mostly consist of vector shapes, you can place or open a raster image in Illustrator and perform some operations on it. If you're creating Web graphics, your crisp vector shapes will become rasterized when you optimize them for output to a browser.

How objects are made

In Illustrator, the key building blocks that you will be using to compose an illustration are Bézier objects, type, and placed bitmap images. Bézier objects are composed of **anchor points** connected by **curved** or **straight segments**. The edge of an object is called its **path**. A path can be open (with two endpoints) or closed and continuous. You can close an open path by joining its endpoints or open a closed path using the **Scissors** tool.

Some Illustrator tools—like the **Rectangle, Ellipse, Polygon,** and **Star**—produce complete, closed paths simply by clicking on the artboard. The number and position of the anchor points on these paths is determined automatically.

Other tools—like the **Pencil** and **Pen**—produce open *or* closed paths by clicking or dragging with the mouse. The **Pencil** tool creates open freeform lines. The **Paintbrush** tool **3** can be used with its four categories

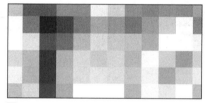

1 *A bitmap image.*

2 *Extreme closeup of a bitmap, showing the individual pixels that make up the image.*

3 *Strokes drawn using the Paintbrush tool, using various brushes.*

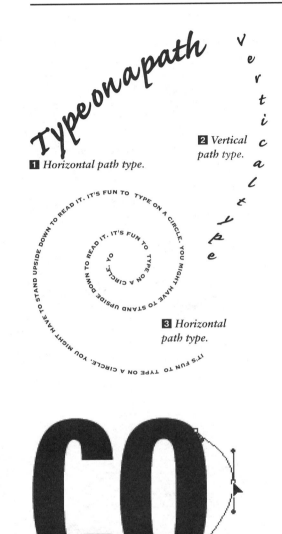

1 *Horizontal path type.*

2 *Vertical path type.*

3 *Horizontal path type.*

4 *After type characters are converted to* ***outlines****, they can be reshaped like any other Illustrator objects.*

of brushes to create **calligraphic, scatter, art,** or **pattern** brushstrokes. You can use Illustrator's brushes or create your own. And using Illustrator's most versatile tool of all—the **Pen**—you can create as many corner or curve anchor points as you need to form an object of any shape.

If you want to use a scanned image as a starting point, you can place it onto a regular layer or a **template layer** in an Illustrator file, and then trace it manually with the Pen tool or trace it automatically using the **Auto Trace** tool.

The written word

Illustrator has six tools for creating PostScript **type**, and a smorgasbord of features with which type can be styled and formatted. Type can be free floating (point type), it can flow along the edge of an object (path type) **1**–**3**, or it can fill the inside of an object of any shape (area type). Depending on which tool is used to create it, type can flow and read vertically or horizontally. It can be repositioned, edited, restyled, recolored, or transformed. And if your text is too long to fit inside one object, it can be linked so it flows into another object.

You can also convert type characters into graphic objects, called **outlines**, which can be reshaped or modified like any other Illustrator object **4**. This is how letter shapes can be personalized.

Editing tools

An object must be **selected** before it can be modified, and there are five tools that do the job: **Selection, Direct-selection,** and **Group-selection, Lasso,** and **Direct-select Lasso.**

An object can be modified using menu commands, filters, dialog boxes, palettes, and tools. There are 53 (yes, 53) tools and 24 movable palettes (Toolbox, Actions, Align, Appearance, Attributes, Brushes, Color, Character, Document Info, Gradient, Info, Layers, Links, MM Design, Navigator, Paragraph, Pathfinder, Stroke, Styles, SVG Interactivity, Swatches, Tab Ruler, Transform, and Transparency). If you need

How Illustrator Works

fast access, leave most of the palettes open while you work. To save screen space, you can dock them together in groups and shrink down the ones you use infrequently.

How everything shapes up

An object's path can be reshaped by moving its anchor points or segments or by converting its curve **anchor points** into corner anchor points (or vice versa). A curve segment can be reshaped by rotating, lengthening, or shortening its **direction lines**. Because a path can be reshaped easily, you can draw a simple shape first and then develop it into a more complicated form later on 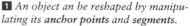. We'll show you how to do this.

Some tools are specifically designed for modifying paths, such as the **Add-anchor-point** tool, which adds points to a path; the **Delete-anchor-point** tool, which deletes points from a path; the **Scissors** tool, which splits a path; and the **Convert-anchor-point** tool, which converts corner points into curve points, and vice versa.

Some tools are used like sculptors' utensils to change the contour of an object. The **Knife** tool carves out sections of an object. The **Smooth** tool removes points to create smoother curves. The **Erase** tool removes whole chunks of a path. And the **Pencil** and **Reshape** tools are used to reshape an object by dragging along the object's edge.

There are two categories of **filters** in Illustrator. The vector filters randomly distort an object's shape or modify its color. The bitmap filters add artistic, painterly touches or textures to a rasterized object or a placed bitmap image.

The **Pathfinder** commands, applied via the Pathfinder palette, combine overlapping objects, divide areas where objects overlap into separate objects, or apply solid colors to areas where objects overlap—and produce a new object in the process ▉.

Other modifications can be made using the **transformation** tools. The **Scale** tool enlarges or reduces an object's dimensions ▉; the **Rotate** tool rotates an object; the **Reflect** tool

How Illustrator Works

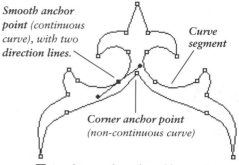

Smooth anchor point *(continuous curve)*, with two direction lines.

Curve segment

Corner anchor point *(non-continuous curve)*

▉ *An object an be reshaped by manipulating its* **anchor points** *and* **segments**.

▉ *The* **Unite** *(Pathfinder) command is used to combine two shapes into one.*

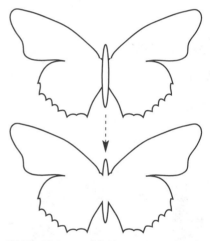

▉ *Illustrator objects are very elastic: They can be* **rotated**, **reflected**, **sheared**, *or, as in this case,* **scaled**.

The original formation.

1 *And after applying the **Transform Each** command.*

2 *A **gradient** applied to multiple text characters.*

3 *Various **opacities** and **blending modes** applied to individual type characters.*

creates a mirror image of an object; the **Shear** tool slants an object; and the **Blend** tool transforms one object into another object by creating a series of transitional shapes. Multiple transformations can be performed at once using the **Free Transform** tool, the **Transform Each** command **1**, or the **Transform** palette.

Still other Illustrator commands combine individual objects into more complex configurations. The **Compound Path** command, for example, "cuts" a hole through an object to reveal underlying shapes. Or an object can be used as a **clipping mask** to hide parts of other objects that extend beyond its edges.

And don't fret about making a mistake: Illustrator has a **multiple-undo** capability. If you want to repeat a series of operations, on the other hand, **actions** can do the work for you.

Coloring

You can **fill** the inside of an open or closed object with a **flat color**, a **gradient** (a smooth gradation of two or more colors) **2**, or a **pattern** of repeating tiles. Patterns and gradients can be produced right in Illustrator. And you can **stroke** the edge of an object with a flat color in a solid or dashed style. If you have a painter's touch, you'll enjoy Illustrator's **gradient mesh** features, which create multicolored, editable gradient mesh objects, and its live, editable **blends**.

A stroke or fill color can be a color from a matching system, like PANTONE, or a CMYK, HSB, or RGB color that you mix yourself. In Illustrator, you can mix, apply, and save colors in either **RGB** or **CMYK Color** mode (not both). This means that a color will be consistent for its model— whether it's a CMYK color being color managed for color separation or a **Web-safe RGB** color chosen for display in a browser.

improved

Using the **Transparency** palette, introduced in Illustrator 9, you can literally change your drawing style **3**. This palette lets you assign **Opacity** levels to any type of object (even a

new

placed raster image or individual type characters); apply **blending modes** to control how objects and layers interact; and use any object as an **opacity mask** to control the transparency of other objects.

How it all stacks up

The **Layers** palette shows the complete stacking configuration of every top-level layer, sublayer, group, and object in an illustration 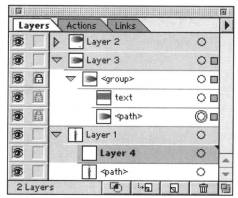. The palette is used to select objects; to target layers, groups, or objects for Appearance palette changes; to restack objects within the same layer; to move or copy objects between layers; and to toggle lock, display, template, and print options on or off for individual layers, sublayers, groups, and objects.

Keeping up appearances

The **Appearance** palette is used to change an object's attributes—but not its actual underlying path **2**. Appearance attributes can include multiple fills and strokes, transparency settings, blending modes, brushstrokes, and Effect menu commands. The point of using appearances is that they can easily be reedited, restacked, or removed at any time.

Gotta have styles

In Illustrator 9.0 or later, you can apply sets of object attributes called **styles**. Styles are saved to the Styles palette and are editable via the Appearance palette. A style can include just about any command that you would apply to a path (e.g., live effects, fill and stroke attributes, transparency, blending modes, and brushstrokes).

It's all for effect

On the **Effect** menu you have access to commands that change an object's appearance without changing its actual path, such as **Feather, Drop Shadow** (improved) **3, Inner Glow,** and **Outer Glow,** as well as effect versions of most of the commands found on the Filter menu. Unlike the Filter commands, which permanently alter an object, however, effects can be edited or removed from an

improved

new

new

new

How Illustrator Works

1 *Layers palette.*

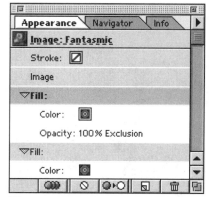

2 *Appearance palette.*

3 *The **Drop Shadow** command from the **Effect** menu was applied to this object.*

1 *Preview view.*

VIEWS

2 *Outline view.*

Adobe Illustrator® document
✓ Amiga IFF (IFF)
AutoCAD Drawing (DWG)
AutoCAD Interchange File (DXF)
BMP (BMP)
Computer Graphics Metafile (CGM)
Enhanced Metafile (EMF)
Flash (SWF)
JPEG (JPG)
Macintosh PICT (PCT)
PCX (PCX)
Photoshop 5 (PSD)
Pixar (PXR)
SVG (SVG)
SVG Compressed (SVGZ)
Targa (TGA)
Text Format (TXT)
TIFF (TIF)
Windows Metafile (WMF)

3 *Formats available in Illustrator's Export dialog box.*

object without causing the object to become permanently altered—only the object's appearance is changed. What's more, there's even a **Convert to Shape** feature that allows you to change its contour without actually reshaping it. You can also create resizable buttons for type using this feature.

On the screen

You can draw an illustration by eye or you can use a variety of Illustrator features to help you work with more precision, such as **Smart Guides, rulers, guides, grids**, the **Measure** tool, the **Move** dialog box, and the **Align** palette.

You can change the **view size** of an illustration as you work to facilitate editing and reduce eyestrain: **Zoom in** to work on a small detail or **Zoom out** to see how the drawing looks as a whole. Illustrator does everything but squint for you. If a drawing is at a large view size, you can move it around in its window using the **Hand** tool or the **Navigator** palette.

An illustration can be displayed and edited in **Preview** view **1**, in which all the fill and stroke colors are displayed. Or to speed up editing and screen redraw and to make it easier to select anchor points, you can display your illustration in **Outline** view **2**, where objects are displayed as wireframe outlines.

If you're a Web designer, you'll use **Pixel** *new* **preview** mode so you can see how your vector objects will look when they're rasterized for the Web.

When all is said and done

There are many options for outputting your Illustrator artwork. It can be **color separated** right from Illustrator or printed on any PostScript output device (e.g., laser printer or imagesetter). If you want to **export** an Illustrator file to a page layout application, like QuarkXPress or InDesign, or to an image editing application, like Photoshop, you can save it in a wide assortment of file formats, including Photoshop, EPS, TIFF, and WMF/EMF **3**.

How Illustrator Works

And last but by no means least, Illustrator 9 introduces a vastly expanded collection of features for optimizing graphics for the Web, included in the **Save for Web** dialog box . This dialog box gives you access to features previously found only in Photoshop and ImageReady. You can optimize a file, save it as a GIF or JPEG, and then preview it in a browser. You can also use Illustrator to assign a URL to an object to create an image map GIF, and export the file for use as a clickable element on a Web page.

And still one more option you'll want to explore is Illustrator's **Release to Layers** command, which releases groups and objects to individual layers. The released layers can be exported to Adobe LiveMotion or Macromedia Flash for use in Web animations.

Well, now that you have a taste of what's come, it's time to get down to basics—Startup (Chapter 3).

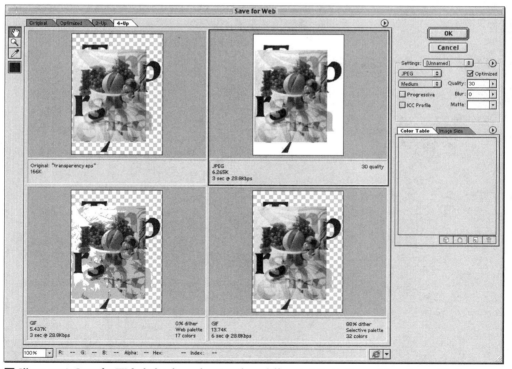

1 Illustrator's **Save for Web** dialog box, showing three different **optimization** settings for an illustration, with the 4-Up tab chosen. The original illustration is shown in the upper left corner.

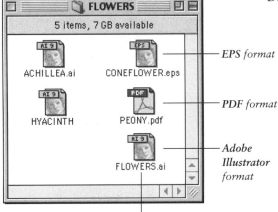

STARTUP 3

In this chapter you will learn how to launch Illustrator, create a new illustration, define the working and printable areas of a document, save an illustration in three different file formats, open an existing illustration, close an illustration, and quit/exit Illustrator.

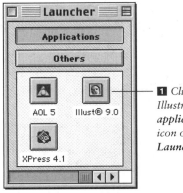

1 *Click the Illustrator application icon on the Launcher.*

Creating new files

Note: A new document window doesn't appear automatically when you launch Illustrator. To create a new document *improved* after launching, see the instructions on the following page.

To launch Illustrator (Mac OS):

Open the Adobe Illustrator 9 folder on the desktop, then double-click the Illustrator 9 application icon.

or

Click the Illustrator application icon on the Launcher **1**.

or

Double-click an Illustrator file icon **2**.

EPS format

PDF format

Adobe Illustrator format

2 *Or double-click an Illustrator file icon.*

Note: A new document window doesn't appear automatically when you launch Illustrator. To create a new document after launching, see the instructions on the next page.

To launch Illustrator (Windows):

Open the Adobe Illustrator folder in My Computer, then double-click the Illustrator application icon.
or
Double-click an Illustrator file icon ■.
or
Click the Start button on the Taskbar, choose Programs, then click the Adobe Illustrator 9.0 shortcut ■.

■ *Double-click an Illustrator **file** icon.*

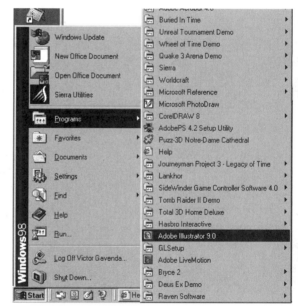

■ *Click the **Start** button, then locate and click the **application**.*

Launch Illustrator (Windows)

Tracing

You'll learn more about tracing on pages 191–194, but here's a sneak preview. To trace over a bitmap image, create or open an Illustrator document, then use File menu > **Place** to import a TIFF, PICT, or EPS with the **Template** box checked. Then, on another layer, use the **Pen**, **Pencil**, or **Auto Trace** tool to produce path shapes above the placed image.

To convert an existing layer into a template layer, click the layer name on the Layers palette, then choose Template from the Layers palette menu. On a template layer, image objects are dimmed and all objects are uneditable.

1 *In the New Document dialog box, type a* **name**, *choose a* **Color Mode**, *and change the* **Artboard Size**, *if desired.*

To create a new document:

1. Choose File menu > New (Command-N/ Ctrl-N).
2. Type a name for the new file **1**.
3. Click CMYK Color for print output.
   or
   Click RGB Color for video or Web output.
4. *Optional:* Change the Artboard Size: Width and Height. *Note:* For Web output, enter "800 px" for the Width and "600 px" for the Height. The units will convert to the current units chosen in Edit menu > Preferences > Units & Undo > Units: General. You can enter points or pixels—you'll get the same result.
5. Click OK (Return/Enter). A new document window will open, at the maximum view size for your monitor.

In the center of every Illustrator document is one non-movable artboard work area **1**. The default artboard area is 8½ inches wide by 11 inches high.

The printable page size is the Paper [size] currently chosen in File menu > Page Setup/ Print Setup. Letter size, for example, is 8½ x 11. Other sizes are available, depending on which printer you're using. You're not limited to an 8½ x11 artboard or to the portrait format; the artboard doesn't have to match the Paper size. You can tile (subdivide) an oversized illustration into a grid so it can be printed in sections on standard-size paper, and you can create a landscape artboard.

To change the artboard dimensions:

1. Choose File menu > Document Setup (Command-Option-P/Ctrl-Alt-P).
2. Choose Artboard from the topmost pop-up menu.
3. Choose a preset size from the Setup: Size pop-up menu (**2**).
   or
   Enter numbers in the Width and Height fields in any unit of measurement (Custom will become the choice on the Size pop-up menu). The maximum work area is 227 x 227 inches. For the current document, the Units chosen in this dialog box override the Units chosen in Edit menu > Preferences > Units & Undo.
   or

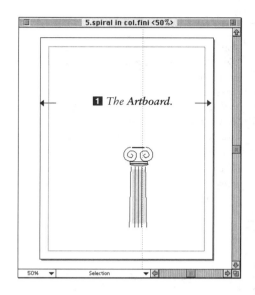

1 *The Artboard.*

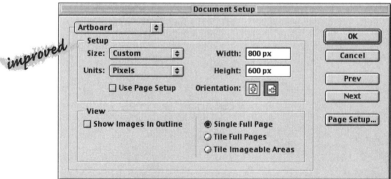

2 *In the Document Setup dialog box, choose a preset **Artboard Size**, or enter custom **Width** and **Height** values, or check the **Use Page Setup/ Use Print Setup** box to use the Paper size currently chosen in the Page Setup/Print Setup dialog box.*

Change Artboard Dimensions

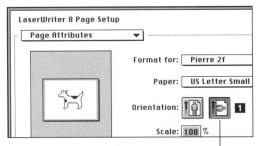

*Click the landscape **Orientation** icon in the **Page Setup** dialog box (Mac OS).*

Page size   Printable area

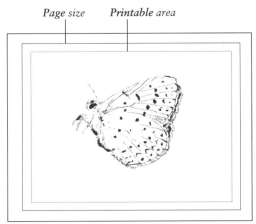

 *The printable page in **landscape** Orientation.*

Check the Use Page Setup/Use Print Setup box to make the artboard dimensions match the Paper size currently chosen in Page Setup/Print Setup. (Click Page Setup/Print Setup to view that setting.) *Note:* The Use Page Setup/Print Setup box will become unchecked automatically if you specify an Artboard size that differs from the current Page Setup/Print Setup size (the page boundary will still match the current Page Setup/Print Setup size, however).

4. Click OK (Return/Enter).

➤ Objects (or parts of objects) outside the artboard will save with the illustration, but they won't print.

➤ If the Page Setup/Print Setup Scale percentage is other than 100%, the page size and artboard will resize and the illustration will print proportionately smaller or larger. If the Use Page Setup/Use Print Setup box is unchecked in the Document Setup dialog box, the artboard will match the Artboard: Size option, but the Page boundary will match the current Page Setup/Print Setup size. If Use Page Setup/Use Print Setup is checked, the artboard dimensions can only match the Page Setup/Print Setup printout size.

You can switch the printable area of an illustration from a vertical (portrait) to a landscape orientation. Then you'll need to make the artboard conform to the new orientation.

To create a landscape page:

1. Choose File menu > Document Setup (Command-Option-P/Ctrl-Alt-P).

2. *Mac OS:* Click Page Setup, then choose Page Attributes from the topmost pop-up menu.

   Windows: Click Print Setup.

3. Click the landscape Orientation icon .

4. Click OK (Return/Enter).

5. Click OK (Return/Enter) again to close the Document Setup dialog box .

Change Artboard Dimensions

To reposition the printable area on the artboard:

1. Choose the Page tool (it's on the Hand tool pop-out menu) 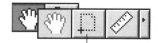.

2. Drag in the document window. *Note:* Any part of a page that extends outside the artboard won't print.

➤ Double-click the Page tool to reset the printable area to its default position.

➤ Double-click the Hand tool to display the entire artboard in the document window.

1 *The Page tool.*

To create a landscape artboard:

1. Choose File menu > Document Setup.

2. Click the landscape Orientation icon, if it isn't already highlighted.

3. Click OK (Return/Enter). (See the tips above.)

4. If the entire page isn't visible on the artboard **2**, reopen Document Setup and enter new Width and Height values to enlarge the artboard to accommodate the new orientation. And remember, objects outside the artboard area won't print.

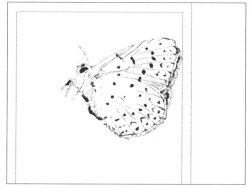

2 *The artboard in landscape Orientation. The printable page, which is in portrait Orientation, doesn't extend beyond the artboard.*

By default, a new document contains a single page, but you can turn it into a multi-page document. If you turn on the Tile Full Pages option, as many full page borders as can fit in the current size of the artboard will be drawn. Changing the artboard size will then increase or decrease the number of page borders.

To divide the artboard into multiple pages:

1. Choose a view size of 50% or smaller from the Zoom pop-up menu at the bottom of the illustration window.

2. Choose File menu > Document Setup.

3. Choose Artboard from the topmost pop-up menu.

4. Enter a new Width that's at least double the existing single-page width.

5. Click View: Tile Full Pages **3**.

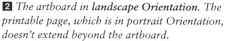

3 *Click the Tile full pages button in the Document Setup dialog box.*

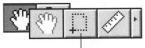

1 *The **Page** tool.*

Parts of objects that fall within this "gutter" area won't print.

2 *The **artboard divided** into two pages.*

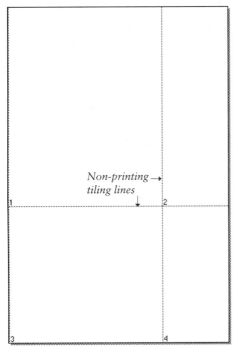

Non-printing → tiling lines

3 *An oversized illustration **tiled** into sections for printing (see page 396).*

6. Click OK (Return/Enter).

7. *Optional:* Choose the Page tool (it's on the Hand tool pop-out menu) **1**, then click or drag near the left edge of the artboard. New page borders will be drawn **2**. (If the tile lines aren't showing, choose View menu > Show Page Tiling.)

➤ You can also tile full pages in landscape mode by clicking the landscape Orientation icon in the Document Setup dialog box and in the Page Setup/Print Setup dialog box and choosing Artboard Size: Tabloid. Then, if necessary, click with the Page tool near the top or bottom of the artboard to cause the new page borders to be drawn.

➤ To tile an entire artboard page into the printer's paper size, create an artboard size that's large enough to hold several print paper sizes, and then click Tile Imageable Areas in the Document Setup dialog box **3**.

➤ If you're going to need trim, crop, or registration marks, make the artboard larger than the page.

Divide the Artboard

Saving files

You have three options for saving a file from Illustrator: Adobe Illustrator document (simply "Illustrator" in Windows), Illustrator EPS (EPS), and Adobe PDF (PDF). If you're going to print your file directly from Illustrator, use the native Illustrator format. If you're going to export your file to another application (e.g., a layout application for print or Web output), you'll need to choose one of the other two options, because not all applications can read native Illustrator files. The native Illustrator format is now based on the PDF format. PDF files can be transferred to and from Illustrator and other PDF applications while retaining full object editability. Other formats are discussed on pages 44–49.

To save a file in the native Illustrator format:

1. If the file has not yet been saved, choose File menu > Save (Command-S/Ctrl-S). If the file has already been saved in a different format, choose File menu > Save As.

2. Enter a Name (Mac) **1**/ File Name (Win) **2**.

3. *Mac:* Open the disk and/or folder in which you want to save the file. Or to create a new folder, choose a location in which to save the new folder, click New, enter a name for the folder, then click Create.

   Win: Use the Save in pop-up menu to navigate to the folder in which you want to save the file.

4. Mac OS: Make sure "Adobe Illustrator document" is chosen as the Format; Windows: Choose Save as Type: Illustrator. Click Save (Return/Enter).

5. Choose a Compatibility option **3**. *Note:* If you downgrade to an earlier version, some elements of your illustration (e.g., gradient meshes and effects) may be altered if the file is subsequently reopened in Illustrator 9. Use Save a Copy to save a copy of the file in an earlier version instead.

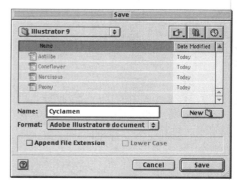

1 *The Mac OS Save dialog box.*

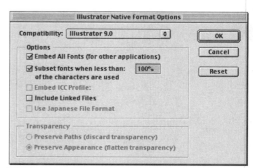

2 *The Windows Save dialog box.*

3 *Choose a Compatibility option (Illustrator version) and check other Options, if applicable, in the Illustrator Native Format Options dialog box. (The Transparency buttons are available only if you save to an earlier version of Illustrator.)*

The Save shortcuts

	Mac OS	Windows
Save	Command-S	Ctrl-S
Save As	Command-Shift-S	Ctrl-Shift-S
Save a Copy	Command-Option-S	Ctrl-Alt-S

6. *Optional:* Check the Include Linked Files box to save a copy of any linked files in the illustration. (Read about linking on pages 242–246.)

7. Click OK (Return/Enter).

Note: For the other options in this dialog box, see page 48.

You can use the Save As or Save a Copy command to save an existing file in a different format (i.e., Adobe Illustrator document, Acrobat PDF, or Adobe EPS) or to convert a file to an earlier Illustrator version.

➤ If you use **Save As,** the new version will stay open on screen. The original file will close, but it will be preserved on disk.

➤ If you use **Save a Copy,** the original version will stay open on screen, but a copy of the file will be saved to disk.

The prior version of a file is overwritten when the Save command is executed. Don't be shy—save frequently. And back up!

To save an existing file:

Choose File menu > Save (Command-S/Ctrl-S).

To save a copy of an existing file:

1. Choose File menu > Save A Copy (Command-Option-S/Ctrl-Alt-S).

2. Follow the instructions starting on the previous page to save the file in the native Illustrator format. Other file formats are discussed on pages 44–49.

To revert to the last saved version:

1. Choose File menu > Revert.

2. Click Revert.

Save; Save a Copy; Revert

Not all applications can read native Illustrator files, and no preview options are available for that format. To prepare an Illustrator file for export to a print or Web page layout application or another drawing application, you should save it in the Illustrator EPS format or the PDF format. First, EPS.

The EPS (Encapsulated PostScript) format is supported by most illustration and page-layout programs and it preserves most graphic elements. Thus, it is a good choice if your file is going to be used in another application. In addition, you can reopen and edit an Illustrator EPS file in Illustrator. Since the files are based on the PostScript language, they can be used for vector and bitmap objects.

To save a file as an EPS:

1. If the file has not yet been saved, choose File menu > Save (Command-S/Ctrl-S). If the file has already been saved in a different format, choose File menu > Save As or Save a Copy (see the previous page).

2. Choose Format/Save as Type: Illustrator EPS (EPS) **1**.

3. Click Save (Return/Enter).

4. Choose from the **Compatibility** pop-up menu **2**. If you choose an earlier version, some elements in your illustration may be altered. For example, transparency effects and appearances with multiple fills and strokes are preserved only in Illustrator version 9.

5. Choose a **Preview** Format:
   None—no preview. The EPS won't display on screen in any other application, but it will print.
   TIFF (**Black & White**)—black and white preview.
   TIFF (**8-bit Color**)—color preview.
   Mac OS: **Macintosh (Black & White)**—black and white preview (a PICT format).
   Mac OS: **Macintosh (8-bit Color)**—color preview (a PICT format).

1 *Choose Format:* **Illustrator EPS (EPS),** *then click Save.*

2 *There are many options to choose from in the EPS Format dialog box.*

Include linked files?

If you check the **Include Linked Files** box in the EPS Format dialog box, and you print, from another program (e.g., QuarkXPress or PageMaker), an Illustrator file containing a linked, placed EPS image, you won't need the original EPS image. You will still need the original EPS image to print the file from Illustrator, though.

If your Illustrator file contains linked, placed images and you *don't* check the Include Linked Files option when saving, you'll get a second chance to save with placed files, because an alert box will open. Just say yes.

Note: Regardless of which preview option you choose, color information will be saved with the file and the illustration will print normally from Illustrator or any other application into which it's imported.

If you chose the TIFF (8-bit Color) format, click **Transparent** to save the file *new* with a transparent background or click **Opaque** to save it with a solid background. *Note:* Choose Opaque if you're going to import the file into a Microsoft Office application.

6. *Optional steps:*

Check the **Include Linked Files** box to save a copy of any linked, placed files with the illustration (see the sidebar).

Check the **Include Document Thumbnails** box to save a thumbnail with the file for previewing in Illustrator's Open or Place dialog box.

Check the **Include Document Fonts** box to save any fonts used in the document as a part of the document. Only individual characters used in the font are saved, not the whole character set. Included fonts will show and print on any system, even where they aren't installed. Be sure to check this option if your Illustrator file contains type and you're going to import it into a layout application.

Check the **CMYK PostScript** box to enable RGB files to print from programs that output only CMYK color. RGB fills will be preserved if the EPS file is reopened in Illustrator 9.

7. Choose a **PostScript** level that conforms to your printing device from the drop-down menu. Levels 2 and 3 are the preferred choices, with Level 3 being the best option for printing gradient meshes. If you are saving an Illustrator EPS file that contains gradient meshes and you will be outputting to a Level 3 printer, choose PostScript Level 3. Level 1 is not

(Continued on the following page)

Save as EPS

available for Illustrator Version 9, and it produces a significantly larger file size.

8. When saving in Illustrator Version 8 or earlier, click Transparency: **Preserve Paths** (discard transparency) to reset all objects to 100% opacity and discard all transparency effects (e.g., blending modes, opacity masks).

   or

   Click Transparency: **Preserve Appearance** (flatten transparency) to flatten the artwork while preserving the appearance of transparency. Transparency attributes will no longer be editable.

9. Click OK (Return/Enter). If you didn't check the Include Linked Files box and your file contains placed, linked images, an alert prompt will appear. Click "Save with linked files" or "Save without linked files." **1**

   Note: If your illustration is in CMYK mode (File menu > Document Color Mode > CMYK color document) and it contains a placed, drag-and-dropped, or rasterized RGB image, you'll get a warning prompt if you save it as an EPS **2**, whether the CMYK PostScript option is checked or not. RGB color objects are saved as RGB in an Illustrator EPS file and will separate correctly from Illustrator. An image that is drag-copied from Photoshop to Illustrator is automatically converted to RGB. For the CMYK Illustrator file, to prevent this color mode change, save the file in Photoshop in CMYK Color mode and in the TIFF or EPS format, then place it into Illustrator.

Backward incompatibility

If you save an illustration in an earlier version of Illustrator, but it was created using features that are not present in that earlier version, the illustration may be altered, flattened, or information may be deleted from it to make it compatible with the earlier version. For example, a gradient fill or gradient mesh may be converted into a blend, vertical type may become horizontal type, or transparency effects will be flattened or discarded. The earlier the Illustrator version you save to, the more drastically the illustration could change.

1 *This prompt will appear if you **didn't** check the Include Linked Files box in the EPS Format dialog box and your file contains placed, linked images. Here's your second chance to include those placed files.*

2 *This prompt will appear if you save, as EPS, a CMYK Illustrator file that contains RGB images from other applications or objects with applied RGB colors that were rasterized in Illustrator.*

Reopening a PDF

PDF is now the basis for the native Illustrator file format. If you save a file in Adobe PDF format and then reopen it in Illustrator 9, all object attributes will remain present and editable and Linked images will be preserved.

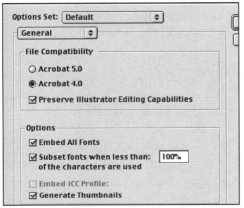

1 *General options for the Default PDF Options Set.*

2 *Compression options for the Default PDF Options Set.*

Use Adobe PDF (Portable Document Format) to prepare an Illustrator file for display on the Web or for transfer to another application or another computer platform that reads PostScript-based Adobe PDF files. All users will need to view your PDF file is the free Acrobat Reader (they don't need the Illustrator application), and the artwork will look as it was originally designed. The PDF format preserves all object attributes, groups, fonts, text, and layering information; it saves RGB colors as RGB and CMYK colors as CMYK. A PDF file can also be edited using Acrobat Exchange. The PDF format also supports document text search and navigation features.

You can open one page of a multi-page PDF file in Illustrator, edit any vector graphics or bitmap images on the page, and then resave the page in PDF format. If you save an Illustrator file as PDF and then reopen or place it in Illustrator, you'll still be able to edit individual objects by the usual means.

To save a file as an Adobe PDF: *improved*

1. If the file has not yet been saved, choose File menu > Save (Command-S/Ctrl-S). If the file has already been saved in a different format, choose File menu > Save As or Save a Copy (see page 43).

2. Enter a Name/File Name, choose a location in which to save the file, choose Format/Save as Type: Adobe PDF (PDF), then click Save.

3. Choose a PDF **Options Set** (the dialog box will reconfigure automatically):

   Default for print output. All fonts are automatically embedded, Compression is ZIP, and Quality is 8 bit. Custom color and high-end image options are preserved. This set produces maximum image quality, but the resulting file size is larger than the Screen Optimized option produces.

   Screen Optimized for on-screen display. The document color mode and any images are converted to RGB color; fonts are embedded; and transparency,

(Continued on the following page)

Save as PDF

appearances, effects, opacity masks, and other attributes are removed. The image resolution is 72 ppi, and the resulting file size is the smallest possible.

Note: If you want to manually change any of the preset settings, proceed with the remaining steps. If you're satisfied with the current settings, skip to step 8.

4. Choose **General** from the second drop-down menu.

5. Check **File Compatibility**: Acrobat 5.0 or Acrobat 4.0. Transparency effects will be preserved with either option if the PDF is reopened in Illustrator 9. Transparency effects will also be preserved if the PDF is saved in the Acrobat 5.0 compability option and then opened in the latest version of Acrobat. Check the **Preserve Illustrator Editing Capabilities** box if you want the option to reopen and edit the file in Illustrator.

6. Check **Embed All Fonts** to have the fonts used in the file embedded in the file. If not all the characters in a particular font were actually used in your artwork, you can choose to embed just a subset of characters to help reduce the PDF file size. To do this, with the Embed All Fonts option checked, check "Subset fonts when less than [%] of the characters are used," then enter a percentage.

For example, let's say you enter 50%. The entire font will be embedded if you use more than 50% of its characters in the file; the Subset option will be used if you use fewer than 50% of its characters in the file. *Note:* Adobe recommends not using the "Subset fonts..." option for TrueType fonts. If you do so, those fonts will be substituted if the PDF file is reopened in Illustrator.

If a Profile was chosen in Edit menu > Assign Profile, check **Embed ICC Profile** to embed that profile into the file.

Check **Generate Thumbnails** to save a thumbnail of the file (or the page).

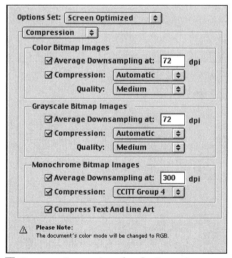

This warning will appear if you save a CMYK document as Screen Optimized.

3 *General options for the Screen Optimized PDF Options Set.*

4 *Compression options for the Screen Optimized PDF Options Set.*

Linking transparency

If a file contains a linked image that overlaps objects containing transparency and you save it as PDF, an alert box will appear. The linked image can't be flattened to preserve the appearance of transparency unless the image is embedded into the file via the Links palette. You will be asked to continue the save without flattening the transparency effect or cancel the save operation. If you continue without flattening and then reopen the saved PDF file in Illustrator 9, the transparency will be preserved. Transparency will be removed if you open the PDF file in another PDF application. Whether or not you embed the image depends on how and where the PDF file will be used.

7. Choose **Compression** from the second pop-up menu.

8. On the whole, the preset compression settings for the Default set and the Screen Optimized set are acceptable choices for PDF files. If you're satisfied with the preset settings, click OK. If you want to enter custom settings, do the following:

Check all the Average Downsampling at [ ] dpi boxes and enter your own value for the final resolution of color and grayscale bitmap images in the file.

For screen output, keep the value at 72 dpi (the default for the Screen Optimized set).

For print output, ask your print specialist how much lower than the 300 dpi default you should downsample your images. Downsampling reduces the image resolution by averaging nearby pixels and combining them to form one pixel. If an image is downsampled too much, its quality will become too low for print output.

For compression methods, choose Automatic from the pop-up menus to have Illustrator choose the appropriate compression and quality settings for your file. (For information on the individual compression methods, read pages 348–349 in the Illustrator User Guide.)

Leave the Compress Text And Line Art box checked to have the ZIP compression method be used on all text and line art in the file.

9. Click OK (Return/Enter).

Save as PDF

Opening files

Follow these instructions to open an existing Illustrator file. Follow the instructions on pages 235–241 to open a non-Illustrator file in Illustrator.

To open a file from within Illustrator:

1. Choose File menu > Open (Command-O/ Ctrl-O).

2. *Mac OS:* Check the Show Preview box to display a thumbnail of the illustration, if it contains a preview that Illustrator can display **1**. QuickTime must be installed for the preview to display.

3. *Mac OS:* Choose Show: All Readable Documents to list only files in the formats Illustrator can read. *Windows:* Choose Files of Type: All Formats.

4. Locate and highlight a file name, then click Open (Return/Enter) or double-click a file name. *Note:* If you get a warning prompt about a linked file, see page 239.

Ending a work session

To close a file:

Mac OS: Click the close box in the upper left corner of the document window (Command-W). *Windows:* Click the close box in the upper right corner of the docu-ment window (Ctrl-W).

If the illustration was modified since it was last saved, a warning prompt will appear **2**. You can close the file without saving (click Don't Save); save the file (click Save); or cancel the close operation (click Cancel).

➤ Hold down Option/Alt and choose Close (or Option/Alt click the close box) to close all open files.

To quit/exit Illustrator:

Mac OS: Choose File menu > Quit (Command-Q).

Windows: Choose File menu > Exit (Ctrl-Q).

All open Illustrator files will close. If changes were made to any open files since they were last saved, a warning prompt will appear. Save the file(s) or quit/exit without saving.

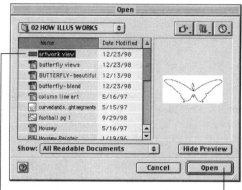

1 *Highlight a file name.*   *Then click* **Open**.

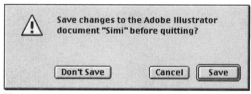

2 *If you try to close a picture that was modified since it was last saved, this prompt will appear.*

VIEWS 4

In this chapter you will learn how to change view sizes, change views (Preview, Outline, or Pixel Preview), create custom view settings, move an illustration in its window, and change screen display modes.

Change views

To use the Navigator palette to change the view size of an illustration:

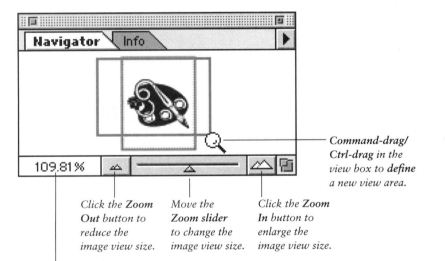

Command-drag/ Ctrl-drag in the view box to define a new view area.

*Click the **Zoom Out** button to reduce the image view size.*

*Move the **Zoom slider** to change the image view size.*

*Click the **Zoom In** button to enlarge the image view size.*

Enter the desired zoom percentage between 3.13% and 6400%, then press Return/Enter. To zoom to a percentage and keep the field highlighted, press Shift-Return/Shift-Enter.

➤ You can also change the view size by double-clicking the zoom field in the lower left corner of the document window, typing the desired zoom percentage (up to 6400%), and then pressing Return/Enter.

➤ To separate the Navigator from its palette group, drag its tab name.

Within the document window, you can display the entire artboard or an enlarged detail of an illustration, or any view size in between. The view size (3.13%–6400%) is indicated as a percentage on the title bar and in the lower left corner of the document/ application window. 100% is actual size. An illustration's view size has no bearing on its printout size.

To choose a preset view size:

Choose View menu > Zoom In (Command-+/Ctrl-+). Repeat to magnify further.

or

Choose View menu > Zoom Out (Command--/Ctrl--). Repeat, if desired.

or

Make sure no objects are selected, Control-click/Right-click on the image, then choose Zoom In or Zoom Out from the context menu .

or

Choose a preset percentage from the zoom pop-up menu in the lower left corner of the document/program window 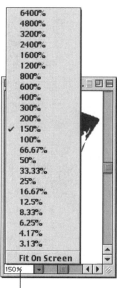. Or choose Fit On Screen from the same pop-up menu to make the artboard fit within the current document window size.

or

Double-click in the Zoom field in the lower-left corner of the document/program window, type in the desired magnification, then press Return/Enter.

➤ Choose View menu > Fit In Window (Command-0/Ctrl-0) or double-click the Hand tool to display the entire artboard in the document window.

➤ To apply a new Zoom value without exiting the Zoom field, press Shift-Return/ Shift-Enter.

1 *Make sure no objects are selected, then Control-click/ Right-click on an image and choose Zoom In or Zoom Out from the context menu.*

new

2 *Choose a **preset percentage** from the Zoom pop-up menu in the lower left corner of the document/program window.*

1 *The Zoom tool.*

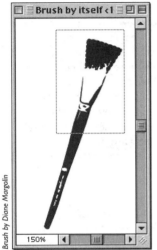

2 *Drag with the Zoom tool.*

Brush by Diane Margolin

3 *The view is enlarged.*

To change the view size using the Zoom tool:

1. Choose the Zoom tool (Z) **1**.
2. Click on the illustration in the center of the area that you want to enlarge or drag a marquee across an area to magnify that area **2**–**3**. The smaller the marquee, the greater the degree of magnification. (To move the illustration in the document window, see pages 57–58.)
   or
   Option-click/Alt-click on the illustration to reduce the view size.
   or
   Drag a marquee, then, without releasing the mouse, press and hold down Spacebar, move the marquee over the area you want to magnify, then release the mouse.

➤ To display an illustration at Actual Size (100%), double-click the Zoom tool or choose View menu > Actual Size (Command-1/Ctrl-1). *Note:* If you double-click the Zoom tool when your illustration is in a small view size, the white area around the artboard may appear in the document window instead of the illustration. Use the Navigator palette or the Hand tool to reposition the illustration in the document window.

 ➤ You can click to change the view size while the screen is redrawing.

This is the method to master for speedy picture editing.

To change the view size using the keyboard:

To magnify the illustration with any tool other than Zoom selected, Command-Spacebar-click/Ctrl-Spacebar-click or -drag in the document window.
or
To reduce the display size, Command-Option-Spacebar-click/Ctrl-Alt-Spacebar-click.

Zoom Tool; Zoom Shortcuts

An illustration can be displayed and edited in any of these four views: Preview, Outline, Pixel Preview, or Overprint Preview. In all views, the other View menu commands—Hide/Show Page Tiling, Edges, Guides, and Grid—are accessible, and any selection tool can be used. (Overprint Preview view is discussed on page 430.)

To change the view:

From the View menu, toggle between…

Preview (Command-Y/Ctrl-Y) to display all the objects with their fill and stroke colors, as well as all placed images.
or
Outline (Command-Y/Ctrl-Y) to display all the objects as wire frames with no fill or stroke colors. The screen redraws more quickly in Outline view.

Or make sure no objects are selected, then Control-click/Right-click and choose Outline or Preview from the context menu.

Choose **Pixel Preview** (Command-Option-Y/ Ctrl-Alt-Y toggle) to turn on a 72 ppi display. Use this view for Web graphics. *new*

➤ Use the Layers palette to choose a view for an individual layer (see page 184).

➤ The display of placed images is discussed on page 239.

➤ Let's say you've got a large file on a slow machine and you start to Preview it in all it's glory—nah, on second thought, you decide to preview it later. Command-. (period)/Ctrl-. to cancel the preview.

➤ Command-click/Ctrl-click an eye icon for a layer on the Layers palette to toggle between Preview and Outline views just for that layer.

It's a snap *new*

In **Pixel Preview** view, you can get a good inkling of what your vector graphics will look like when they're rasterized for the Web (choose View menu > Actual Size first). But Pixel Preview is more than just a preview. When you choose this view, View menu > **Snap To Pixel** is turned on automatically, causing the edges of objects to snap to the nearest pixel edge. Also uncheck **Use Preview Bounds** in Edit menu > Preferences > General for this. Snap To Pixel diminishes the need for anti-aliasing and thus helps keep edges crisp. (Anti-aliasing adds pixels along the edges of objects to make them look smoother, but it also can diminish their crispness.)

1 *Deselect all objects, then choose* **Outline** *(or* **Preview***) from the context menu. This is* **Preview** *view.*

| Undo Clear |
| Redo |
| Zoom In |
| Zoom Out |
| Show Rulers |
| Show Grid |
| Hide Guides |
| ✓ Lock Guides |
| Select ▶ |
| Outline |

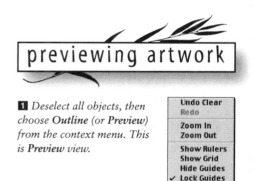

2 *Outline view.*

3 *Pixel Preview view.*

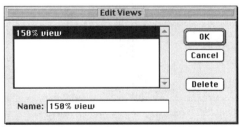

1 *Enter a* **Name** *for the view setting in the* **New View** *dialog box.*

View
Outline ⌘Y
Overprint Preview ⌥⇧⌘Y
Pixel Preview ⌥⌘Y
Proof Setup ▶
Proof Colors
Zoom In ⌘+
Zoom Out ⌘-
Fit In Window ⌘0
Actual Size ⌘1
Hide Edges ⌘H
Hide Artboard
Hide Page Tiling
Hide Template ⇧⌘W
Show Rulers ⌘R
Hide Bounding Box ⇧⌘B
Show Transparency Grid ⇧⌘D
Guides ▶
✓ Smart Guides ⌘U
Show Grid ⌘"
Snap To Grid ⇧⌘"
Snap To Point ⌥⌘"
New View...
Edit Views...
125% View
75% View
175% View

2 *Choose a* **custom view** *setting from the bottom of the* **View** *menu.*

Edit Views
150% view
Name: 150% view

OK   Cancel   Delete

3 *In the* **Edit Views** *dialog box, highlight a view, then change the* **Name** *or click* **Delete**.

You can define and save up to 25 custom view settings that you can switch to quickly using an assigned shortcut, and you can specify whether your illustration will be in Preview view or Outline view for each setting that you define.

To define a custom view setting:

1. Display your illustration at the desired view size and choose scroll bar positions.
2. Put your illustration into Preview or Outline view (Command-Y/Ctrl-Y).
3. Choose View menu > New View.
4. Enter a descriptive name for the new view in the Name field, as in "40% view" **1**.
5. Click OK (Return/Enter).

To choose a custom view setting:

Choose the view name from the bottom of the View menu **2**.

➤ You can switch views at any time. For example, if your illustration is in a custom view setting for which you chose Outline view but you want to display your illustration in Preview view, choose View menu > Preview.

To rename or delete a custom view setting:

1. Choose View menu > Edit Views.
2. Click on the name of the view you want to change **3**.
3. Type a new name in the Name field.
   or
   Click Delete to delete the view setting.
4. Click OK (Return/Enter). The View menu will update to reflect your changes.

➤ If you want to rename more than one view setting, you have to click OK, then reopen the dialog box.

Custom Views

The number of Illustrator documents that can be open at a time is limited only by the amount of RAM (Random Access Memory) currently available to Illustrator. To activate a currently open window, choose the document name from the list of open documents at the bottom of the Window menu **1**.

You can open the same illustration in two windows, one in a large view size, such as 200%, to edit small details, and the other in a smaller view size so you can see the whole illustration. In one window you could hide individual layers or display individual layers in Outline view and in another window you could Preview all the layers together.

Note: The illustration in the window for which Preview view is selected will redraw each time you modify the illustration in the window for which Artwork view is selected, which means you won't save processing or redraw time when you work in the Outline window.

To display an illustration in two windows:

1. Open an illustration.

2. Choose Window menu > New Window. A new window of the same size will appear on top of the first window, and with the same title followed by ":2" **2**.

3. *Mac OS:* Reposition the new window by dragging its title bar so the original and new windows are side by side, and resize one or both windows.

   Windows: Choose any of these Window menu commands: Cascade to arrange the currently open illustrations in a stair-step configuration; Tile to tile open windows side by side; or Arrange Icons to move the minimized windows to the bottom of the application window.

➤ If you save the file, close both windows, and then later reopen the file, both windows will reopen.

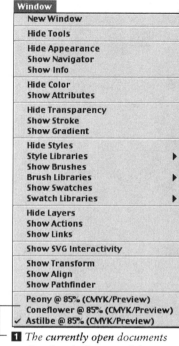

1 *The **currently open** documents are listed at the bottom of the Window menu.*

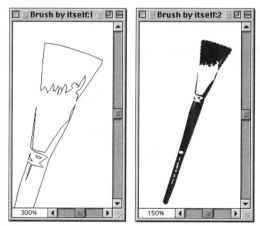

2 *One illustration displayed in **two windows**.*

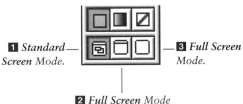

1 *Standard Screen Mode.*

3 *Full Screen Mode.*

2 *Full Screen Mode with Menu Bar.*

4 *Hand tool.*

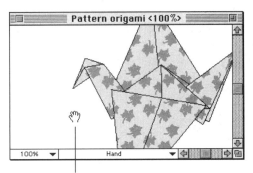

5 *Spacebar-drag in the document window to move the illustration.*

To change the screen display mode:

Click the **Standard Screen Mode** button at the bottom of the Toolbox to display the image, menu bar, and scroll bars in the document window **1**. This is the default mode.
or
Click the **Full Screen Mode with Menu Bar** (second) button to display the image and the menu bar, but no scroll bars **2**. The area around the image will be white.
or
Click the **Full Screen Mode** (third) button to display the image, but no menu bar or scroll bars **3**. The area around the image will be white.

➤ Press "F" to cycle through the three modes.

➤ Press Tab to hide (or show) all currently open palettes, including the Toolbox; press Shift-Tab to hide (or show) all the palettes except the Toolbox.

➤ Choose View menu > Hide Artboard. Choose the command again to redisplay the artboard. *new*

Get around

To move an illustration in its window using the Hand tool:

Click the up or down scroll arrow.
or
Choose the Hand tool (H) **4** (or hold down Spacebar to turn any other tool into the Hand tool temporarily), then drag the illustration to the desired position **5**.

➤ Double-click the Hand tool to fit the entire artboard in the document window.

Screen Display Modes; Move the Illustration

To move the illustration in its window using the Navigator palette:

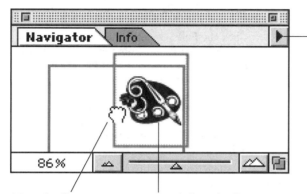

*Choose **View Artboard Only** from the palette menu to have the palette display only objects on the artboard. This is like a quick print preview.*

*__Move__ the illustration in its window by dragging the **view box**.*

*Or **click** on the illustration **thumbnail** to display that area of the illustration.*

➤ To change the color of the view box frame from its default red, choose Palette Options from the Navigator palette menu, then choose a preset color from the Color pop-up menu or double-click the color swatch and choose a color from the Color Picker.

➤ The proportions of the view box match the proportions of the document window.

➤ The Navigator palette will display multiple pages, if any, and tiling of the imageable area.

➤ To stop a slow screen redraw on Mac OS, press Command-. (period). On Windows, press Esc. The display will change to Outline view. Choose View menu > Preview (Command-Y/Ctrl-Y) to restart the redraw.

Move the Illustration

OBJECTS BASICS 5

A path (object) is a shape that is composed of anchor points connected by straight and/or curved line segments. A path can be open or closed. Rectangles and ovals are closed paths because they have no endpoints. A line is an open path. As you'll learn in Chapter 8, any path can be reshaped.

In this chapter you will learn how to delete objects; draw rectangles and ovals; round the corners of any existing path; use the Polygon, Spiral, and Star tools to create simple geometric shapes; and draw in a freehand style using the Pencil tool.

Once you've learned the basics in this chapter, check out these related chapters:

Daniel Pelavin

Artist and designer Danny Pelavin builds crisp, effective images from geometric shapes.

Deleting objects

You'll be creating lots of different shapes in this chapter, and your artboard may start to get crowded with junk. To remove an object that you've just created, Undo (Command-Z/Ctrl-Z). To remove an object that's been lying around, follow these instructions.

To delete one object:

1. Choose the Selection tool (V), ▶ then click on the object you want to delete.
   or
   Choose the Lasso tool (Y), ☂ then drag around the object you want to delete. *new*

2. Press Delete/Backspace or Del or choose Edit menu > Clear or Cut.

➤ If you're using the Direct-selection tool and only some of the object's points are selected, press Delete twice.

To delete a bunch of objects:

1. Marquee the objects you want to remove using the Selection tool (V) or use any of the other methods for selecting multiple objects that are described in the next chapter.

2. Press Delete/Backspace or Del.

Create a Rectangle or Ellipse

Drawing geometric objects

To create a rectangle or an ellipse by dragging:

1. Choose the Rectangle tool (M) **1** or the Ellipse tool (L) **2**.

2. Press and drag diagonally **3**. As you drag, you'll see a wire frame representation of the rectangle or oval. When you release the mouse, the rectangle or oval will be selected, and it will be colored with the current fill and stroke settings (Preview view).

➤ To create a series of perfectly-aligned, equal-size rectangles, create and select a rectangle, then use Type menu > Rows & Columns (see page 226).

To create a rectangle or an ellipse by specifying dimensions:

1. Choose the Rectangle tool (M) **1** or the Ellipse tool (L) **2**.

2. Click on the artboard where you want the object to appear.

3. In the Rectangle or Ellipse dialog box, enter dimensions in the Width and Height fields **4**. To create a circle or a square, enter a number in the Width field, then click the word Height (or vice versa)— the value in one field will copy into the other field.

4. Click OK (Return/Enter).

➤ Values in dialog boxes are displayed in the unit of measure that is currently selected in Edit menu > Preferences > Units & Undo (General pop-up menu) for the application as a whole. The Units setting in File menu > Document Setup for an individual document will supercede the Units & Undo setting.

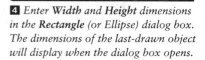

Circles, rectangles, and polygons (triangles).

Daniel Pelavin

Extras

Draw a rectangle or oval from its center	Option-drag/Alt-drag
Move a rectangle or ellipse as you draw it	Spacebar-drag
Draw a square with the Rectangle tool or a circle with the Ellipse tool	Shift-drag

Recoloring: sneak preview

You'll learn all about Illustrator's fill and stroke controls in Chapter 9, but here's a sneak preview. Select an object, activate the **Fill** or **Stroke** box (square) on the **Toolbox** or the **Color** palette, then click a swatch on the **Swatches** palette or click the color bar on the **Color** palette.

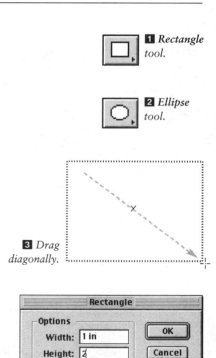

1 *Rectangle tool.*

2 *Ellipse tool.*

3 *Drag diagonally.*

4 *Enter* **Width** *and* **Height** *dimensions in the* **Rectangle** *(or Ellipse) dialog box. The dimensions of the last-drawn object will display when the dialog box opens.*

1 *Rounded Rectangle tool.*

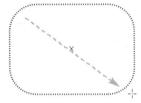

2 *Drag diagonally.*

3 *The rectangle is automatically painted with the current fill and stroke settings.*

*A **great** use of rounded rectangles!*

Chris Spollen

Daniel Pelavin

To create a rounded rectangle:

1. Choose the Rounded Rectangle tool **1**.

2. Drag diagonally. As you drag, you'll see a wireframe representation of the rounded rectangle **2**. When you release the mouse, the rounded rectangle will be selected and colored with the current fill and stroke settings (Preview view) **3**.

   Note: Keep the mouse down as you draw the rectangle and press or hold down the up arrow to make the corners rounder or the down arrow to make them more square. Press the left or right arrow to toggle between square and round corners.

➤ To draw a rectangle of a specific size, choose the Rounded Rectangle tool, click on the artboard, then enter Width, Height, and Corner Radius values.

➤ The current Corner Radius value in Edit menu > Preferences > General, which controls how curved the corners of a rectangle will be, is entered automatically in the Corner Radius field in the Rectangle dialog box, and vice versa.

Create a Rounded Rectangle

Here's a quick introduction to one of the Illustrator filters: Round Corners. For other ways to reshape objects, see Chapter 8, Reshape.

To round the corners of an existing object:

1. Select the object.
2. Choose Filter menu > Stylize > Round Corners (on the top portion of the filters menu).
   or
   Choose Effect menu > Stylize > Round Corners to create an editable appearance (not a permanent change to the object). You'll learn lots more about effects in Chapter 18.
3. Enter a Radius value (the radius of the curve, in points).
4. Click OK (Return/Enter) .

Using the Polygon, Spiral, or Star tool, you can easily create geometric objects without having to draw with the mouse. The current fill and stroke settings are automatically applied to objects that are produced using these tools.

To create a polygon by clicking:

1. Choose the Polygon tool 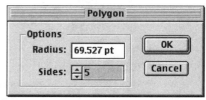.
2. Click where you want the center of the polygon to be.
3. Enter a value in the Radius field (the distance from the center of the object to the corner points) 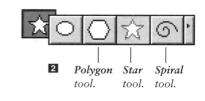.
4. Choose a number of Sides for the polygon by clicking the up or down arrow or by entering a number (3–1000). The sides will be of equal length.
5. Click OK (Return/Enter) 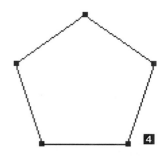.

1 *Top row: the original objects; second row: after applying the* **Round Corners** *filter (30pt).*

2 *Polygon tool.   Star tool.   Spiral tool.*

3 *In the Polygon dialog box, choose a Radius distance and a number of Sides.*

Round Corners; Create a Polygon

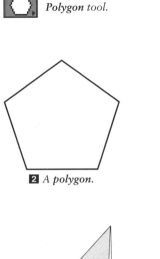

1 *The Polygon tool.*

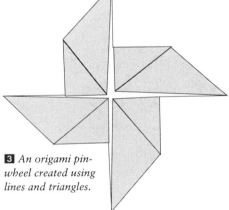

2 *A polygon.*

3 *An origami pin-wheel created using lines and triangles.*

To create a polygon by dragging:

1. Choose the Polygon tool **1**.

2. Drag on the artboard, starting from where you want the center of the polygon to be **2**–**3**.

   While dragging, do any of the following:

   Drag away from or towards the center to increase or decrease the **size** of the polygon, respectively.

   Drag in a circular fashion to **rotate** the polygon.

   Hold down Shift while dragging to **constrain** the bottom side of the polygon to the horizontal axis.

   With the mouse still held down, press or hold down the up or down arrow key to **add** or **delete sides** from the polygon.

   Hold down Spacebar and **move** the polygon.

3. When you release the mouse, the polygon will be selected and it will be colored with the current fill and stroke settings.

➤ To align a new object with an existing object as you draw it, use Smart Guides (see pages 76–77).

Create a Polygon

To create a spiral by clicking:

1. Choose the Spiral tool .

2. Click roughly where you want the center of the spiral to be.

3. Enter a number in the Radius field (the distance from the center of the spiral to the outermost point) **2**.

4. Enter a percentage in the Decay field (5–150) to specify how tightly the spiral will wind.

5. Choose a number of Segments for the spiral (the number of quarter revolutions around the center point) by clicking the up or down arrow or by entering a number.

6. Click a Style button (the direction the spiral will wind from the center point).

7. Click OK (Return/Enter) **3**.

8. Apply a stroke color to the spiral (see pages 126–128).

To create a spiral by dragging:

1. Choose the Spiral tool .

2. Drag on the artboard, starting from where you want the center of the spiral to be.

3. While dragging, do any of the following:

Drag away from or towards the center to increase or decrease the **size** of the spiral.

Option-drag/Alt-drag outward to **add segments** from the center of the spiral as you change its size. Option-drag/Alt-drag inward to **delete segments**.

With the mouse still held down, press or hold down the up or down arrow key to **add** to or **delete segments** from the center of the spiral.

Drag in a circular fashion to **rotate** the spiral.

Hold down Shift while dragging to **constrain** the rotation of the entire spiral to an increment of 45°.

Hold down Spacebar while dragging to **move** the spiral.

1 *The Spiral tool.*

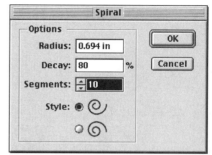

2 *In the Spiral dialog box, enter numbers in the Radius and Decay fields, choose a number of Segments, and click a Style button.*

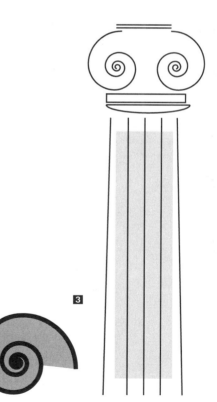

1 *A spiral.*

After applying Filter menu > Distort > Punk and Bloat (Bloat 15%)...

...and then reversing the fill and stroke colors.

2 *The Star tool.*

3

Hold down Command/Ctrl and drag away from/towards the center to control how **tightly** the spiral winds (the Decay value).

4. When you release the mouse, the spiral will be selected and it will be colored with the current fill and stroke colors **1**.

To create a star by clicking:

1. Choose the Star tool **2**.
2. Click where you want the center of the star to be.
3. Enter a number in the Radius 1 and Radius 2 fields **3**. Whichever value is higher will become the distance from the center of the star to its outermost points. The lower value will become the distance from the center of the star to the innermost points. The greater the difference between the Radius 1 and Radius 2 values, the thinner will be the arms of the star.
4. Choose a number of Points for the star by clicking the up or down arrow or entering a number (3–1000).
5. Click OK (Return/Enter) **4**.
➤ You can use the Rotate tool to rotate the completed star.

Star

Options
Radius 1: 0.347 in
Radius 2: 0.69 in
Points: 5

OK
Cancel

After putting circles on top of the points and then clicking the Unite button on the Pathfinder palette to join the shapes.

4 *Classic, five-point star.*

Create a Star

To create a star by dragging:

1. Choose the Star tool.

2. Drag on the artboard, starting from where you want the center of the star to be **1**–**2**.

   While dragging, do any of the following:

   Drag away from or towards the center to increase or decrease the **size** of the star.

   Drag in a circular fashion to **rotate** the star.

   Hold down Shift while dragging to **constrain** one or two points to the horizontal axis.

   With the mouse still held down, press the up or down arrow key to **add** or **delete points** from the star.

   Hold down Spacebar while dragging to **move** the star.

   Hold down Option/Alt to make the shoulders (opposite segments) **parallel 3**.

   Hold down Command/Ctrl and drag away from/towards the center to increase/decrease the **length** of the **arms** of the star, while keeping the inner radius points constant.

3. When you release the mouse, the star will be selected and it will be colored with the current fill and stroke settings.

➤ Hold down "~" while dragging with the Star or Polygon tool to create progressively larger copies of the shape **4**. Drag quickly. Apply a stroke color to distinguish the different shapes. Try using the Twirl tool to twirl the shapes around their center.

1 *Drawing a star.*

2 *Stars.*

3

4 *Multiple polygons drawn with the Polygon tool with "~" held down.*

Create a Star

1 *Pencil tool.*

 **2** *Blue-footed booby, drawn with the **Pencil** tool.*

 3 *The booby in Outline view.*

Drawing freeform objects

Lines drawn with the Pencil tool look hand drawn or quickly sketched. A path drawn with the Pencil can be reshaped like any other path (see Chapter 8). Use the Pencil tool for freehand drawing, but not to create straight lines—that's not what it's designed for. If you need to draw straight lines and smooth curves, use the Pen tool.

Note: The Pencil tool performs two distinctly different functions. If you drag over an empty area of the artboard with the Pencil, you'll create a new, open path. If you drag along the edge of a selected path (open or closed), the Pencil will reshape the path (see page 111).

To draw using the Pencil tool:

1. Choose the Pencil tool (N) **1**.

2. Click the Stroke color box ▣ on the Color palette, then choose a stroke color. Choose stroke attributes from the Stroke palette. (See Chapter 9.)

3. Click the Fill Color box ■ and the None button ⊘ on the Color palette so the curves on the path won't fill in.

4. Draw a line. A dotted line will appear as you draw. When you release the mouse, the line will be colored with the current fill and stroke settings and its anchor points will be selected (Preview view) **2**. In Outline view, you'll see only a wire-frame representation of the line **3**.

Note: To create a closed path with the Pencil tool, hold down Option/Alt before you release the mouse.

➤ To add to a Pencil line, start drawing from the endpoint of a selected open path.

➤ Read about the Pencil tool settings on the next page.

To close an existing Pencil line using a command:

1. Choose the Selection tool (V).

2. Select the line.

3. Click the Unite (first) button ▥ on the Pathfinder palette.

If you change the Fidelity and Smoothness settings for the Pencil tool, which control the number of anchor points and the size of the curve segments the tool produces, only subsequently drawn lines will be affected—not existing lines.

To choose Pencil tool settings:

1. Double-click the Pencil tool (or press "N" to choose the tool, then press Return/Enter).

2. Choose a Fidelity value (0.5–20) 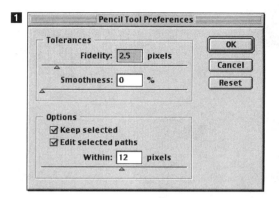–3. The lower the Fidelity, the more closely the line will follow the movement of the mouse and the greater the number of anchor points will be created. The higher the Fidelity, the smoother the path.

3. Choose a Smoothness value (0–100). The higher the Smoothness, the smoother the curves; the lower the smoothness, the more bends and twists in the path.

4. *Optional:* Leave the "Keep selected" box checked to keep a Pencil path selected after it's created. This is handy if you like to add to a path after it's drawn.

5. Check the "Edit selected paths" box to make it possible to edit a path only if the pointer is within the specified distance (within [ ] pixels). Turn this option off if you want to prevent the Pencil from reshaping paths.

6. Click OK (Return/Enter).

➤ Click Reset in the Pencil Tool Preferences dialog box to restore the tool's default preferences.

To smooth a path, use the Smooth tool (see page 112).

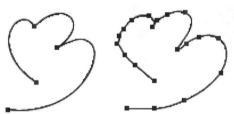

2 *A line drawn with a high Fidelity value.*   **3** *A line drawn with a low Fidelity value.*

Diane Margolin

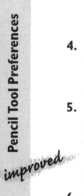

In Chapter 5 you learned basic methods for creating objects. In later chapters you will learn how to reshape, recolor, and transform objects. Objects can't be modified unless they're selected, though, so the first thing you'll learn in this chapter is how to select and deselect objects. You'll also learn how to move objects; how to use Smart Guides to align objects; how to hide an object's anchor points and direction lines; how to hide/show objects; how to lock/unlock objects; how to copy objects within the same file or between files; and how to offset a copy of a path.

If you like to move or position objects by entering values or measuring distances, after you learn the fundamental techniques in this chapter, read Chapter 21, Precision Tools.

A few pointers

The pointer over an unselected segment.

The pointer over a selected segment.

The pointer over a selected point.

Selection tool

Direct-selection tool

Selecting

The five selection tools

The **Selection (V)** tool is used to select or move whole paths and to resize or rotate a path using its bounding box. If you click on the edge (or the fill*) of an object with the Selection tool, you will select all the points on that object.

The **Direct-selection (A)** tool is used to select one or more individual anchor points or segments of a path. If you click on a curve segment with the Direct-selection tool, that segment's direction lines and anchor points will become visible. (Straight line segments don't have direction lines—they only have anchor points.) If you click on the fill* of an object in Preview view using this tool, all the points on the object will become selected.

*If the Use Area Select option is turned on in Edit menu > Preferences > General.

(Continued on the following page)

The **Group-selection** tool can be used to select all the anchor points on a path, but its primary use is to select groups nested inside larger groups. Click once to select an object; click twice to select that object's group; click three times to select the next group that was added to the larger group, and so on.

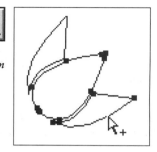

Group-selection tool

➤ The easiest way to access the Group-selection tool is by holding down Option/Alt when the Direct-selection tool is active.

The **Lasso** tool is used to select whole paths (open or closed) by dragging a freeform marquee around them.

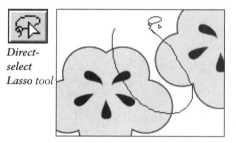

Lasso tool

The **Direct-select Lasso** tool is used to select points or segments on one or more paths by dragging a freeform marquee around those points or segments.

To select all the objects in an illustration:

Choose Edit menu > Select All (Command-A/Ctrl-A). All unlocked objects in your illustration will be selected, whether they are on the artboard or on the scratch area. Objects on hidden layers (eye icon turned off) won't become selected.

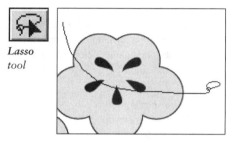

Direct-select Lasso tool

➤ If the pointer is in a text block when the Select All command is executed, the entire text story will become selected—not all the objects in the illustration.

Quick select

To select all the objects on a **layer** or **sublayer** (even in a one-layer document), click the selection area for that layer at the far right side of the **Layers palette**. You can also click the selection area for an individual object or group. Read all about layers in Chapter 11.

Select All Objects

Using area select

If the **Use Area Select** box is checked in Edit menu > Preferences > General and you click on an object's fill when your illustration is in Preview view, the entire path will become selected. If you find this feature to be unnecessary or annoying, by all means turn it off. If the Use Area Select box is unchecked or the path has no fill, you must click on the edge of the path to select it. ("Fill" and "Stroke" are defined in Chapter 9.)

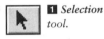 Selection tool.   Group-selection tool.

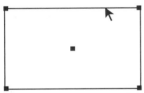

3 Using the Selection tool to select a path and all its anchor points.

4 Marqueeing two paths with the Selection tool.

To select an object or objects:

1. Choose the Selection tool (V) **1** or the Group-selection tool **2**.
2. Click on the edge of the path **3**.
   or
   If the path has a color fill, your illustration is in Preview view, and the Use Area Select option is on (see the sidebar), click on the fill.
   or
   Position the pointer outside the path(s) you want to select, then drag a marquee across all or part of it **4**. The whole path will be selected, even if you only marquee a portion of it.
   or
   If the illustration is in Outline view, click on the edge of the path.
➤ Hold down Option/Alt to use the Group-selection tool while the Direct-selection tool is chosen, and vice versa.

Be sure to read more about the Lasso tools on page 74!

To add or subtract objects from a selection:

Choose the Selection tool (V), then Shift-click or Shift-drag (marquee) any selected objects to deselect them or do the same for any unselected objects to add them to the selection.
or
Choose the Lasso tool (Y), then Shift-drag partially or completely around or across any unselected objects to add them to the selection. Or Option-drag/Alt-drag around selected objects to deselect them.

Select an Object; Add to Selection

Select Anchor Points or Segments

To select anchor points or segments:

1. Choose the Direct-selection tool (A) **1**.

2. Click on the edge of the path (not the fill!). A **segment** will become selected. If you click on a curve segment, the direction lines for that segment will become visible.

or

If the path isn't already selected, click on the edge of the path (not the fill!). Then click on an anchor **point 2**–**3**.

or

Position the pointer outside the object or objects whose **points** you want to select, then drag a marquee across them (a dotted marquee will define the area as you drag over it). Only the anchor points you marquee will be selected **4**–**5**.

3. *Optional:* To select additional anchor points or segments or to deselect selected anchor points or segments individually, Shift-click or Shift-marquee them with the Direct-selection tool.

Or choose the Direct-select Lasso tool (Q), then Shift-drag partially or completely around any unselected points or segments to select them or Option-drag/Alt-drag around any selected points or segments to deselect them.

➤ Hold down Command/Ctrl to use the last highlighted selection tool while a non-selection tool is highlighted. With Command/Ctrl held down, you can click to select or deselect an object.

➤ If you select or move a curve segment without moving its corresponding anchor points, you will reshape the curve and the anchor points will remain stationary. You'll learn more about reshaping curves in the next chapter.

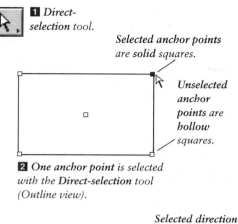

1 *Direct-selection tool.*

Selected anchor points are solid squares.

Unselected anchor points are hollow squares.

2 *One anchor point is selected with the Direct-selection tool (Outline view).*

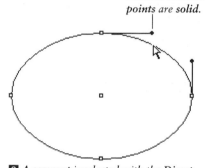

Selected direction points are solid.

3 *A segment is selected with the Direct-selection tool.*

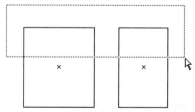

4 *A marquee selection is being made with the Direct-selection tool.*

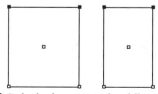

5 *Only the four points that fell within the marquee became selected.*

Reselect

You just used a Select submenu command and you loved it so much you want to choose it again. **Command-6/Ctrl-6** makes it happen. Unlike the Undo command, it doesn't need to be executed right away; you can perform other operations, and Illustrator will still remember which Select submenu command was used last. *Note:* This command may produce unexpected results, depending on what is currently selected.

Undo Styles	⌘Z
Redo	⇧⌘Z
Cut	⌘X
Copy	⌘C
Paste	⌘V
Paste In Front	⌘F
Paste In Back	⌘B
Clear	
Select All	⌘A
Deselect All	⇧⌘A
Select ▶	
Define Pattern...	
Edit Original	
Assign Profile...	
Color Settings...	
Keyboard Shortcuts...	⌥⇧⌘K
Preferences ▶	

Select Again   ⌘6
Same Style
Same Fill & Stroke
Same Fill Color
Same Stroke Color
Same Stroke Weight
Same Blending Mode
Same Opacity
Masks
Stray Points
Brush Strokes
Inverse

1 *Choose from the Select submenu under the Edit menu.*

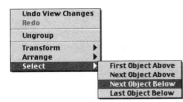

Undo View Changes	
Redo	
Ungroup	
Transform ▶	
Arrange ▶	
Select ▶	

First Object Above
Next Object Above
Next Object Below
Last Object Below

2 *Control-click/Right-click and choose from the Select submenu.*

Use the Select commands to select objects with characteristics similar to the last (or currently) selected object. Each command is named for the attributes it searches for.

To select using a command:

1. If no object is selected, attributes will be searched for based on the last selected object (except for Masks and Stray Points). Or select an object now, if desired.

2. From the Edit menu > Select submenu **1**, choose:

   Same Style to select only paths with the same applied style.

   Same Fill & Stroke to select only paths with the same fill and stroke attributes.

   Same Fill Color to select only paths with the same fill color.

   Same Stroke Color to select only paths with the same stroke color.

   Same Stroke Weight to select only strokes of the same weight.

   Same Blending Mode to select only paths with the same blending mode.

   Same Opacity to select only paths with the same opacity percentage.

   Masks to select masking objects. This one is handy, because the edges of a masking object display in Preview view only when the object is selected.

   Stray Points to select single points that are not part of any paths so they can be deleted easily.

   Brush Strokes to select only objects with the same brushstrokes.

   Inverse to select all the currently deselected objects, and vice versa.
   or
   Control-click/Right-click, then choose Select > **First Object Above, Next Object Above, Next Object Below, or Last Object Below 2**. This works only if you click in the spot where the object you want to select is located and if that object has a fill color, or if the pointer is directly over the lower object's path.

Select Using a Command

new

Let's say you need to select a few points on one path and a couple of points on a nearby path. Until now you would probably grab the Direct-selection tool and click on the points individually (tedious) or marquee them (works only if the points in question fall conveniently within the rectangular marquee). With the Direct-select Lasso tool, you can weave an irregular pathway around just the points you want to select. With the Lasso tool, you can select just the whole paths you drag over. Both tools are very handy for selecting paths that are close to or overlapping other paths.

To select using a lasso tool:

1. Deselect.

2. Choose the Lasso tool (Y) 🔾, then drag around the paths you want to select **1**–**2**. You can drag right through a path or around a path. You don't need to "close" the lasso path.
   or
   Choose the Direct-select Lasso tool (Q) 🔾, then drag around just the points you want to select **3**–**4**.

➤ To move the newly-selected path or points, use a selection tool.

To prevent objects from being modified, you must deselect them.

To deselect all objects:

1. Choose a selection tool.

2. Click outside the selected object or objects.
   or
   Choose Edit menu > Deselect All (Command-Shift-A/Ctrl-Shift-A).

➤ To deselect an individual object within a multiple object selection, see page 71.

➤ To deselect an object in a group, Shift-click it with the Direct-selection tool. Grouping is discussed on pages 167–175.

1 *Drag through or around the object you want to select with the* **Lasso** *tool.*

2 *The* **whole object** *becomes selected.*

3 *You can wend your way around parts of objects with the* **Direct-select Lasso** *tool.*

4 *Only the* **points** *you surround become selected.*

Give it a nudge

Press any arrow key to move a selected object the current Keyboard Increment: **Keyboard Increment** value in Edit menu > Preferences > General. The default increment is 1 pt.

 1 *Selection* tool.

2 *You can drag the **edge** of an object using the Selection tool.*

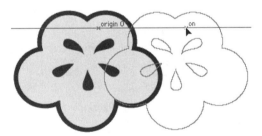

3 *Or with the **Use Area Select** option on, you can drag an object's fill. Here, **Smart Guides** are used to move the object along the horizontal axis.*

Moving

There are many ways to move objects: By dragging, nudging (arrow keys), or using a dialog box. Precise methods for positioning objects, such as the Move dialog box, the Transform palette, and Transform Each, are covered in Chapter 21, Precision Tools. We'll start with the most direct approach first.

To move an object by dragging:

1. Choose the Selection tool (V) **1**.
2. Drag the object's **edge** (Outline or Preview view) **2**.
   or
   If the Use Area Select option is on in Edit menu > Preferences > General, the illustration is in Preview view, and the object has a fill color, drag the **fill 3**. This can also be done with the Direct-selection tool!
   or
   Use **Smart Guides** to guide you! (View menu > Smart Guides.)

➤ If View menu > Snap To Point is on (Command-Option-"/Ctrl-Alt-"), the part of an object that is directly under-neath the pointer will snap to the nearest guide if it comes within two pixels of that guide (the pointer will turn white when it's over the guide).

➤ Hold down Shift while dragging to con-strain the movement to a multiple of 45° or the current Constrain Angle in Edit menu > Preferences > General.

Smart guides are temporary guides that appear when you draw, move, duplicate, or transform an object. They are designed to help you align objects with one another or along a particular axis. And Smart Guides have magnetism: Drag an object near one, and the pointer will snap to it.

To turn smart guides on or off, choose View menu > Smart Guides (Command-U/Ctrl-U). Smart guides settings are chosen in Edit menu > Preferences > Smart Guides **1** (see page 387). You'll understand smart guides pretty quickly once you start working with them—they're easier done than said.

You can start by using Smart Guides to move an object along an axis or align one object with points on another object. Here's how it works.

To use smart guides to align objects:

1. Make sure View menu > Smart Guides (Command-U/Ctrl-U) is turned on (has a check mark). And make sure View menu > Snap to Grid is turned off (if Snap to Grid is on, you won't see the smart guides).

2. Make sure Text Label Hints **2** and Object Highlighting **3** are turned on in Edit menu > Preferences > Smart Guides. (The Construction Guides and Transform Tools options are discussed on page 387.)

3. Choose the Selection tool (V).

4. To use angle lines to position an object: Start dragging an object. Smart Guide angle line guides will appear as you move the object (e.g., 0°, 45°, 90°). Release the mouse any time the word "**on**" appears, to position the object along that angle. You don't need to hold down Shift to constrain the movement—that's the whole point!
   or
   To align one object to another, start dragging an object, position the pointer over the edge of another path, and release the

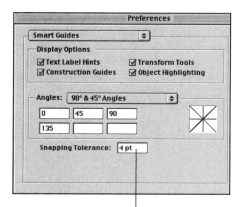

1 *The* ***Snapping Tolerance*** *is the maximum distance the pointer can be from an object for the snap function to work.*

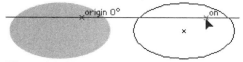

2 ***Text label hints*** *display when an object is moved along one of the axes.*

3 *The edge of the* ***object highlights*** *when the pointer is moved over it (button up).*

Interesting angle

You can specify the angle for smart guides in Edit menu > Preferences > Smart Guides. You can choose a predefined Angles set or you can enter your own angles. If you switch from Custom Angles to a predefined set and then switch back to Custom Angles at a later time, the last-used custom settings will be restored.

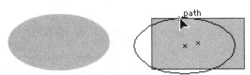

4 *An ellipse is moved over a rectangle. As the mouse is dragged over the rectangle's path, the word "path" appears on the unselected object.*

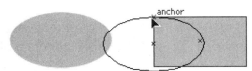

5 *An ellipse is dragged by an anchor point and is aligned to an anchor point (as revealed by the word "anchor") on the rectangle.*

mouse when the word "**path**" appears **4**. You can also align an object's **center** point or path to another object's center point or path. The word "center" will appear. *Note:* In order for the center point to show up as a Smart Guide, the object's center point must be visible (see the following page).

or

To move objects by anchor points: Make sure the object you want to move is not selected, then position the pointer over one of its anchor points (the word "**anchor**" will appear). Drag the object over an anchor point on another object, and release the mouse when the word "anchor" appears on the second object **5**.

Note: You could also align a path of one object to an anchor point or the center point on another object or an anchor point of one object to the path of another object.

➤ You can't lock smart guides—they vanish as quickly as they appear. To create guides that stay on screen, drag from the horizontal or vertical ruler.

➤ Smart Guides are the same color as the current Guides color, which is chosen in Edit menu > Preferences > Guides & Grid.

improved

Use Smart Guides

Hiding and locking

When the Hide Edges feature is turned on, anchor points and direction lines are invisible, yet objects are still fully editable. Try hiding edges to see how different stroke attributes look on an object in Preview view or to make distracting points invisible when you're working in Outline view.

Note: The Hide Edges command won't hide the bounding box. To hide the bounding boxes of all objects in a document, choose View menu > Hide Bounding Box (Command-Shift-B/Ctrl-Shift-B). **1**–**2**. Rechoose the command to redisplay the boxes.

To hide the anchor points and direction lines of an object or objects:

1. Select the object or objects.

2. Choose View menu > Hide Edges (Command-H/Ctrl-H). To redisplay the anchor points and direction lines, choose View menu > Show Edges.

You can use an object's center point like a handle to drag the object. You can also align objects via their center points using Smart Guides, but the objects' center points must be visible in order to do this (see the previous page).

To show or hide an object's center point:

1. Select the object (or objects) whose center point you want to show or hide. To show or hide the center point for all the objects in the document, choose Edit menu > Select All (Command-A/Ctrl-A).

2. Show the Attributes palette **3**.

3. If the Show Center point options aren't visible on the palette, choose Show All from the palette menu.

4. Click the Show Center button ▣ **4**.
   or
   Click the Don't Show Center button ▣ **5**.

5. Deselect the object(s).

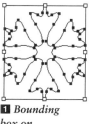
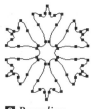

1 *Bounding box on.*

2 *Bounding box off.*

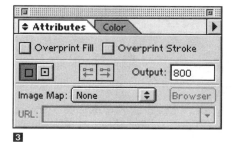

3

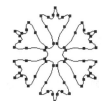

4 *Center point showing.*

5 *Center point hidden.*

Use the Layers palette!

Here we go again, singing the praises of the **Layers** palette. It can be used to quickly show/hide or lock/unlock a layer, a group, or an individual object. For show/hide, see page 183. For lock/unlock, see page 182.

If your illustrations tend to be complex, you'll find the Hide Selection command to be useful for isolating the objects you want to work on and for boosting screen redraw. Hidden objects don't print, and are invisible in both Outline and Preview views. When you close and reopen a file, previously hidden objects redisplay automatically.

If you prefer commands to palettes, this page is for you. Frankly, we think the methods on this page are outdated (see the sidebar).

To hide an object or objects:

1. Select the object or objects to be hidden.
2. Choose Object menu > Hide Selection (Command-3/Ctrl-3).

Individual hidden objects *cannot* be selectively redisplayed (read the sidebar for a workaround).

To redisplay all hidden objects:

Choose Object menu > Show All (Command-Option-3/Ctrl-Alt-3).

A locked object cannot be selected or modified. If you close and reopen the file, locked objects remain locked.

To lock an object or objects:

1. Select the whole object or objects to be locked. You can't lock or hide part of a path.
2. Choose Object menu > Lock (Command-2/Ctrl-2).

Locked objects can't be unlocked individually using a command, but they can be unlocked individually using the Layers palette.

To unlock all locked objects:

Choose Object menu > Unlock All (Command-Option-2/Ctrl-Alt-2). The newly unlocked objects will be selected; any previously selected, unlocked objects will be deselected.

Hide/Show Objects; Lock Objects

Copying

On this page we discuss the most straight-forward methods for copying: By dragging and by nudging. To copy objects via the Clipboard, see the next page; to copy objects using the Transform tools, see the next chapter; to copy an object to a different layer, see page 178; to copy an entire layer with all the objects on that layer, see page 178; and to copy objects using the Move dialog box, see page 365. To copy an object in a group, see page 173.

To drag-copy an object:

1. Choose the Selection tool (V).

2. Option-drag/Alt-drag the fill or the edge of the object you want to copy (the pointer will turn into a double arrowhead). Don't drag a bounding box handle!
   or
   To constrain the position of the copy, start dragging the object, then Option-Shift-drag/Alt-Shift-drag. Or use Smart Guides instead.

3. Release the mouse, then release Option/Alt. A copy of the object will appear in the new location **1**–**2**.

➤ To create additional copies of the object, choose Object menu > Transform > Transform Again (Command-D/Ctrl-D) as many times as you like.

To copy an object by nudging:

1. Choose the Selection tool (V).

2. Select the object (or objects) you want to copy.

3. Press Option-arrow/Alt-arrow to copy the object and move the copy by the Keyboard Increment currently specified in Edit menu > Preferences > General. The default unit is one point.
   or
   Press Option-Shift-arrow/Alt-Shift-arrow to copy the object and move it ten times the current Keyboard Increment.

Copying grouped objects

If you copy an object in a group by dragging (start dragging with the Direct-selection tool, then continue dragging with Option/Alt held down), the copy will be **part** of that group. If you use the **Clipboard** to copy and paste an object that was in a group, the object will paste **outside** the group. The Group command is discussed on page 167.

1 *To copy an object, **Option-drag/Alt-drag** it. Note the double arrowhead pointer.*

2 *The object is copied.*

Copy Objects

If you select an object or a group and then choose the Cut or Copy command, that object or group will be placed onto the Clipboard, a temporary storage area in memory. The previous contents of the Clipboard are replaced each time you choose Cut or Copy.

The Paste command places the current Clipboard contents in the center of the currently active document window. The Paste in Front and Paste in Back commands paste the object in its original *x/y* location, but in the new stacking position. The same Clipboard contents can be pasted an unlimited number of times.

 Objects are automatically copied to the Clipboard in PICT format. They may also be copied in the PDF or AICB format, depending on which of those options is currently chosen in Edit menu > Preferences > Files & Clipboard (see page 390).

Note: Be sure to also read about the drag-and-drop method for copying objects (see the previous page).

To copy or move objects from one document to another (Clipboard):

1. Open both documents.

2. Select the object or group that you want to copy or move.

3. Choose Edit menu > Cut (Command-X/Ctrl-X). The object or group will be removed from the current document.
   or
   To move a copy of the object or group, choose Edit menu > Copy (Command-C/Ctrl-C).

4. Click in the destination document, and click a layer to make it active.

5. *Optional:* Select an object whose stacking position you want to paste the copied object in front of or behind.

6. Choose Edit menu > Paste (Command-V/Ctrl-V).
   or
   If you've selected an object in the destination document, choose Edit menu > Paste in Front (Command-F/Ctrl-F) or Paste in Back (Command/B/Ctrl-B).

Use the Clipboard

81

The Offset Path command copies a path and offsets the copy around or inside the original path by a specified distance. The copy is also reshaped automatically so it fits nicely around the original path.

Note: Try using this command on a path that has a stroke, but no fill.

To offset a copy of a path:

1. Select an object 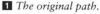.

2. Choose Object menu > Path > Offset Path.

3. In the Offset field, enter the distance you want the offset path to be from the original path 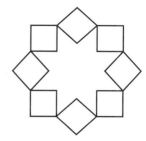. Be sure your Offset value is larger or smaller than the stroke weight of the original path so the original and offset paths won't overlap.

4. Choose a Joins (bend) style: Miter (pointed), Round (semicircular), or Bevel (square-cornered).

5. *Optional:* Enter a different Miter Limit for the maximum amount the offset path's line weight (as measured from the inside to the outside of the corner point) can be enlarged before the miter join becomes a bevel join. The Miter limit value times the stroke weight value equals the maximum inner-to-outer corner measurement. Use a high Miter Limit to create long, pointy corners; use a low Miter limit to create bevel joins.

6. Click OK (Return/Enter) –. The offset path will be a separate path from, and stacked behind, the original path. And regardless of whether the original object was open or closed, the offset path will be a closed path.

Offset a Copy of a Path

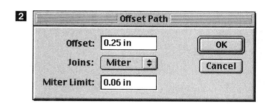

1 *The original path.*

3 *After applying the Offset Path command.*

4 *After recoloring the objects.*

TRANSFORM 7

This chapter covers methods for transforming an object. You'll learn how to use the five individual transformation tools (Rotate, Scale, Reflect, Shear, and Blend), the Free Transform tool, an object's bounding box, the Transform Each command, the Transform Effect command, and the Make Blend command. The Transform palette is discussed on page 366, the Move command on page 365.

The tools

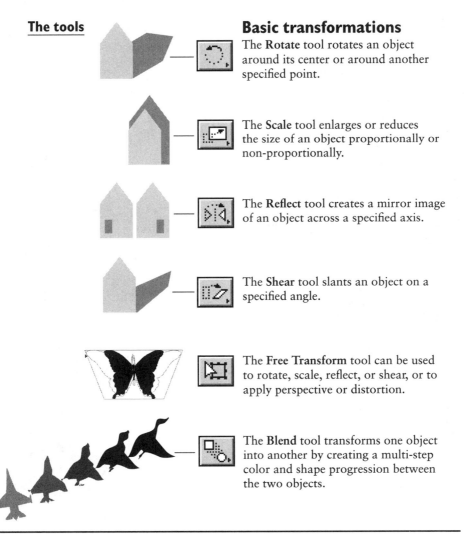

Basic transformations

The **Rotate** tool rotates an object around its center or around another specified point.

The **Scale** tool enlarges or reduces the size of an object proportionally or non-proportionally.

The **Reflect** tool creates a mirror image of an object across a specified axis.

The **Shear** tool slants an object on a specified angle.

The **Free Transform** tool can be used to rotate, scale, reflect, or shear, or to apply perspective or distortion.

The **Blend** tool transforms one object into another by creating a multi-step color and shape progression between the two objects.

Using the transformation tools

Before we delve into the transformation tools
in detail, here's a summary of the basic ways
to use them.

Dialog box method

Select the whole object, and double-click
the Rotate, Scale, Reflect, or Shear tool to
open the tool's dialog box or Control-click/
Right-click in the document window and
choose from the Transform submenu on the
context menu **1**. The default point of origin
at the object's center will now be visible.
Check the Preview box in the tool dialog
box, enter numbers (press Tab to apply a
value and move to the next field), then click
OK or click Copy.

To use a point of origin other than the
object's center, select the object, choose a
transform tool, then Option-click/Alt-click
on or near the object to establish a new point
of origin. A dialog box will open.

Dragging method

Select the whole object; choose the Rotate,
Scale, Reflect, Shear, or Free Transform
tool; position the pointer outside the object;
then drag.

➤ Once the point of origin is established, for
finer control position the pointer (arrowhead) far from the point of origin before
dragging. You can use Smart Guides
(Command-U/Ctrl-U) for positioning.

To use a point of origin other than the
object's center **2**, select the object, choose
an individual transform tool (not the Free
Transform tool), and click to establish a new
point of origin **3**. Reposition the mouse **4**,
then drag to complete the transformation **5**.
The point of origin can also be dragged to a
different location.

Hold down Option/Alt while dragging with
an individual transform tool to transform a
copy of the original (release the mouse first).

To transform an object using its bounding
box, see page 91.

➤ Watch the rotate angle or other readouts
on the Info palette as you transform an
object.

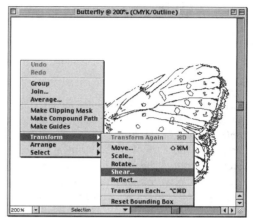

1 *Select an object, and then choose a command
from the* **Transform** *submenu on the* **context** *menu.*

2 *Point of origin
indicator.*

3 *Click to establish
a point of origin.*

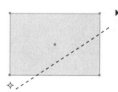

4 *Reposition
the mouse.*

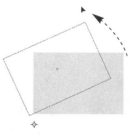

5 *Drag to
transform.*

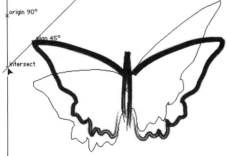

1 *Check the **Transform Tools** box in Edit menu > Preferences > **Smart Guides Preferences.***

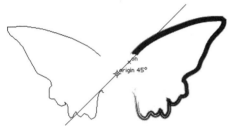

2 *Using Smart Guides with the **Reflect** tool.*

3 *Using Smart Guides with the **Scale** tool.*

4 *Using Smart Guides with the **Shear** tool.*

Repeating a transformation

Once you have performed a transformation on an object (other than a blend), you can repeat the transformation using the same values by choosing Object menu > Transform > **Transform Again** (Command-D/Ctrl-D). If you make a copy of an object while transforming it and then apply Transform Again, a new copy will be transformed.

➤ To constrain all transform commands to a custom angle, change the Constrain Angle in Edit menu > Preferences > General (Command-K/Ctrl-K).

Transforming fill patterns

If you transform an object that contains a pattern fill and the Patterns box is checked in the transformation tool dialog box or the Transform Pattern Tiles box is checked in Edit menu > Preferences > General, the pattern will also transform. Checking or unchecking this option in one location automatically resets it in the other location.

To transform a pattern but not the object, uncheck the Objects box in the transformation tool's dialog box. Or, choose any individual transformation tool except Free Transform, click to establish the point of origin, then hold down "~" and drag.

To use smart guides as you rotate, scale, or shear an object:

1. Choose Edit menu > Preferences > Smart Guides, and make sure the Transform Tools box has a check mark **1**. You can also choose a different Angles set or enter custom angles, if you like.

2. Make sure View menu > Smart Guides is turned on (has a check mark).

3. Select the object to be transformed using the Selection (V) tool or Lasso (Y) tool.

4. Choose any individual transform tool except the Free Transform tool.

5. As you drag the mouse to transform the object, Smart Guides will appear temporarily **2**–**4**. Move the pointer along a Smart Guide to transform along that axis.

Use Smart Guides as you Transform

To rotate an object using a dialog box:

1. Select an object (or objects) using the Selection tool or the Lasso tool **1**.

2. Double-click the Rotate tool if you want to rotate the object around its center **2**.
   or
   Choose the Rotate tool, then Option/Alt click near the object to establish a new point of origin.

3. Check the Preview box.

4. Enter a positive Angle (then press Tab) to rotate the object counterclockwise or a negative Angle to rotate the object clockwise (-360–360) **3**.

5. *Optional:* If the object contains a pattern fill and you check the Patterns box, the pattern will rotate with the object. (This option can also be turned on or off via the Transform Pattern Tiles box in Edit menu > Preferences > General.)

6. Click Copy to rotate a copy of the original (not the original object) and close the dialog box.
   or
   Click OK (Return/Enter) **4**–**6**.

To rotate an object by dragging:

1. Select an object (or objects) using the Selection tool or the Lasso tool **1**.

2. Choose the Rotate tool (R) **2**.

3. Drag around the object to use the object's center as the point of origin.
   or
   Click to establish a new point of origin (the pointer will turn into an arrowhead), reposition the mouse as far from the origin as possible for better control, then drag to rotate the object.

   Start dragging, then press Option/Alt to rotate a **copy** of the object (release the mouse before you release Option/Alt).

   Hold down Shift while dragging to rotate in 45° increments. Release the mouse before you release Shift.

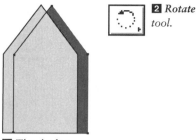

2 *Rotate tool.*

1 *The shadow object is selected.*

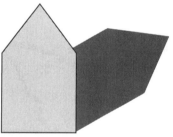

3 *Enter an Angle in the Rotate dialog box. Click Copy to rotate a copy of the object.*

4 *The shadow was rotated –60°, and then moved.*

5 *An object is copy-rotated.*

6 *And then the Transform Again command is applied twice (Command-D/Ctrl-D).*

Scale tool.

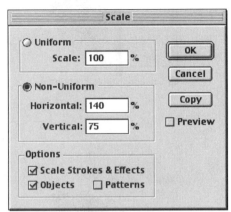

2 *The Scale dialog box.*

3 *The original object.*

4 *The object scaled Uniformly, Patterns box checked.*

5 *The original object scaled Non-uniformly, Patterns box checked.*

6 *The original object scaled Non-uniformly, Patterns box unchecked.*

To scale an object using a dialog box:

1. Select an object (or objects) using the Selection tool or the Lasso tool.

2. To scale the object from its center, double-click the Scale tool **1**.
   or
   Choose the Scale tool, then Option/Alt click near the object to establish a new point of origin.

3. Check the Preview box.

4. To scale the object proportionally, click Uniform, then enter a percentage in the Scale field (press Tab) **2**.
   or
   To scale the object non-proportionally, click Non-Uniform, then enter a percentage in the Horizontal and Vertical fields (press Tab).

   Note: Enter 100 to leave a dimension unchanged. Enter a negative value to flip the object(s).

5. *Optional:* Check the Scale Strokes & Effects box to also scale the stroke thickness and effects from the Effects menu by the same percentage. This option can also be turned on in Edit menu > Preferences > General.

6. *Optional:* Check the Patterns box if the object contains a pattern fill and you want the pattern to scale with the object.

7. Click Copy to scale a copy of the original (not the original object) and close the dialog box.
   or
   Click OK (Return/Enter) **3**–**6**.

➤ You can enter any number into the Angle field in any Transform tool dialog box. Illustrator will substitute the nearest acceptable value between 360 and -360.

improved

Scale

When you scale an object, the stroke may or may not scale accordingly depending on whether the Scale Strokes & Effects box is checked in Edit menu > Preferences > General or in the Scale dialog box. Turning this option on in one location automatically turns it on in the other location.

To scale an object by dragging:

1. Select an object (or objects) using the Selection tool or the Lasso tool.

2. Choose the Scale tool (S).

3. To scale from the object's center, drag (without clicking first) away from or toward the object.
   or
   Click near the object to establish a point of origin **1** (the pointer will turn into an arrowhead), reposition the mouse **2**, then drag away from the object to enlarge it or drag toward the object to shrink it **3**.

   Start dragging, then press Option/Alt to scale a **copy** of the object **4**.

   Shift-drag diagonally to scale the object **proportionally**. Release the mouse before you release Shift.

➤ To flip and scale simultaneously, drag completely across the object with the Scale tool.

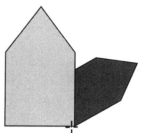

1 *Click to establish a point of origin.*

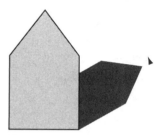

2 *Reposition the mouse...*

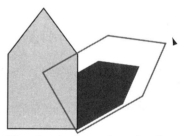

3 *...then drag away from the object.*

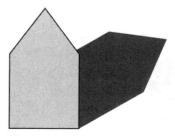

4 *The shadow object is enlarged.*

Scale

Default angle

The default Horizontal angle is 0°; the default Vertical angle is 90°. The default starting point for measuring the degree of an angle is the horizontal *(x)* axis (the three o'clock position).

1 *Reflect tool.*

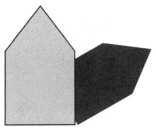
2 *In the Reflect dialog box, click* **Horizontal** *or* **Vertical**, *or enter a number in the* **Angle** *field.*

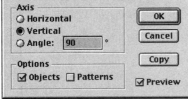
3 *The original objects.*

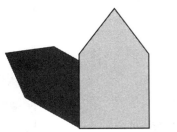
4 *The shadow reflected across the* **Vertical Axis** *(90°).*

To reflect (flip) an object using a dialog box:

1. Select an object (or objects) using the Selection tool or the Lasso tool.
2. To reflect from the object's center, double-click the Reflect tool **1**.
   or
   Choose the Reflect tool, then Option/Alt click near the object to establish a new point of origin.
3. Check the Preview box.
4. Click Axis: Horizontal or Vertical (the axis the mirror image will flip across) **2**.
   or
   Enter a number between 360 and –360 in the Angle field (press Tab). Enter a positive number to reflect the object counterclockwise or a negative number to reflect the object clockwise. The angle is measured from the horizontal *(x)* axis.
5. *Optional:* Check the Patterns box if the object contains a pattern fill and you want the pattern to reflect with the object.
6. Click Copy to reflect a copy of the original (not the original object) and close the dialog box.
   or
   Click OK (Return/Enter) **3**–**4**.
➤ You can enter any Angle. Illustrator will substitute the nearest acceptable value.

To reflect an object by dragging:

1. Select the object (or objects) using the Selection tool or the Lasso tool.
2. Choose the Reflect tool (O) **1**.
3. Click near the object to establish a new point of origin (the pointer will turn into an arrowhead), reposition the mouse, then drag horizontally or vertically toward, across, or around the point of origin. The object will flip across the axis you create by dragging.

   Start dragging, then press Option/Alt to reflect a **copy** of the object **4**.

   Shift-drag to **reflect** the object along a multiple of 45°. Release the mouse first.

Reflect

To shear (slant) an object using a dialog box:

1. Select an object (or objects) using the Selection tool or the Lasso tool 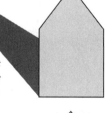.

2. To shear the object from its center, double-click the Shear tool (it's on the Reflect tool pop-out menu) **2**.
   or
   Choose the Shear tool, then Option-click/Alt-click near the object to establish a new point of origin.

3. Check the Preview box.

4. Enter a number between 360 and −360 in the Shear Angle field (press Tab) **3**.

5. Click Axis: Horizontal or Vertical (the axis along which the object will be sheared) **4**.
   or
   Click Axis: Angle, then enter a number in the Angle field (press Tab). The angle will be calculated clockwise relative to the horizontal *(x)* axis **5**.

6. *Optional:* Check the Patterns box to shear a pattern fill with the object.

7. Click Copy to shear a copy of the original (not the original object) and close the dialog box.
   or
   Click OK (Return/Enter).

To shear an object by dragging:

1. Select an object (or objects) using the Selection tool or the Lasso tool.

2. Choose the Shear tool **2**.

3. To slant from the object's center, without clicking first, position the pointer outside the object, then drag away from the object.
   or
   Click near the object to establish a new point of origin, reposition the mouse, then drag.

   Start dragging, then press Option/Alt to shear a **copy** of the object. To shear the object to a multiple of 45°, start dragging, then hold down Shift. Release the mouse button first.

Get the numbers

Each transformation dialog box displays the last-used values for that type of transformation (whether a tool or a dialog box was used) until those values are changed or you quit/exit Illustrator.

1 *The shadow object is selected.*

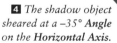 **2** *Shear tool*

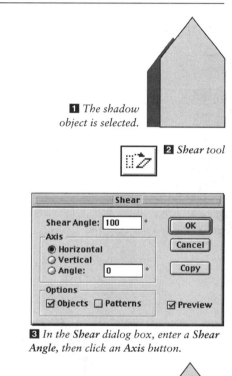

3 *In the Shear dialog box, enter a Shear Angle, then click an Axis button.*

4 *The shadow object sheared at a −35° Angle on the Horizontal Axis.*

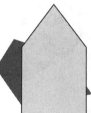

5 *The shadow object sheared at a −35° Angle on a 35° Axis Angle.*

Shear

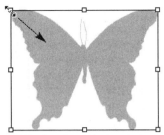

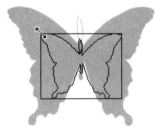

1 *Option-drag/Alt-drag to* **scale** *a path from its center.*

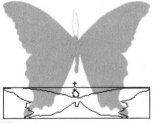

2 *The path is scaled down.*

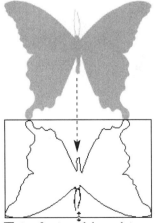

3 *To* **flip** *a path, drag a bounding box handle all the way across it.*

4 *A reflection of the path is made.*

To transform an object using its bounding box:

1. If bounding boxes are hidden, choose View menu > Show Bounding Box. *new*

2. Select an object (or objects) using the Selection tool or the Lasso tool. A rectangular box with eight handles will surround the object(s). The handles and box will be drawn in the color of the object's layer.

3. To **scale** the object along two axes, drag a corner handle; to resize along one axis, drag a side handle. Shift-drag to resize proportionally. Option-drag/Alt-drag to scale the object from its center **1**–**2**. Option-Shift-drag/Alt-Shift-drag to do both. *Note:* You can't choose a point of origin.
    or
    To create a **reflection** (mirror image) of the object, drag a side handle all the way across it.
    or
    To **flip** the object, drag a corner handle all the way across the object or Shift-drag a side handle to reflect and flip **3**–**4**. Option-drag/Alt-drag to reflect or flip from the object's center.
    or
    To **rotate** the object, move the pointer slightly to the right of a corner handle, (the pointer will be a *curved* double-arrow), then drag in a circular direction.

➤ If all of an object's anchor points are selected and then the Selection tool is chosen, the bounding box will appear.

If you rotate a box using either the Rotate tool or the Free Transform tool, the bounding box will no longer align with the *x/y* axes of the page. The Reset Bounding Box command resets the orientation of the bounding box (but not the orientation of the object).

To square off the bounding box:

With the object selected, choose Object menu > Transform > Reset Bounding Box or Control-click/Right-click and choose Transform > Reset Bounding Box.

Transform using Bounding Box

Free Transform

The Free Transform tool does what all the transformation tools do, plus distort and perspective.

Note: The Free Transform tool always works from the center of the object or objects. You can't choose a different point of origin.

To use the Free Transform tool:

1. Select an object(s) or a group. The Free Transform tool won't clone, so copy the object now if you want to transform a copy of it.

2. Choose the Free Transform tool (E) 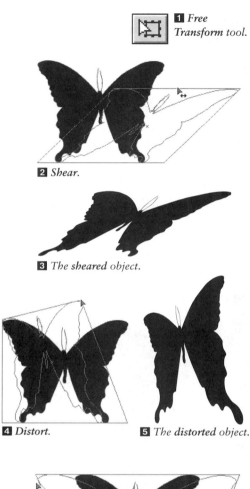.

1 *Free Transform tool.*

3. To **scale** in two dimensions, drag a corner handle. Shift-drag to resize proportionally. Option-drag/Alt-drag to resize the object from its center. Or to resize the object in one dimension, drag a side handle.

   To **rotate**, position the pointer outside the object, then drag in a circular motion. Shift-drag to rotate in 45° increments.

   To **shear**, drag a side handle then hold down Command/Ctrl and continue to drag **2**–**3**. To constrain the movement, drag a side handle, then hold down Command-Shift/Ctrl-Shift and continue to drag. To shear along the *x* or *y* axis from the object's center, drag, then hold down Command-Option-Shift/ Ctrl-Alt-Shift and continue to drag.

   To **reflect**, drag a side handle all the way across the object. To flip the object, drag a corner handle all the way across it. To reflect or flip from the object's center, Alt-drag/Option-drag a side or corner handle. Include the Shift key to reflect and flip proportionally.

   To **distort**, drag a corner (not a side) handle, then hold down Command/Ctrl and continue to drag **4**–**5**. *Note:* This won't work on type.

   To apply **perspective**, drag a corner handle, then hold down Command-Option-Shift/Ctrl-Alt-Shift and continue to drag **6**–**7**. The perspective will occur along the *x* or *y* axis, depending on which direction you drag. *Note:* You can't apply perspective to type.

2 *Shear.*

3 *The sheared object.*

4 *Distort.*   **5** *The distorted object.*

6 *Perspective.*

7 *The object with applied perspective.*

The original formation.

*The formation rotated 15° via the **Rotate** tool.*

*The formation rotated 15° via the **Transform Each** command with the Random box unchecked.*

1 *The **Transform Each** command vs. the **Rotate** tool.*

[The Transform Each dialog box with fields:]

Transform Each

Scale
Horizontal: 140 %
Vertical: 66 %

Move
Horizontal: 32 pt
Vertical: 0 pt

Rotate
Angle: 359 °

OK
Cancel
Copy

☐ Reflect X
☐ Reflect Y
☐ Random
☑ Preview

2 *The **Transform Each** dialog box.*

Point of origin

(See also the illustrations on the following page.)

The Transform Each command modifies one or more selected objects relative to their *individual* center points. The transformation tools, by contrast, transform multiple objects relative to a single, *common* center point **1**. To make your illustration look less regular and more hand drawn, apply the Transform Each command to multiple objects with the Random box checked.

To apply multiple transformation commands via Transform Each:

1. Select one or more objects. Objects in a group can't be transformed individually.

2. Choose Object menu > Transform > Transform Each (Command-Option-D/ Ctrl-Alt-D).
   or
   Control-click/Right-click and choose Transform > Transform Each.

3. Check the Preview box, and move the dialog box out of the way, if necessary.

4. Do any of the following **2**:

   Move the Horizontal or Vertical **Scale** slider (or enter a percentage and press Tab) to scale the objects' horizontally and/or vertically from their center point.

   Choose a higher Horizontal Move value to move the objects to the right, or vice versa. Choose a higher Vertical Move value to move the objects upward, or vice versa.

   Enter a number in the **Rotate** Angle field and press Tab, or rotate the dial.

   Check the **Reflect X** or **Reflect Y** box to create a mirror reflection of the objects.

   Check the **Random** box to have Illustrator apply random transformations within the range of the slider values you've chosen *improved* for Scale, Move, or Rotate. For example, at a Rotate Angle of 35°, a different angle between 0° and 35° will be used for each selected object. Turn the Preview box on and off to get different random effects.

   Click a different **point of origin** (the point that will remain stationary) for the transformation.

5. Click OK (Return/Enter).

Transform Each

new

If you apply transformations via the Transform Effect dialog box, you will be able to edit (not just undo) those transformations long after you've closed the dialog box, or even closed or reopened the file.

To use the Transform Effect dialog box to apply editable effects:

1. Select one or more objects.

2. Choose Effect menu > Distort & Transform > Transform.

3. Follow the instructions for the Transform Each dialog box on the previous page. The Transform Effect dialog box looks and behaves just like the Transform Each dialog box, with one exception: In the Transform Effect dialog box, you can specify how many copies you want **1**.

4. To edit the transformation, select the object, then double-click "Transform" on the Appearance palette **2**. This is a sneak preview of what's to come in Chapter 18, Appearances/Styles.

1 *Apply* **editable** *effects via the* **Transform Effect** *dialog box.*

2 *Double-click* **"Transform"** *on the* **Appearance** *palette to edit a transformation.*

Transform Effect

The original objects.

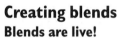

After applying **Transform Each**
(**Horizontal Scale** 120, **Vertical Scale** 80,
Horizontal Move 13, **Vertical Move** –13,
and **Rotate** 17°—*non-matching*
Horizontal and Vertical Scale values).

Creating blends
Blends are live!

Both the Blend tool and the Make Blend command create a multi-step color and shape progression between two or more objects. Using the Blend tool, you control which parts of the objects are calculated for the blend, whereas the Make Blend command controls this function automatically.

If you reshape, recolor, or reposition any of the individual objects in a blend or reshape, reposition, or transform the overall blend shape, the blend will update automatically. You can also alter the appearance of an existing blend by reshaping the straight path (spine) that the Blend tool or command creates using any path editing tool, or by selecting the blend and changing the number of steps or other options in the Blend Options dialog box.

To blend colors between objects without blending their shapes, use a Blend filter (see page 150).

Process or spot?

■ If one of the original blend objects contains a **process** color and another object contains a **spot** color, the intermediate objects will be painted with **process** colors.

■ If you blend objects containing more than one **spot** color, the intermediate objects will be painted with **process** colors.

■ If you blend **tints** of the **same spot** color, the intermediate objects will be painted with graduated **tints** of that color. To blend between a spot color and white, apply 0% of the spot color to the white object.

Before you create a blend, keep these guide-
lines in mind:

■ You can blend non-matching shapes
and shapes with different fill and stroke
attributes, **even brushstrokes.**

■ You can blend gradients or other blends,
but not gradient meshes.

■ You can blend two open paths, two
closed paths, or a closed path and an
open path.

■ Don't blend a closed path and an unfilled,
open path. You'll get something strange
and ugly.

To blend between objects using the Make Blend command:

1. Position two or more open paths or two
or more closed paths (or even groups),
allowing room for the transition shapes
that will be created between them,
and select the objects using the Selection
tool or the Lasso tool **1**.

2. Choose Object menu > Blend > Make
(Command-Option-B/Ctrl-Alt-B) **2**–**3**.

3. To change the appearance of the blend,
read the instructions on the next two
pages.

➤ If you don't like the blend, use the Undo
command or release the blend (instructions below).

➤ To prevent banding, see pages 97 and 99.

To release a blend:

1. Select the blend with the Selection tool
(or using the Layers palette).

2. Choose Object menu > Blend >
Release (Command-Option-Shift-B/
Ctrl-Alt-Shift-B). The original objects and
the *path* created by the blend will remain;
the transition objects will be deleted.

Recoloring blend objects

To recolor **all** the objects in a blend, use Filter
menu > Colors > **Adjust Colors**. To recolor
one of the **original** blend objects, deselect the
blend, choose the **Direct-selection** tool, select
one of the original objects, then choose a color
from the Color or Swatches palette. The transitional objects can't be recolored individually.

1 *The original objects: A white butterfly on top of a black butterfly.*

2 *After choosing Object menu > **Blend** > **Make**, with Spacing: **Smooth Color** chosen in the Blend Options dialog box (see the following page).*

3 *The original objects after choosing Object menu > **Blend** > **Make**, with Spacing: **Specified Steps** (7) chosen in the Blend Options dialog box (see the following page).*

Make Blend; Release Blend

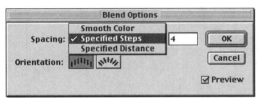

1 *Blend tool.*

2 *Choose* **Spacing** *and* **Orientation** *options for existing and future blends in the* **Blend Options** *dialog box.*

3 *Spacing:* **Smooth Color.**

4 *Spacing:* **Specified Steps** *(7).*

5 *Orientation:* **Align to Page.**

Note: If you change the Blend Options settings, any currently selected blends will update automatically. The new settings will also affect any subsequently created blends.

To choose or change blend options:

1. Double-click the Blend tool (not the Gradient tool!) **1**.
   or
   Select an existing blend and choose Object menu > Blend > Blend Options.

2. Check the Preview box to preview changes on any currently selected blends.

3. Choose an option from the Spacing pop-up menu **2**:

   Smooth Color to have Illustrator automatically calculate the necessary number of blend steps (transition shapes) to produce smooth, non-banding color transitions **3**. This option may take a moment to preview on existing objects.

   Specified Steps, and enter the desired number of transition steps for the blend (press Tab to preview). Use this option if you want to create distinct, discernible transition shapes **4**.

   Specified Distance to enter the desired distance between the transition shapes in the blend. The Specified Distance has no effect on the overall length of the blend.

4. Click the **Align to Page** Orientation (first) button to keep the blend objects perpendicular to the page (horizontal axis) **5**.
   or
   Click the **Align to Path** Orientation (second) button to keep the blend objects perpendicular to the blend path **6**. (To place blend objects on a user-drawn spine, see page 101.)

5. Click OK (Enter/Return).

6 *Orientation:* **Align to Path.**

Blend Options

Editing blends

➤ Recolor any of the original objects in a blend using the **Direct-selection** tool.

➤ Recolor all the objects in a blend using a filter on the Filter menu > **Colors** submenu.

➤ Transform an entire blend using a **transform** tool or the **Free Transform** tool.

➤ Reshape a blend path by **moving** one of the original objects (Direct-selection tool) or using any of the **path-reshaping** tools (e.g., Direct-selection, Add-anchor-point, or Convert-anchor-point-tool).

The original blend.

The same blend after recoloring the rightmost snowflake, adding points to the blend path, and reshaping the path.

Editing Blends

The 39 Steps

To **print** a Smooth Color blend, Illustrator automatically calculates the number of steps needed to produce a smooth blend based on the difference in CMYK color-component percentages between the blend objects (e.g., changes in the percentage of Magenta between each object), and based on the assumption that the blend will be output on a high-resolution device (1200 dpi or higher). To specify the number of steps for a blend, enter the desired number (1–1000) in the Blend Options dialog box in the Spacing pop-up menu: Specified Steps field. Banding is more likely to occur in a color blend if it spans a wide distance (more than seven inches). For better results, use Adobe Photoshop to create a wide color blend, then place it into Illustrator.

Outputting blends to the **Web** is a whole different story. See pages 442 and 444.

The Reverse Front to Back command changes the stacking order of blend objects—not their *x/y* locations.

To reverse the stacking position of objects in a blend:

1. Select the blend with the Selection tool (or using the Layers palette) **1**.
2. Choose Object menu > Blend > Reverse Front to Back **2**. The original and transitional objects will now be in their reverse stacking order (e.g., what was originally the backmost object will now be the frontmost object, and vice versa).

The Reverse Spine command swaps the *x/y* location of all the blend objects, but it doesn't change their stacking position.

To reverse the location of objects in a blend:

1. Select the blend with the Selection tool (or using the Layers palette) **1**.
2. Choose Object menu > Blend > Reverse Spine. The blend objects will swap locations **3**.

1 *The original blend.*

2 *After applying the **Reverse Front to Back** command.*

3 *Figure **2** after applying the **Reverse Spine** command.*

To blend objects using the Blend tool:

1. Position two or more different-shaped open paths or two or more closed paths, allowing room for the transition shapes that will be created between them. You can apply different colors or gradients to each object.

2. Choose the Blend tool (W) .

3. To let Illustrator decide which anchor points to use for the blend, click on the fill of the first object (but not on the center point).
   or
   If you want to control which anchor point will be used, click on an anchor point on the first object **2**. The little square on the Blend tool pointer will change from hollow to filled when it's over an anchor point.

4. Click on the fill or on an anchor point on the next object **3**. If the path is open, click on an endpoint. For the smoothest shape transitions, click on corresponding points on all the objects (e.g., the top left corner point of all the objects; not the top left corner point of one object and the lower right corner point of another object). You can add points, if necessary, so the objects have an equal number of points. The blend will appear **4**–**5**.

   Repeat this step for any other objects that you want to include in the blend. The blend will update automatically! See "Blends are live" on page 95.

5. To change the appearance of the blend, (e.g., change Specified Steps to Smooth Color), see page 97.

➤ If you don't like the blend, use Undo or choose Object menu > Blend > Release.

➤ If the original objects contain different pattern fills, the transition shapes will be filled automatically with the pattern fill from the topmost object.

➤ Apply a stroke color to the blend if you want the transition shapes to be clearly delineated. To do this after the blend is created, use the Selection tool, click the blend, then apply a stroke.

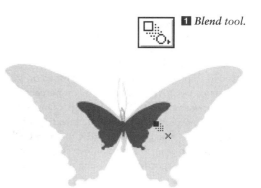

1 *Blend tool.*

2 *Click on the fill or an anchor point of one object.*

3 *Then click on the fill or an anchor point of another object.*

4 *The blend appears.*

5 *This is what happens if you click on non-corresponding points.*

Blend Tool

1 *Select a user-drawn path and a blend.*

2 *After choosing **Replace Spine**, the blend flows along the user-drawn path.*

To apply an existing blend to a path:

1. Create a blend, then draw a separate path along which you want the blend to flow. The path you draw can be closed or open. If it's closed, the blend will wrap around the object as best as it can.

2. Select both the blend and the path using the Selection tool or the Lasso tool **1**.

3. Choose Object menu > Blend > Replace Spine. The blend will now follow along the user-drawn path **2**.

➤ If you release the blend from a user-drawn path (Object menu > Blend > Release), the path will be preserved, but it won't have a stroke. You can locate the path in Outline view or using Smart Guides (Object Highlighting).

➤ To change the orientation of the blend objects, select the blend, choose Object menu > Blend > Blend Options, then click the non-highlighted Orientation button (see **5** and **6** on page 97).

➤ Blends can contain appearances and effects. To learn more about blends and appearances, see page 297.

Use a blend to create a 3-D effect:

1. Select an object , and apply a fill color and a stroke of None.

2. Double-click the Scale tool.

3. Click Uniform, enter a number between 60 and 80 in the Scale field, then click Copy.

4. With the copy still selected, choose a lighter or darker variation of the original fill color (or black or white) . (For a process color, you can Shift-drag a process color slider on the Color palette to lighten or darken the color.)

5. Make sure the smaller object is in front of the larger object so you'll be able to see the blend, then select both objects using the Selection tool or the Lasso tool.

6. Choose Object menu > Blend > Make (Command-Option-B/Ctrl-Alt-B) –. If the resulting blend doesn't look smooth, select it, double-click the Blend tool, choose Smooth Color from the Spacing pop-up menu, then click OK.

➤ You can modify either blend object at any time. Select the object using the Direct-selection tool, and then reposition or recolor it. You can resize the selected object using the Free Transform or the Scale tool. The blend will redraw automatically.

➤ A similar effect can be achieved on a single object using Object menu > Create Gradient Mesh (choose Appearance: To Center).

➤ To create a 3-D surface-modeling effect the old-fashioned way, draw a line and copy it to a new location. Reshape the copy, if desired, and recolor it. Make sure the Smooth Color option is chosen in the Blend Options dialog box, then create the blend using the two lines and the Make Blend command or the Blend tool.

1 *The original object.*

2 *A reduced-size copy of the object is created, and a white fill is applied.*

3 *The two objects are blended together.*

4 *Here's another variation.*

RESHAPE | 8

In Chapter 5 you learned how to draw closed and open paths without thinking about their individual components. In this important chapter, you will learn how to reshape paths using the nuts and bolts that all paths are composed of: direction lines, direction points, anchor points, and segments. Once you learn how to alter the profile of an object by changing the number, position, or type of anchor points on its path, you'll be able to create just about any shape imaginable.

In this chapter you will learn how to move anchor points, direction lines, or path segments to reshape a path; how to convert a corner anchor point into a curve anchor point (or vice versa) to reshape the segments that it connects; how to add or delete anchor points and segments; and how to use the Erase, Pencil, Paintbrush, Smooth, or Reshape tool to quickly reshape part of a path. You will also learn how to average anchor points; how to join endpoints; how to combine paths using the Unite command; how to split a path; how to make cutout shapes using the Slice command; and how to carve away parts of a path using the Knife tool. Also included in this chapter are three practice exercises.

The path building blocks

Paths are composed of curved and/or straight segments. A curve consists of two anchor points connected by a curve segment, with at least one direction point and one direction line attached to each anchor point. An anchor point that connects a curve and a straight line segment has one direction line. An anchor point that connects two curve segments has a pair of direction lines.

Path Building Blocks

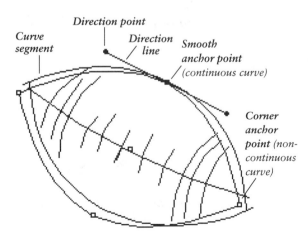

Curve segment

Direction point

Direction line

Smooth anchor point (continuous curve)

Corner anchor point (non-continuous curve)

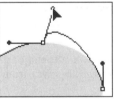

*The **angle** of a direction line affects the **slope** of the curve into the anchor point.*

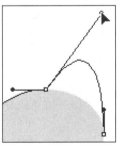

*The **length** of a direction line affects the **height** of the curve.*

Corners and curves

If you move an anchor point, the segments that are connected to it will reshape. If you move a curve segment, the connecting anchor points will remain stationary. If you move a straight line segment, connecting anchor points *will* move.

To move an anchor point or a segment:

1. Choose the Direct-selection tool (A) 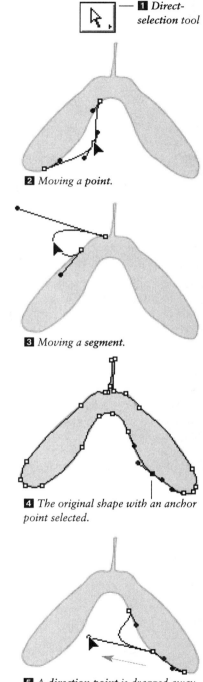.
   Note: You can move more than one point at a time, even points on different paths. To select them, Shift-click them or drag a marquee around them.

2. Drag an anchor point **2**, or drag the middle of a segment **3**, or press an arrow key. You can use Smart Guides for precise positioning (Command-U/Ctrl-U).

➤ Shift-drag to constrain the movement of an anchor point to a multiple of 45°.

➤ If all the anchor points on a path are selected, you will not be able to move an individual point or segment. Deselect the object, then reselect an individual point.

In the instructions above, you learned that you can drag a curve segment or an anchor point to reshape a curve. A more precise way to reshape a curve is to lengthen, shorten, or change the angle of its direction lines.

To reshape a curve segment:

1. Choose the Direct-selection tool (A).

2. Click on an anchor point or a curve segment **4**.

3. Drag a direction point (the end of the direction line) toward or away from the anchor point **5**.
   or
   Rotate the direction point around the anchor point. The anchor point will remain selected when you release the mouse. Use Shift to constrain the angle.

➤ Direction line antennae on a smooth curve always move in tandem. They'll stay in a straight line even if the curve segment or anchor point they are connected to is moved.

1 *Direct-selection tool*

2 *Moving a point.*

3 *Moving a segment.*

4 *The original shape with an anchor point selected.*

5 *A direction point is dragged away from its anchor point.*

104

1 *Convert-anchor-point tool.*

To convert a corner anchor point into a smooth anchor point:

1. Choose the Convert-anchor-point tool (Shift-C) **1**. (This works better for right-handed mousers than left-handed mousers—grrr...)

   improved
   Not!

   or

   Choose the Pen tool (P).

2. Command-click/Ctrl-click the edge of the object to display its anchor points.

3. If you're using the Convert-anchor-point tool, press on an anchor point **2**, then drag away from it **3**. Direction lines will appear as you drag. If you're using the Pen tool, do the same thing with Option/Alt held down.

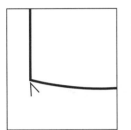

2 *To convert a corner point into a curve point, press with the Convert-anchor-point tool on the anchor point...*

3 *...then drag away from the point.*

5. *Optional:* To further modify the curve, choose the Direct-selection tool, then drag the anchor point or a direction line **4**.

   Note: If the new curve segment twists around the anchor point as you drag, keep the mouse button down, rotate the direction line back around the anchor point to undo the twist, then continue to drag in the new direction **5**.

➤ To reshape paths using a vector filter, try Filter menu > Stylize > Round Corners. To reshape paths using the effect version, try Effect menu > Stylize > Round Corners.

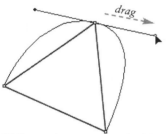

4 *Converting a **corner** point into a **smooth** point.*

Convert a Corner Point into a Curve Point

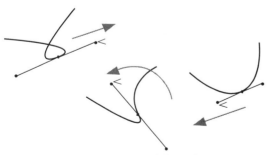

5 *If the curve twists around the anchor point, rotate the direction line to un-twist it.*

To convert a curve anchor point into a corner anchor point:

improved

1. Choose the Convert-anchor-point tool (Shift-C).
   or
   Choose the Pen tool (P).
2. Command-click/Ctrl-click the edge of the object to display its anchor points.
3. If you're using the Convert-anchor-point-tool, click on a curve anchor point—don't drag! Its direction lines will be deleted **1**–**2**. If you're using the Pen tool, do the same thing with Option/Alt held down.

1 *Click with the Convert-anchor-point tool on a curve point…*

2 *…to convert it into a corner point.*

The direction lines in a pinched curve rotate independently of each other—they don't stay in a straight line.

To pinch a curve inward:

1. Choose the Direct-selection tool (A).
2. Click the edge of an object to display its anchor points, then click a point **3**.
3. Choose the Convert-anchor-point tool (Shift-C).
   or
   Choose the Pen tool (P) and hold down Option/Alt.
4. Drag a direction point at the end of one of the direction lines. The curve segment will reshape as you drag **4**. Release Option/Alt, if it's pressed down.
5. Choose the Direct-selection tool, if it isn't already chosen, click on the anchor point, then drag the other direction line for that anchor point **5**.

➤ To revert an independent-rotating direction line pair back to its previous straight-line alignment and produce a smooth, unpinched curve segment, choose the Convert-anchor-point tool, then press on, and drag away from, the anchor point.

3 *A point is selected on an object.*

4 *A direction line is moved independently using the Convert-anchor-point tool.*

5 *The second direction line is moved.*

Convert a Curve into a Corner; Pinch a Curve

Nice curves

It's hard to get a symmetrical curve if you place points at the high point of a curve.

You'll get a more symmetrical curve if you place points only at the ends.

1 *Add-anchor-point tool.*

2 *Click on a segment to add a new point…*

3 *…and then move the new anchor point, if desired.*

Adding points

Another way to reshape a path is to manually add or delete anchor points from it. Adding or deleting points from a closed path won't split or open it.

Note: If you want to use the Pen tool to add points to a path, make sure the Disable Auto Add/Delete box is unchecked in Edit menu > Preferences > General. Then all you have to do is click a segment on a selected path to add a point to it.

To add anchor points to a path manually:

1. Choose the Selection tool (V) or the Lasso tool (Y), then select the object to which you want to add a point or points.

2. Choose the Add-anchor-point tool (+) **1**.
   or
   Choose the Pen tool (P). See the Note, above.

3. Click on the edge of the object. A new, selected anchor point will appear **2**. Repeat, if desired, to add more points.

   Note: An anchor point added to a curve segment will be a curve point with direction lines. An anchor point added to a straight segment will be a corner point.

4. *Optional:* Use the Direct-selection tool (A) to move the new anchor point (or its direction lines) **3**.

➤ Hold down Shift to disable the Auto Add/Delete function of the Pen tool. Release Shift before releasing the mouse.

➤ If you don't click precisely on a path segment, a warning prompt may appear. Click OK, then try again.

➤ Hold down Option/Alt to use the Delete-anchor-point tool when the Add-anchor-point tool is selected, and vice versa.

The Add Anchor Points command inserts one anchor point midway between every two existing anchor points.

To add anchor points to a path using a command:

1. Choose the Selection tool (V) or the Lasso tool (Y), then select the object or objects to which you want to add points.

2. Choose Object menu > Path > Add Anchor Points **1**–**3**. Repeat, if desired.

1 *The original object.*

2 *After adding anchor points to the original object and then applying the Punk and Bloat filter (Punk 70%).*

Diane Margolin

3 *After adding more anchor points and then applying the Punk and Bloat filter (Bloat 70%).*

Pen shortcuts new

Pen tool	**P**
Add-anchor-point-tool	**+**
Delete-anchor-point-tool	**-**
Convert-direction-point tool	**Shift-C**
Pencil tool	**N**
Paintbrush tool	**B**
Scissors tool	**C**
Direct-select Lasso tool	**Q**
Access Convert-direction-point tool with Pen tool chosen	**Option/Alt**
Disable Auto Add/Delete function of Pen tool	**Shift**
Access last-used selection tool with Pen tool chosen	**Command/Ctrl**
Use Delete-anchor-point tool when Add-anchor-point tool is chosen, and vice versa	**Option/Alt**
Access Smooth tool with Pencil or Paintbrush tool chosen	**Option/Alt**
Average points	**Command-Option-J/Ctrl-Alt-J**
Join points	**Command-J/Ctrl-J**
Average and join points	**Command-Option-Shift-J/ Ctrl-Alt-Shift-J**

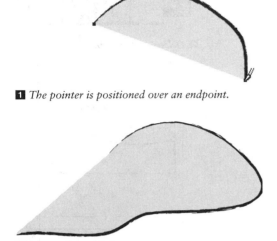

1 *The pointer is positioned over an endpoint.*

2 *The path is added to.*

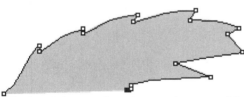

3 *The pointer is positioned over an endpoint. Note the slash next to the pen.*

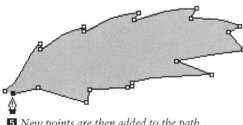

4 *After clicking on the endpoint, it becomes solid.*

5 *New points are then added to the path.*

You can use the Pencil tool to add to any open path. It doesn't matter which tool was used to draw the path initially, and the path can have a brushstroke.

To add to an open path using the Pencil tool:

1. Choose the Selection tool (V), then select an open path.

2. Choose the Pencil tool (N).

3. Position the pointer directly over an endpoint, then draw an addition to it. When you release the mouse, the path will remain selected.

➤ If you end up with a separate path instead of an addition to an existing path, delete the new path and try again.

To add to a brushstroke path using the Paintbrush tool:

1. Choose the Selection tool (V), then select an open path that has a brushstroke.

2. Choose the Paintbrush tool (B).

3. Position the pointer directly over an endpoint, then draw an addition to it **1**. When you release the mouse, the path will remain selected **2**.

To add a segment to an open path:

1. Choose the Pen tool (P).

2. Position the pointer over the endpoint of one of the paths to which you want to add a segment (the path doesn't have to be selected). A slash will appear next to the Pen pointer when the tool is positioned correctly **3**.

3. Click on the endpoint. The point will become solid **4**.

4. Position the pointer where you want a new anchor point to appear.

5. Drag to create a smooth point.
   or
   Click to create a corner point **5**.

6. Continue to add points, if desired. Choose another tool when you're done.

➤ To close a path or join two separate paths using the Pen tool, see page 118.

Deleting points

Note: If you want to use the Pen tool to delete points from a path, make sure the Disable Auto Add/Delete box is unchecked in Edit menu > Preferences > General. Then all you have to do is click on a point to delete it.

To delete anchor points from a path:

1. Choose the Delete-anchor-point tool (-) .
   or
   Choose the Pen tool (P).

2. Command-click/Ctrl-click the edge of the object from which you want to delete anchor points.

3. Click an anchor point (don't press Delete!). The point will be deleted and an adjacent point will become selected 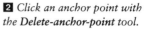. Repeat to delete other anchor points, if desired.

➤ Hold down Shift to disable the add/ delete function of the Pen tool. Release Shift before releasing the mouse button.

➤ If you don't click precisely on an anchor point with the Delete-anchor-point tool, you'll either hear a beep (if the Disable Warnings box is checked in General Preferences) or a prompt will appear (if the Disable Warnings box is unchecked).

1 *Delete-anchor-point tool*

2 *Click an anchor point with the Delete-anchor-point tool.*

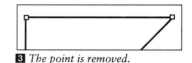

3 *The point is removed.*

Delete Anchor Points

1 *Erase tool*

2 *The original objects.*

3 *Using the Erase tool.*

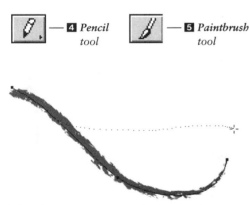

4 *Pencil tool*   **5** *Paintbrush tool*

6 *Reshaping a path using the Pencil tool. (Caps Lock was pressed to turn the cursor into a crosshair.)*

7 *The path is reshaped.*

Quick reshaping

The Erase tool deletes points, too—but you don't have to click on them individually.

To erase part of a path using the Erase tool:

1. Choose the Erase tool from the Pencil tool pop-out menu **1**.

2. Command-click/Ctrl-click an object (not a gradient mesh or a text path).

3. Position the eraser (black) part of the pencil pointer directly over the area from which you want to remove points, then drag once across that area **2**–**3**. If you erase points from a closed path, you'll end up with an open path. If you erase points from an open path, you'll end up with two separate paths.

You already know how to use the Pencil and Paintbrush tools to draw freehand shapes. Now we'll show you how they can be used for quick-n-easy reshaping.

To reshape a path using the Pencil or Paintbrush tool:

1. To reshape a non-brushstroked path, choose the Pencil tool (N) **4**.
   or
   To reshape a brushstroked path, choose the Pencil tool (N) or the Paintbrush tool (B) **5**.

2. Command-click/Ctrl-click on a path to select it.

3. Position the pointer directly over the edge of the path, then start dragging **6**. If you want the path to close up or stay closed, finish up over another edge of the path. The path will reshape instantly **7**.

➤ Be sure to position the pointer right on the edge of the path. If you don't, you'll create a new path instead of a reshaped path. Press Caps Lock and nudge the mouse to turn the pointer into a Precise Cursor (crosshair). Press Caps Lock again to restore the default cursors.

➤ To add to an open path using the Pencil or Paintbrush tool, see page 109.

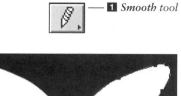

1 *Smooth tool*

To smooth part of an existing path:

1. Choose the Selection tool (V) or the Lasso tool (Y), select an open or closed path, then choose the Smooth tool (it's on the Pencil tool pop-out menu) **1**.
or
If the Pencil or Paintbrush tool is currently chosen, Command-click/Ctrl-click an open or closed path to select it, then hold down Option/Alt to access the Smooth tool.

2. Drag along the path. The bumps on the path will be smoothed out **2**–**4**. Some anchor points may be removed. Now read about the Smooth Tool Preferences, which affects how drastic an effect this tool has on a path.

2 *Using the Smooth tool.*

To choose settings for the Smooth tool:

1. Double-click the Smooth tool **1**.

2. Choose a Fidelity value (0.5–20) **5**. Higher values mean more anchor points will be removed.

3. Choose a Smoothness value (0–100). The higher the Smoothness value, logically, the greater the amount of smoothing; the lower the smoothness, the less drastic the reshaping.

4. Click OK (Return/Enter).

➤ Click Reset to reset the preferences to their defaults.

3 *The Smooth tool used with **high Fidelity** and **Smoothness** settings.*

4 *The Smooth tool used on the original object with **moderate Fidelity** and **Smoothness** settings.*

5 *Smooth Tool Preferences.*

Smooth Tool

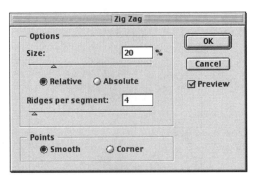

1 *The Zig Zag dialog box.*

The original line.

Zigzag, Smooth Points.

Zigzag, Corner Points.

Some of the Illustrator filters and effects can be used to explode a simple shape into a more complex one in one fell swoop. The Zig Zag filter, for example, adds anchor points to a path or line and then moves those points to produce waves or zigzags. The Effect menu version applies the Zig Zag effect without actually altering the path. Effect menu commands are reeditable; Filter menu commands are not. (This is just a preview. Read more about filters in Chapter 20; Effects in Chapter 18.)

To apply the Zig Zag effect: *improved*

1. Select a path.

2. Choose Effect menu > Distort & Transform (upper part of the menu) > Zig Zag.

3. Check the Preview box **1**.

4. Click Points: Smooth (bottom of the dialog box) to make curvy waves or click Corner to create sharp-cornered zigzags.

5. To move the added points by a percentage of the size of the object, click Relative, then choose a Size percentage.
   or
   To move the added points a specified distance, click Absolute, then choose the actual distance via the Size slider or field (the increment is chosen in File menu > Document Setup: Units).

6. Choose a number of Ridges for the number of anchor points to be added between existing points. If you enter a number, press Tab to preview.

7. Click OK (Return/Enter).

The original star.

Size 45, Ridges 4, Smooth.

The original circle.

Size 24, Ridges 20, Corner.

Zig Zag Effect

The Reshape tool is hard to describe in words. It's the best tool for gentle reshaping because it causes the least amount of distortion. Our favorite way to use this tool is to select a handful of points with it, then drag. That portion of the path will keep its overall contour while it elongates or contracts, and the rest of the path will stay put.

To use the Reshape tool:

1. Click on the edge of a path using the Direct-selection tool. Only one point or segment should be selected.

2. Choose the Reshape tool on the Scale tool pop-out menu **1**.

3. Drag any visible point. A square border will display around the point when you release the mouse.
   or
   Drag any segment of the path. A new square border point will be created.
   or
   Try this: Shift-click or marquee multiple points on the path using the Reshape tool (squares will display around these points), then drag. For smooth reshaping, leave at least one point on the path unselected (with no square around it) to act as an anchor for the shape **2**–**3**.

➤ Option-drag with the Reshape tool to copy the object as it's reshaped.

➤ Choose Edit menu > Undo to undo the last Reshape.

➤ To reshape multiple paths at the same time, leave at least one point on each path unselected by the Reshape tool (with no square around it) to act as an anchor. For fun, try this on a series of lines. Their endpoints will remain stationary.

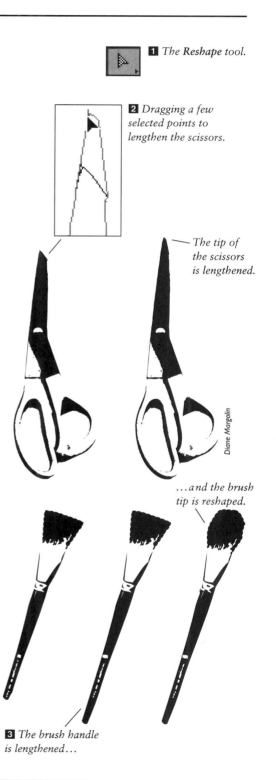

1 *The Reshape tool.*

2 *Dragging a few selected points to lengthen the scissors.*

The tip of the scissors is lengthened.

Diane Margolin

...and the brush tip is reshaped.

3 *The brush handle is lengthened...*

Reshape Tool

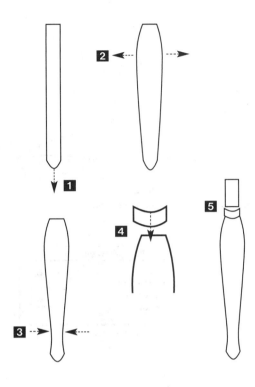

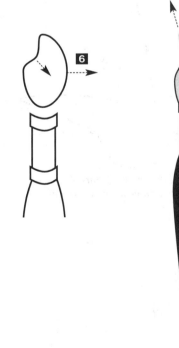

Exercise

Draw a paintbrush using the Reshape tool

1. Using the Rectangle tool, draw a narrow vertical rectangle, white fill, black stroke.

2. Choose the Direct-selection tool (A), deselect the shape, then click on the edge of the path.

3. Choose the Reshape tool (Scale tool pop-out menu), then drag downward from the middle of the bottom segment **1**.

4. Drag the upper middle of the right vertical segment slightly outward and drag the upper middle part of the left vertical segment outward the same distance **2**.

5. Drag each side of the bottom vertical segments inward to pinch the stem **3**.

6. Draw a small horizontal rectangle. Then choose the Direct-selection tool, deselect the rectangle, and click on the path.

7. Choose the Reshape tool again, click the middle of the top segment, Shift-click the middle of the bottom segment, then drag downward **4**.

8. Choose the Selection tool (V), place the rectangle over the top of the brush stem, scale it to fit, and fill it with white.

9. Draw a vertical rectangle above the horizontal rectangle in a slightly narrower width. Choose Object menu > Arrange > Send to Back **5**.

10. Option-Shift/Alt-Shift drag the horizontal rectangle upward. Move the copy to the top of the vertical rectangle.

11. Using the Ellipse tool, draw an oval for brush tip. Choose the Direct-selection tool, deselect the oval, then click on the edge of the path.

12. Choose the Reshape tool, drag the right middle point outward, drag the upper left segment inward **6**, and drag the top point upward to lengthen the tip **7**.

13. Position the brush tip shape over the brush stem, then choose Object menu > Arrange > Send To Back.

Reshape Tool

Averaging points

The Average command reshapes one or more paths by precisely realigning their endpoints or anchor points along the horizontal and/or vertical axis.

To average points:

1. Choose the Direct-selection tool (A) or Direct-select Lasso tool (Q).

2. Shift-click or marquee two or more anchor points 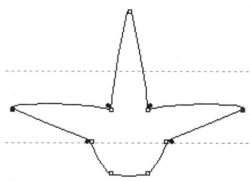. They can be on different paths.

3. Choose Object menu > Path > Average (Command-Option-J/Ctrl-Alt-J).
   or
   Control-click/Right-click on the artboard and choose Average from the context menu.

4. Click **Horizontal** to align the points along the horizontal *(x)* axis **2**. Points will move vertically.
   or
   Click **Vertical** to align the points along the vertical *(y)* axis. Points will move horizontally.
   or
   Click **Both** to overlap the points along both the horizontal and vertical axes. Choose this option if you're going to join them into one point (instructions on the following page).

5. Click OK (Return/Enter) **3**.

1 *Two anchor points are selected.*

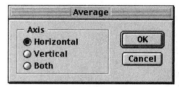

2 *Click an **Axis** button in the Average dialog box.*

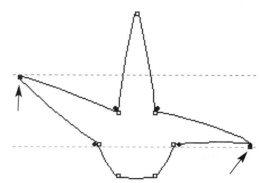

3 *After averaging the selected points, **Axis: Horizontal**, the points now align horizontally.*

All at once

To **average** and **join** two selected endpoints using one keystroke: Command-Option-Shift-J/ Ctrl-Alt-Shift-J. Don't apply this to a selected path. *Note:* To undo this, use the Undo command twice!

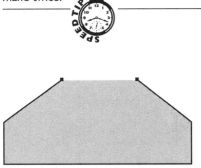

1 *Two endpoints are selected.*

2 *The endpoints are joined, and a segment is added between them automatically.*

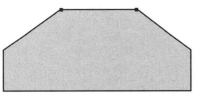

3 *Click **Points: Corner** or **Smooth** in the Join dialog box.*

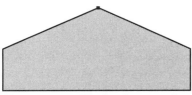

4 *This is Figure **1** after the two endpoints were **averaged** and then **joined** into **one** point.*

Joining

If you align two endpoints on top of each other and then execute the Join command with the endpoints selected, they will combine into one anchor point (that's method 1, below). If the endpoints are not on top of each other when they're joined, a new straight segment will be created between them. The Join command will not add direction lines to the new anchor point.

Note: The endpoints you join can be on separate open paths or one open path. If you join an open path with a path in a group, the resulting path will be outside the group.

To join two endpoints:

Method 1

1. Choose the Direct-selection tool (A).

2. *Optional:* If you want to combine two endpoints into one, move one endpoint on top of the other manually and marquee them to select them both, or use the Average command (Axis: Both) to align them (instructions are on the previous page).

3. Shift-click or marquee two endpoints **1**.

4. Choose Object menu > Path > Join (Command-J/Ctrl-J) or Control-click/ Right-click on the artboard and choose Join from the context menu. If the endpoints are not on top of each other, the Join command will connect them with a straight line segment **2**.

   If the endpoints are right on top of each other, the Join dialog box will open **3**. In the Join dialog box:

   Click **Corner** to join corner points into one corner point with no direction lines or to connect two curve points (or a corner point and a curve point) into one curve point with independent-moving direction lines. This is the default setting.
   or
   Click **Smooth** to connect two curve points into a curve point with direction lines that move in tandem.

5. Click OK (Return/Enter).

(Method 2 is on the following page)

Join Endpoints

Method 2

1. Choose the Pen tool (P).

2. Position the pointer over the endpoint of one of the paths you want to join. A small slash will appear next to the Pen pointer when the tool is positioned correctly **1**.

3. Click on the endpoint.

4. Position the pointer over the other endpoint of the same path or an endpoint on another path. A small hollow circle will appear next to the Pen pointer **2**.

5. Click on the second endpoint. A new segment will appear between the two points you clicked on **3**.

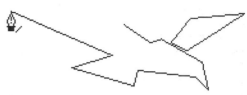

1 *To join two endpoints, position the Pen over one* **endpoint**...

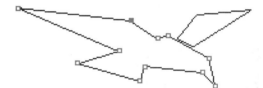

2 *...then click on the other* **endpoint**.

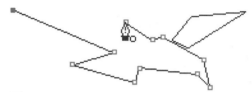

3 *The two points are joined by a* **new segment**.

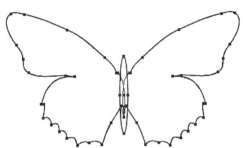

1 *Two or more objects are arranged so they overlap, and then they're selected.*

2 *After clicking the **Unite** button on the Pathfinder palette, the individual shapes are combined into a single shape.*

3 *The original objects.*

4 *After applying the **Unite** command.*

5 *The original objects.*

6 *After applying the **Unite** command.*

Rather than joining individual points, the Pathfinder commands combine whole objects into one new object. Here's an introduction to one of the most straightforward and useful ones: The Unite command. (Read more about the Pathfinders on pages 271–274.)

To combine two or more objects into one using the Unite command:

1. Position two or more objects so they overlap **1**.

2. Choose any Selection tool.

3. Marquee at least some portion of all the objects.

4. On the Pathfinder palette, click the Unite button ▨. The individual objects will combine into one closed object **2**–**6**, and will be colored with the topmost object's paint attributes.

➤ If you apply a stroke color to the new object, you will see that the previously overlapping segments were removed.

➤ You can use the new closed object as a masking object. (You could not have created a single mask with the original objects before they were united.)

Unite Command

Slicing and dicing

The Scissors tool can be used to open a closed path or split an open path into two paths (method 1). A path can be split at an anchor point or in the middle of a segment.

1 *Scissors tool.*

To split a path:

1. Choose any selection tool.
2. Click on an object to display its points. *Note:* You can split a closed path with text inside it (area text), but you can't split an open path that has text on it or inside it.
3. Choose the Scissors tool (C) **1**.
4. Click on the object's path **2**. If you click once on a **closed** path, it will turn into a single, open path. If you click in **two** different spots on a closed path, the object will be split into two open paths. If you click once on an **open** path, it will split into two paths.

   If you click on a **segment**, two new endpoints will appear, one on top of the other. If you click on an anchor **point**, a new anchor point will appear on top of the existing one, and it will be selected.

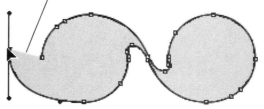

2 *Click with the Scissors tool on an anchor point or a segment.*

There is no segment, and thus no stroke, between the endpoints.

To move the two new endpoints apart:

5. Choose the Direct-selection tool (A).
6. Drag the selected point away to reveal the other new endpoint underneath it **3**. (To move the bottom endpoint instead, marquee both endpoints, Shift-click the top one, then press and hold an arrow key.)

3 *The new endpoint is moved. If you apply a stroke color to an open path, you'll be able to see where the missing segment is. An open path can have a fill.*

To split a path by deleting a point or a segment:

1. Deselect the object you want to split.
2. Choose the Direct-selection tool (A).
3. Click on an anchor point or a segment. *Note:* If you delete an endpoint from an open path, the adjacent segment will also be deleted. If you delete a segment at the end of an open path, the endpoint will be left behind.
4. Press Delete/Backspace.

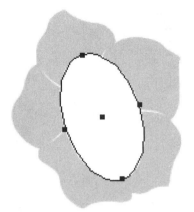

1 *The white oval is the cutting object.*

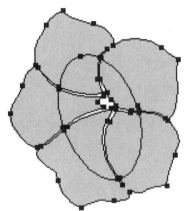

2 *After applying the Slice command, all the resulting objects become selected.*

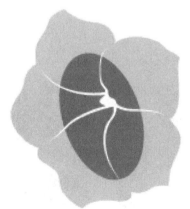

3 *After recoloring the five separate paths that originally formed an oval.*

The Slice command uses an object like a cookie cutter to cut the objects underneath it, and then deletes the cutting object.

To cut objects using the Slice command:

1. Create or select an object to be used as the cutting shape. The Slice command will cause this object to be deleted, so make a copy of it now if you want to preserve it.

2. Place the cutting object on top of the objects you want to cut **1**.

3. Make sure no other objects are selected except the cutting object.

4. Choose Object menu > Path > Slice. The topmost shape (cutting object) will be deleted automatically and the underlying objects will be cut into separate paths where they meet the edge of the cutting object **2**–**3**. New path layers will be created for the newly cut shapes.

➤ To prevent an object from being affected, hide or lock that path layer (see pages 182–183). *new*

Slice Objects

The Knife tool reshapes paths like a carving knife, and is a wonderful tool for artists who have a freehand drawing style.

Note: The Knife tool works on a closed path or a filled, open path, but not on an unfilled open path. To carve up type, first convert it to outlines.

To cut an object into separate shapes:

1. *Optional:* If you select an object (or objects) before using the Knife tool, the tool won't cut any of the unselected objects. This is useful if there are many objects close together in the illustration and you don't want them all to be cut. If you don't select any objects first, any object the Knife passes through is fair game.

2. Choose the Knife tool from the Scissors tool pop-out menu **1**.

3. Starting from outside the object(s), drag completely across it to divide it in two or end up outside the object again to carve off a chunk of it **2**–**4**.

   Option-drag/Alt-drag to cut in a straight line. (Press and hold Option/Alt before dragging.) Add Shift to constrain the cutting strokes to a multiple of 45°.

➤ If you make a curved or circular cut completely inside the object (not across its edges) with the Knife, the resulting shape will be a compound. The line you created using the Knife will be like a rip or tear in the object. To open up the tear, use the Direct-selection tool to select it, then pull on its direction lines or segments.

➤ Choose Object menu > Group to group the newly separated shapes together, and then use the Direct-selection tool if you need to select individual shapes within the group.

1 *Knife tool.*

2 *The original mother and child elephants.*

3 *After carving hills and valleys using the **Knife** tool to create more realistic elephant shapes.*

Diane Margolin

4 *The final image, after applying a black fill.*

Knife Tool

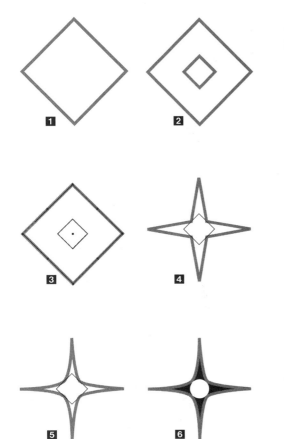

Exercise

Change a square into a star

1. Choose the Rectangle tool (M). Set up the Color palette to have a fill of None and a stroke of 2 points (see Chapter 9).

2. Click on the artboard.

3. In the Rectangle dialog box, enter 2″ in the Width field, click the word Height, then click OK.

4. Double-click the Rotate tool, enter 45 in the Angle field, then click OK **1**.

5. Double-click the Scale tool, enter 30 in the Uniform Scale field, then click Copy **2**.

6. Choose View menu > Guides > Make Guides (Command-5/Ctrl-5) to turn the small diamond into a guide.

7. Select the large diamond shape. Choose Object menu > Path > Add Anchor Points **3**.

8. Choose the Direct-selection tool (A). Deselect, then click on the edge of the diamond.

9. Drag each of the new midpoints inward until it touches the guide shape. Use Smart Guides to drag on a 45° angle **4**.

10. Choose the Convert-direction-point tool, and drag each of the inner midpoints to create a curve. Drag clockwise and drag along the edge of the guide shape **5**.

11. Choose the Ellipse tool (L), position the pointer over the center point of the star shape, then Option-Shift-drag/Alt-Shift-drag until the circle touches the curves of the star.

12. Fill the circle with white, stroke of None. Apply a black fill and a gray stroke to the star shape **6**.

13. *Optional:* Select the circle. Choose the Scale tool (S). Start dragging, hold down Option-Shift/Alt-Shift, and continue to drag until the copy of the circle touches the outer tips of the star. Fill the large circle with None, and apply a 2-point stroke **7**.

Exercise: Square to Star

Exercise

Draw a light bulb

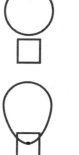

1. *Draw a **circle** (about 1" dia.) and a **rectangle** (about .5" x .5"). Apply a fill of None and a 4-point black stroke to both objects.*

2. *Select the bottom point of the circle with the **Direct-selection** tool (A), and drag the point downward. Select **both** objects using the Selection tool.*

3. *Click the **Unite** button on the Pathfinder palette. Use the **Add-anchor-point** tool (+) to add a point on the bottom segment (1), then use the **Direct-selection** tool to drag the new point downward.*

4. *Click on each point where the curve meets the straight line segment (2). Rotate the direction line upward to 90° vertical. Use Smart Guides for this.*

5. *Make sure the bulb has a white fill.*

6. *Create a rounded rectangle or an oval that's wider than the base of the bulb. Rotate it using the **Rotation** tool (R). Choose the Selection tool, and Option-Shift/Alt–Shift drag two copies downward.*

7. *Fill the ovals (no stroke), and position them on the bottom area of the bulb.*

8. *Use the **Star** tool to create a 20-point star (Radius 1: .4", Radius 2: .69"). Apply a light fill color and a stroke of None. Scale the star, if necessary, so it's larger than the bulb.*

9. *Position the star over the bulb. On the Layers palette, drag the star path layer below the bulb path layer.*

10. *Select the star. Choose Effect menu > Distort & Transform > Roughen (Size: 2, Detail: 3–6, Relative). On the Transparency palette, set the blend mode to Overlay.*

11. *Use the **Pencil** tool (N). Choose a fill of None, a black stroke, and a stroke Weight of 1–2 pt. Draw a filament line inside the bulb. It should be the topmost object layer.*

12. *Select the bulb. On the Transparency palette, set the Opacity slider to 60-70%, Normal mode.*

13. *Select the bulb, star, and filament. Choose Effect menu > Stylize > Drop Shadow (Opacity 50–60%, Blur 1–3 pt.).*

FILL & STROKE 9

In this chapter you will learn to fill the inside or stroke the edge
of an object with a color, shade, or pattern, and choose stroke
attributes like dashes and joins. You'll learn how to change a document's color mode and choose colors for print or Web output.
You'll learn to save, copy, edit, replace, delete, merge, move, and
duplicate color swatches. You'll learn to select objects for recoloring; globally replace or edit a color; apply fill and stroke colors
simultaneously using the Paint Bucket tool; sample colors using
the Eyedropper tool; and blend fill colors between objects. You'll
also learn to invert, adjust, convert, and saturate/desaturate
colors. Finally, you'll learn how to create and modify fill patterns.

Related topics

Mixing and applying colors
Fills and strokes

The flat color, pattern, or gradient that's
applied to the inside of a closed or open
shape is called the **fill**. The color or brushstroke that's applied to the edge of a closed
or open path is called the **stroke**. A stroke
can be solid or dashed, and it can have an
applied brushstroke, but not a gradient.

Colors and patterns can be applied using the
Color or **Swatches** palette, buttons on the
Toolbox, or the **Paint Bucket** tool. The **Stroke**
palette is also used to apply characteristics
such as stroke thickness (weight) and style
(dashed, solid). You can store any color, pattern, or gradient on the Swatches palette for
later use. The color attributes of a selected
object are displayed on the Toolbox and the
Color and Appearance palettes. The current
fill and stroke colors are automatically
applied to any new object you create.

Note: Before you start working with color,
you should calibrate your monitor (see pages
421–422). Then, for the instructions in this
chapter, open the Color, Stroke, and Swatches
palettes. And of course work with your illustration in Preview view so you can see colors
on screen as you apply them.

Chris Spollen

Fills and Strokes

Here's a quick method for applying color, just to get you started. The beauty of this method is that you don't need to choose any particular tool or select anything in your document. Try this method, then keep on reading—there's a lot more to this chapter!

QuickStart drag-color:

Click the Fill **1** or Stroke **2** box on the Toolbox or the Color palette, click a color on the spectrum bar on the Color palette **4**, then drag from the active box right over an object's fill or stroke—whichever element you want to recolor. The object doesn't have to be selected. If the object is selected, clicking a color swatch or a color on the spectrum bar will automatically change the fill or stroke, whichever box is currently active.

➤ You could also drag from the Color box on the expanded Gradient palette or drag a swatch from the Swatches palette **6**.

➤ Shift-drag to apply a stroke color if the fill box is active or apply a fill color if the stroke box is active.

To apply a fill or stroke of black or white:

1. Select an object.

2. Click the Fill or Stroke box on the Color palette **1**–**2**, then click the white or black selector at the right end of the spectrum bar on the Color palette **5** or click the white or black swatch on the Swatches palette **6**.

   or

   To apply a white fill *and* a black stroke, click the Default Colors button (D) on the Toolbox **3**.

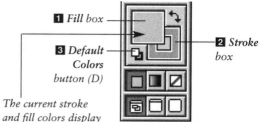

1 *Fill box*

2 *Stroke box*

3 *Default Colors button (D)*

The current stroke and fill colors display on the Toolbox and the Color palette.

Toolbox

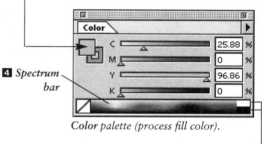

4 *Spectrum bar*

Color palette (process fill color).

5 *White and black selectors*

White swatch   *Black swatch*

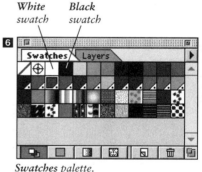

Swatches palette.

Drag-Color; Apply Black or White

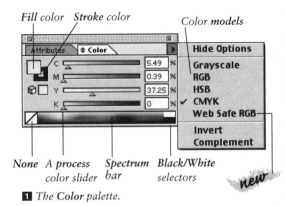

Fill color   Stroke color

Color models

None   A process   Spectrum   Black/White
color slider   bar   selectors

new

1 *The Color palette.*

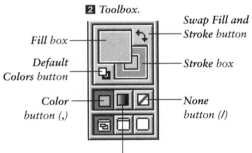

2 *Toolbox.*

Fill box —

Default
Colors button

Swap Fill and
Stroke button

Stroke box

Color
button (,)

None
button (/)

Gradient button (.)

A gradient   A pattern   A global process
color has a
white corner
with no dot.

A non-global
process color

A spot color
has a dot.

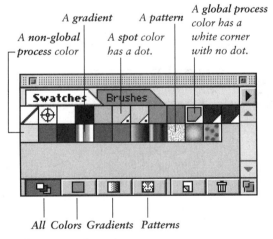

All Colors Gradients Patterns

3 *The Swatches palette.*

The palettes you'll use for coloring
Color palette
The Color palette is used to mix and choose solid colors. The color boxes on the Color palette display the current fill and stroke colors of the currently or last-selected object **1**. The palette options change depending on whether the Grayscale, RGB, HSB, CMYK, or Web Safe RGB color model is chosen from the palette menu. You can click a color on the spectrum bar or mix a process color using exact percentages. Choosing a color model for the palette doesn't change the document color mode (see page 132).

Toolbox
The Fill and Stroke boxes on the Toolbox display the attributes of the currently or last-selected object, as well as any changes you make to the current fill or stroke color via the Color or Swatches palette **2**. Click the Color or Gradient button to reapply the last chosen solid color or gradient.

Swatches palette
The Swatches palette contains process color (RGB or CMYK, depending on the current document color mode), spot color, pattern, and gradient swatches **3**. You can append additional swatches from other libraries (e.g., PANTONE). If you click a swatch, that color will appear on the current Fill or Stroke box (whichever is currently active) on the Toolbox and on the Color palette, and it will apply immediately to all currently selected objects. If a selected object contains a color or colors from the Swatches palette, those swatches will be highlighted on the palette.

improved

A default set of process color, spot color, pattern, and gradient swatches is supplied with Illustrator. You can also create your own swatches, which will save with the file in which they're created.

None
The None button is located on the Color palette, the Swatches palettes, and the Toolbox. Select an object and then click this button to remove any fill or stroke color, depending on which color box is currently active on the Color palette and the Toolbox.

Color Palette; Toolbox; Swatches Palette

The basic coloring steps

Open the Toolbox, Color, Swatches, and Stroke palettes.

1. Select the objects whose color attributes you want to change.

2. Make sure the box for the attribute that you want to change is active on the Color palette or the Toolbox—Fill or Stroke.

3. To choose a solid color, choose a color model from the Color palette menu, then click the Spectrum bar on the palette or choose specific color percentages.
   or
   Click a swatch on the Swatches palette to assign a saved color or pattern to a selected object. (You can also drag a swatch over an unselected object.)

4. Adjust the line Weight and other stroke attributes using the Stroke palette.

5. To save the current color, follow the instructions below.

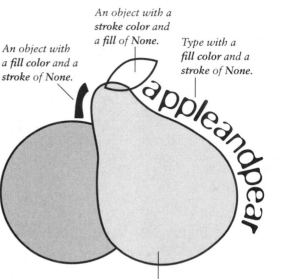

An object with a stroke color and a fill of None.

An object with a fill color and a stroke of None.

Type with a fill color and a stroke of None.

An object with a fill color and a stroke color.

Swatches that are stored on the Swatches palette are saved only with the current file.

To save the current fill or stroke color as a swatch:

Drag the Fill or Stroke box from the Color palette or the Toolbox to an empty area of the Swatches palette to make it the last swatch **1** or release the mouse between two colors to insert the new color between them.
or
Make sure the Fill or Stroke button is active on the Color palette—whichever you want to save as a swatch—then click the New Swatch button on the Swatches palette **2**.
or
To choose options for the new swatch as you save it, Option-click/Alt-click the New Swatch button, enter a Swatch Name, choose a Color Type (Process Color or Spot Color), check or uncheck the Global box, choose a Color Mode, then click OK. Command-click/Ctrl-click the New Swatch button to save the color as a spot color.

➤ Command-drag/Ctrl-drag to convert a process color into a spot color as you save it as a swatch.

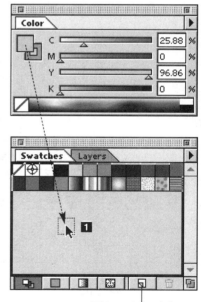

2 *New Swatch button*

Don't be fooled

Illustrator's **Color Settings** command works with the system's color management software to ensure more accurate color matching between the on-screen display of CMYK or RGB colors and the printed version of those colors. This command utilizes monitor and printer device profiles and output intents, all chosen by the user, to better translate color between particular devices. However, the profiles won't produce a perfectly reliable on-screen proof.

For print output, you shouldn't mix or choose process colors or choose spot colors (e.g., PANTONE) based on how they look on the screen, because screen colors don't look like printed colors. Instead, use **matching system books** to choose spot colors or mix process colors, and be sure to run a color **proof** (or two or three) of your document. Really.

1 *The Registration color appears on all plates when a file is color separated.*

Global process colors have a white triangle with no dot in the lower right corner (see the next page).

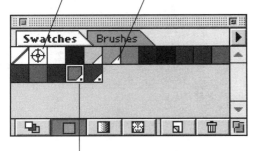

Spot colors have a dot in the lower right corner.

Colors for print

Spot colors are used for offset printing. Each **spot** color appears on its own plate after color separation. On a rare occasion you might mix a spot color yourself, but normally you'll pick a named, numbered, pre-mixed spot color from a matching system book (e.g., PANTONE). You can use spot colors exclusively if your illustration doesn't contain any continuous-tone (raster) images. Your only limitation is your budget.

➤ If you mix your own spot color, to ensure that it separates onto its own plate, double-click the swatch for the color on the Swatches palette, choose Color Type: **Spot Color,** then click OK.

➤ You can achieve a pleasing range of tints using a black plate and a single spot color plate by using varying tint percentages of that spot color throughout your illustration.

A **process** color, on the other hand, is printed from four plates, one each for Cyan (C), Magenta (M), Yellow (Y), and Black (K). You can enter process color percentages yourself or you can choose a pre-mixed process color from a matching system (e.g., TRUMATCH or PANTONE Process). (FOCOLTONE, DIC Color, and Toyo are not usually used in the United States.)

Process printing *must* be used for any document that contains continuous-tone images, because it's the only way to achieve a range of graduated tones. Budget permitting, you can use both: four-color process and a few spot color plates.

➤ The Registration color is used for crop marks and the like **1**. To change the Registration color (let's say your illustration is very dark and you need white Registration marks), double-click the swatch and adjust the sliders.

➤ Double-click a spot color swatch to display its process color breakdown.

Note: Normally, Illustrator converts all spot colors into process colors when they're color separated. To make your spot colors separate

(Continued on the following page)

Colors for Print

to their own plates—which is what they *should* do—uncheck the **Convert to Process** box in File menu > Separation Setup.

To define a color as process or spot, double-click the swatch on the Swatches palette, choose Color Type: Spot Color or Process Color, decide whether the process color will be Global or not, choose a Color Mode, then click OK **1**.

Global colors

If a process color is **global** (the Global box is checked for that color in the Swatch Options dialog box) and you modify its swatch, it will update on all objects to which it was previously applied. If you modify a **non-global** color (Global box unchecked), that color will update only on currently selected objects. See page 146.

Colors for the Web

The Mac OS, Windows, and other platforms have 216 colors in common. These colors are called "Web safe," which means they won't shift when viewed in the popular Web browsers.

If you mix a color in the RGB model that is not Web safe, the **Out of Web Color** warning (cube) alert button will appear on the palette, and the closest Web safe version of that color will appear in the little swatch next to it **3**. Click the cube or the swatch to convert the color to the closest Web safe version.

If you create images only for the Web, you should choose the **Web Safe RGB** color model for the Color palette. Note how the sliders align with the vertical notches **2**.

➤ The Info palette shows the color breakdowns for the currently selected object. The breakdown on the left is the current fill color; the breakdown on the right is the current stroke color **4**. The palette also shows the Hexadecimal equivalent of the current fill and stroke colors. If the palette is blank, it means two or more objects with different color values are selected at the same time.

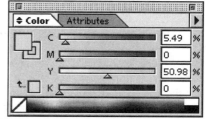

1 Use the CMYK color model for print design.

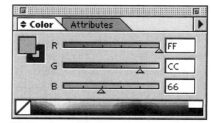

2 Use the **Web Safe RGB** color model for Web design.

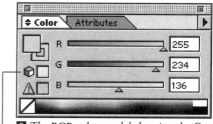

3 The RGB color model showing the **Out of Web Color** warning.

Global Colors; Colors for the Web

130

Recoloring type

■ To recolor **all** the type in a block, highlight it with the Selection tool.

■ To recolor only a **portion** of a type block, select it with a Type tool.

■ To recolor a **type object** (not the type), click on the edge of it with the Direct-selection tool. See pages 208–209.

1 *Fill box*

2 *Stroke box*   *Tint slider*

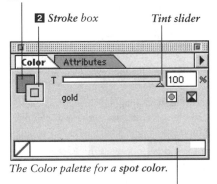

The Color palette for a spot color.

3 *Tint Ramp*

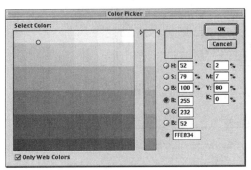

4 *In the Color Picker, you can enter HSB, RGB, or CMYK percentages. Check the Only Web Colors box to choose Web safe colors. This is the Adobe Color Picker on Mac OS.*

To choose a fill or stroke for a path before or after you create it:

1. Select an existing object (not all the anchor points need to be solid).
   or
   Choose the tool with which you want to draw a new object.

2. Click the Fill **1** or Stroke **2** box on the Color palette or the Toolbox. To toggle between these two boxes, press "X".

3. Click a color or pattern swatch on the Swatches palette. If you chose a spot color swatch or a global process color swatch, you can move the Tint (T) slider on the Color palette or click or drag inside the Tint Ramp to adjust the percentage of that color **3**.
   or
   Choose a color model from the Color palette menu and choose color percentages (instructions on the next page).
   or
   Double-click the Fill or Stroke box on the Color palette, then mix a color from the Color Picker **4**.

   To choose a color from a matching system (e.g., PANTONE), see page 135.

4. If you're applying a stroke color, define stroke attributes using the Stroke palette (see page 136).

5. Your color is chosen. If you didn't select an existing object for step 1, now you're ready to draw it. It will have the current Color and Stroke palette attributes.

➤ You can fill an object with any of the patterns that are supplied with Illustrator or you can create and use your own patterns (see pages 152–154). Just remember not to apply a path pattern as a fill—it won't look right.

➤ A gradient cannot be applied as a stroke. For a workaround, see page 274.

new

new

When you created your new document, you were asked to choose a Color Mode: CMYK or RGB. (The current color mode displays in the document title bar.) Any colors you mix or choose in a document automatically conform to the current document color mode. If you want to create two versions of an illustration, one for Web output (RGB mode) and one for print output (CMYK mode), you can make a copy of the file and then change the color mode for the copy.

Note: Changing the color mode changes all colors in the illustration to the new mode, and color shifts will occur, particularly if you go in the direction of CMYK to RGB. That's why we suggest you copy your file first, and leave the original file unchanged. To reverse a document mode change, *don't* re-choose the prior color mode. To restore the original colors, use Edit menu > Undo.

To change a document's color mode:

1. Use File menu > Save As to create a copy of your illustration.

2. Choose File menu > Document Color Mode > CMYK Color or RGB Color.

In the mode

➤ Any process or spot colors you create for a document will be in the document color mode—regardless of which mode is currently chosen on the Color Mode pop-up menu in the Swatch Options dialog box (see page 151). You can create colors in your illustration in either CMYK or RGB—but not both.   *new*

➤ When a spot color is displayed on the Color palette, a current document mode icon will also display on the palette ■.

➤ The Swatches palette uses the default palette for the current document color mode (CMYK or RGB).

➤ Blend and gradient colors conform automatically to the current document color mode: all CMYK or all RGB.

➤ Placed and pasted images, linked or embedded, are converted to the current document color mode.

➤ The color mode options in the Rasterize dialog box change depending on the current document color mode.

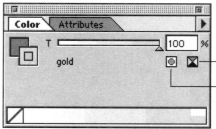

Document color mode indicator

Color type indicator: A circle for a spot color, a solid gray square for a global process color.

■ *Click either indicator to convert a spot or global process color in a selected object to the current document mode. In our testing, both buttons seem to do the same thing. To convert the colors on selected objects, choose Filter menu > Colors > Convert to Grayscale or Convert to CMYK or Convert to RGB.*

Document Color Mode

What's the gamut?

If your document is in CMYK color mode and an exclamation point appears below the Color boxes on the Color palette **3**, you have mixed an RGB or HSB color that has no **CMYK** equivalent, which means it's not **printable** on a four-color press. If you click the exclamation point, Illustrator will substitute the closest CMYK (printable) equivalent. If you're outputting **online**, your document color mode is **RGB**, and the exclamation point appears, it means the current color is out of the Web-safe gamut.

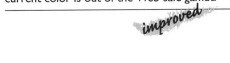

Fill box   *Stroke box*   **1** *Color models*

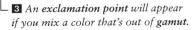

2 *Spectrum bar*

None *Process*   *Black/White*
         color sliders   *selectors*

 3 *An exclamation point will appear if you mix a color that's out of gamut.*

If the fill or stroke colors differ among currently selected objects, a question mark will appear in the corresponding Fill or Stroke box on the Color palette and the Toolbox, but you can go ahead and apply a new fill and/or stroke color to all the selected objects.

Follow these instructions to mix your own process color. *Note:* To apply a color from a color matching system, like TRUMATCH or FOCOLTONE, see page 135.

To mix a process color:

1. *Optional:* To recolor an existing object or objects, select them now, and click the Fill or Stroke box on the Color palette (X). To choose a color for an object you're about to draw, make sure no objects are selected.

2. Choose a color model from the Color palette menu **1**:

   Choose **Grayscale** to remove color from any selected objects or to choose a gray shade.

   Choose **RGB** to mix colors for video output.

   Choose **HSB** to individually adjust a color's hue (location on the color wheel), saturation (purity), or brightness.

   Choose **CMYK** to create process colors for output on a four-color press. Use a matching system book for this.

   Choose **Web Safe RGB** to choose colors for the Web.

3. Click a color on the spectrum bar at the bottom of the Color palette **2**.
   and/or
   Move the sliders to adjust the individual color percentages (0–255 for RGB; 0–100 for CMYK).

4. *Optional:* To save the newly mixed color as a swatch, see page 128.

➤ Premixed swatches and colors that are applied to objects remain associated with their color model. If you click on a swatch or on an object to which a color is applied, the Color palette will reset to reflect that color's model.

Mix a Process Color

Color editing shortcuts

➤ Shift-click the spectrum bar on the Color palette to cycle through the color **models**. You can also convert the current color by choosing a different color model from the palette menu. If a color has been saved as a swatch, the swatch itself won't change.

➤ Press "X" to toggle between the **Fill** and **Stroke** boxes on the Toolbox and the Color palette.

➤ To make the fill color the **same** as the stroke color, or vice versa, drag one box over the other on the Toolbox or the Color palette.

➤ If you've chosen a fill or stroke of None for a path and then want to restore the last-applied colors to the path, click the **Last Color** button on the Color palette **1**.

➤ Choose Complement from the Color palette menu to convert the current color into its **complement**. This won't change the color model.

➤ Shift-drag any RGB or CMYK slider on the Color palette to change that color's **strength**—the other sliders will readjust automatically.

➤ To select objects with the same paint attributes via a command, see page 145.

The Color, Gradient, and None buttons

Click the Color, Gradient, or None button on the Toolbox to change the current fill color (if the Fill box is active) to a solid color, a gradient, or a fill of none, respectively, or to change the current stroke to a solid color or none. The Color button displays the last chosen solid color; the Gradient button displays the last chosen gradient. If an object is selected, it will be recolored (or its color removed) when you click a different button. If you click the Color button on the Toolbox, the Color palette and any other palettes that are grouped with or docked to the Color palette will display.

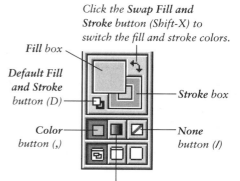

Click the Swap Fill and Stroke button (Shift-X) to switch the fill and stroke colors.

Fill box

Default Fill and Stroke button (D)

Stroke box

Color button (,)

None button (/)

Gradient button (.)

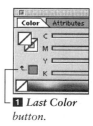

1 *Last Color button.*

Become a speed demon

These are the shortcuts for activating the Color, Gradient, and None buttons:

Color , (comma)

Gradient . (period)

None / (slash)

The comma, period, and slash keys appear next to each other on the keyboard, which makes them easy to remember. Let's say the Fill box on the Toolbox happens to be selected and you want to remove a stroke from a selected object. Press "X", then "/", then "X" again. No mousing around.

➤ **Option-drag/Alt-drag** on the **spectrum bar** to modify the stroke while the Fill box is active, or vice versa.

➤ Press "**X**" to toggle between the Fill and Stroke boxes on the Toolbox and Color palette.

➤ Press **Shift-X** to swap the Fill and Stroke colors.

Quick-append

If you apply a color to a path directly from some library palettes, the color is added to the current document's Swatches palette automatically. This doesn't work for some libraries (e.g., Pastels, Web). If you want to keep a color that you've applied to a path that didn't copy to the Swatches palette automatically, but you've already closed the library palette, select the object, then drag the Fill or Stroke box from the Color palette to the Swatches palette.

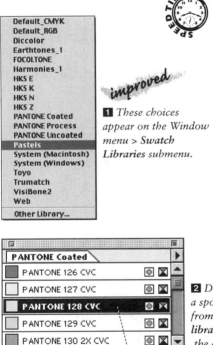

1 *These choices appear on the Window menu > Swatch Libraries submenu.*

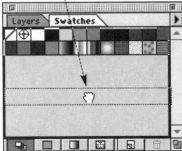

2 *Dragging a spot color from a swatch library to the current document.*

In order to apply a color from a matching system, like the PANTONE or TRUMATCH, or from the Web palette, you must open the swatch library that contains the swatch you want to use and then drag the swatch from the library palette onto the Swatches palette for your document. Colors will convert to the current document color mode.

Note: The Web palette contains the 216 Web safe RGB colors commonly used by Web browsers.

To add matching system or Web colors to the Swatches palette:

1. Display the Swatches palette.

2. Choose a color matching system name from the Window menu > Swatch Libraries submenu **1**.

3. Locate the desired color on the newly opened swatch library palette (scroll downward or expand the palette, if necessary), and drag it onto your document's Swatches palette **2**. (To locate a color, Command-Option-click/Ctrl-Alt-click in the library palette or choose Show Find Field from the palette menu, then start typing the color name or number.) *improved*
or
Click a swatch (or swatches) on the swatch library palette, then choose Add to Swatches from the swatch library palette menu. The new color will be added to your document's Swatches palette.

Note: To add multiple swatches at a time, before dragging, Command-click/Ctrl-click them individually. Or click, then Shift-click a contiguous series of them.

➤ If two or more swatch libraries are grouped in the same palette and you want to close one library in a group, drag its tab out of the palette, then click that palette's close box.

➤ You can't modify swatches on a swatch library palette (note the non-edit icon in lower left corner of palette)—the Swatch Options dialog box won't be available. You *can* edit any swatch once it's saved to your document's Swatches palette.

Use Matching System or Web Colors

135

Changing stroke attributes

You can change a stroke's color, weight (thickness), and style (dashed or solid, rounded or sharp corners, flat or rounded ends). First, the width.

To change the width of a stroke:

1. Select an object or objects.

2. On the Stroke palette:

   Click the up or down arrow on the palette to change the current stroke weight one unit at a time. Or click in the Weight field, then press the up or down arrow on the keyboard.

   or

   Choose a preset weight from the Weight pop-up menu.

   or

   Enter a width in the Weight field (.01–1000 pt) **1**. *Note:* A stroke narrower than .25 pt. may not print. A weight of 0 produces a stroke of None. The stroke will be balanced on the path: Half the stroke width on one side of the path, the other half on the other side of the path **2**–**3**.

➤ Don't apply a wide stroke to small type—it will distort the letterforms.

➤ You can enter a number in inches (in), millimeters (mm), centimeters (cm), or picas (p) in the stroke Weight field. When you click Return/Enter or Tab, the value you enter will be converted automatically to the Stroke unit currently chosen in Edit menu > Preferences > Units & Undo.

1 *To change a stroke's thickness, enter a value in the stroke Weight field, or click the up or down arrow, or choose from the pop-up menu.*

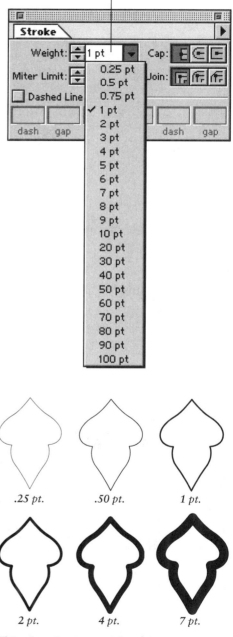

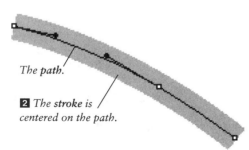

The path.

2 *The stroke is centered on the path.*

.25 pt.   .50 pt.   1 pt.

2 pt.   4 pt.   7 pt.

3 *Strokes of various weights.*

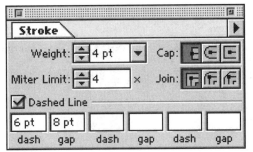

1 *Stroke palette settings for a **dashed line** with a 6-pt. dash **length** and an 8-pt. **gap** between dashes.*

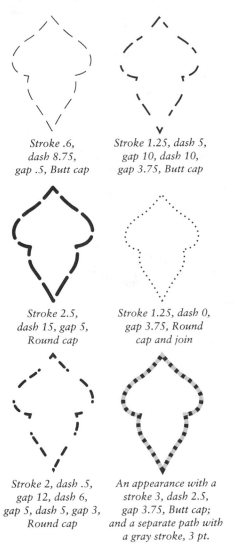

Stroke .6,
dash 8.75,
gap .5, Butt cap

Stroke 1.25, dash 5,
gap 10, dash 10,
gap 3.75, Butt cap

Stroke 2.5,
dash 15, gap 5,
Round cap

Stroke 1.25, dash 0,
gap 3.75, Round
cap and join

Stroke 2, dash .5,
gap 12, dash 6,
gap 5, dash 5, gap 3,
Round cap

An appearance with a
stroke 3, dash 2.5,
gap 3.75, Butt cap;
and a separate path with
a gray stroke, 3 pt.

Using Illustrator's Dashed Line feature, you can easily edit a line for any individual path.

To create a dashed stroke:

1. Select an object. Make sure it has a stroke color and its stroke is wider than zero.

2. If the Stroke palette options aren't fully displayed, choose Show Options from the palette menu.

3. Click a Cap button for the dash shape **1**.

4. Check the Dashed Line box.

5. Enter a number in the first dash field (the length of the first dash, in points), then press Tab to proceed to the next field. If you don't enter values in any of the other dash fields, the first dash value will be used for all the dashes. The default first dash unit is 12 pt.

6. *Optional:* Enter an amount in the first gap field (the length of the first gap after the first dash), then press Tab to proceed to the next field or press Return/Enter to exit the palette. If you don't enter a gap value, the dash value will also be used as the gap value.

7. *Optional:* To create dashes of varying lengths, enter values in the other dash fields. The more different values you enter, the more irregular the dashes will look.

8. *Optional:* Enter different amounts in the other gap fields to create gaps of varying lengths. If you enter an amount only in the first gap field, that amount will be used for all the gaps.

➤ To create a dotted line, click the second Cap button, enter 0 for the Dash value, and enter a Gap value that is greater than or equal to the stroke Weight.

➤ You can enter a value in inches (in), millimeters (mm), centimeters (cm), or picas (p) in the dash or gap fields. That number will be translated automatically into the Stroke unit currently chosen in Edit menu > Preferences > Units & Undo.

➤ User-defined values will remain in effect until you change them or quit/exit Illustrator.

Dashed Stroke

Stroke Caps and Joins

To modify stroke caps and/or joins:

1. Select an object. Make sure it has a stroke color and its stroke is wider than zero.

2. If the Stroke palette options aren't fully displayed, choose Show Options from the palette menu.

3. To modify the endpoints of a solid line or all the dashes in a dashed line:

Click the left **Cap** button **1** to create square-cornered ends in which the stroke stops at the endpoints, or to create thin rectangular dashes. Use this option if you need to align your paths very precisely.

Click the middle **Cap** button to create semicircular ends or dashes that end in a semicircle.

Click the right **Cap** button to create square-cornered ends in which the stroke extends beyond the endpoints or to create rectangular dashes.

4. To modify the bends on corner points (not curve ponits) of the path:

Click the left **Join** button to produce pointed bends (miter joins) **2**.

Click the middle **Join** button to produce semicircular bends (round joins).

Click the right **Join** button to produce square-cornered bends (bevel joins). The sharper the angle, the wider the bevel.

5. *Optional:* Enter a different Miter Limit (1–500) to specify when a miter (pointed) corner becomes a bevel corner. When the measurement from the inside to the outside of the corner point becomes greater than the miter limit value times the stroke weight, the miter corner is replaced with a bevel corner. Use a high Miter Limit to create long, pointy corners; use a low Miter limit to create bevel join corners.

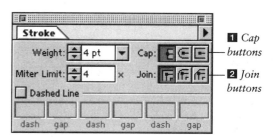

1 *Cap buttons*

2 *Join buttons*

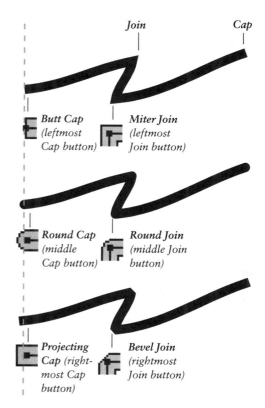

Butt Cap (leftmost Cap button)

Miter Join (leftmost Join button)

Round Cap (middle Cap button)

Round Join (middle Join button)

Projecting Cap (rightmost Cap button)

Bevel Join (rightmost Join button)

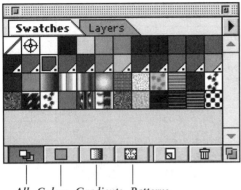

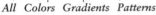

All   Colors   Gradients   Patterns

1 *The Swatches palette display buttons.*

*A **spot** color
has a dot.*

*A **global process** color has
a white corner with no dot.*

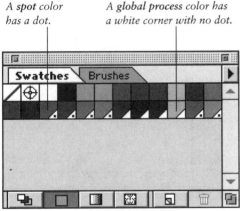

2 *Color swatches displayed.*

Non-global process

*RGB document
color mode*

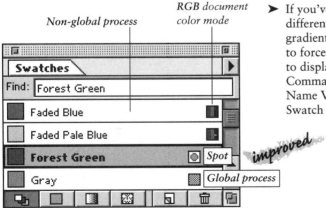

3 *The swatches displayed by **Name**.*

Using the Swatches palette

You can control whether the Swatches palette displays all types of swatches or only certain categories of swatches, and whether the swatches are large or small.

To choose swatch display options:

1. Click a display button at the bottom of the Swatches palette to control which category of swatches is displayed **1**: Show All, for all types (colors, gradients, and patterns); Show Color, for solid colors only **2**; Show Gradient, for gradients only; or Show Pattern, for patterns only.

2. Choose a view for the currently chosen category of swatches from the palette menu: Name View **3**, Small Swatch View, or Large Swatch View.

   ➤ Choose Large Swatch for gradients and patterns.

   Note: In Name view, the palette also displays an icon for the color's color model.

3. From the palette menu, choose Sort by Kind to sort swatches into color, then gradient, then pattern groups (use when all the categories of swatches are displayed).
   or
   Choose Sort by Name to sort the swatches alphabetically by name.

   ➤ To choose a swatch by typing, choose Show Find Field from the palette menu, click in the field, then start typing. A swatch will become selected.

   ➤ If you've chosen different views for the different categories of swatches (colors, gradients, and patterns) and you want to force all the categories of swatches to display in the same view, hold down Command-Option/Ctrl-Alt as you choose Name View, Small Swatch View, or Large Swatch View from the palette menu.

Swatches Palette Display

Whatever swatches are on the Swatches palette will save with the current file. (To load matching system colors, see page 135.)

To load swatches from one Illustrator file to another:

1. With the file into which you want to load swatches open, choose Window menu > Swatch Libraries > Other Library.

2. Locate the Illustrator file from which you want to copy the swatches (that file should not be open), then click Open.

3. Drag a swatch from the newly opened (secondary) swatch palette into the current document's Swatches palette **1**. To add multiple swatches at a time, first Command/Ctrl click them individually or click, then Shift-click, a contiguous series of them.

or

Click the swatch you want to load, then choose Add to Swatches from the secondary swatch palette's option menu. The selected color will appear on the current document's Swatches palette.

➤ You'll find pattern library files in the Adobe Illustrator 9 > Other Libraries > Pattern Samples folder and gradients in the Gradients folder.

Auto copy

If you **drag-and-drop** an object from one file to another, any swatches that are applied to that object will also copy to the destination file.

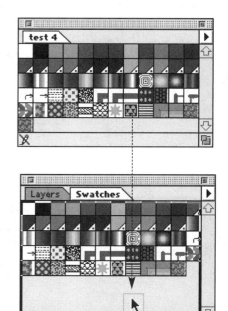

1 *Moving a swatch from a **library** to the Swatches palette.*

Swatches at launchtime

If you want to control which colors appear on the Swatches palette when the application is launched, add those colors to the **Startup** file (see page 381).

If you turn on the **Persistent** command from a swatch library palette menu, that swatch library palette will reopen automatically when you re-launch Illustrator, with the same tab in front.

There's no simple way to restore the Swatches palette to its default state. You have to manually drag swatches from the Default palette.

To restore default swatches to the current Swatches palette:

1. *Optional:* To completely clear the current document's Swatches palette first, click, then Shift-click all the swatches except None and Registration, then click the Delete button.

2. Choose Window menu > Swatch Libraries > Default_CMYK or Default_RGB (depending on the current document color mode).

3. On the Default_CMYK or Default_RGB palette that you just opened, select the swatches you want to restore to your document (Click, then Shift-click to select multiple, contiguous swatches).

4. Choose Add to Swatches from the Default_CMYK or Default_RGB palette option menu **1**–**2**.
   or
   Drag those swatches to the current document's Swatches palette.

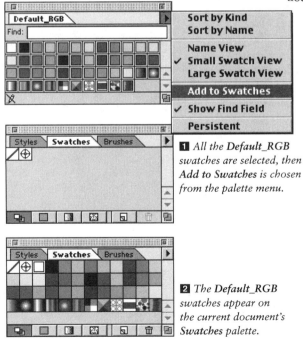

1 *All the Default_RGB swatches are selected, then* **Add to Swatches** *is chosen from the palette menu.*

2 *The Default_RGB swatches appear on the current document's Swatches palette.*

To delete swatches:

1. Click the swatch you want to delete. Or click, then Shift-click a series of contiguous swatches or Command-click/ Ctrl-click individual swatches.

   or

   To select only swatches that are not currently applied to objects in your document, choose Select All Unused from the palette menu. To limit the selection to a particular category (e.g., patterns or gradients), make sure only those swatches are displayed on the palette before choosing Select All Unused.

2. Click the Delete button at the bottom of the Swatches palette, then click Yes **1**.

   or

   Choose Delete Swatch from the palette menu, then click Yes.

   or

   Option-click/Alt-click the Delete button to bypass the warning dialog box.

   or

   Drag the swatch(es) you want to delete over the Delete button.

➤ If you delete a global process color or a spot color that is currently applied to a path or paths, the paths will be recolored with the non-global process color equivalent to the deleted colors.

➤ Choose Undo to restore a deleted swatch or swatches.

Quick fix

If you delete a color, gradient, or pattern swatch that was applied to an object in the current file, you can retrieve it by selecting the object and then dragging the Fill box from the Toolbox or the Color palette onto the Swatches palette.

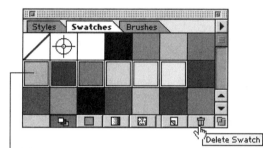

1 *Select the swatch or swatches that you want to delete from the Swatches palette, then click or Option-click/Alt-click the* **Delete Swatch** *button.*

Delete Swatches

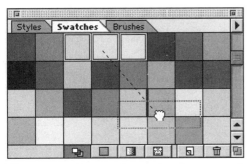

1 *Three swatches are selected, then they're **moved** to a new location on the palette.*

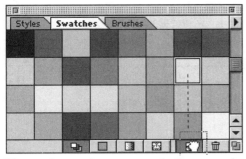

1 *Drag the swatch you want to **duplicate** over the New Swatch button.*

To move a swatch or swatches:

Drag a swatch to a new location on the palette **1**. A dark vertical line will show the swatch location as you drag it. (To select multiple swatches, click a swatch, then Shift-click the last swatch in a series of contiguous swatches, or Command-click/Ctrl-click to select individual swatches.)

To duplicate a swatch:

Select the swatch you want to duplicate, then choose Duplicate Swatch from the palette menu or click the New Swatch button. The duplicate swatch will appear at the bottom of the palette.

or

Drag the swatch to be duplicated over the New Swatch button **2**.

➤ If no swatch is selected when you click the New Swatch button, a new swatch will be created for the current fill or stroke color.

➤ Option-drag/Alt-drag one swatch over another to replace the existing swatch with the one you're dragging.

Move Swatch; Duplicate Swatch

Resolving swatch conflicts

If you copy and paste or drag-and-drop an object from one document window to another, that object's colors will appear as swatches on the target document's Swatches palette. If a global process or spot color on the copied object contains the same name, but different color percentages, as an existing global process or spot color swatch in the target document, the Swatch Conflict dialog box will open . Here's what to do:

Click **Merge swatches** to apply the existing swatch in the target document to the copied objects. Or click **Add swatches** to add the new swatch to the Swatches palette in the target document (colors in the copied objects won't change).

Check the **Apply to all** box to have the current Options setting apply to any other name conflicts that crop up for other objects being copied. This will prevent the alert dialog from opening repeatedly if more than one name conflict crops up.

Normally, if there are two spot colors that have the same color breakdown, but different names, Illustrator will color separate each of those colors to a separate sheet of film. You can use the Merge Swatches command to selectively merge colors into one swatch so it will print from one plate.

To merge spot color swatches:

1. Select the swatches on the Swatches palette that you want to merge. Click, then Shift-click to select contiguous swatches or Command-click/Ctrl-click to select non-contiguous swatches 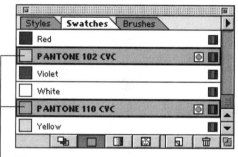. The **first** swatch you select will replace all the other selected swatches, so strategize as you do this.

2. Choose Merge Swatches from the Swatches palette menu 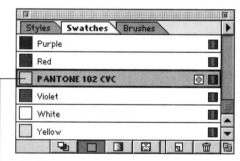. If any of the merged swatches were applied to objects in the file, the first swatch that was selected for merging will be applied to all those objects.

 Select the spot colors you want to merge.

 After choosing **Merge Swatches** from the palette menu, the swatches are merged into the first swatch that was selected.

Select Same Tint Percentage new

When the **Select Same Tint Percentage** box is checked in Edit menu > Preferences > General, the Edit menu > Select > Same Fill Color and Same Stroke Color commands will select only colors with the same tint percentage (spot color percentage) as the selected object.

Deselect All	⇧⌘A
Select	▶
Define Pattern...	
Edit Original	
Assign Profile...	
Color Settings...	
Keyboard Shortcuts...	⌥⇧⌘K
Preferences	▶

Select Again	⌘6
Same Style	
Same Fill & Stroke	
Same Fill Color	
Same Stroke Color	
Same Stroke Weight	
Same Blending Mode	
Same Opacity	
Masks	
Stray Points	
Brush Strokes	
Inverse	

1 *Choose from the Select submenu on the Edit menu.*

2 *The original group of objects.*

3 *All the colors inverted.*

Changing colors

To select objects with the same paint attributes for recoloring:

1. Select an object whose paint attributes you want to change (fill color, stroke color, stroke weight).
   or
   With no object selected, choose the attributes that you want to search for from the Swatches palette, the Color palette, or the Stroke palette.

2. Choose Edit menu > Select > Same Fill & Stroke, or Same Fill Color, or Same Stroke Color, or Same Stroke Weight to select objects with the same paint attributes as you chose in the previous step **1**. All objects with those paint attributes will now be selected. A spot color in different tint percentages is considered one color.

3. With the objects still selected, mix a new color using the Color palette.
   or
   Click a new swatch on the Swatches palette.
   or
   Choose a new Weight or other attributes from the Stroke palette.

➤ To globally change a spot color or a global process color by replacing its swatch, see the next page.

The Invert command converts each color in an object into its color negative.

To invert colors:

1. Select the object or objects whose colors you want to invert.

2. Choose Filter menu > Colors > Invert Colors **2**–**3**. This filter converts only *non-global process colors*. It will not convert spot colors, global process colors, gradients, or patterns.
   or
   To invert only the object's *fill* or *stroke* color, click either box on the Color palette, then choose Invert from the Color palette menu. This command will convert *any* kind of solid color—spot, global process, or non-global process.

This is what happens when colors are replaced:

➤ If you replace a spot or global process color swatch with a different swatch, that color (or tint of that color) will automatically update in *all* the objects to which it is currently applied—whether or not those objects are selected. The object's original tint value will be preserved.

➤ If you replace a non-global process color swatch, only the currently *selected* object or objects containing that color will be recolored.

To replace a swatch globally:

On the Color palette, mix a brand new color (not merely a tint variation of the global process or spot color that you want to replace). Then Option-drag/Alt-drag the Fill or Stroke box from the Color palette over the swatch on the Swatches palette that you want to replace.

or

Option-drag/Alt-drag one swatch over another swatch.

or

To edit a gradient swatch, use the Gradient palette (see page 278). To edit a pattern swatch, follow the instructions on page 153.

The new color will replace the old color in all objects to which the original swatch is currently applied.

Follow these instructions to edit a process color globally. To change spot colors in multiple objects, use the method described in the sidebar instead (select the objects, then choose a new swatch).

To edit a color globally:

1. Double-click a global process swatch on the Swatches palette.

2. Modify the color using the Color Type menu, the Color Mode menu, or by moving the sliders, and then click OK (Return/Enter). The color will update in all objects to which it is currently applied. Individual tint variations will be preserved.

Change without changing

If you want to globally change a color without changing the swatch from which it originated, use an Edit menu > Select submenu command to select all the objects that contain that color (see page 145), then choose a new swatch or mix a new color for the selected objects. Use this method to assign a different spot color to existing objects.

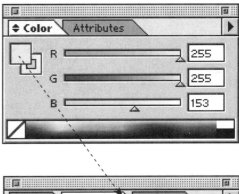

1 *Option-drag/Alt-drag the current color from the **Fill** or **Stroke** box over the **spot** or **global process** swatch you want to replace. Objects to which that color is currently applied will update.*

Replace, Edit Colors Globally

Recolor using Pathfinders

You can use the **Hard Mix** or **Soft Mix** command on the **Pathfinders** palette to change colors in overlapping paths (see page 335–336).

1

Use the Adjust Colors filter to adjust color percentages or convert color modes in one or more selected path objects; text objects; or an opened or placed Photoshop TIFF, EPS, or flattened .psd image—but not gradients or patterns. To adjust individual .psd layers, convert them into separate Illustrator objects (see page 240).

To adjust or convert colors:

1. Select the object or objects whose colors you want to adjust or convert.

2. Choose Filter menu > Colors > Adjust Colors.

3. Check the Preview box to preview color adjustments in your illustration while the dialog box is open **1**.

4. Check the Adjust Options: Fill and/or Stroke box to adjust one or both of those attributes.

5. The sliders will reflect the color mode of the currently selected object or objects. If the selected objects' colors are in more than one mode, the sliders will display in the first mode that's present, in the following order: Global mode, then either CMYK mode or RGB mode, then Grayscale mode. Make sure Convert is unchecked, then move the sliders or enter new percentages in the fields. Only colors in that mode will be adjusted. After you adjust colors in one mode, you can choose another mode and adjust other colors.
   or
   To convert all the currently selected objects to the same color mode, regardless of their original mode, check the Convert box, choose a Color Mode, then move the sliders.

6. Click OK (Return/Enter).

To convert an object's colors to a different mode:

1. Select the object or objects whose colors you want to convert.

2. Choose Filter menu > Colors > Convert to Grayscale, or either Convert to CMYK or Convert to RGB. Spot colors will be converted into process colors.

improved

147

Adjust Colors; Convert Colors

If you click with the Paint Bucket tool on an object, that object will be filled *and* stroked using the current Color and Stroke palette settings. Neither palette needs to be displayed for you to use the Paint Bucket.

To use the Paint Bucket tool:

1. With no objects selected, choose the Paint Bucket tool (K) .

2. Choose fill and stroke colors from the Color or Swatches palette.
   or
   Option-click/Alt-click on a color anywhere in any open Illustrator window (this is a temporary Eyedropper).

3. Choose a stroke weight, and choose other stroke options, if desired.

4. Click on an object (the object does not have to be selected). The object will become colored with the current Color and Stroke palette attributes **2**–**3**. For an object without a fill color, or if you're working in Outline view, position the black spill of the Paint Bucket pointer on the path outline before clicking.

Use the Eyedropper/Paint Bucket Options dialog box to change the default attributes for either or both tools.

To choose paint attributes the *improved* Eyedropper picks up or the Paint Bucket applies:

1. Double-click the Eyedropper or Paint Bucket tool.

2. Click check box options on or off **4**.

3. Click OK (Return/Enter).

 1 *Paint Bucket tool.*

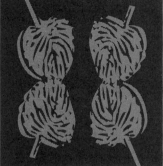

2 *The original illustration.*

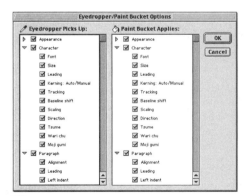

Diane Margolin

3 *After using the Paint Bucket to apply a white fill and a dashed stroke to the leaves on the left side.*

4 *Eyedropper/Paint Options.*

Grab a color from another application

Open the application from which you want to sample colors. If that application's color palette stays open even if the application isn't currently active (as in Director), open that palette, too.

Move the window or palette that you want to sample from over to one side of the screen and move the Illustrator document window so that you can see the other application window behind it. Choose the Eyedropper tool, drag from the Illustrator document window over to a color in another application window, then release the mouse (the color will appear on Illustrator's Toolbox and Color palette). Save the color as a swatch. Repeat for other colors.

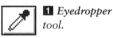 **1** *Eyedropper tool.*

If you click on a path or a placed image with the Eyedropper tool, it will sample the object's paint attributes and style (if any), display them on the Toolbox and the Color and Stroke palettes, and apply them to any currently selected objects.

To use the Eyedropper tool:

1. *Optional:* Select an object or objects if you want to recolor them immediately with the attributes you pick up with the Eyedropper.

2. Choose the Eyedropper tool (I) **1**.

3. Click on an object in any open Illustrator window that contains the color, gradient, or pattern you want to sample. The object doesn't have to be selected.

   Note: If the object you're sampling from has an applied style, the Eyedropper will pick up the style. If you want the tool to pick up only the color it clicks on—not the style—Shift-click the color. The color will be copied to the fill or stroke of any selected objects, depending on whether the Fill or Stroke box is currently active on the Color palette.
   or
   Drag from the Illustrator document window into any location on your screen— in another application or on the Desktop.

   If you selected any objects (step 1), they will be given the paint attributes of the object you click on.

➤ Hold down Option/Alt to use the Paint Bucket tool while the Eyedropper is selected, or vice versa.

➤ To preserve the sampled color to use again, drag the Fill or Stroke box from the Toolbox or the Color palette onto the Swatches palette.

Eyedropper Tool

The Saturate filter deepens or fades colors in selected objects by a relative percentage.

To saturate or desaturate colors:

1. Select the object(s) whose solid colors you want to saturate or desaturate.

2. Choose Filter menu > Colors > Saturate.

3. Check the Preview box to preview color changes in your illustration.

4. Move the Intensity slider or enter a percentage for the amount you want to intensify or fade the color or colors 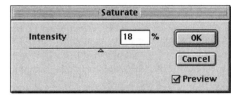. A 100% tint cannot be further saturated.

5. Click OK (Return/Enter).

To blend fill colors between objects:

1. Select three or more objects that contain a fill color. Objects with a fill of None won't be recolored. The more objects you use, the more gradual will be the blend.

   Note: The two objects that are farthest apart (or frontmost and backmost) cannot contain gradients, patterns, global colors, or different spot colors. The frontmost and backmost objects can contain different tints of the same spot color. Objects will stay on their respective layers.

2. From the Colors submenu under the Filter menu, choose:

   Blend Front to Back to create a color blend using the fill colors of the frontmost and backmost objects as the starting and ending colors.

   Blend Horizontally to create a color blend using the fill colors of the leftmost and rightmost objects as the starting and ending colors **2**–**3**.

   Blend Vertically to create a color blend using the fill colors of the topmost and bottommost objects as the starting and ending colors.

   Any selected objects that are stacked between the frontmost and backmost objects (or between the leftmost and rightmost or topmost and bottommost objects) will be assigned intermediate blend colors. Stroke colors won't change.

1 *Change a color's **Intensity** in the **Saturate** dialog box.*

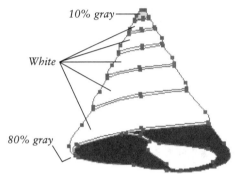

2 *Seven objects are selected.*

3 *After applying the **Blend Vertically** filter.*

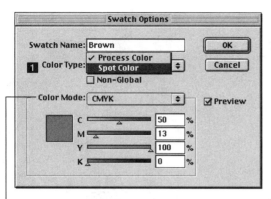

Regardless of whether CMYK or RGB is chosen from the Color Mode pop-up menu, only the option that matches the document's color mode will be applied when you click OK.

improved

Quick conversion

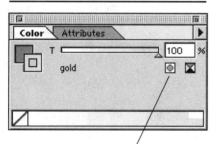

Click this button to convert the spot color on the currently selected object to the current document color mode (CMYK or RGB). This won't change the original spot swatch.

To convert a process color into a spot color or vice versa:

1. Mix a color on the Color palette.
   or
   Select the object that contains the color you want to convert.
2. If the color isn't already on the Swatches palette, drag the Fill or Stroke box from the Color palette or the Toolbox onto the Swatches palette.
3. Double-click the swatch to open the Swatch Options dialog box.
4. Choose Color Type: Spot Color or Process Color **1**, and rename the color, if desired.
5. For a process color, choose whether it will be Global (checked) or non-global (unchecked). If you edit a global process color that has been applied to objects in a file, the color will update on those objects.
6. Choose Color Mode: Grayscale, RGB, HSB, CMYK, or Web Safe RGB.
7. Click OK (Return/Enter).
➤ By default, spot colors are converted to process colors during color separation. To prevent this conversion, uncheck the Convert to Process box in File menu > Separation Setup.

A 1-bit TIFF or 1-bit Photoshop (.psd) image that is opened or placed in Illustrator (not drag-and-dropped) can be colorized via the Color palette. Black areas in the TIFF will recolor; white areas will remain transparent.

To colorize a 1-bit TIFF image:

1. Use File menu > Open or Place to open a 1-bit TIFF image in Illustrator (a 1-bit image has only black and white areas). The image can be linked or embedded.
2. Select the <image> layer on the Layers palette. (A .psd file will be a group of layers.)
3. Apply a fill color (not a stroke).
➤ To make transparent areas in a 1-bit TIFF look as if they're colorized, create an object with the desired background color and send it behind the TIFF.

Creating fill patterns

To create a fill pattern:

1. Draw an object or objects to be used as the pattern . They may not contain a gradient, gradient mesh, mask, pattern, or EPS file. Simple shapes are least likely to cause a printing error. As of Illustrator 9, the objects can contain **brushstrokes**.

2. *Strictly optional:* Apply Filter > Distort > Roughen or Effect menu > Distort & Transform > Roughen at a low setting to make the pattern shapes look more hand drawn.

3. Marquee all the objects with the Selection tool (V).

4. Choose Edit menu > Define Pattern.
   or
   Drag the selection onto the Swatches palette **2**, deselect the objects, then double-click the new swatch.

5. Type a name in the Swatch Name field.

6. Click OK (Return/Enter) **3**.

You can use a rectangle to control the amount of white space around a pattern or to crop parts of the objects that you want to eliminate from the pattern.

To use a rectangle to define a fill pattern:

1. Draw objects to be used as the pattern.

2. Choose the Rectangle tool (M or Shift-M).

3. Drag a rectangle or Shift-drag a half-inch to one-inch square around the objects (use the Info palette to check the dimensions). Fit the rectangle closely around the objects if you don't want any blank space to be part of the pattern (use Smart Guides to assist you) **4**. If the pattern is complex, make the rectangle small to crop the objects to facilitate printing.

4. Choose Object menu > Arrange > Send to Back. The rectangle must be behind the pattern objects.

5. Apply a fill and stroke of None to the rectangle if you don't want it to become

1 *Select one or more objects. You can use anything from geometric objects to freehand lines. The simpler, the better.*

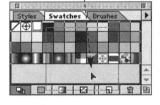

2 *Drag the selected objects onto the* **Swatches** *palette.*

3 *An object is filled with the new pattern.*

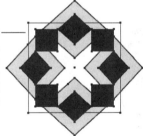

4 *Draw a rectangle around the objects, and send it to the back. (All the objects are selected in this figure.)*

5 *An object is filled with the new pattern.*

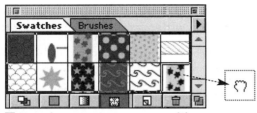

1 Drag the pattern you want to modify out of the **Swatches** palette.

2 The original pattern swatch.

3 The pattern is modified, then selected, then dragged back over the original swatch.

The modified pattern is used as a fill.

part of the pattern. Apply a fill color to the rectangle if you want it to become the background color in the pattern.

6. Follow steps 3–6 in the previous set of instructions **5**.

You can modify any pattern, including any pattern that's supplied with Illustrator. To change an existing pattern, first drag its swatch back into a document.

Note: Patterns are fun, patterns are beautiful, patterns choke printers. Try to keep it simple.

To modify a fill pattern:

1. Display a blank area in your document window, then drag the pattern swatch out of the Swatches palette **1**. The pattern is now a group with a bounding rectangle (with a fill and stroke of None) added behind it **2**.

2. Modify the pattern object. Her

3.

4.

5.

➤ Read about transforming patterns on page 85.

Note: To create a pattern that repeats seamlessly, see the Illustrator User Guide.

To create a geometric fill pattern:

1. Create a symmetrical arrangement of geometric objects – using the Rectangle, Ellipse, Polygon, Spiral, Star, or any other tool.

   To copy an object, Option-drag/Alt-drag it using a selection tool. Add Shift to constrain the movement horizontally or vertically. Position objects so they abut each other. To help you align the objects, show the grid or use Smart Guides (see page 76).

2. *Optional:* Apply assorted fill colors to add variety to the pattern.

3. Choose the Rectangle tool (M).

4. Choose a fill and stroke of None, then carefully draw a rectangle around the objects, preserving the symmetry so the pattern will repeat properly ■.

5. With the rectangle still selected, choose Object menu > Arrange > Send to Back.

6. Marquee all the objects with the Selection tool (V), drag the selection onto the Swatches palette, and use it as a fill in any object ■.

To expand a pattern fill into individual objects:

1. Select an object that contains a pattern fill ■–■.

2. Choose Object menu > Expand.

3. Check the Fill and Stroke boxes, then click OK ■. The pattern fill will be divided into the original shapes that made up the pattern tile. Any stroke will become a compound path. The expanded shapes will now be a group inside a clipping mask. You can release the mask, change the mask shape, or delete it.

shifting patterns

To reposition the pattern fill in an object without moving the object itself, hold down "~" and drag inside it with the Selection tool.

1 *Draw geometric objects.*

2 *Copy the object(s) and arrange the copies symmetrically.*

3 *Draw a rectangle and position it so it will create symmetry in the pattern tile.*

4 *The **geometric** pattern fill.*

5 *The original pattern.*

6 *A detail of the pattern expanded (Artwork view).*

Diane Margolin

7 *After applying the **Expand** command, releasing the mask, and applying Effect menu > Distort & Transform > Roughen (low settings).*

Mastering the Pen tool—Illustrator's most difficult tool—requires patience and practice. Once you become comfortable creating Pen tool paths, read Chapter 8 to learn how to reshape them. If you find the Pen tool too difficult to use, remember that you can always transform a simple shape into a complex shape or draw a freehand shape using the Pencil or Paintbrush tool. Simpler methods for creating shapes are covered in Chapter 5.

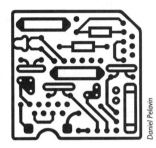

Daniel Pelavin

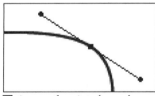

1 *This **corner** point joins two **straight** segments. It has **no** direction lines.*

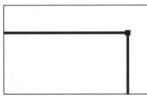

2 *A **smooth** point always has a pair of direction lines that move in **tandem**. This is a continuous curve.*

3 *This **corner** point has direction lines that move **independently**. This is a non-continuous curve.*

Drawing with the Pen tool
What the Pen tool does

The Pen tool creates precise curved and straight line segments connected by anchor points. If you click with the Pen tool, you will create corner points and straight line segments with *no* direction lines **1**. If you drag with the Pen tool, you will create smooth curve points and curve segments *with* direction lines **2**–**3**. The distance and direction in which you drag the mouse determine the shape of the curve segment.

In the instructions on the following pages, you'll learn how to draw straight sides, continuous curves, and non-continuous curves using the Pen tool. Once you master these three types of path shapes and start using the Pen tool as an illustrator, you'll naturally combine all three techniques without really thinking about it. Drag-drag-click, drag, click-click-drag...

Click with the Pen tool to create an open or closed straight-sided polygon.

To draw a straight-sided object using the Pen tool:

1. If a color is selected for the Fill box on the Color palette (not None), the Pen path will be filled as soon as three points are created (you'll see this only in Preview view, of course). To create segments that appear as lines only, choose a stroke color and a fill of None now (or at any time while you're drawing the path).

2. Choose the Pen tool (P) 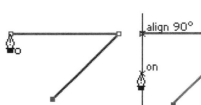.

3. Click to create an anchor point.

4. Click to create a second anchor point. A straight line segment will now connect the two points.

5. Click to create additional anchor points. They will be also connected by straight line segments.

6. To complete the shape as an **open** path:

   Click the Pen tool or any other tool on the Toolbox.
   or
   Hold down Command/Ctrl and click outside the new shape to deselect it.
   or
   Choose Edit menu > Deselect All (Command-Shift-A/Ctrl-Shift-A).

   To complete the shape as a **closed** path, position the Pen pointer over the starting point (a small circle will appear next to the pointer), and click on it **2**.

➤ Hold down Shift while clicking with the Pen tool to constrain a segment to a multiple of 45°.

➤ Use smart guides to help you align points and segments (see page 76) **3**.

➤ If the artboard starts to get filled with extraneous points, Use the Object > Path > Cleanup command with only the Stray Points box checked.

1 *Pen tool.*

2 *The Pen tool pointer is positioned over the starting point to close the new shape.*

3 *You can use **Smart Guides** to align points as you create them.*

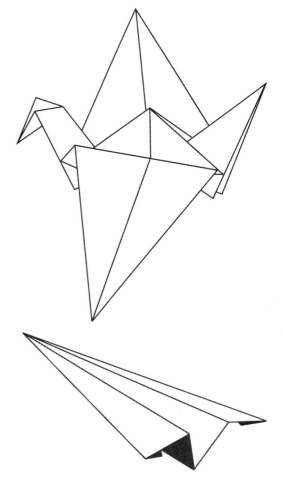

Draw a Straight-Sided Object

1 *Drag to create the first anchor point.*

2 *Release and reposition the mouse, then drag in the direction you wish the curve to follow.*

3 *Continue to reposition and drag the mouse.*

4 *Continue to reposition and drag.*

Follow these instructions to create continuous curves, which consist of smooth anchor points connected by smooth curve segments, each with a pair of direction lines that move in tandem. The longer the direction lines, the steeper or wider the curve. You can practice drawing curves by tracing over a placed image that contains curve shapes or by converting curved objects into guides and then tracing over the guide lines (see page 194).

To draw continuous curves using the Pen tool:

1. Choose the Pen tool (P). *Optional:* Turn on Smart Guides (Command-U/Ctrl-U toggle).

2. Drag to create the first anchor point **1**. The angle of the pair of direction lines that you create will be determined by the direction you drag.

3. **Release** the mouse, **move** it away from the last anchor point, then drag a short distance in the direction in which you want the curve to follow to create a second anchor point **2**. A curve segment will connect the first and second anchor points, and a second pair of direction lines will be created. The shape of the curve segment will be defined by the length and direction you drag the mouse.

   Remember, you can always reshape the curves later (see Chapter 8). When you drag a direction line after it's drawn, only one of the curves that the smooth point connects will reshape.

4. Drag to create additional anchor points and direction lines **3**–**4**. The points will be connected by curve segments.

(Continued on the following page)

Draw Continuous Curves

5. To complete the object as an **open** path:

Choose a different tool.
or
Click a selection tool (or hold down Command/Ctrl), then click away from the new object to deselect it.
or
Choose Edit menu > Deselect All (Command-Shift-A/Ctrl-Shift-A).

To complete the object as a **closed** path, position the Pen pointer over the starting point (a small loop will appear next to the pointer; if Text Label Hints is on in Edit menu > Preferences > Smart Guides, the word "anchor" will appear), drag, then release the mouse.

➤ The fewer the anchor points, the smoother the shape. Too many anchor points will produce bumpy curves, and also could cause printing errors. Also, don't make your direction lines too long. You can always lengthen them later.

Adjust as you go

■ If the last-created anchor point was a **curve** point and you want to convert it into a **corner** point, click on it with the Pen tool, move the mouse, and continue to draw. One direction line from that point will disappear.

■ If the last-created point was a **corner** point and you want to convert it into a **curve** point, position the Pen tool pointer over it, then drag. A direction line will appear. Continue to draw.

■ To move a point as it's being created, keep the mouse button down, hold down **Spacebar**, and drag the point.

Favorite toggles (Pen tool selected)

Convert-direction-point tool	Option/Alt
Last-used selection tool	Command/Ctrl

Be smart with your pen

Smart Guide angle lines will appear for existing points as you click or drag with the Pen tool to produce new points **1**. Make sure the **Construction Guides** box is checked in Edit menu > Preferences > Smart Guides.

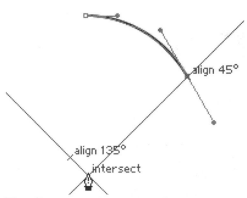

1 *To align new anchor points with existing, unselected anchor points, use* ***Smart Guides.***

1 *Drag to create the first anchor point.*

2 *Release the mouse, reposition it, then drag to create a second anchor point.*

3 *Hold down Option/Alt and drag from the last anchor point in the direction you want the new curve to follow. The direction lines are on the same side of the curve segment.*

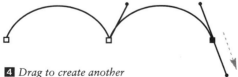

4 *Drag to create another anchor point, and so on.*

You can use the Pen tool to create corner points that join non-continuous curves, which are segments that curve on the same side of an anchor point. (Segments curve on both sides of a smooth anchor point.) If you move one direction line from a corner point, only the curve on that side of the point will reshape. Smooth points and corner points can be combined in the same path, of course. You can convert smooth points into corner points (or vice versa) as you draw them (instructions on this page) or after you draw them (instructions on the next page).

To convert smooth points into corner points as you draw them:

1. Choose the Pen tool (P).

2. Drag to create the first anchor point **1**.

3. **Release** the mouse, **move** it away from the last anchor point, then drag to create a second anchor point **2**. A curve segment will connect the first and second anchor points, and a second pair of direction lines will be created. The shape of the curve segment will be determined by the length and direction you drag.

4. Option-drag/Alt-drag from the last anchor point to create a new independent-moving direction line. Drag in the direction in which you want the curve to follow **3**.
or
Click on the last anchor point to remove one of the direction lines from that point.

5. Repeat the previous two steps to draw a series of anchor points and curves **4**.

6. To close the shape:
Drag on the starting point to keep it as a smooth point.
or
To convert the starting point to a corner, click on it.

Convert Points as You Draw Them

This is a recap of the various ways to use the Convert-anchor-point tool. These techniques were covered in three separate sets of instructions in Chapter 8.

To convert points in an existing object:

1. Choose the Direct-selection tool (A).

2. Click on the path.

3. Choose the Convert-anchor-point tool (Shift-C) **2**.
   or
   Choose the Pen tool (P), then hold down Option/Alt.

4. Position the pointer over the anchor point that you want to convert.

5. Drag new direction lines from a corner point to convert it into a smooth point **3**.
   or
   To convert a smooth point into a corner point with a non-continuous curve, rotate a direction line from the anchor point so it forms a "V" shape with the other direction line **4**.
   or
   Click on a smooth point to convert it into a corner point with no direction lines **5**–**6**.

6. Repeat the previous step to convert other anchor points.

Convert Existing Points

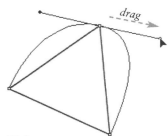

1 *Direct-selection tool.*

2 *Convert-anchor-point tool.*

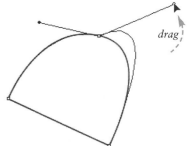

3 *Converting a **corner** point into a **smooth** point.*

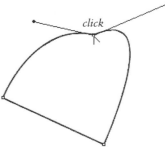

4 *Converting a **smooth** point into a **corner** point (**non-continuous** curve).*

5 *Converting a **non-continuous** curve into a **corner** point with **no** direction lines.*

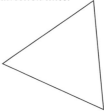

6 *Back to the original triangle.*

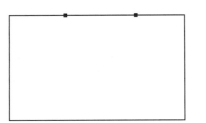

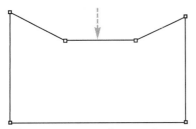

1 *Click to add two anchor points at the ⅓ points along the rectangle's top segment.*

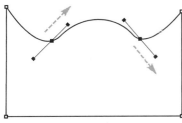

2 *Drag the segment between the new points downward.*

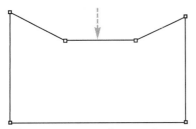

3 *Convert each new point into a curve point.*

Exercise

Convert a rectangle into a costume mask

The outer mask shape

1. Draw a rectangle with a fill of None and a 1 pt. black stroke, and select it using the Direct-selection tool.

2. Choose the Pen tool (P), and make sure the Disable Auto Add/Delete box is unchecked in Edit menu > Preferences > General.

3. Click to add two anchor points at the ⅓ points along the rectangle's top segment **1**.

4. Command-drag/Ctrl-drag the segment between the new points downward **2**.

5. Option-drag/Alt-drag the new point on the left upward and to the right to convert it into a smooth point, and drag the new point on the right downward and to the right **3**.

6. Option-drag/Alt-drag the left corner point upward and to the left and the right corner point downward and to the left **4**.

7. Release Option/Alt, then click to add a point in the middle of the bottommost segment.

8. Hold down Command/Ctrl, click on the new center point, then drag it slightly upward **5**.

(Continued on the following page)

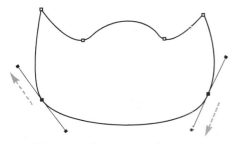

4 *Convert the rectangle's bottom corner points into curve points.*

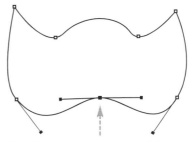

5 *Add a point in the center of the rectangle's bottom segment, then drag the new center point upward.*

Exercise: Rectangle into Costume Mask

The eye holes

1. Choose the Ellipse tool (L), then draw a small ellipse for an eye hole **1**.

2. Choose the Direct-selection tool (A). Deselect, click on the leftmost anchor point of the ellipse, then drag it upward to form an eye shape **2**.

3. Click on the bottommost anchor point of the ellipse, then drag the left handle of that point to the left to widen the bottom segment **3**.

4. Click on the top middle point of the ellipse, then drag the right handle of that point upward and to the right to widen the top right segment **4**.

5. Choose the Selection tool (V), then move the ellipse to the left side of the mask shape.

6. Choose the Reflect tool (O).

7. Option-click/Alt-click in the center of the mask shape. In the dialog box, check the Preview box, click Vertical, enter 90° in the Angle field, press Tab to force a preview, if desired, then click Copy. Shift-drag the copy to the right (Shift will constrain the movement) **5**.

8. Use the Selection tool to marquee all three shapes, and fill the shapes with a color. Leave them selected.

9. Choose Object menu > Compound Path > Make (Command-8/Ctrl-8). The eye holes will now cut through the mask shape **6**.

1 *Create a small ellipse for the eye holes.*

2 *Drag the leftmost anchor point upward with the Direct-selection tool.*

3 *Drag the left direction handle of the bottommost anchor point to the left.*

4 *Drag the right handle of the top middle anchor point point upward and to the right.*

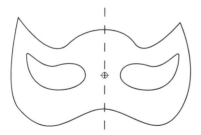

5 *To create the second eye hole, Option-click/ Alt-click in the center of the mask shape with the Reflect tool. Check Preview, click Vertical, enter 90° in the Angle field, then click Copy.*

6 *All the shapes are selected and made into a compound. A fill color is applied to the compound shape. (The gray rectangle behind reveals the transparency in the compound.)*

LAYERS 11

In this chapter you will learn how to create top-level layers, sublayers, groups, and template layers. How to activate layers. How to select objects using the Layers palette. How to create and edit groups. How to restack, duplicate, and delete layers and objects. How to choose layer options, such as hide/show, lock/unlock, view, and print. How to merge and flatten layers. And how to trace objects manually or using the Auto Trace tool.

All the features covered in this chapter are new or substantially improved!

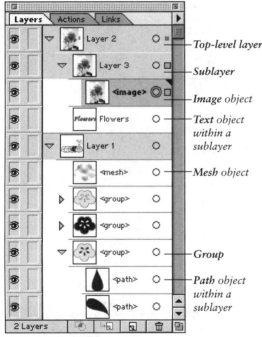

Top-level layer — Layer 2
Sublayer — Layer 3
Image *object* — <image>
Text *object within a sublayer* — Flowers
 — Layer 1
Mesh *object* — <mesh>
 — <group>
 — <group>
Group — <group>
Path *object within a sublayer* — <path>
 — <path>

2 Layers

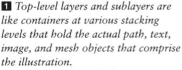
1 *Top-level layers and sublayers are like containers at various stacking levels that hold the actual path, text, image, and mesh objects that comprise the illustration.*

Layer upon layer

Until now (unless you snuck ahead to this chapter), you've been creating objects on a single, default layer that was created automatically when you created your document. Each new path you drew was added on top of the next path in the document's stacking order.

Now it's time to get acquainted with the feature that displays the stacking order—the Layers palette. It has a number of powerful new features. With a document open, click the Layer 1 triangle on the Layers palette to expand that list and reveal its path objects. Layer 1 is called a **top-level layer** (meaning it's not nested within another layer) **1**.

You can add as many layers as you like to an illustration (okay, memory permitting). You can also create your own **sublayers** within the top-level layers and you can nest groups, objects, and even other sublayers within sublayers. Best of all, you can activate, select, restack, show/hide, lock/unlock, and print any of those components individually.

Objects in the illustration are nested within the top-level layer that was selected when the object was created. Nesting is displayed as

(Continued on the following page)

Layers Palette Options

indenting on the Layers palette. Up to 29 indent levels can be created.

By default, each new vector object you create is assigned the name **<path>**; each placed raster image or rasterized objects is assigned the name **<image>**; each new mesh object is assigned the name **<mesh>**; and each new **text** object is assigned the first few characters in that particular text object (e.g., "The planting season has started" might be shortened to "The plan").

➤ Double-click an object or layer to assign a custom name to it. Leave the word "group" or "path" in the name to help you identify it later.

You may say "Whoa!" when you first see the long list of names on the redesigned Layers palette. Once you get used to working with it, though, you may become enamoured with its clean, logical design. It makes even simple tasks like selecting and restacking objects much easier than before.

➤ Layers and sublayers are numbered in the order in which they are created, regardless of their position in the stacking order or whether they are at the top level or indented.

You can choose different Layers palette options for each document.

To choose Layers Palette Options:

1. Choose Palette Options from the Layers palette menu.

2. Do any of the following ◾1–◾2:

   Check Show Layers Only to list top-level layers and sublayers only—not individual objects.

   Click a Row Size for layer names and thumbnails. Choose Other to enter a custom size (12–100 pixels).

   Check which Thumbnails you want to show: Layers (Top Level Only, or top level layers and sublayers, with that box unchecked), Groups, or Objects.

3. Click OK (Return/Enter).

One catchall name

In this book, we refer to paths, images, mesh objects, and text objects collectively as **objects**. If we need to refer to one of these categories individually for some reason, we will.

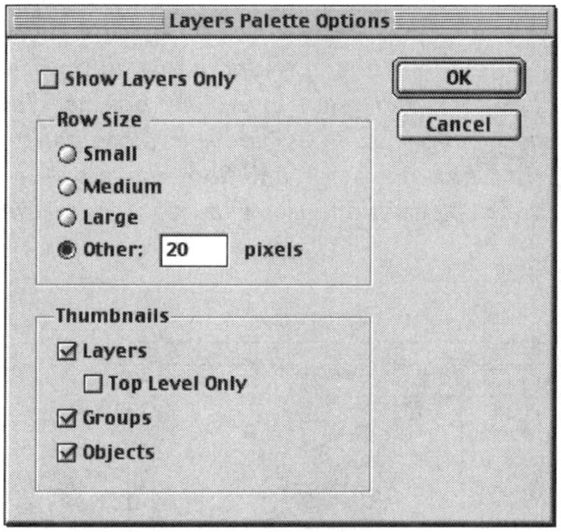

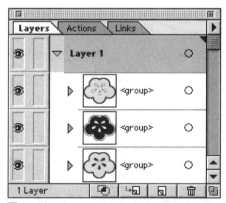

◾1 *You can customize the Layers palette for each file.*

◾2 *For this document, we chose a large, custom thumbnail size (40 pixels), with no thumbnails for layers.*

Quick layer

To insert a new top-level layer in the topmost layer palette position, Command-click/Ctrl-click the New Layer button.

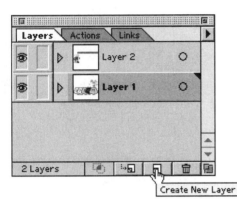

1 *Option-click/Alt-click the **Create New Layer** button on the **Layers** palette to choose options for or rename a new layer as you create it.*

2 *The new Layer 4 appears above Layer 1.*

Creating layers

In these instructions, you'll learn how to create the granddaddy of layers—top-level layers.

To create a new top-level layer:

Method 1 (quick, no options)

1. On the Layers palette, click on the top-level layer name above which you want the new layer to appear.

2. To create a layer without choosing options for it, click the Create New Layer button **1**–**2**. Illustrator will assign to the new layer the next number in order and the next available color from the Color pop-up menu in the Layer Options dialog box.

Method 2 (choose options)

1. On the Layers palette, click on the top-level layer name above which you want the new layer to appear.

2. Option-click/Alt-click the Create New Layer button.
   or
   Choose New Layer from the Layers palette menu.

3. Do any of the following:

   Enter a **Name** for the new layer.

   Choose a different selection border color for objects on a layer via the **Color** pop-up menu. Colors are assigned to new layers in the order in which they appear on the Color pop-up menu. The different selection colors help to make it easier to tell on which layer or sublayer a selected object is located. If the fill or stroke colors are similar to the selection border colors, it may be difficult to distinguish among them. In that case, choosing a different selection color helps.

   Choose other layer options (see page 180).

4. Click OK (Return/Enter).

➤ A group or an object will always be nested within a top-level layer or a sublayer—it can't float around by itself.

Once you're accustomed to adding and using top-level layers, you're ready for the next level of intricacy: sublayers. Each sublayer is nested within (indented under) a top-level layer or under another sublayer, and layer options can be chosen for individual sublayers. When you create a new object or group of objects while a sublayer is selected, the new object or group will be nested within that sublayer.

Note: By default, every sublayer is assigned the name "Layer," the same name as top-level layers, which can be very confusing. But remember, you can always rename layers and sublayers to help you distinguish among them (e.g., "poem" or "order form" or "tyrannosaurus").

To create a sublayer:

Method 1 (quick, no options)
1. On the Layers palette, click the top-level layer (or sublayer) name within which you want the new sublayer to appear.

2. To create a new layer without choosing options for it, click the Create New Sublayer button **1**–**2**.

Method 2 (choose options)
1. On the Layers palette, click the top-level (or sublayer) layer within which you want the new sublayer to appear.

2. To create a new sublayer and choose options for it, Option-click/Alt-click the Create New Sublayer button or choose New Sublayer from the Layers palette menu.

3. Enter a Name for the new sublayer.

4. *Optional:* Change the selection Color for the sublayer, and check or uncheck any of the Template, Show, Preview, Lock, Print, or Dim Images to options (see page 180).

5. Click OK (Return/Enter).

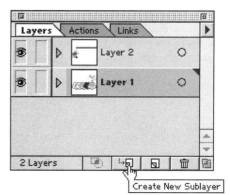

1 *Activate a layer name, then click the* **Create New Sublayer** *button.*

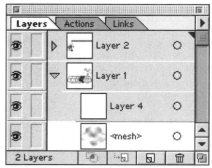

2 *A new sublayer name (Layer 4) appears within Layer 1.*

Create a Sublayer

1 *Draw a marquee around the objects to be grouped to select them...*

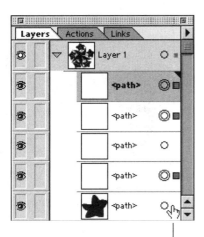

2 *...or Shift-click in the selection area on the Layers palette for each object.*

If you group objects together, you can easily select, cut, copy, paste, transform, recolor, or move them as a unit. When objects are grouped, they are automatically placed on the same top-level layer (the top-level layer of the frontmost object in the group) and are assigned the same selection color. You can group any types of objects together (e.g., text objects with placed images) and you can select and edit any individual object in a group at any time.

To create a group:

1. Choose the Selection tool (V). Then, in the illustration window, Shift-click or marquee all the objects to be grouped **1**.
   or
   Shift-click the selection area at the far right side of the Layers palette for each object you want to join in a group. A selection square will appear for each of those objects **2**. (You'll learn more about the selection area later.)

2. Choose Object menu > Group (Command-G/Ctrl-G) **3**.
   or
   Control-click/Right-click on the artboard and choose Group from the context menu.

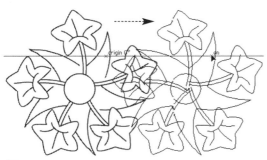

3 *If you move a group using the selection tool, all the objects in the group will move in unison.*

Activating layers

In order to control where a newly created (or pasted) path will be positioned in the stacking order, you need to activate (highlight) a top-level layer, sublayer, group, or object on the Layers palette.

Note: Activating a top-level layer or sublayer will not cause objects on those layers to become selected. To learn how to select objects using the Layers palette, see pages 170–173.

➤ If a top-level layer is active when a new object is created but no sublayer is active, the new object name (e.g., "<path>" or "<mesh>") will be nested just below that top-level layer name.

➤ If a sublayer is active when a new object is created but no objects in the sublayer are selected, the new object will appear at the top of that sublayer.

➤ If an object or group is active when a new object is created, the new object will appear directly above the active object or group. This doesn't work for placed images.

To activate a layer, sublayer, group, or object:

Click a top-level layer, sublayer, group, or object name. Click the name—not the selection area at the far right side of the palette. The current-layer indicator will appear at the far right side of the palette **1**.

To activate more than one layer, group, or object at a time, see the following page.

Quick activate

Command-Option click/Ctrl-Alt-click anywhere on the Layers palette list, then start typing a layer, group, or object name. You can type a layer number without typing the word "Layer." Caveat: You can't select a sublayer, group, or object unless its name is visible on the palette (its layer list is expanded).

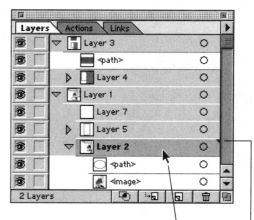

1 *Click to the right of the name of the layer, sublayer, group, or object you want to activate.*

Current-layer indicator

Circles and squares

The column of little circles on the far side of the Layers palette are used to **target** an object, group, or layer for applying appearance attributes. You'll learn all about appearances in Chapter 18. For now, just remember to use the selection area to **select** objects for modification—not the target circle (see the next page).

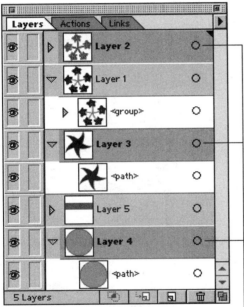

1 *Three **non-contiguous** top-level layers are activated (note the darker highlight color).*

When more than one layer or sublayer is active, they can be restacked on the palette en masse and the same layer options can be applied to them. *Note:* Selecting an object won't cause its layer to become active, and vice versa. Activating and selecting are two different functions.

First, some rules.

➤ You can activate more than one sublayer within the same top-level layer, but you can't activate sublayers from different top-level layers.

➤ You can activate more than one layer of the same category (e.g., all top-level layers), but you can't activate layers from different nesting levels at the same time (e.g., not top-level layers with sublayers).

➤ You can activate multiple paths in the same top-level layer, but not from different top-level layers.

To activate multiple layers:

1. Click a top-level layer (or a sublayer) on the Layers palette.

2. Shift-click another layer (or sublayer). The layers you clicked on and all layers in between them of a similar kind will become active (highlighted).
   or
   Command-click/Ctrl-click non-contiguous layer (or sublayer) names **1**. Only the layers you click on will become active.

➤ Command-click/Ctrl-click to deactivate one layer when more than one layer is active.

Activate Layers

Selecting objects

One of our favorite new features in the Layers palette is that it can be used to select paths or groups. Here we're talking about selecting for editing or reshaping—selection handles and all—not just activating, which we discussed on the previous two pages.

To select all the objects in one layer:

Click the selection area for a top-level layer or sublayer at the far right side of the Layers palette. A selection square will appear for every sublayer, group, and object on that layer, and every object on the layer, regardless of its indent level, will become selected in the illustration window **1**–**2**.

➤ To deselect any selected object individually, Shift-click its selection square.

To deselect all the objects in a layer:

Shift-click the selection square for the layer. All the objects in the layer will be deselected, including any objects in any of its sublayers or groups.

To select one object:

1. Make sure the object name is visible on the palette. Expand any top-level layer, sublayer, or group list, if necessary.

2. At the far right side of the Layers palette, click the selection area for the object you want to select **3**.

   To select multiple objects on different layers, see the instructions on the following page.

➤ If you click the selection area for a top-level layer or sublayer but there is no object on that layer or sublayer (its thumbnail is blank), no selection square will appear.

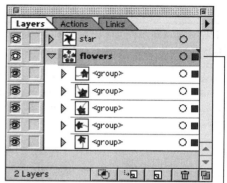

1 *Click the **selection area** for a layer to select all the paths and groups on that layer.*

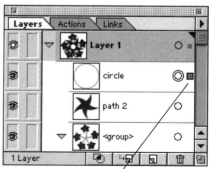

2 *All the paths (and path groups, in this case) on our "flowers" layer became selected in the illustration window.*

3 *One object is selected.*

Seelect Objects

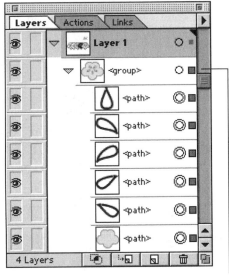

1 *Objects from non-consecutive stacking levels are selected (note the selection squares).*

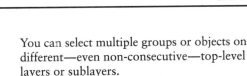

2 *If you click the selection area for a group, all the objects in the group will become selected.*

You can select multiple groups or objects on different—even non-consecutive—top-level layers or sublayers.

Note: Selecting an object won't cause its layer to become active, and vice versa. Activating and selecting are two different functions.

To select multiple objects on different layers:

Method 1
Expand any layer or group lists so the names of all the nested objects you want to select are visible. Click the **selection area** for any object, then Shift-click any other individual groups or objects you want to add to the selection **1**. The groups or objects can be non-consecutive.

Method 2
Option-drag/Alt-drag through a series of consecutive top-level or sublayer **names** to select all the objects on those layers.
or
Or expand a sublayer or group list, then Option-drag/Alt-drag through a series of consecutive object **names**.

➤ To deselect any selected object individually, Shift-click its selection square.

Working with groups
To select all the objects in a group:

Method 1 (Layers palette)
1. Expand a top-level layer on the palette that contains a nested group.
2. To select all the objects in a group, (including any objects in groups that may be nested inside it), click the group's selection area at the far right side of the Layers palette **2**.
   or
   To select all the objects in a group that's nested inside another group, expand the list for the larger group, then click the selection area only for the nested group.

(For the illustration window selection method, see the following page.)

Select Multiple Objects

Select Grouped Objects

Method 2 (illustration window)

To select an entire group, click any item in the group with the Selection tool (V) **1**.

or

To select individual anchor points or segments of an object within a group, click on them with the Direct-selection tool (A).

or

To select groups that are nested within a larger, parent group, use the Direct-selection tool while holding down Option/Alt or use the Group-selection tool (it's on the Direct-selection tool pop-out menu). Click once to select an object in a group **2**; click again on the same object to select the whole group that object is part of **3**; click a third time on the object to select the next larger group in the hierarchy that the newly selected group is a part of **4**, and so on.

➤ To see the selection's bounding box, leave the objects selected and choose the Selection tool.

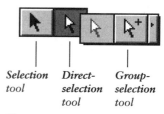

Selection   Direct-   Group-
tool   selection   selection
           tool   tool

1 *Illustrator's selection tools.*

2 *One object in a group is selected.*

3 *Click again to select the remaining objects in the same group.*

4 *Keep clicking to select other groups that are nested inside the larger group.*

1 To *select multiple objects in a group,* expand the group list, then Shift-click the *selection area* for each object. A *selection square* will appear for each object. ─────

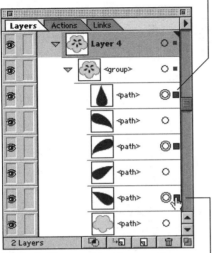

2 To *deselect an object in a group,* Shift-click its selection square.

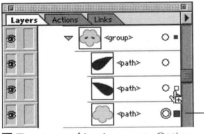

3 To *copy an object in a group,* Option-drag/Alt-drag its selection square upward or downward (note the plus sign).

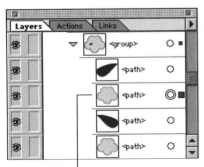

4 *The duplicate appears.*

To select some objects in a group:

Expand the group's list on the Layers palette, then Shift-click the selection area at the far right side of the palette for each object in the group you want to select **1**.

or

Choose the Group-selection tool (on the Direct-selection tool pop-out menu), then Shift-click objects in a group (or nested groups) in the illustration window.

or

Choose the Direct-selection tool (A), then Command-Shift-click/Ctrl-Shift-click multiple items (or nested groups) in the illustration window.

To deselect an object in a group:

On the Layers palette, expand the group list, then Shift-click the selection square for an object in the group **2**.

or

Choose the Direct-Selection tool, then Shift-click the object in the illustration window.

To copy an object in a group:

Method 1 (Layers palette)

1. Expand the group list.

2. Click the selection area for the object you want to copy.

3. Option-drag/Alt-drag the selection square upward or downward, then release the mouse when the little outline square is at the desired stacking position inside the same group or in another sublayer or top-level layer **3–4**. (To restack the copy after it's created, see page 176.)

Method 2 (illustration window)

1. Select the object you want to copy.

2. To keep the copy inside the group, Option-drag/Alt-drag the object.

   or

   To make the copy fall outside the group, copy the object (Command-C/Ctrl-C), deselect, then paste (Command-V/Ctrl-V).

Select Grouped Objects: Copy Object in Group

Follow these instructions to add an existing object to a group. The object will stay in its original *x/y* position.

To move an existing object (or group) into a group:

Method 1 (the easier way)

1. Make sure the name of the object you want to add to the group is visible on the Layers palette.

2. Drag the object name upward or downward in the palette. Release the mouse when the large, black arrowhead points to the name of the group you want to move it to **1**. The group list will expand, if it isn't already expanded **2**.

Method 2 (the old way)

1. Choose the Selection tool (V).

2. Select the object (or group) to be added to the group.

3. Choose Edit menu > Cut (Command-X/Ctrl-X).

4. Select the object in the group in front of or behind which you want the object to appear.

5. Choose Edit menu > Paste in Front (Command-F/Ctrl-F) or Paste in Back (Command-B/Ctrl-B).

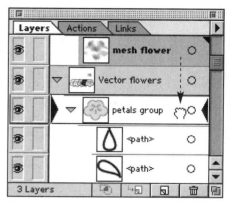

1 The "mesh flower" **object** is dragged to the "petals group."

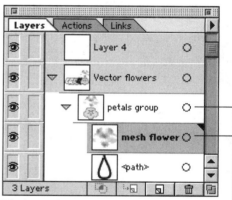

2 The petals **group** list expands; the mesh flower is now **inside** it.

Move Object into a Group

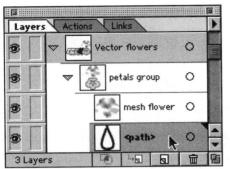

1 *The name of an object in a group is clicked on.*

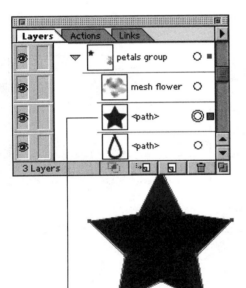

2 *A new object is drawn in the illustration window. The word "<path>" appears within the group list.*

You can choose a group for an object before it's created. *Note:* This works only for path objects drawn in Illustrator—not placed images.

To add a new object to a group:

1. Deselect all objects (Command-Shift-A/ Ctrl-Shift-A).

2. On the Layers palette, expand the list for the group to which you want to add a new object.

3. Click the object name (not the selection area) above which you want the new object to appear **1**. This is now the active layer.

4. Draw a new object. The object name will appear on the group list, above the object you chose in the previous step **2**.

Sometimes there comes a time when a group has be disbanded.

To ungroup a group:

1. If the group isn't already selected:

   Choose the Selection tool (V), then click the group in the illustration window.
   or
   Click the selection area for the group on the Layers palette.

2. Choose Object menu > Ungroup (Command-Shift-G/Ctrl-Shift-G).
   or
   Control-click/Right-click on the artboard and choose Ungroup from the context menu. If the command isn't available, it means no group is currently selected.

➤ Keep choosing the same command again to ungroup nested groups.

Add New Object to Group: Ungroup

Restacking

The order of layer names on the Layers palette matches the front-to-back order of layers in the illustration. You can move a group or object to a different stacking position within the same layer, move a group or object to a different top-level layer or sublayer, or even move a whole top-level layer or sublayer upward or downward on the list.

On this page you'll use the Layers palette for restacking. On the next page, you'll use commands. Shop and compare.

To restack a layer, group, or object:

Drag a top-level layer, sublayer, group, or object name upward or downward on the Layers palette (the pointer will turn into a hand icon). Release the mouse between layers or objects to keep the object on the same level of indent (e.g., keep a path within a group) **1–2**. Or release the mouse when the large black arrowhead points to a different group or layer **3–4**. The illustration will redraw with the objects in their new stacking position.

Beware! If you move an object that's part of a group or clipping mask to a different top-level layer, the object will be released from the group or mask.

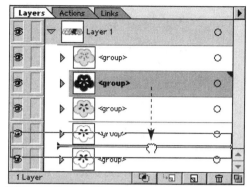

1 *Drag a layer, sublayer, group, or object name upward or downward on the list. Here the mouse is released at the **same indent level.***

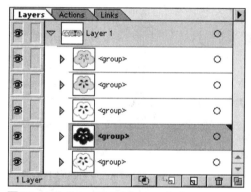

2 *The dark flower group is restacked.*

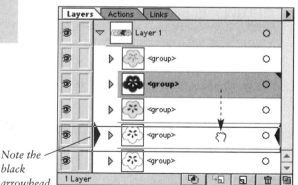

Note the black arrowhead

3 *The dark flower group is moved into a **different** group.*

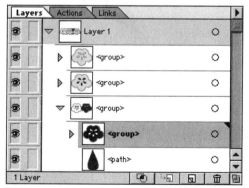

4 *The dark flower group is in a new stacking position and indent level.*

Restack

Upside down

To reverse the order of sublayers, groups, and objects within a layer, make all the elements you want to reverse active (active—not selected). To activate non-contiguous items, Command-click/Ctrl-click them; to activate contiguous items, Shift, then Shift-click. Then choose **Reverse Order** from the Layers palette menu.

1 Select the object you want to restack, then choose Edit menu > **Cut.**

2 Select the object that you want to paste directly in front of or directly behind.

3 Choose Edit menu > **Paste In Front** or **Paste in Back.** (In this case, Paste in Back was chosen.)

The Paste In Front and Paste In Back commands paste the Clipboard contents directly in front of or directly behind the currently selected object within the selected object's layer in the same horizontal and vertical (x/y) position from which it was cut.

To restack an object in front of or behind another object:

1. Choose the Selection tool (V), then select an object **1**.

2. Choose Edit menu > Cut (Command-X/Ctrl-X).

3. Select the object (in the same document or a different document) that you want to paste directly in front of or directly behind **2**. If you don't select an object, the Clipboard contents will be pasted to the top or bottom of the currently active top-level layer.

4. Choose Edit menu > Paste In Front (Command-F/Ctrl-F).
   or
   Choose Edit menu > Paste In Back (Command-B/Ctrl-B) **3**.

This is the old-fashioned way to restack. We like the method on the previous page better.

To restack using a command:

1. Choose the Selection tool (V), then select the object or group you want to restack.

2. To move the object to the bottom or top of the same layer, choose Object menu > Arrange > Send To Back or Bring To Front.
   or
   To shift the object one level at a time within the same layer, choose Object menu > Arrange > Bring Forward or Send Backward.

➤ You can also Control-click/Right-click and choose a restacking command from the Arrange submenu on the context menu.

➤ If you restack an object in a group, it will stay in the group.

Restack

Duplicating

If you duplicate an entire top-level layer, all the sublayers and objects from that layer will appear in the duplicate. The duplicate layer will be stacked directly above the original from which it is made.

To duplicate a layer, sublayer, or object:

Activate the layer, sublayer, or object you want to duplicate, then choose Duplicate "[name]" from the Layers palette menu.
or
Drag a layer, sublayer, or object name over the Create New Layer button **1**–**2**. If you duplicate a top-level layer or sublayer, the word "copy" will appear in the duplicate name.

Follow these instructions to copy all the objects from a top-level layer and any sublayers or groups contained within it to an existing layer or sublayer of your choice. (In the previous set of instructions, the duplicate objects appeared in a brand new layer.)

To copy objects between layers:

1. Click the selection area for a top-level layer, sublayer, group, or object.

2. Option-drag/Alt-drag the selection square for the layer, sublayer, group, or object upward or downward on the list. Release the mouse when the selection square is in the desired location **3**. The duplicate objects will appear in the same *x/y* location as the original objects.

➤ If you Option-drag/Alt-drag a <clipping path> (a mask) into a different top-level layer, the mask copy won't clip any objects below it. It will be a basic path with a Fill and Stroke of None.

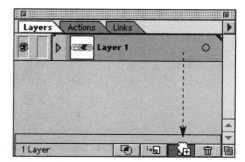

1 *To **duplicate** a layer, sublayer, group, or object, drag it over the **Create New Layer** button (note the plus sign).*

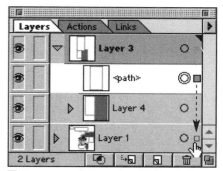

2 *A copy of Layer 1 is made.*

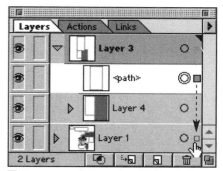

3 *To copy an object to another layer, Option-drag/Alt-drag its **selection square** upward or downward to the desired location.*

1 *Activate the layer you want to* **delete**, *then click the* **Delete Selection** *(trash) button.*

Deleting

You know how to make 'em. Now you need to learn how to get rid of 'em.

Beware! If you delete a top-level layer or a sublayer, any and all objects on that layer will be removed from the file.

To delete a layer, sublayer, object, or group:

1. Activate all the layers, sublayers, groups, and objects you want to delete. To activate more than one, Command-click/Ctrl-click them. Remember, you can activate more than one layer of the same category (e.g., all top-level layers), but not different kinds of layers (e.g., not a top-level layer and objects from a different top-level layer).

2. Choose Delete "[layer name]" or Delete Selection from the Layers palette menu or click the Delete Selection (trash) button at the bottom of the palette **1**. If there are any objects on a layer or sublayer you're deleting, a warning dialog box will appear. Click Yes (Return/Enter).
   or
   Drag the activated layers or objects over the Delete Selection (trash) button. No warning dialog box will appear.

➤ To retrieve a deleted layer and the objects it contained, choose Edit menu > Undo Deletion (Command-Z/Ctrl-Z) immediately.

Delete Layer or Object

Choosing layer options

To choose more than one option (e.g., color, show/hide, lock, and print) for a layer or an object at the same time, use the Layer Options dialog box, which is discussed on this page and the next page (one-stop shopping). To learn how to choose individual options for a layer or an object (e.g., hide a layer or change its view mode), read through pages 182–184.

If you choose Layer Options for a top-level layer, those options will apply to all the sublayers and objects within that layer. You can also choose options for a sublayer, a group, or even an individual object.

To choose layer or object options:

1. Double-click a layer, sublayer, group, or object on the Layers palette.
   or
   Click a layer, sublayer, group, or object on the Layers palette, then choose Options for "[layer name]" from the palette menu.
   or
   Activate more than one layer, sublayer, group, or object, then choose Options for Selection from the palette menu.

2. For the active layer, sublayer, group, or object, do any of the following **1**–**2**:

   Type a different **Name** for the layer, sublayer, group, or object.

   Check **Show** to display that object or all the objects on the layer or sublayer; uncheck to hide the object or objects. Hidden layers won't print.

   Check **Lock** to prevent that object or all the objects on that layer or sublayer from being edited; uncheck to allow the objects to be edited.

   ➤ You can also lock/unlock a layer or sublayer by clicking in the second column on the Layers palette. It's faster! (See page 182.)

   ➤ You can unlock a whole illustration via an Object menu command, but not individual objects. Using the

Making layers non-printable

There are three ways to make a layer non-printable, and there are significant differences among them:

➤ If you **hide** a layer, the layer won't print, export, or be editable.

➤ If you turn a layer into a **template**, it won't print, export, or be editable, but it will be visible (images on the layer can be dimmed).

➤ If you turn off the **Print** option in the Layer Options dialog box, the layer won't print, but it will export and it will be visible and editable.

1 *The Layer Options dialog box for a layer.*

2 *The Options dialog box for a path.*

Choose Layer/Object Options (side tab)

Layers palette, however, you can unlock one object at a time.

For a layer or sublayer, do any of the following:

Choose a different **Color** for the object's selection border in the illustration and its selection square on the Layers palette. This is handy if the current selection color is very similar to the artwork color, and thus hard to distinguish easily. You can choose a color from the pop-up menu or double-click the color swatch and mix a color yourself using the color picker.

Choose **Template** to convert a layer or sublayer into a tracing layer. It will be uneditable and non-printable. Any images and raster objects on the layer will be dimmed (more about templates on page 185). Template layer names appear in italics.

Check **Preview** to display the layer in Preview view; uncheck to display the layer in Outline view.

➤ To switch views for a layer without opening the Layer Options dialog box, see "To change the view for a top-level layer" on page 184.

Check **Print** to make the layer printable; uncheck to prevent all the objects on that layer from printing. The names of non-printable layers appear in italics.

➤ Another way to make a layer non-printable is to hide it (click the eye icon on the Layers palette).

Check **Dim Images to** to dim any placed images or rasterized objects on that layer and specify a percentage by which you want those images dimmed (use this for tracing); uncheck this option to display placed images normally. Unlike template layers, dimmed images are editable and print normally.

➤ Layer options (e.g., hide/show, preview, print. lock/unlock) that are applied to a sublayer or the top-level layer that contains a group will apply automatically to all the objects in that group.

Choose Layer/Object Options

If you lock an object, it will be unselectable and uneditable. If you lock a whole layer, all the objects on that layer will be uneditable. Locked layers stay locked even if you close and reopen the file.

To lock/unlock a layer or an object:

Click in the edit column for a layer, sublayer, group, or object to make the padlock icon appear **1**. Click the padlock icon to unlock.

or

To lock multiple layers, sublayers, groups, or objects, drag upward or downward in the edit column. Drag back over the padlock icons to unlock 'em.

or

Option-click/Alt-click in the edit column for a top-level layer to lock or unlock all the other top-level layers except the one you click on.

Note: You can't unlock an object individually if the top-level layer in which the object is nested is locked; you have to unlock the top-level layer before you can unlock the object.

➤ To lock a selected object via a command, choose Object menu > Lock (Command-2/ Ctrl-2). There is no Object menu command for unlocking an individual object.

➤ To Unlock All: Command-Option-2/ Ctrl-Alt-2.

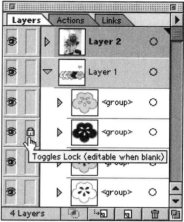

1 *Click in the edit column to **lock a layer**, group, or object (the padlock icon will appear).*

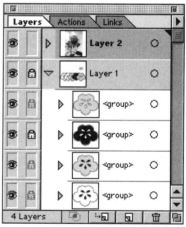

2 *If you lock an entire **layer**, all the objects on that layer will be uneditable.*

Lock Layer or Object

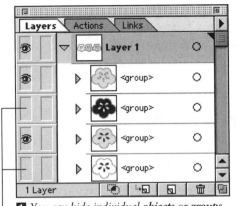

1 *You can hide individual objects or groups...*

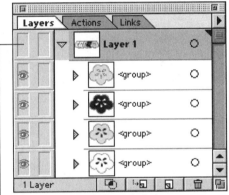

2 *...or you can hide a whole layer.*

What have you got to hide? Well, for one thing, if you've got a lot of stuff happening in an illustration, hiding the parts you're not working on will make your screen redraw faster. For another, it will make it easier to locate and focus on the parts of your illustration that you're working on. You can hide a top-level layer and all its nested layers; hide a group; or hide an individual object. If it's hidden, it won't print.

To hide/show a layer or an object:

Click the eye icon (first column) for a top-level layer, a sublayer, a group, or an object **1**–**2**. If you hide a top-level layer or a sublayer, any objects nested within that layer or sublayer will be hidden, whether or not they are selected. To redisplay what was hidden, click where the eye icon was.

Note: If you want to show an object but its top-level layer is hidden, you must show the top-level layer first.
or
To hide multiple, consecutive top-level layers, sublayers, groups, or objects, drag upward or downward in the eye column.
To redisplay what was hidden, drag again.

➤ To hide a selected object via a command, choose Object menu > Hide Selection (Command-3/Ctrl-3). There is no command for showing an individual object.

➤ To make a visible layer non-printable, uncheck the Print box in the Layer Options dialog box. You can also show or hide an entire layer via that dialog box.

To hide all the top-level layers except one:

Option-click/Alt-click in the eye column to hide/show all the top-level layers except the one you click on.
or
Make sure all the layers are visible (choose Show All Layers from the Layers palette menu), make the top-level layer you want to remain visible active (click its name), then choose Layers palette menu > Hide Others.

Hide Layer or Object

If you change the view for a top-level layer, all of its nested layers and objects will be displayed in that view.

To change the view for a top-level layer:

To display a top-level layer in Outline view, regardless of the current view for the illustration, Command-click/Ctrl-click the eye icon for that layer. The eye will become hollow **1**. To redisplay the layer in Preview view, Command-click/Ctrl-click the eye icon again.
or
Double-click the layer name, then check or uncheck the Preview box.

To display all top-level layers in Outline view except one:

Command-Option-click/Ctrl-Alt-click a top-level layer eye icon to display all layers in Outline view except the one you click on.
or
Click the top-level layer that you want to display in Preview view, then choose Outline Others from the Layers palette menu.

➤ Template layers continue to display in Preview view when View menu > Outline is chosen. To display a template layer in Outline view, Command-click/Ctrl-click its eye column on the Layers palette.

➤ To display all layers in Preview view, choose Preview All Layers from the Layers palette menu.

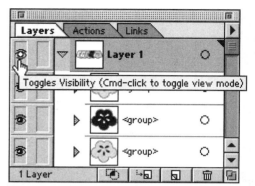

1 *Command/Ctrl click the eye icon to toggle between* **Outline** *and* **Preview** *views for that top-level layer.*

Show or hide 'em

To show/hide all template layers, use this shortcut: Command-Shift-W/Ctrl-Shift-W.

1 *The* **template** *layer icon. The template layer name is in italics.*

Objects on template layers are locked, non-printable, and non-exportable. Any images are dimmed. Use a template layer to trace an object or a placed image using the Auto Trace tool or use a template as a guide to draw new objects. Read about tracing on pages 191–194.

To create a template layer:

Method 1

1. Double-click an existing top-level layer name.

   or

   To create a new top-level layer to become the template layer, Option-click/Alt-click the Create New Layer button at the bottom of the Layers palette.

2. Check the Template box.

3. *Optional:* Choose a "Dim Images to" percentage for any placed images or rasterized objects on the template layer.

4. Click OK (Return/Enter). A template icon will appear in place of the eye icon for the layer and any nested layers or objects in that layer will be locked **1**.

Method 2

1. Click an existing layer name.

2. Choose Template from the Layers palette menu.

Method 3

To create a template layer as you place an image into Illustrator, check the Template box in the File menu > Place dialog box.

Create Template

Layer management

With the abundance of information on the new Layers palette comes one minor drawback: Sometimes it's hard to find things. Luckily, Adobe built in a locator command. Now, how about a locator command for the contents of Elaine's handbag?

To locate an object on the Layers palette:

1. Choose the Selection tool (V).

2. Select the object in the illustration window that you want to locate on the Layers palette. You can select more than one object; they will all be found.

3. Choose Locate Object from the Layers palette menu. The selected object's top-level layer will become expanded, and a selection square will appear for the object.

➤ If "Locate Layer" appears on the palette menu instead of "Locate Object," choose Palette Options from the palette menu and uncheck the Show Layers Only option. The Locate Object command will then become available.

The Collect to New Layer command moves all the currently highlighted top-level layers, sublayers, groups, or objects into a brand new layer.

To move layers, sublayers, groups, or objects to a new layer:

1. Command-click/Ctrl-click the layer, group, or object names you want to gather together ▇. They all have to be at the same indent level (e.g., all objects from the same sublayer or a series of consecutive sublayers). Don't select the layers!

2. Choose Collect in New Layer from the Layers palette menu. Active sublayers, groups, or objects will be nested inside a new sublayer within the same top-level layer ▇. Active top-level layers will be nested as sublayers within a new top-level layer.

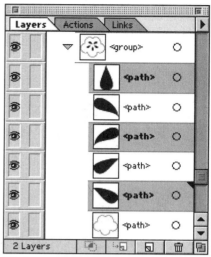

▇ *Three paths are made active.*

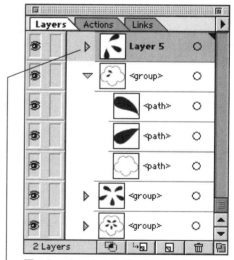

▇ *After choosing* **Collect in New Layer,** *the three active paths are gathered into a new top-level layer (Layer 5, in this case).*

Export to LiveMotion or Flash

If you're planning to export your Illustrator drawing to Adobe LiveMotion or Macromedia Flash to use as the contents of an object or frame animation, first release any groups and expand any appearances or blends, and then release the object sublayers to individual layers nested within a top-level layer via the Release to Layers command. Flash or LiveMotion will then be able to convert the layers from the placed file into separate objects or into a sequence. See pages 409 and 413.

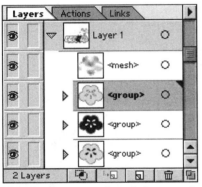

1 *A group is activated on the Layers palette. You could also activate a layer or sublayer.*

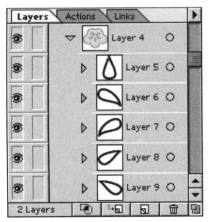

2 *After choosing the Release to Layers command, each object from the group is now on a separate layer.*

The Release to Layers command moves all the objects or groups that are nested within the currently active layer onto separate layers within that active layer.

To move objects to new, separate layers:

1. On the Layers palette, click a top-level layer, sublayer, or group name (not an object) **1**.

2. Choose Release to Layers from the Layers palette menu. Each object in the currently active layer or group will be moved to its own sublayer within that layer **2**. If the original objects were originally in a group, that group name ("<group>") will be removed from the palette.

➤ If you release a layer or a sublayer that contains a clipping mask object, the mask will still clip the objects within the same sublayer.

➤ If you release a layer or group that contains a scatter brush, the brush object will remain as a single <path> layer. If you activate only the brush object layer and release to layers, each object in the scatter brush will be moved to a separate layer. The original scatter brush path will be preserved. If the brush object was originally within a group, its new released layer will no longer be within the group.

Release to Layers

Here's the old-fashioned horse-and-buggy method again. We're probably just holding onto this page for nostalgic reasons. See our new and improved instructions on page 187. You can use this page for doodling.

To move an object to a different layer using the Clipboard:

1. Make sure Paste Remembers Layers is unchecked on the Layers palette menu.

2. Choose the Selection tool (V), then in the illustration window, select the object or objects you want to restack. The objects can be from different layers or sublayers.

3. Choose Edit menu > Cut (Command-X/ Ctrl-X).

4. Click the name of the top-level layer or sublayer on the Layers palette to which you want to move the object, then choose Edit menu > Paste (Command-V/ Ctrl-V). The object will reappear at the top of the stack in the center of the active layer.
    or
    Click the name of an object or group, then choose Edit menu > Paste in Front (Command-F/Ctrl-F) or Edit menu > or Paste in Back (Command-B/Ctrl-B). The Clipboard contents will reappear in front of (or behind) the selected object or group layer. The *x/y* location won't change.
    or
    Choose the Direct-selection tool (A), select an object in a group, then choose Edit menu > Paste in Front or Paste in Back. The pasted object(s) will become part of that group.

Remembering layers

If you want to paste an object to the top of its own layer or sublayer rather than to a different layer, turn on the **Paste Remembers Layers** option via the Layers palette menu. If this option is on and the original layer is deleted after object is copied, but before the Paste command is used, the object(s) will paste onto a brand new layer.

Move Object to Different Layer

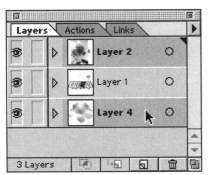

1 *Activate the layers, sublayers, groups, or objects you want to merge, then choose* **Merge Selected** *from the Layers palette menu.*

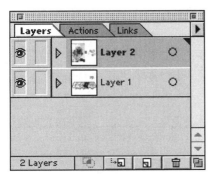

2 *After choosing the* **Merge Selected** *command, the two layers are merged into the topmost of the currently active layers (or groups).*

Merging and flattening

Dire warning! If there's a chance you're going to want to work with the individual layers in your illustration again, save a copy of it using File menu > Save As before you apply the Merge Selected or Flatten Artwork command.

If you have more layers and sublayers on the Layers palette than you can comfortably handle, you can merge some of them together. You can also merge two or more groups, or merge a group with individual non-grouped objects (the objects will become part of the group and will appear at the top or bottom in the group).

Note: A non-grouped object can be merged with a sublayer or a group, but not with another object.

To merge layers, group, or object sublayers:

1. Activate two or more layers, sublayers, or groups. You can merge non-contiguous top-level layers or sublayers (Command-click/Ctrl-click to activate them). Locked and/or hidden layers can be merged.

2. Choose Merge Selected from the Layers palette menu **1**–**2**.

➤ If you merge two groups and one of the groups contains a clipping path, that clipping path may be released, depending on the original stacking order of the groups.

Merge

Warning! The Flatten Artwork command *discards* hidden top-level layers (read that again) and flattens all layers into one top-level layer. Actually, you'll get a warning dialog box which will give you the option to keep the hidden artwork when layers are flattened, but you still need to think ahead. Existing sublayers and groups will be nested within the resulting single top-level layer.

Warning! Flatten Artwork also removes transparency, effects, and paint attributes from top-level layers. Otherwise, the appearance of the artwork in the illustration window won't change. The objects will be fully editable, though they will all be on the same layer.

To flatten artwork:

1. Make sure there are no hidden top-level layers that you want to keep **1**.

2. By default, if no layers are active, the Flatten Artwork command merges all the currently visible layers into the *bottommost* top-level layer. To flatten into a layer of your choice, activate it now.

3. Choose Flatten Artwork from the Layers palette menu. If there are any hidden layers that contain artwork, a warning dialog box will appear **2**–**3**. Click Yes to discard the hidden artwork or click No to preserve the artwork in the flattened document.

   Note: If you try to flatten artwork into a hidden, locked, or template layer, all the layers will be flattened into the next higher top-level layer that isn't hidden, locked, or a template.

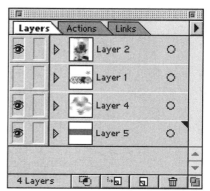

1 *The original four-layer illustration. Since at least one layer is hidden (Layer 1), a warning prompt will appear when the Flatten Artwork command is chosen.*

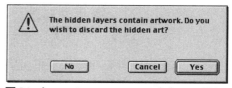

2 *It's always nice to get a second chance. This warning dialog will appear if you choose the* **Flatten Artwork** *command for an illustration that contains artwork on a hidden layer.*

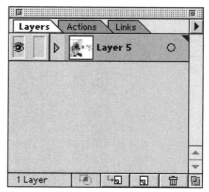

3 *After choosing the* **Flatten Artwork** *command, all the layers are flattened into the bottommost layer (Layer 5, in this case).*

Flatten

1 *The placed artwork in the document window. When placing an EPS for tracing, do not link the file, as this will produce either an inferior screen image or no screen image at all. A template layer isn't required for auto tracing a placed image.*

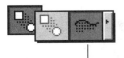

2 *Auto Trace tool.*

Tracing

You can use the **Auto Trace** tool to trace any image that's opened via the File menu > **Place** command (e.g., a scanned photo or drawing). This tool tends to create extraneous anchor points and places points in inappropriate locations, so you'll need to do some cleanup afterwards. If your artwork is simple (high contrast) or if you're deliberately looking for a rough, hand-drawn look, this is the tool to use. You're better off tracing photographs, on the other hand, with the **Pen** or **Pencil** tool (see page 194). P.S. Adobe **Streamline** traces more accurately and offers many more options than Illustrator's Auto Trace tool, and you can also color-adjust your image in Streamline before you trace.

Note: To control the exactness with which the Auto Trace tool traces a path, go to Edit menu > Preferences > Type & Auto Tracing. The higher the **Auto Trace Tolerance** (0–10 pt), the less precisely an object will be traced, and the fewer anchor points will be created. The **Tracing Gap** (0–2 pt) is the minimum width a gap in linework must be in order to be traced. With a high Tracing Gap setting, you'll probably get a lot of extraneous points.

To use the Auto Trace tool:

1. Open a file, then choose File menu > Place.

2. Locate and highlight an EPS, PDF, TIFF, or PSD file, check the Template box (if desired), then click Place **1**. You can also create a template layer later (see page 185).

3. On the Layers palette, create or click on a layer above the template layer.

4. *Optional:* Choose a fill of None and a black stroke.

5. Choose the Auto Trace tool on the Blend tool pop-out menu **2**.

6. Click on areas or edges of the placed image or drag the Auto Trace tool over the area to be traced. The shape will be traced automatically **3**–**4**. Experiment!

7. Fill the traced shapes, as desired **5**. To hide a template layer, click its template icon on the Layers palette 🖺; to hide an image layer, click its eye icon.

3 *After tracing the outer path. Apply a fill of None to prevent the new tracing shapes from blocking out the placed image.*

4 *The outer and inner paths traced.*

5 *The final objects after applying black and white fills.*

To trace letters manually:

The Auto Trace tool traces quickly and is useful if the feel of the relatively coarse rendering it produces is appropriate for your particular project. If you need to create smoother shapes, you can either refine the Auto Trace tool paths or trace the template manually **1**. What follows is a description of how you can use Illustrator to produce your own letterforms using the Pen tool.

1. *Scan the artwork*

To make sure the baseline of your letterwork squares with the horizontal guides in Illustrator, trim the edge of your drawing parallel to the baseline, then slide it against the glass frame of the scanner. Scan your artwork at a resolution between 72 and 150 ppi. Save it as a PICT, TIFF, EPS, or PSD. Even at 300% view, you will see only a minor difference in crispness between a placed 72-ppi PICT and a placed, non-linked, 250-ppi EPS.

2. *Trace manually*

Place an image in an Illustrator file via File menu > Place, the Template box checked **2**.

Use the Pen tool to trace the upright letters. In the illustration at right, anchor points were placed on the topmost, bottommost, leftmost, and rightmost parts of the curve **3**. Most rounded shapes can be created using as few as four anchor points. Hold down Shift to draw out the direction lines horizontally or vertically.

To create the inclined letter shown in **3**, choose the Measure tool, click the base of a letter (e.g., the lowercase "t"), then click the top of the letter. The Info palette will show that angle. Choose Edit menu > Preferences > General, enter that angle in the Constrain Angle field, then click OK. Choose View menu > Show Grid. The grid lines will now follow the slope of the letters. Extend the direction lines of the leftmost and rightmost points of the letter to align with the grid.

Here's an alternate method: Choose File menu > Preferences > Smart Guides, and enter that angle into the first blank field in

Peter Fahrni

1 *A closeup of an Auto Trace of the letters. Note the non-systematic distribution of anchor points and direction lines.*

2 *A closeup of the placed artwork.*

3 *The letters drawn manually (the artwork is hidden). All the direction lines are horizontal or on the same diagonal.*

Manual Tracing

1 *The hand-drawn "B."*

the Angles area. Smart Guides will display on that angle as you drag with the Pen tool.

3. *Fine tune the flow of curves*
Select an anchor point, then move it by pressing the arrow keys. The length and the angle of the direction lines won't change. Select a curve segment, and press the arrow keys to adjust its shape. The length, but not the angle, of the direction lines will change.

The manually traced "B" consisted of two closed, crisscrossing paths **1**. The Unite command was applied to combine the two paths into one **2**.

2 *The final "B" after applying the Unite command.*

A comparison between an Auto Traced character and an Adobe font character

Placed artwork in Illustrator.

The character Auto Traced.

A character in the Goudy 100 Adobe PostScript font, created as type in Illustrator.

Using the Pen or Pencil tool, you can manually trace over any placed image. When you manually trace an image, you can organize and simplify path shapes as well as control their stacking order. If you create separate paths on separate layers, you'll be able to restack and edit them more easily later on.

To manually trace over a placed image:

1. Create or open an Illustrator document, then choose File menu > Place **1**.
2. Locate and highlight the image you want to trace, check the Template box (if desired), then click Place (Return/Enter). The image will appear dimmed on its own uneditable layer. These layer options can be changed at any time.
3. Create a new layer above the template.
4. Choose the Pen (P) or Pencil (N) tool.
5. Trace the placed image **2**. You can periodically hide the image or template to help you see what you're doing (View menu > Hide Template or Command-Shift-W/ Ctrl-Shift-W), then redisplay it to resume tracing.

➤ If you're using the Pencil tool, double-click the tool to change its Tolerances: Smoothness or Fidelity settings.

➤ You can transform a placed image before you trace it.

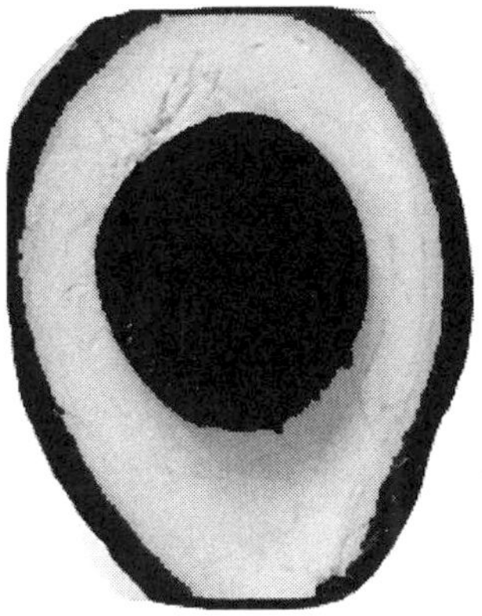

1 *A **placed** image.*

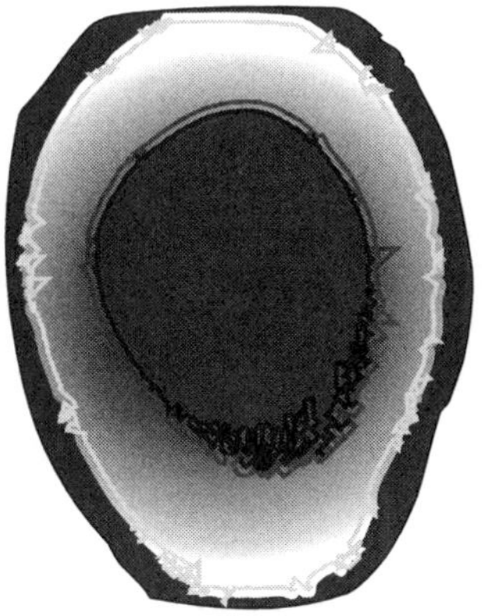

2 *After **tracing** the image using the **Pen** tool, filling and stroking the paths with various shades of black, applying the Roughen effect with low Size and Detail settings to give the path strokes a more handmade appearance, and adding a radial gradient.*

CREATE TYPE 12

This chapter is an introduction to Illustrator's impressive type creation tools. You will learn how to create type that stands by itself and how to enter type inside an object or along a path. You'll also learn how to import type from another application, link type, copy type or a type object, and convert type into graphic outlines. Typographic attributes are modified using the Character, Paragraph, and MM (Multiple Master) Design palettes, which are covered in the next chapter, along with methods for selecting type.

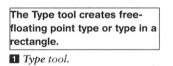

The Type tool creates free-floating point type or type in a rectangle.

1 *Type tool.*

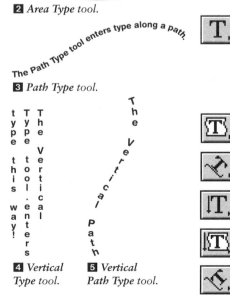

2 *Area Type tool.*

3 *Path Type tool.*

4 *Vertical Type tool.* **5** *Vertical Path Type tool.*

Creating type
The type tools

There are three horizontal type tools: The Type tool, the Area Type tool, and the Path Type tool. Each of these tools has a counterpart for creating vertical type: The Vertical Type tool, the Vertical Area Type tool, and the Vertical Path Type tool. Vertical type reads from right to left, making it useful for typesetting text in languages that read in that direction. Some of these tools' functions overlap, but each of them has unique characteristics for producing a particular kind of type object.

The **Type** tool creates a free-floating block of type, called **point** type, that is not associated with a path **1**. You can also draw a rectangle with it and enter type inside the rectangle; you can use it to enter type along the edge of an open path; or you can use it to enter type inside a closed path. It's the most versatile of the type tools.

The **Area Type** tool creates type *inside* an open or closed path. Lines of type created with the Area Type tool automatically wrap inside the path **2**.

The **Path Type** tool creates a line of type along the outside *edge* of an open or closed path **3**.

The **Vertical Type** tool has the same function as the Type tool, except that it creates vertical type **4**.

The **Vertical Area Type** tool creates vertical type *inside* an open or closed path.

The **Vertical Path Type** tool creates vertical type along the outside *edge* of an open or closed path **5**.

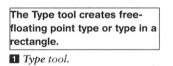

A few things to know about fonts

Some fonts, such as Helvetica, Courier, Arial, and Times, are automatically installed in the System Folder > Application Support > Adobe > Fonts > Reqrd > Base folder (Mac)/ Program Files > Common Files > Adobe > Fonts > Reqrd > Base (Win). Only Adobe products can access and utilize this folder. Type rasterization and font management are performed internally within Illustrator (not by Adobe Type Manager). You must have the printer fonts for a typeface in a location that Illustrator can find in order to print that typeface from Illustrator.

If you open a file that uses a font that is unavailable to the System, an alert message will appear **1**. You can Open the document as is, Cancel, or Obtain Fonts. If the missing font subsequently becomes available to the System, it will reappear on Illustrator's font list and the type should display correctly. Illustrator 9 supports the activation and deactivation of fonts of ATM 4.0 Deluxe (and later).

Point type stands by itself—it's neither inside an object nor along a path. Use this tool to set a type block that doesn't need to be aligned with any neighboring type blocks (e.g., a picture caption or a pull quote).

To create point type:

1. Choose the Type or Vertical Type tool **2**.

2. Click on a blank area of the artboard where you want the type to start (not on an object). A flashing insertion marker will appear.

3. Enter type. Press Return/Enter when you want to start a new line **3**.

4. Choose a selection tool and click away from the type block to deselect it.
   or
   Click the Type tool again to complete the type block and start a new one.

➤ To align separate blocks of point type, use the Align palette (see page 368.)

Choose type attributes first?

If you like to choose character and paragraph attributes before you create type, use the Character and Paragraph palettes. They're discussed in depth in the next chapter.

Recolor after?

When type is entered inside an object or on a path, the object becomes filled and stroked with None. You can then apply fill and/or stroke colors to the type object—just deselect then reselect it with the Direct-selection tool (click on the edge). To recolor the type itself, first select it using a type tool or a selection tool (type selection methods are discussed in the next chapter).

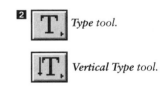

1 *The* **Font Problems** *alert dialog box will appear if you open a file that uses fonts that are unavailable.*

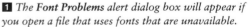

Type tool.

Vertical Type tool.

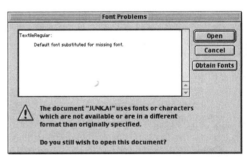

3 **Point** *type created using the* **Type** *tool.*

No going back

Once you place type inside or along a graphic object, it becomes a type object, and it can only be converted back into a graphic object via the Undo command. To preserve the original graphic object, Option-drag/Alt-drag it to copy it, then convert the copy into a type path. You can't enter type into a compound path, a mask object, a gradient mesh object, or a blend, and you can't make a compound path from a type object. If you create type on a brushstroke path, the brushstroke will be removed.

'It spoils people's clothes to squeeze under a gate; the proper way to get in, is to climb down a pear tree.'

1 *Drag with the **Type** tool to create a rectangle, then enter type. To see the edges of the rectangle, go to Outline view or use Smart Guides (Object Highlighting).*

2 *Drag with the **Vertical Type** tool, then enter type. Type flows from top to bottom and from right to left.*

a p e a R   T r e E . . .

C l i m B   d o w N

'It spoils people's clothes to squeeze under a gate; the proper way to get in, is to climb down a pear tree.'

3 *After reshaping the type rectangle using the Direct-selection tool.*

Use this method if you want to define the shape of the type container before creating the type. To enter type in a non-rectangular shape, see page 198.

To create a type rectangle:

1. Choose the Type tool (T) or the Vertical Type tool.

2. Drag to create a rectangle (Shift-drag to create vertical type in a rectangle). When you release the mouse, a flashing insertion marker will appear.

3. Enter type. Press Return/Enter only when you need to create a new paragraph. The type will automatically wrap to fit into the shape of the rectangle **1**–**2**.

4. Choose a selection tool and click away from the type block to deselect it.
   or
   To keep the type tool selected so as to create another, separate type rectangle, press Command/Ctrl (to temporarily access the last-used selection tool) and click away from the type block to deselect it. Release Command/Ctrl, then click again to start the new type block. (You could also click the Type tool again to complete the type object.)

   Note: If the overflow symbol appears (tiny cross in a tiny square) and you want to reveal the hidden type, you can reshape the rectangle using the Direct-selection tool (deselect it first). Use Smart Guides (with Object Highlighting) or choose Outline view to locate the rectangle. The type will reflow to fit the new shape **3**. Another option is to spill the overflow type into another object via linking (see page 201).

➤ To turn a path created with the Rectangle tool into a type rectangle, click on the edge of the path with the horizontal or vertical Type or Area Type tool, then enter type.

➤ **Watch** where your pointer is. If it's in a palette field, you won't be able to edit text in your illustration window.

Type Rectangle

Use the Area Type or Vertical Area Type tool to place type inside a rectangle or an irregular shaped path, or on an open path. The object you use will turn into a type path.

Area Type tool.

Vertical Area Type tool.

To enter type inside an object:

1. Choose the horizontal or vertical Area Type tool **1** if the object is an open or closed path, or choose either Type tool if the object is a closed path.

2. Click precisely on the edge of the path. A flashing insertion marker will appear, and any fill or stroke on the object will be removed. The object's layer will now be listed as <text> (not <path>) on the Layers palette.

3. Enter type on the path, or copy and paste text from a text editing application onto the path. The text will stay inside the object and conform to its shape **2**–**3**. The smaller the type, the more snugly it will fit inside the shape. Justify it to make it hug both sides of the object, and turn on hyphenation. Vertical area type flows from top to bottom and from right to left.

4. Choose a selection tool and click away from the type object to deselect it.
   or
   To keep the type tool selected so as to enter type in another object, press Command/Ctrl to temporarily access the last-used selection tool and click away from the type block to deselect it, then release Command/Ctrl and click on the next type object. You could also click again on the type tool you used to create the type object.

➤ With any type tool selected, you can press Shift to toggle between the vertical or horizontal equivalent of that tool.

To make a horizontal type block vertical, or vice versa:

1. Choose the Selection tool.

2. Click on a type block.

3. Choose Type menu > Type Orientation > Vertical or Horizontal.

This is text in a copy of a light bulb shape. You can use the Area-Type tool to place type into any shape you can create. When fitting type into a round shape, place small words at the top and the bottom. This is text in a copy of a light bulb shape. You can use the Area-Type tool to place type into

2 *Area type.*

The kiss of memory made pictures of love and light against the wall. Here was peace. She pulled in her horizon like a great fish-net. Pulled it from around the waist of the world and draped it over her shoulder. So much of life in its meshes! She called in her soul to come and see.
ZORA NEALE HURSTON

3 *Type in a circle.*

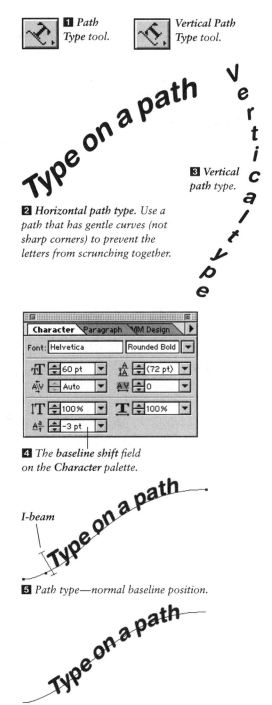

1 *Path Type tool.*

Vertical Path Type tool.

3 *Vertical path type.*

2 *Horizontal path type. Use a path that has gentle curves (not sharp corners) to prevent the letters from scrunching together.*

4 *The baseline shift field on the Character palette.*

I-beam

5 *Path type—normal baseline position.*

6 *Path type—Baseline shifted downward.*

Use the Path Type tool to place type on the inside or outside edge of a path. Type cannot be placed on both sides of the same path, but it can be moved from one side to the other after it's created. Only one line of type can be created per path.

To place type on an object's path:

1. Choose the Type, Path Type, Vertical Type, or Vertical Path Type tool **1**, then click the top or bottom edge of an open or closed path. The path can be selected, but it doesn't have to be.

2. When the flashing insertion marker appears, enter type. Don't press Return/ Enter. The type will appear along the edge of the object, and the object will now have a fill and stroke of None **2**–**3**.

3. Choose a selection tool and click away from the type object to deselect it.
   or
   Click the type tool again if you want to enter type into a new type block.

To adjust the position of type on a path:

1. Choose the Selection tool (V) or Direct-selection tool (A).

2. Click on the type.

3. Drag the I-beam to the left or the right along the edge of the path.
   or
   To flip the type to the other side of the path, move the I-beam inside the path or double-click the I-beam.
   or
   To shift *all* the characters slightly toward or away from the center of the path, but keep their orientation, click or marquee the path with the Selection tool; to shift *some* but not all of the characters, double-click the type with the Selection or Direct-selection tool, and highlight the desired characters. Then change the baseline shift value on the Character palette **4**–**6**.

➤ To convert vertical path type to horizontal, select the characters you want to convert, then choose Direction: Rotate from the Character palette.

Path Type

Importing type

You can import Microsoft Word, WordPad (Win), SimpleText (Mac), or ASCII text. In Illustrator 9.0 or later, the text will appear in a rectangle, which can be reshaped using the Direct-selection tool. To place text into a custom path, Place it, then copy and paste it into or onto the custom path (see "To move type from one object to another" on page 203).

To import type into an object from another application:

1. Choose File menu > Place.

2. Highlight the name of the text file you want to import.

3. Click Place. The text file will appear in a rectangle, with its original font, size, and paragraph breaks, but not necessarily the same line breaks **1**.

➤ Type styling will be lost if you open or place a Text Only format file (as used in SimpleText). Both the Word Document and the Rich Text Format, on the other hand, preserve most type styling.

➤ To export text, see page 224.

➤ To create columns and rows of type, see page 226.

➤ If you create type in a layout program, save the file in EPS format, and then open the EPS file using Illustrator's Open command, you'll be able to manipulate it as you would any type in Illustrator. Beware, though: a new point type block will be created for each word in the imported text, and the blocks will be grouped.

improved

Import Type

Don't space out!

If you press Spacebar to access the Hand tool while a Text tool is chosen, you'll end up adding spaces to your text instead of moving the illustration. Instead, press Command-Spacebar/Ctrl-Spacebar, then quickly release Command/Ctrl, and you'll have your Hand tool.

May the day come (soon perhaps) when I'll flee to the woods on an island in Oceania, there to live on ecstasy, calm, and art. With a new family by my side, far from this European scramble for money. There, in Tahiti, in the silence of the beautiful tropical nights, I will be able to listen to the soft murmuring music of the movements of my heart in amorous harmony with the mysterious beings around me. Free at last, without financial worries and able to love, sing, and die.

Paul Gauguin

1 *Placed type appears in a rectangle.*

Overflow path type

To reveal hidden overflow path type text, you can do one of three things: Make the type smaller (Select All first); make the path longer (to extend a path, see page 109); or delete some words (the old standby!).

1 *Rectangle tool.*

Here was peace. She pulled in her horizon like a great fish-net. Pulled it from around the waist of the world and draped it over

/

The overflow symbol.

2 *Create a new rectangle with the Rectangle tool.*

Here was peace. She pulled in her horizon like a great fish-net. Pulled it from around the waist of the world and draped it over

her shoulder. So much of life in its meshes! She called in her soul to come and see.

Zora Neale Hurston

3 *The objects are linked, and the overflow type spills from the first object into the second object.*

Linking type

If your type overfloweth

If a type rectangle is almost, but not quite, large enough to display all the type inside it, you can enlarge it to reveal the hidden type.

➤ Click on the type block with the **Selection** tool, then drag a **bounding box handle**.

➤ Or select only the rectangle—not the type—with the **Direct-selection** tool (turn on Smart Guides with Object Highlighting or go to Outline view to locate the rectangle), then **Shift-drag** a **segment**.

Another way to deal with overflow type that was created using a horizontal or vertical Type or Area Type tool is to spill it into a rectangular object (instructions on this page) or spill it into a non-rectangular object (instructions on the next page).

To link overflow type to another type object:

1. You can link to an existing type object, even one that contains type, or you can choose the Rectangle tool **1**, then drag diagonally to create a new rectangle **2**.

2. Choose any selection tool.

3. Shift-click or marquee the original type rectangle and the second rectangle.

4. Choose Type menu > Blocks > Link. Overflow type from the first rectangle will flow into the second rectangle **3**.

Linking causes text blocks to be stacked consecutively behind the frontmost text block.

To change the order in which type flows from one object to another:

1. Choose the Direct-selection tool (A), then click on the type object whose stacking order you want to change.

2. Choose Object menu > Arrange > Bring to Front, Send to Back, Bring Forward, or Send Backward.

➤ A series of linked text blocks will occupy the same layer on the Layers palette.

Link Type; Unlink Type; Reflow Type

To link overflow type to a copy of an existing object:

1. Turn on Smart Guides (check the Object Highlighting box in Edit menu > Preferences > Smart Guides) or put your illustration into Outline view.

2. Choose the Direct-selection tool (A) .

3. Click away from the type object to deselect it.

4. Click on the edge of the type object. The type should not be underlined after you click. Don't move the mouse yet!

5. Option-drag/Alt-drag a copy of the type object away from the original object. Option-Shift-drag/Alt-Shift-drag to constrain the movement to a multiple of 45°. Release the mouse, then release Option/Alt (and Shift, if used). The overflow type will appear inside the new object **2**.

6. *Optional:* Choose Object menu > Transform > Transform Again (Command-D/Ctrl-D) to create additional linked copies.

➤ If both the type and the type object are selected when you drag, a copy of the object and type will be created, but the original and copy won't be linked.

To unlink two or more type objects:

1. Choose the Selection tool (V), then click one of the linked type objects (all the linked objects will become selected).

2. Choose Type menu > Blocks > Unlink. All the objects will unlink; the type in each object will be separate and unlinked.

➤ To rejoin the type, cut and paste it back into the original object using a type tool.

To remove one type object from a chain and keep the text stream intact:

1. Choose the Direct-selection tool (A).

2. Click the edge of the type object to be removed.

3. Press Delete/Backspace twice. The type will reflow into the remaining objects.

1 *Direct-selection tool.*

The
kiss of
memory made pic-
tures of love and light
against the wall. Here was peace.

She
pulled in her
horizon like a great
fish-net. Pulled it from
around the waist of the world and

2 *Overflow type from the first object appears in a **linked copy** of that object. (A paragraph indent was applied to the type to move it away from the edge of the objects.)*

Italics into Photoshop

If you copy or drag-and-drop italic type characters from Illustrator into Photoshop, part of the rightmost character in some fonts may be cropped. To prevent this from happening, convert the characters into outlines before copying them.

To test whether an italic character will copy properly, select the character with any Type tool. Any portion of the character that extends beyond the highlight will be cropped.

1 *Point type is **highlighted** and put on the Clipboard via the Cut command.*

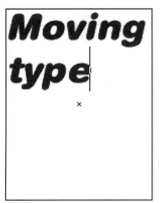

2 *Then it's **pasted** into a rectangle.*

Copying type

To copy or move type with or without its object, use the Clipboard, a temporary storage area in memory. The Clipboard commands are Cut, Copy, and Paste. You could also use the drag-and-drop method to move a type object (see page 247).

To copy type and its object between Illustrator documents or between Illustrator and Photoshop:

1. Choose the Selection tool (V).
2. Click on the edge of the object, on the type, or on the baseline of the type you want to copy.
3. Choose Edit menu > Copy (Command-C/Ctrl-C).
4. Click in another Illustrator document window, then choose Edit menu > Paste (Command-V/Ctrl-V). The type and its object will appear.
   or
   Click in a Photoshop document window, choose Edit menu > Paste, click Paste As Pixels, check the Anti-alias box, then click OK. The type and its object will appear on a new layer.

To move type from one object to another:

1. Choose the Type or Vertical Type tool.
2. Highlight the type (or a portion of the type) you want to move **1**.
3. Choose Edit menu > Cut (Command-X/Ctrl-X). The object you cut the type from will remain a type object.
4. Hold down Command/Ctrl, click another object, then release Command/Ctrl.
5. Click inside or on the edge of the second object. A flashing insertion marker will appear.
   or
   Drag to create a type rectangle.
6. Choose Edit menu > Paste (Command-V/Ctrl-V) **2**.

Creating outlines

The Create Outlines command converts each letter into a separate graphic object. As outlines, the paths can be reshaped, used in a compound or as a mask, or filled with a gradient, or gradient mesh—like any non-type object. Once type is converted into outlines, unless you Undo immediately, you can't change the font or other typographic attributes or convert them back into type.

To create type outlines:

1. Create type using any type tool. *All* the characters in the type object or on the path are going to be converted.

2. Choose the Selection tool (V).

3. If the type isn't already selected, click a character or the baseline.

4. Choose Type menu > Create Outlines (Command-Shift-O/Ctrl-Shift-O) –.
   or
   Control-click/Right-click and choose Create Outlines from the context menu.

   The characters' original fill and stroke attributes will be preserved, but the path object, if any, will be deleted.

➤ To create accurate outlines, the Type 1 font (screen font and printer outlines) or the TrueType font for the typeface you are using must be installed in your system or in the Adobe Font folder (see page 196). Otherwise, Illustrator will use a substitute font to recreate the missing font and font outlines.

➤ Group multiple type outline paths together (Object menu > Group) to make it easier to select and move them.

➤ If the original character had an interior counter—as in an "A" or a "P"—the outside and inside shapes will form a compound path after conversion to outlines. To release the compound into separate objects, choose Object menu > Compound Paths > Release; to reassemble them, select them both, then choose Object menu > Compound Paths > Make.

Converter beware

The Create Outlines command is most suitable for creating logos or other large characters that require reshaping. Printer fonts are not required in order to print type outlines properly from another application. *Note:* Small type (i.e., body type) shouldn't be made into outlines, because the Create Outlines command removes the hinting information that is designed to preserve character shapes during printing. Outline "characters" are also slightly heavier than their pre-outline counterparts, and thus less legible, particularly if a stroke is applied to them. Also, outlines occupy more file storage space.

1 *The original type.*

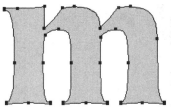

2 *The type converted into **outlines**.*

3 *The outlines reshaped and filled with a gradient.*

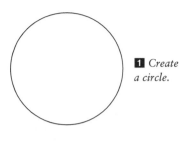

1 *Create a circle.*

— **2** *Path Type tool*

3 *Create path type on the top of the circle. The circle will have a stroke of None. (This is Artwork view.)*

4 *Option-drag/ Alt-drag the type I-beam to the bottom of the circle.*

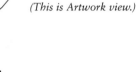

5 *Select the type on the bottom of the circle, and type the words that you want to appear on the bottom.*

Exercise

Putting type on both sides of a circle, and having all of it read vertically, requires creating two circles.

Type on a circle

Type on the top

1. Open the Character and Color palettes.
2. Choose File menu > Preferences > Units & Undo, then choose General: Inches.
3. Choose the Ellipse tool (L), then click on the artboard (don't drag).
4. Enter "3" in the Width field, click the word "Height," then click OK **1**.
5. On the Character palette, enter 24 in the Size field and choose a font.
6. Choose the Path Type tool **2**.
7. Click the top of the circle, then type the text that you want to appear on the top of the circle ("TYPE ON THE TOP," in our example) **3**.
8. Choose the Selection tool, then drag the I–beam to the left to reposition the type.

Type on the bottom

1. Option-drag/Alt-drag the I-beam downward into the circle (the type and its path will be duplicated) **4**. Center the bottom type.
2. Double-click the bottom type with the Selection tool (the Type tool will be chosen automatically), type the words that you want to appear there **5**, then choose the Selection tool.

(Continued on the following page)

Exercise: Type on a Circle

3. On the Character palette, click the down arrow for baseline shift to move the type downward (the appropriate amount will depend on the typeface and type size) **6**. Then deselect the type.

4. Reposition the bottom type as necessary, but don't drag it outside the circle.

5. Marquee both circles.

6. *Optional:* To recolor the type, apply a fill color and a stroke of None to each string of characters. The type will be easier to select if the Type Area Select box is checked in Edit menu > Preferences > Type & Auto Tracing.

7. Choose Object menu > Group (Command-G/Ctrl-G) **7**. To recolor either circle, use the Direct-selection tool.

➤ Set the baseline shift field back to zero (with no type selected) to prevent the negative baseline shift value from being applied to any subsequently created type.

➤ To select either type block separately, click on it with the Direct-selection tool or click the selection area for that type layer on the Layers palette.

➤ If type is part of a group, double-clicking it with the Selection tool will select the group—not the Type tool.

6 *Baseline shift the path type on the bottom of the circle copy downward, and center it on the circle.*

type on the top

7 *The final type. The circles still have a stroke of None.*

STYLE & EDIT TYPE

In this chapter you will learn how to select type and apply character-based typographic attributes using the Character palette (font, size, leading, kerning, tracking, baseline shift, and horizontal and vertical scaling) and apply paragraph-wide attributes using the Paragraph palette (alignment, indentation, inter-paragraph spacing, hanging punctuation, and word and letter spacing).

You'll learn to use Illustrator's word processing features to check spelling, export text, find and replace fonts or text, create text rows and columns, apply professional typesetter's marks, auto hyphenate, and apply tabs. And finally, you'll learn how to sample and apply type attributes using the Eyedropper and Paint Bucket tools, wrap text around an object, create type with a shadow, and create slanted type.

To apply styles or appearances to type, see Chapter 18. To change type opacity, see Chapter 19.

Selecting type

Before you can modify type, you must select it. If you use the **Selection** tool, both the type and its object will be selected **1**. If you use the **Direct-selection** tool, you can select the type object alone or the type object *and* the type **2**. If you use a **type** tool to select type, only the type itself will be selected, not the type object **3**.

> *If we*
> *shadows*
> *have*
> *offended,*
> *Think but*
> *this—*
> *and all is*
> *mended—*

1 *Type and type object selected with the Selection tool.*

> If we
> shadows
> have
> offended,
> Think but
> this—
> and all is
> mended—

2 *Type object selected with the Direct-selection tool.*

> If we
> shadows
> have
> offended,
> Think but
> this—
> and all is
> mended—

William Shakespeare

3 *Type (but not its object) selected with the Type tool.*

Select Type

Note: Use this selection method if you want to move, transform, restyle, or recolor a *whole type block*. To reshape or recolor a type *object*, use the first selection method on the next page. To edit type or to restyle or recolor *part* of a type *block*, use the second selection method on the next page.

To select type and its object:

1. Choose the Selection tool (V) **1**.

2. Turn on Smart Guides (Command-U/ Ctrl-U), with Object Highlighting (Edit menu > Preferences > Smart Guides).

3. With the Type Area Select box checked in Edit menu > Preferences > Type & Auto Tracing, click on the type. Or click inside the type object if the object has a fill **2**.
   or
   In Outline view, click on the edge of the type object. In Preview view, click on the Smart Guide (Object Highlighting).
   or
   Click on the baseline of any character **3**.

   If you select point type (type that's created by clicking, then entering text with the Type or Vertical Type tool), the type will have a solid anchor point before the first character and each line will be underlined. The bounding box will also display, if that option is turned on (View menu).

   If you select a linked type object, all the objects that are linked to it will also become selected.

➤ To modify the paint attributes of type, use the Color palette (see the sidebar on page 131).

➤ To move, scale, rotate, shear, or reflect type, use a command on the Object menu > Transform submenu or use a transform tool.

➤ If type and its object are selected, but you only want the object selected, Shift-click the type with the Direct-selection tool.

Hot tip

Double-click a type character in an existing type object with any selection tool. The type and the Type tool will become selected automatically.

1 *Selection* tool.

ₓ*Think but this—and all is mended—*

2 *To select **point type** in **Outline** view, click on the "**x**." Or click on the type itself if Type Area Select is turned on.*

Baseline —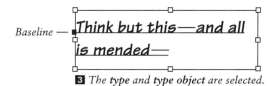

3 *The type and type object are selected.*

Appearances can be deceiving

The relationship between type color and appearances is confusing, to say the least. If you look at the Appearance palette when a type object is selected, the Stroke and Fill will be listed as None, but if you click the "Text" listing on the Appearance palette, the type's default or user-defined color will display on the Color palette. You'll learn about the Appearance palette in Chapter 18. To work specifically with type color and appearances, see page 312 (steps 1–3) in that chapter. *new*

Inserting and deleting

To **add** more type to an existing block, choose a Type tool, click to create an insertion point, then type away.

To **delete** one character at a time, choose a Type tool, click to the right of the character you want to delete, then press Delete/Backspace. To delete a text string, select it with a Type tool, then press Delete/Backspace.

1 *Direct-selection* tool.

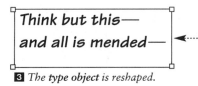

2 *The type object is selected; the type is not.*

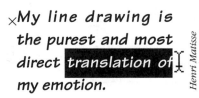

3 *The type object is reshaped.*

×**My line drawing is the purest and most direct translation of my emotion.**

Henri Matisse

4 *Two words are selected.*

Use this selection method if you want to reshape a type object (and thus reflow the type) or recolor a type object.

To select a type object but not the type:

1. Choose the Direct-selection tool (A) **1**.
2. Click on the edge of the type object **2**–**3**. Use Smart Guides (Object Highlighting) to assist you, or go to Outline view. Now, modifications you make will affect only the type object—not the type.

Use this selection method to select only the type—not the object—so you can edit the text or change its character, paragraph, or paint attributes.

To select type but not its object:

1. Choose any type tool.
2. For horizontal type, drag horizontally with the I-beam pointer to select and highlight a word or a line of type **4**. For vertical type, drag vertically.
   or
   For horizontal type, drag vertically to select whole lines of type. For vertical type, drag horizontally to select lines.
   or
   Double-click to select a word.
   or
   Triple-click to select a paragraph.
   or
   Click in the text block, then choose Edit menu > Select All (Command-A/Ctrl-A) to select all the type in the block or on the path, including any type to which it is linked.
   or
   Click to start the selection, then Shift-click where you want the selection to end. (Shift-click again to extend the selection.)
3. After modifying the type, click anywhere on the type block to deselect it and keep the flashing insertion marker in the type block for further editing.
   or
   Choose a selection tool and click away from the type object to deselect it.

Applying type attributes

The type palettes

Press **Tab** to apply a value in a highlighted field on a palette and move to the next field on that palette. Press **Return/Enter** to apply a value and exit the palette. Press **Shift-Return/ Shift-Enter** to apply a value and keep the field highlighted. Shift-Tab to move backward.

Character palette

Use the Character palette (Command-T/ Ctrl-T) to modify font, type size, leading, kerning, and tracking values in one or more highlighted text characters **1**. Choose Show Options from the palette menu to expand the palette for baseline shift, and horizontal and vertical scale adjustments.

Paragraph palette

Use the Paragraph palette (Command-M/ Ctrl-M) to modify paragraph-wide attributes, such as alignment and indentation **2**. Choose Show Options from the palette menu to expand the palette for word spacing, letter spacing, auto hyphenation, hanging punctuation, and East Asian font options.

To change the paragraph attributes of *all* the text in a type object or on a path, select the object or path with the Selection tool. To isolate a paragraph or series of paragraphs, select just those paragraphs with a type tool.

Note: A paragraph is created when the Return/Enter key is pressed within a type block. Choose Type menu > Show Hidden Characters to reveal symbols for line breaks and spaces.

MM Design palette

Use the **Multiple Master** Palette to modify the weight and width of characters in a multiple master (MM) font **3**. Choose Type menu > MM Design when text in a MM font is highlighted. The axes that can be adjusted vary depending on the MM font. Use a Multiple Master font if you require a type style that's slightly slimmer or heavier than an existing style. The palette will combine two existing weights to produce the desired weight.

The Type Palettes

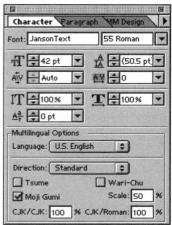

1 *The Character palette.*

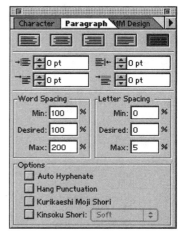

2 *The Paragraph palette.*

3 *The MM Design palette.*

Fast info

The size, font, and tracking info for selected type are listed on the **Info** palette 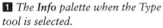.

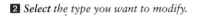

1 *The Info palette when the Type tool is selected.*

2 *Select the type you want to modify.*

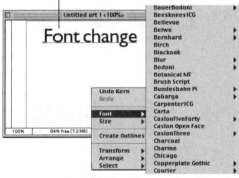

3 *Then choose a font from the context menu.*

4 *The font is changed from Gill Sans Bold to Bodoni Poster.*

Or choose from the Font drop-down menu.

5 *Enter a **font name** and **style**.*

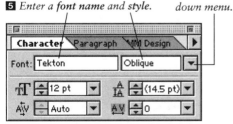

*The **Character** palette on **Mac OS**.*

You can, of course, choose a font before entering your text—just skip the type selection step.

To choose a font:

1. Choose any type tool, then select the type you want to modify **2**.
   or
   Choose the Selection tool, then click on the type object.

2. Control-click/Right-click on the type and choose a font from the Font submenu on the context menu **3**–**4**.
   or
   On the Character palette, *Mac OS:* Choose a font from the Font drop-down menu (and from a submenu if the font name has an arrowhead next to it). *Windows:* Choose from the Font and style drop-down menus.
   or
   Double-click the Font field on the Character palette, then start typing the first few characters of the desired font name. When the name appears, press Tab. For a style other than Roman (or Regular), start typing the style name, then press Return/Enter. You need only enter the first few letters of the font name or style—the name or style with the closest spelling match will appear in the field **5**–**6**.

➤ You can also choose from the Type menu > Font submenu.

➤ Press Command-Option-Shift-M/ Ctrl-Alt-Shift-M to quickly highlight the Font field on the Character palette. The palette will open, if it isn't open already.

6 *Enter or choose a **font**.*   *Enter or choose a **style**.*

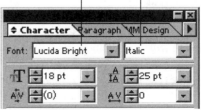

*The **Character** palette in **Windows**.*

To resize type:

1. Choose any type tool, then select the type you want to modify.
or
Choose the Selection tool, then click on the type object.

2. *On the Character palette:*

Enter a point size in the Font Size field (.1–1296), then press Return/Enter to apply and exit the palette or press Tab to apply the value and highlight the next field **1**–**2**. You don't need to reenter the unit of measure.

Note: If the selected type is in more than one point size, the Font Size field will be blank. Entering a size now will change all selected type to the new size.
or
Choose a preset size from the Font Size drop-down menu or click the up or down arrow. Or click in the Font Size field, then press the up or down arrow (keyboard).
or
To resize type via the keyboard, hold down Command-Shift/Ctrl-Shift and press ">" to enlarge or "<" to reduce. The increment the type resizes each time you use this shortcut is specified in the Size/Leading field in Edit menu > Preferences > Type & Auto Tracing. Two points is the default increment. Command-Option-Shift/Ctrl-Alt-Shift increases/decreases the point size by five times the current Size/Leading increment.

To choose a size via the context menu:
Control-click/Right-click on the type and choose a preset size from the context menu. Choosing Other from the context menu highlights the size field on the Character palette.

➤ If you use the Undo command while entering a value on the Character palette, that field will stay highlighted.

➤ You can also choose a preset type size from the Type menu > Size submenu.

Resize by dragging

Select point or path type using the Selection tool, then drag a **bounding box** handle. Or scale type and its object using the **Scale** tool. To scale uniformly using either method, hold down Shift.

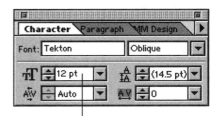

1 *On the Character palette, enter a number in the Font Size field, or click the up or down arrow, or choose a preset size from the drop-down menu.*

2 *Type enlarged.*

Resize Type

1 On the **Character** palette, enter the desired leading in points in the **Leading** field, or choose Auto or a preset leading amount from the drop-down menu.

ACT III

Scene I

The Wood. The QUEEN OF FAIRIES *lying asleep.*

Enter QUINCE, SNUG, BOTTOM, FLUTE, SNOUT, *and* STARVELING.

Bot. Are we all met?

Quin. Pat, pat; and here is a marvel-lous convenient place for our rehearsal. This green plot shall be our stage, this hawthorn brake our tiring-house; and we will do it in action, as we will do it before the duke.

2

Loose leading (8-point type; 12 point leading)

ACT III

Scene I

The Wood. The QUEEN OF FAIRIES *lying asleep.*

Enter QUINCE, SNUG, BOTTOM, FLUTE, SNOUT, *and* STARVELING.

Bot. Are we all met?

Quin. Pat, pat; and here is a marvel-lous convenient place for our rehearsal. This green plot shall be our stage, this hawthorn brake our tiring-house; and we will do it in action, as we will do it before the duke.

3

Tight leading (8-point type; 8.75 point leading)

Leading is the distance from baseline to baseline between lines of type, and it is tradi-tionally measured in points. Each line of type in a block can have a different leading amount. (To add space between whole para-graphs, follow the instructions on page 220.)

Note: To change the vertical spacing in verti-cal type, change the horizontal tracking (see the next page). Changing the leading for vertical type changes the horizontal spacing between vertical columns.

To change leading via the Character palette:

1. *Select the type you want to modify:*

   Click anywhere in a type block with the Selection tool to change the leading of the entire block.
   or
   Highlight an entire paragraph with a type tool (triple-click anywhere in the para-graph) to change the leading of all the lines in that paragraph.
   or
   Highlight an entire line with a type tool (including any space at the end) to change the leading of only that line.

2. *On the Character palette:*

   Enter a number in the Leading field, then press Return/Enter or Tab to apply **1**–**3**.
   or
   Choose a preset leading amount from the Leading drop-down menu or click the up or down arrow.
   or
   Choose Auto from the drop-down menu to set the leading to 120% of the largest type size on each line.
   or
   To make the leading value match the point size of the type, make sure all the type in the block is the same point size, then double-click the leading button . This is called "solid" leading.

Leading

To change leading via the keyboard:

1. Select the type you want to modify (see step 1 on the previous page).

2. Option-press/Alt-press the up arrow on the keyboard to decrease the leading or the down arrow to increase the leading. The increment leading changes each time you use this shortcut is specified in the Size/Leading field in Edit menu > Preferences > Type & Auto Tracing.

   Hold down Command-Option/Ctrl-Alt as you press an arrow to change leading in five times the Size/Leading increment.

Kerning is the addition or removal of space between a *pair* of adjacent characters. Kerning values for specific character pairs (e.g., the uppercase "T" and the lowercase "a") are built into all fonts. The built-in kerning values are adequate for small text (e.g., body type), but not for large type (e.g., headlines and logos). This awkward spacing can be remedied by careful manual kerning. To kern a pair of characters, the cursor must be inserted between them.

Note: Built-in kerning can be turned on or off for individual groups of characters, and this should be done before the text is kerned manually. Select the text, then choose Auto from the Kerning drop-down menu on the Character palette (**1**, next page). Choose or enter 0 to turn this feature off.

Tracking is the simultaneous adjustment of the space between each of *three or more* characters. It's normally applied to a range of type—a paragraph or a line. To track type, first highlight the range of type you want to track using a type tool or select an entire type block with a selection tool.

To kern or track type:

1. Choose a type tool, then click to create an insertion point between the two characters you want to kern or highlight the range of text you want to track. Zoom in.
   or
   To track all the type in an object, choose the Selection tool, then click on the object.

spacing out

➤ To adjust the **overall** word or letter spacing in a text block, use the Word Spacing and Letter Spacing fields on the Paragraph palette (see page 220).

➤ Tracking/kerning changes the vertical spacing of characters in **vertical** type.

Quick un-kern/un-track

To restore 0 kerning to a selected pair of characters or 0 tracking to a selected text string, use this shortcut: **Command-Shift-Q/Ctrl-Shift-Q.**

1 *Kerning field and drop-down menu.* *Tracking field and drop-down menu.*

Simona

2 *Normal type.*

Simona

3 *Space added between the first two characters (kerning).*

Simona

4 *Space removed between the last five characters (kerning or tracking).*

5 *Click an option in the* **Change Case** *dialog box.*

2. In the Kerning or Tracking field on the Character palette, enter a positive number to add space between characters or a negative number to remove space, then press Return/Enter or Tab to apply **1**–**4**.
or
Choose a preset kerning or tracking amount from the drop-down menu or click the up or down arrow.
or
Hold down Option/Alt and press the right arrow on the keyboard to add space between letters or the left arrow to remove space between letters. The amount of space that is added or removed each time you press an arrow is specified in the Tracking field in Edit menu > Preferences > Type & Auto Tracing. Hold down Command-Option/Ctrl-Alt to track in larger increments.
or
Use this shortcut: Command-Shift-[or]/ Ctrl-Shift-[or].

The Change Case command changes selected text to all UPPER CASE, all lower case, or Mixed Case (initial capitals).

To change case:
1. Highlight the text you want to modify with a type tool.

2. Choose Type menu > Change Case.

3. Click Upper Case (ABC); Lower Case (abc); or Mixed Case (Abc; the first character in each word is uppercase) **5**.

4. Click OK (Return/Enter).

Change Case

Change Selection To:
- ● Upper Case (ABC)
- ○ Lower Case (abc)
- ○ Mixed Case (Abc)

OK
Cancel

Change Case

The Fit Headline command is used to track a one-line paragraph of horizontal or vertical type outward to the edges of its container.

To fit type to its container:

1. Choose any type tool.

2. Highlight a one-line paragraph (not a line in a larger paragraph; we're talking about a standalone line).

3. Choose Type menu > Fit Headline – When applied to a Multiple Master font, Fit Headline adjusts both the weight and the tracking.

The Horizontal Scale feature extends (widens) or condenses (narrows) type. The Vertical Scale feature makes type taller or shorter. The default scale is 100%.

Note: In the Multiple Master typefaces and the typefaces that are narrow or wide by design (e.g., Univers Extended or Helvetica Narrow), the weight, proportions, and counters (interior spaces) are adjusted along with the width. For this reason, they look better than Regular characters that are extended or narrowed via Illustrator's Horizontal or Vertical Scale command. That being said…

To scale type horizontally and/or vertically:

Select the type you want to modify, enter a higher or lower percentage in the Horizontal or Vertical Scale field on the Character palette, then press Return/Enter or Tab to apply **5** and **6**. Or choose a preset amount from the drop-down menu or click the up or down arrow.
or
To scale point or path type manually, select it using the Selection tool, then drag a side handle of the bounding box.
or
To scale a selected type block, double-click the Scale tool and change the Non-Uniform: Horizontal or Vertical value.

To restore normal scaling:

Select the type, then choose 100% from both Scale fields on the Character palette.

1 *The original, selected characters.*

2 *The **Fit Headline** command adds **space** between characters in non-Multiple Master type.*

3 *The original, selected Multiple Master characters.*

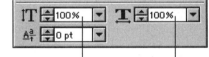

4 *The **Fit Headline** command adds **space** between, and changes the **weight** of, Multiple Master characters.*

Vertical Scale field.   **5** *Horizontal Scale field.*

6 DANIELLE
Normal type (no scaling).

DANIELLE
75% horizontal scale.

DANIELLE
125% horizontal scale.

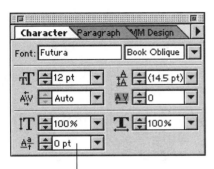

1 *Baseline Shift field.*

2 *Characters on a path, baseline shifted downward.*

*A*licia

3 *The "A" is baseline shifted 9 points downward.*

Hanging
punctuation

'Lo! all these trophies of affections hot,
Of pensiv'd and subdued desires the tender,
Nature hath charg'd me that I hoard them not,
But yield them up where I myself must render,
That is, to you, my origin and ender:
For these, of force, must your oblations be,
Since I their altar, you enpatron me.

William Shakespeare

4 *Let it hang out.*

The Baseline Shift command repositions characters above or below the baseline. You can use this command to offset curved path type from its path or to create superscript or subscript characters (there is no superscript or subscript type style in Illustrator).

To baseline shift type:

1. Highlight the type you want to modify.

2. In the Baseline Shift field on the Character palette (choose Show Options from the palette menu if the field isn't visible), enter a positive number to baseline shift characters upward or a negative number to baseline shift characters downward, then press Return/Enter to apply **1**–**3**. Or choose a preset amount from the drop-down menu or click the up or down arrow.
   or
   Option-Shift-press/Alt-Shift-press the up arrow to shift highlighted characters upward or the down arrow to shift characters downward. The amount type shifts each time you press an arrow is specified in the Baseline Shift field in Edit menu > Preferences > Type & Auto Tracing. (Command-Option-Shift-press/Ctrl-Alt-Shift-press to shift in larger increments.)

Use hanging punctuation to make the edges of your paragraphs look more uniform. This option works only with area type. The period, comma, quotation mark, apostrophe, hyphen, dash, colon, and semicolon are affected.

To hang punctuation:

1. Select a paragraph with a type tool.
   or
   Select a type object with a selection tool.

2. Check the Hang Punctuation box in the Options area at the bottom of the Paragraph palette **4**. If this option isn't visible, choose Show Options from the palette menu.

Alignment and indent values affect whole paragraphs.

➤ To create a new paragraph (hard return) in a text block, press **Return/Enter**. Type preceding a return is part of one paragraph; type following a return is part of the next paragraph. Type that wraps automatically is part of the same paragraph.

➤ To create a line break (soft return) within a paragraph in non-tabular text, press **Shift-Return** or press **Enter** (on the keypad).

To change paragraph alignment:

1. Choose a type tool, then click in a paragraph or drag through a series of paragraphs.
or
Choose a selection tool and select a type object.

2. At the top of the Paragraph palette, click the Align Left, Align Center, Align Right, Justify Full Lines, or Justify All Lines alignment button ▉–▇.
or
Use one of the keyboard shortcuts listed in the sidebar on this page.

➤ Don't apply Justify Full Lines or Justify All Lines alignment to path type or to point type (type that's not in an object or in a block). Those type objects don't have edges, thus nothing to justify the type to.

Paragraph Alignment (side tab)

Paragraph alignment shortcuts

Left	Command-Shift-L/Ctrl-Shift-L
Center	Command-Shift-C/Ctrl-Shift-C
Right Justify	Command-Shift-R/Ctrl-Shift-R
Justify Full Lines	Command-Shift-J/Ctrl-Shift-J
Justify All Lines	Command-Shift-F/Ctrl-Shift-F

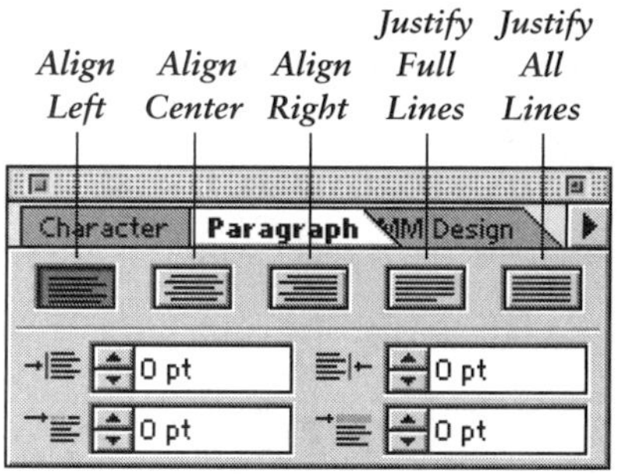

Align Left   Align Center   Align Right   Justify Full Lines   Justify All Lines

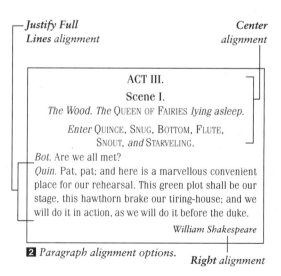

▉ *The five **Alignment** buttons on the Paragraph palette.*

Justify Full Lines alignment   *Center alignment*

ACT III.

Scene I.

The Wood. The QUEEN OF FAIRIES *lying asleep.*

Enter QUINCE, SNUG, BOTTOM, FLUTE, SNOUT, *and* STARVELING.

Bot. Are we all met?

Quin. Pat, pat; and here is a marvellous convenient place for our rehearsal. This green plot shall be our stage, this hawthorn brake our tiring-house; and we will do it in action, as we will do it before the duke.

William Shakespeare

▇ *Paragraph alignment options.*   *Right alignment*

Selecting paragraphs for modification

If you want to change paragraph attributes for *all* the text in a type object or on a path, select the object or path with the Selection tool. To isolate a paragraph or series of paragraphs, select just those paragraphs with a type tool.

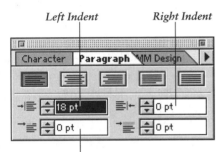

Left Indent   Right Indent

First Line Left Indent

1 *The* **Indent** *fields on the* **Paragraph** *palette. If you forget which one is which, rest the mouse over an icon—the tool tip will remind you.*

Left and Right Indent values affect area type; only a Left Indent value will affect point type.

To change paragraph indentation:

1. Choose a type tool, then select the paragraph(s) you want to modify or click to create an insertion point in a single paragraph.
or
Choose a selection tool, then select a type object.

2. *On the Paragraph palette:*
Enter a new number in the Left or Right Indent field, then press Return/Enter or Tab to apply **1**–**2**.
or
Click the up or down arrow.
or
To indent only the first line of each paragraph, enter a number in the First Line Left Indent field.

➤ You can enter a negative value in the Left Indent, First Line Left Indent, or Right Indent field to expand the measure of each line. The type will be pushed outside its object, but it will still display and print **3**.

ACT II.

Scene I.

A Wood near Athens.

Enter a Fairy *at one door, and* Puck *at another.*
Puck. How now, spirit! whither wander you?
Fai.   Over hill, over dale,
     Thorough bush, thorough brier,
     Over park, over pale,
     Thorough flood, thorough fire,
     I do wander everywhere,
     Swifter than the moon's sphere;

2 *Left Indentation.*

ACT III.

Scene I.

The Wood. *The* Queen of Fairies *lying asleep.*

Enter Quince, Snug, Bottom, Flute, Snout, *and* Starveling.

Bot.   Are we all met?
Quin. Pat, pat; and here is a marvellous convenient place for our rehearsal. This green plot shall be our stage, this hawthorn brake our tiring-house; and we will do it in action, as we will do it before the duke.

William Shakespeare

3 *To create a* **hanging indent,** *as in the last paragraph in this illustration, enter a number in the* **Left Indent** *field and the same number with a minus sign in front of it in the* **First Line Left Indent** *field.*

Paragraph Indents

Use the Space Before Paragraph field on the Paragraph palette to add or subtract space *between* paragraphs in area type. Point type isn't modified by this feature. (To adjust the spacing between lines of type *within* a paragraph (leading), see pages 213–214.)

To adjust inter-paragraph spacing:

1. Select the type you want to modify. To modify the space before only one paragraph in a type block, select the paragraph with a type tool. To change all the type in an object, select the object with the Selection tool.

2. In the Space Before Paragraph field on the Paragraph palette **1**, enter a positive value to move paragraphs apart or a negative value to move them closer together, then press Return/Enter or Tab to apply **2**.
   or
   Click the up or down arrow.

➤ To create a new paragraph (hard return), press Return/Enter. To create a line break within a paragraph (soft return), press Shift-Return/Shift-Enter.

1 *The Space Before Paragraph field on the Paragraph palette.*

ACT III.

Scene I.

The Wood. The Queen of Fairies *lying asleep.*

Enter QUINCE, SNUG, BOTTOM, FLUTE, SNOUT, *and* STARVELING.

Bot. Are we all met?

Quin. Pat, pat; and here is a marvellous convenient place for our rehearsal. This green plot shall be our stage, this hawthorn brake our tiring-house; and we will do it in action, as we will do it before the duke.

William Shakespeare

2 *Higher Space Before Paragraph values were applied to these paragraphs to widen the space above them.*

Word and letter spacing

To change the horizontal word or letter spacing for justified paragraphs, change the percentage in the Minimum, Desired, or Maximum Word Spacing or Letter Spacing fields on the Paragraph palette **3**–**5** (choose Show Options from the Paragraph palette menu if these options aren't visible). Non-justified type is only affected by the Desired value. Headlines are usually improved by reduced word spacing.

Ocean
Body more immaculate than a wave,
salt washing away its own line,
and the brilliant bird
flying without ground roots.

Pablo Neruda

3 *Normal word and letter spacing.*

Ocean
Body more immaculate than a wave,
salt washing away its own line,
and the brilliant bird
flying without ground roots.

4 *Loose letter spacing.*

Ocean
Body more immaculate than a wave,
salt washing away its own line,
and the brilliant bird
flying without ground roots.

5 *Tight word spacing.*

220

Word processing

Use the Find/Change command to search for and replace characters.

To find and replace text:

1. *Optional:* Click with a type tool to create an insertion point from which to start the search. If you don't do this, the search will begin from the most recently created object.

2. Choose Type menu > Find/Change.

3. Enter a word or phrase to search for in the "Find what" field ▮.

4. Enter a replacement word or phrase in the "Change to" field ▮. Leave the "Change to" field blank to delete instances of the "Find what" text altogether.

5. *Do any of these optional steps:*

   Check the Whole Word box to find the "Find what" letters only if they appear as a complete word—not as part of a larger word (e.g., "go" but not "going").

   Check the Case Sensitive box to find only those instances that match the exact uppercase/lowercase configuration of the "Find what" text.

   Check the Wrap Around box to search the whole file from the current cursor position to the end of the text object or string of linked objects and then continue the search from the most recently created object. With Wrap Around unchecked, the search will proceed only from the current cursor position forward to the end of that text object; you'll have to click Find Next to resume the search.

   Check the Search Backward box to search backward from the current cursor position.

6. Click **Find Next** to search for the first instance of the "Find what" word or phrase or to skip over a word ▮.

7. Click **Change** to replace only the currently found instance of the "Find what" text.
   or
   Click **Change All** to replace all the instances at once ▮.
   or
   Click **Change/Find** to replace the current instance and search for the next instance.

8. Click Done (Return/Enter or Esc).

   Beware: The corrected word will take on the styling of the text preceding it and lose its original styling.

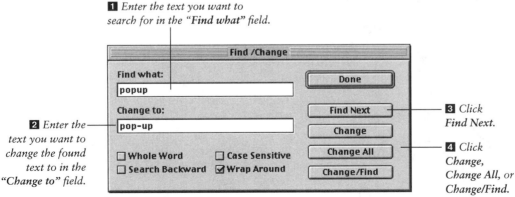

▮ *Enter the text you want to search for in the "**Find what**" field.*

▮ *Enter the text you want to change the found text to in the "Change to" field.*

▮ *Click Find Next.*

▮ *Click Change, Change All, or Change/Find.*

The **Find/Change** dialog box.

The Check Spelling command checks spelling in an entire document using a built-in dictionary. You can also create and edit your own word list.

To check spelling:

1. Choose Type menu > Check Spelling. Any words not found in the application or user dictionary will appear on the Misspelled Words list **1**.

2. Leave the currently highlighted Misspelled Word selected or click a different word on the list. The selected misspelled word will be highlighted in your illustration.

3. *Optional:* Check the Case Sensitive box to display the Misspelled Word both ways if it appears in both upper and lower case (such as *Spelle* and *spelle*).

4. If the correctly spelled word appears on the **Suggested Corrections** list, double-click it **2**. Or to change all instances of the misspelled word instead, click the correctly spelled word, then click **Change All**. The next misspelled word will now become highlighted.
   or
   If the correct word doesn't appear on the list, or no words appear at all (because there are no similar words in the Illustrator dictionary), type the correctly spelled word in the entry field at the bottom of the dialog box. Then click **Change** to change only the first instance of the highlighted Misspelled Word to the currently highlighted Suggested Correction, or click **Change All** to change all instances of the Misspelled Word.

   For any word, you can click **Skip** to leave the current instance of the Misspelled Word as is or click **Skip All** to leave all instances of the Misspelled Word as is.

5. *Optional:* Click Add to List to add the currently highlighted Misspelled Word or Words to the Learned Words list (which is in Plug-ins > Text Filters > AI User Dictionary). To add more than one word at a time, Command-click/Ctrl-click them first.

Check spelling in Dutch?

Click Language in the Check Spelling dialog box, locate and highlight the dictionary you want to use in Adobe Illustrator 9 folder > Plug-ins > Text Filters, then click Open.

Note: The Check Spelling command can only be used with Roman fonts—not with Chinese, Japanese, or Korean fonts.

1 *Misspelled words.*

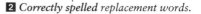

2 *Correctly spelled replacement words.*

Check Spelling

Click Done when you're finished.

Click a Misspelled Word.

Click Change or Change All.

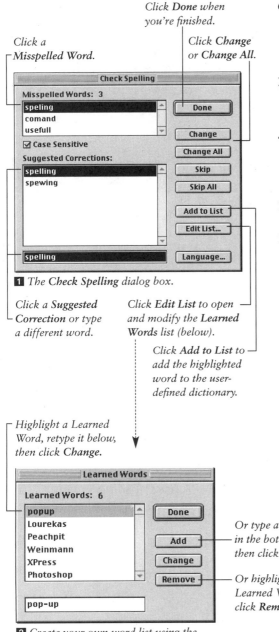

1 *The Check Spelling dialog box.*

Click a Suggested Correction or type a different word.

Click Edit List to open and modify the Learned Words list (below).

Click Add to List to add the highlighted word to the user-defined dictionary.

Highlight a Learned Word, retype it below, then click Change.

Or type a new word in the bottom field, then click Add.

Or highlight a Learned Word, then click Remove.

2 *Create your own word list using the Learned Words dialog box.*

6. If you spell-check all the Misspelled Words, a prompt will appear. Click OK, then click Done (Return/Enter or Esc). You can also click Done at any time to stop spell-checking.

➤ Beware: The corrected word will take on the styling of the text preceding it and lose its original styling.

To edit the user-defined dictionary:

1. If the Check Spelling dialog box isn't open, choose Type menu > Check Spelling **1**.

2. Click Edit List to open the Learned Words list dialog box **2**.

3. Click on a word in the list, correct it in the field at the bottom of the dialog box, then click **Change**.
 or
 Click on a word, then click **Remove**.
 or
 Type a completely new word in the field at the bottom of the dialog box, then click **Add**. Hyphenated words—like "pop-up"—are permitted.

➤ *Mac OS:* The built-in dictionary is saved as USEnglish 9.0 in Adobe Illustrator 9.0 > Plug-Ins folder > Text Filters. The user-defined dictionary is saved as AI User Dictionary.

 Windows: The dictionary is saved as USEnglish.dct in Plug-ins > Text Filters. The user-defined dictionary is saved as AIUser.dct.

Check Spelling: Edit Dictionary

223

Use the Export command to prepare Illustrator text so it can be imported into, and used as text in, another application. Path information isn't included.

To export text:

1. Select the text you want to export with a type tool or a selection tool.

2. Choose File menu > Export.

3. Choose a location in which to save the text file **1**.

4. Enter a Name for the new file.

5. Choose Text Format (TXT) from the Format pop-up menu (Mac OS)/Save as Type drop-down menu (Windows). Text Format is a text only format.

6. Click Export.

1 *Choose **Text Format** (TXT) for your selected text from the **Format** pop-up menu.*

The Find Font command can be used to generate a list of the fonts currently being used in an illustration. Or it can be used to actually replace fonts; the type color, kerning/tracking, and other attributes are retained.

To find and replace a font:

1. Choose Type menu > Find Font.

2. In the Include in List area at the bottom of the dialog box, check the Type 1, Standard, Roman, TrueType, CID, Multiple Master, or OTF box to selectively display only fonts of those types on the scroll lists. For Multiple Master fonts, you must also check the Type 1 box.

3. To have the replacement font list display only fonts of the types checked in step 2 that are currently being used in your document, leave the Replace Font From menu option on Document.

or

Choose System from the Replace Font From pop-up menu to display on the replacement font list all the fonts currently available in your system.

Export Text; Find and Replace Fonts

4. Click a font to search for on the Fonts in Document scroll list 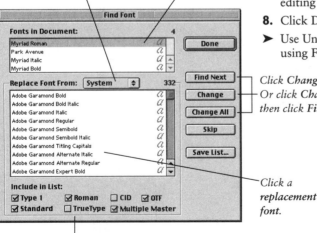. The first instance of that font will be highlighted in your document.

5. Click a replacement font on the replacement font list.

6. Click **Change** to change only the current instance of the currently highlighted font.
or
Click **Change All** to change all instances of the currently highlighted font. Once all the instances of a font are replaced, that font will be removed from the Fonts in Document list.
or
Click **Find Next** to search for the next instance of the currently highlighted font or click the font name on the Fonts in Document list again.
or
Click **Skip** to leave the current instance of the font unchanged and proceed to the next instance of the font.

7. *Optional:* To save a list of the fonts currently being used in the illustration as a text document, click Save List, enter a name, choose a location in which to save the file, then click Save. The text document can later be opened directly from the Desktop or it can be imported into a text editing or layout application.

8. Click Done (Return/Enter).

➤ Use Undo to undo font changes made using Find Font.

*Choose **System** from the **Replace Font From** pop-up menu to display on the replacement font list all available fonts in the System of the types checked, or choose **Document** to list only the fonts currently being used in your illustration.*

1 *Click a font to search for on the Fonts in Document scroll list.*

Click Change All. Or click Change, then click Find Next.

Click a replacement font.

Uncheck any font types to narrow the selection of replacement fonts.

To arrange text in linked rows and columns:

1. Select one text object or a series of linked text objects with the Selection tool. No point type!

2. Choose Type menu > Rows & Columns.

3. Check the Preview box to apply changes immediately **1**. Uncheck Preview if the redraw is tediously slow.

4. Click the up or down arrow or enter values in the fields to choose:

   The total Number of Rows and Columns to be produced.
   and
   The Height of each Row and the Width of each Column.
   and
   The Gutter (space) between each Row and each Column.
   and
   The Total width and Total height of the entire block of Rows and Columns. If you change the Total values, the height or width of the boxes will change, but the gutter values will remain constant.

5. Click a different Text Flow button to control the direction of the text flow.

6. *Optional:* Check the Add Guides box to make guides appear around the text blocks. Make sure the ruler origin is in the correct location.

7. Click OK (Return/Enter) **2**–**3**.

➤ If you select the entire block of rows and columns with the Selection tool and then reopen the Rows & Columns dialog box, the current settings for that block will be displayed.

1 *The Rows & Columns dialog box.*

Hey! diddle, diddle,
The cat and the Fiddle,
The cow jumped over the moon;
The little dog laugh'd
To see such sport,
And the dish ran away with the spoon.

2 *One text object...*

Hey! diddle, diddle,   The cow jumped
The cat and the   over the moon;
Fiddle,   The little dog

laugh'd   away with the
To see such sport,   spoon.
And the dish ran

3 *...is converted into two rows and two columns.*

Dialog box option	Keyboard	Smart punctuation
ff, fi, ffi Ligatures	ff, fi, ffi	ff, fi, ffi
ff, fl, ffl Ligatures	ff, fi, ffl	ff, fi, ffl
Smart Quotes	' "	' " " '
Smart Spaces (one space after a period)	. T	. T
En [dashes]	--	–
Em Dashes	---	—
Ellipses	...	...
Expert Fractions	1/2	½

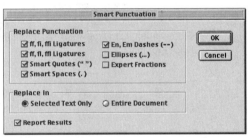

1 Check **Replace Punctuation** options in the **Smart Punctuation** dialog box.

The Smart Punctuation command converts keyboard punctuation into professional typesetter's marks.

Note: With the exception of the "fi" ligature, which is available in most serif fonts on Mac OS, to apply Ligatures and Expert Fractions, the Adobe Expert font set for the font you are using must be available in your system. The Expert set is required for all ligatures in Windows.

To create smart punctuation:

1. *Optional:* Select text with the Type tool to smart-punctuate that text only. Otherwise, the command will affect the entire document.

2. Choose Type menu > Smart Punctuation.

3. Check any of the Replace Punctuation boxes **1** (and see the sidebar).

4. Click Replace In: Selected Text Only if you selected text for step 1, otherwise click Entire Document.

5. *Optional:* Check Report Results to display a list of your changes.

6. Click OK (Return/Enter) **2**–**3**.

➤ Windows users, press Num Lock and one of these keystrokes to produce a fraction: ¼ = Alt-0188; ½ = Alt-0189; ¾ = Alt-0190.

Smart Punctuation

He supposed Miss Petiigrew might have leaned over the sugar bowl and said, "Mayor," which Daddy said was all she ever called him anymore, "I'd be pleased to have a chimpanzee." And Daddy supposed the mayor frumped himself up a little and muddied his expression and said, "Sister darling, your chimpanzee is just around the corner."

"Louis!" Momma said. Daddy was hardly ever a very big hit with Momma.

2 Dumb punctuation: Straight quotes and two spaces after each period.

He supposed Miss Petiigrew might have leaned over the sugar bowl and said, "Mayor," which Daddy said was all she ever called him anymore, "I'd be pleased to have a chimpanzee." And Daddy supposed the mayor frumped himself up a little and muddied his expression and said, "Sister darling, your chimpanzee is just around the corner."

"Louis!" Momma said. Daddy was hardly ever a very big hit with Momma.

T.R. Pearson

3 Smart punctuation: Curly quotes and one space after each period.

To turn on auto hyphenation:

1. Auto hyphenation affects only currently selected or subsequently created text. If you want to hyphenate existing text, select it with a type tool now.

2. On the Paragraph palette, check the Options: Auto Hyphenate box **1**. (If this option isn't visible, choose Show Options from the palette menu.)

3. To choose hyphenation options, choose Hyphenation from the Paragraph palette menu.

4. In the "Hyphenate [ ] letters from beginning" field, enter the minimum number of characters to precede any hyphen **2**. Fewer than three letters before or after a hyphen can impair readability.

5. In the "Hyphenate [ ] letters from end" field, enter the minimum number of characters to carry over onto the next line following a hyphen **3**.

6. In the "Limit consecutive hyphens to" field, enter the maximum allowable number of hyphens in a row **4**. More than two hyphens in a row impairs readability and looks unsightly.

7. Click OK (Return/Enter). Look over the newly hyphenated text, and correct any undesirable breaks.

➤ To hyphenate using rules of a different language for selected text in the current document only, choose Show Multilingual from the Character palette menu, then choose from the Language pop-up menu. You can change the default hyphenation language for the application in Edit menu > Preferences > Hyphenation. You can also enter hyphenation exceptions or specify how particular words are to be hyphenated in that dialog box. Turn Auto Hyphenate off and then on again to apply Preferences changes. See page 388.

➤ To hyphenate a word manually: Command-Shift--(hyphen)/Ctrl-Shift--.

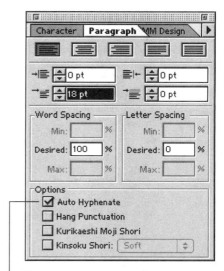

1 *Check the **Auto Hyphenate** box on the* ***Paragraph** palette.*

AN
OVER-
ABUN-
DANCE
OF HY-
PHENS
MAKES
FOR
TIR-
ING
READ-
ING.

2 *Minimum number of characters preceding a hyphen.*

3 *Minimum number of characters after a hyphen.*

4 *Maximum number of hyphens **in a row**.*

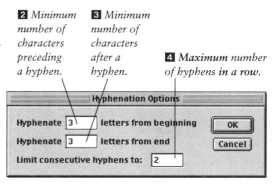

Auto Hyphenation

Out of hiding

To show the tab characters that are hidden in your text, along with other non-printing characters, like paragraph returns, soft returns, and spaces, choose Type menu > **Show Hidden Characters**. Tab characters display as right-pointing arrows **1**. Choose the command again to turn it off.

	Front.9→	Back.9→	Total¶
Tiger→	34→	34→	68¶
Jack→	38→	44→	82¶
David→	34→	38→	72¶
→	35→	38→	73∞

1 *Text aligned using custom tab stops.*

To align columns of text correctly, you must use tabs—not spaces. The Tab Ruler palette is used to set custom left-, center-, right-, and decimal-justified tabs in horizontal type, and top-, center-, bottom-, and decimal-justified tabs in vertical type. The default tab stops are half an inch apart.

To insert tabs into text:

Press Tab **once** as you input copy before typing each new column. The cursor will jump to the next tab stop.

or

To add a tab to already inputted text, click just to the left of the text that is to start a new column, then press Tab. The text will move to the nearest default tab stop.

To set custom tab stops, see the next page.

Set Tabs

To set or modify custom tab stops:

1. Choose the Selection tool, then select a text object that contains tab characters.
   or
   Choose a type tool and select text that contains tab characters.

2. Choose Type menu > Tab Ruler (Command-Shift-T/Ctrl-Shift-T).

3. *Optional:* Check the Snap box to have a tab marker snap to the nearest ruler tick mark as you insert or move it. Or to turn on/off the Snap feature temporarily (the opposite of the current Snap state), Command-drag/Ctrl-drag a marker.

4. Click in the Tab Ruler where you want the tab stop to appear (the selected text will align to the new stop) ■, then click a tab alignment button in the top left corner of the palette. Or Option-click/Alt-click a tab stop to cycle through the alignment types. Repeat for other stops.

5. *Optional:* To delete a tab stop, drag the tab marker upward and out of the ruler. As you drag it, the word *delete* will display on the palette. Shift-drag to delete a marker and all markers to its right.

6. *Optional:* To move a tab stop, drag the marker to the left or the right. Shift-drag a marker to move all the markers to the right of it along with it.

➤ Tab Ruler measurements display in the currently chosen Artboard Units (File menu > Document Setup).

What's the question?

The stops from the first line of selected text are shown on the ruler. If a **question mark** appears in the ruler instead of a tab stop, it means that stop isn't present in one or more lines of the selected text. Click the question mark to apply that stop to all the selected text.

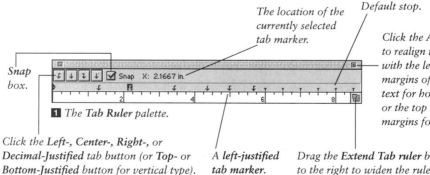

The location of the currently selected tab marker.

Default stop.

*Click the **Alignment** box to realign the tab ruler with the left and right margins of the selected text for horizontal type or the top and bottom margins for vertical type.*

Snap box.

■ *The **Tab Ruler** palette.*

*Click the **Left-, Center-, Right-,** or **Decimal-Justified** tab button (or **Top-** or **Bottom-Justified** button for vertical type).*

*A **left-justified** tab marker.*

*Drag the **Extend Tab ruler** box to the right to widen the ruler.*

1 *Eyedropper tool.*

The more things change, the more they remain the same.

The more things change, the more they₊ remain the same.

Select the type object whose attributes you want to change.

2 *Then click with the Eyedropper on the attributes you want to copy.*

The more things change, the more they remain the same.

The more things change, the more they remain the same.

3 *The attributes are copied to the selected type.*

Copy type attributes

When you click on a type object with the Eyedropper tool, it samples the type's character, paragraph, fill, stroke, and appearance attributes, copies them to the Character, Paragraph, Color, Stroke, and Appearance palettes, and applies them to any currently selected text—a temporary "style sheet" on the fly.

Note: To choose which attributes the Eyedropper picks up or the Paint Bucket applies, see the following page.

To copy type attributes using the Eyedropper or Paint Bucket:

1. Choose the Selection tool, then select the type object or objects whose attributes you want to change.

2. Choose the Eyedropper **1** tool (**don't use the "I" shortcut if type is selected!**).

3. Click on any unselected type in any open document window that contains the desired attributes **2** (a tiny "t" will appear next to the pointer). The type attributes will be copied to the Character, Paragraph, Color, and Stroke palettes and to the selected type **3**.
   or
   To change only fill or stroke attributes, Shift-click unselected text.

4. *Optional:* To apply the newly sampled effects and type attributes to yet another type object, Option-click/Alt-click any other type object (this is a temporary Paint Bucket tool).

Eyedropper and Paint Bucket for Type

To choose which attributes the Eyedropper picks up or the Paint Bucket applies:

1. Double-click the Eyedropper or Paint Bucket tool.

2. Click a triangle to expand the Appearance, Character, or Paragraph list, then check any individual attributes on or off 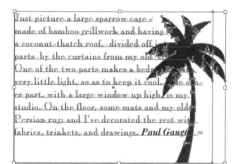. By default, all the attributes are checked on.

   or

   Check or uncheck the Appearance, Fill, Stroke, Character, or Paragraph box to turn all the attributes in that category on or off.

3. Click OK (Return/Enter).

Special effects with type

To wrap type around an object:

1. Create area type inside an object.

2. Choose the Selection tool.

3. Select the object the type is to wrap around **2**. It can even be a placed image with a clipping path from Photoshop.

4. Choose Object menu > Arrange > Bring To Front.

5. Drag a marquee around both objects.

6. Choose Type menu > Wrap > Make **3**. The text block and the object are now listed as a group on the Layers palette.

➤ Use the Direct-selection tool to move the object the type is wrapping around. For multiple objects, first Shift-click them.

➤ To move the type away from the edge of the wrap object, change the value in the Left or Right Indentation field on the Paragraph palette for the type.

➤ To wrap type around part of a placed image or vector object, create a separate object with the desired shape for the wrap with a stroke and fill of None, apply the Wrap command to both objects, then bring the separate placed image to the front. To adjust the wrap, move or adjust the blank object's anchor points using the Direct-selection tool.

improved

Eyedropper Options; Wrap Type

1 *Choose which attributes the **Paint Bucket Applies** or the **Eyedropper Picks Up.***

Unwrap

To undo a type wrap, select both objects using the Selection tool, then choose Type menu > Wrap > **Release**.

2 *Select a type object (not point or path type) and the object the type is going to wrap around.*

Just picture a large sparrow cage made of bamboo grillwork and having a coconut-thatch roof, divided off two parts by the curtains from my old studio. One of the two parts makes a bedroom, with very little light, so as to keep it cool. The other part, with a large window up high, is my studio. On the floor, some mats and my old Persian rug; and I've decorated the rest with fabrics, trinkets, and drawings. *Paul Gauguin*

3 *The type **wraps** around the palm tree.*

Working with the shadow

➤ Use the **Layers palette** to select the type object or its shadow object.

➤ Use the **Free Transform** tool to vertically **scale** or **shear** a type block (move the top center handle for both)(see page 92).

➤ Use the **Free Transform** tool to **reflect** the shadow block. Drag the top center handle across the object.

1 *The shadow is created and sent to the back.*

2 *Scale tool*

3 *The shadow is shortened using the Scale tool.*

4 *Shear tool*

5 *The shadow is slanted using the Shear tool.*

6 *The type is reflected using the Reflect tool.*

An advantage of using the following method instead of Effect menu > Drop Shadow is that here the shadow is an independent object.

To create type with a shadow:

1. Create point type (see page 196).
2. *Optional:* Select the type with the Type tool, then track the characters out (Option/Alt right arrow).
3. Choose the Selection tool, then click on the type block.
4. Apply a dark fill color, stroke of None.
5. Option-drag/Alt-drag the type block slightly to the right and downward. Release the mouse, then Option/Alt.
6. With the copy of the type block still selected, lighten its shade.
7. On the Layers palette, drag the copy of the type below the original **1**.
8. Choose Effect menu > Stylize > Feather. check the Preview box, enter a Radius value, then click OK.
9. Reposition either type block—press any arrow key to move it in small increments.

To *slant the shadow:*
1. Select the shadow object using the Layers palette **2**.
2. Double-click the Scale tool, click Non-uniform, enter 100 in the Horizontal field, enter 60 in the Vertical field, then click OK **3**.
3. With the shadow type still selected, double-click the Shear tool **4**.
4. Enter 45 in the Shear Angle field, click Axis: Horizontal, then click OK.
5. Use the arrow keys to move the baseline of the shadow text so it aligns with the baseline of the original text **5**. You might also need to move it to the right.

To *reflect the shadow:*
1. Select the shadow type.
2. Double-click the Reflect tool, click Axis: Horizontal, then click OK (Return/Enter).
3. Move the two blocks of type together so their baselines meet **6**.

Shadow Type

To slant a type block:

1. Choose the Rectangle tool (M), then draw a rectangle.

2. Choose the Area Type tool.

3. Click on the edge of the rectangle, then enter type **2**.

4. With the rectangle still selected, double-click the Rotation tool.

5. Enter 30 in the Angle field, then click OK (Return/Enter) **3**.

6. Make sure Smart Guides is turned on (Command-U/Ctrl-U) with Object Highlighting (Edit menu > Preferences > Smart Guides). Deselect the object.

7. Choose the Direct-selection tool (A), then Shift-drag the top segment diagonally to the right until the side segments are vertical **4**–**5**.

8. *Optional:* Drag the right segment of the rectangle a little to the right to enlarge the object and reflow the type.

Use the shears

You can use the Shear tool to slant a block of type (it's on the Reflect tool pop-out menu) **1**.

1 *Select the type, click with the **Shear** tool on the center of the type, then drag upward or downward from the edge of the type block. (Hold down Shift to constrain vertically or horizontally.)*

2 *The original type object.*

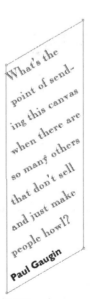

3 *The type rotated 30°.*

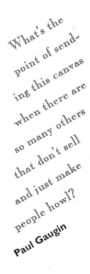

4 *The top segment dragged diagonally to the right.*

5 *The final type object in Preview view.*

ACQUIRE 14

In this chapter you will learn how to get images into Illustrator via the Open command, the Place command, and drag-and-drop. You will also learn how to work with the Links palette to edit, locate, update, replace, and convert linked images.

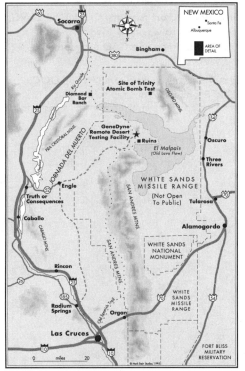

©Mark Stein, Mark Stein Studios

Opening and placing images
How images are acquired

You can use Illustrator to open or import objects or images in a variety of file formats, which means you can work with imagery that was originally created in another application. Methods for acquiring an image from another application include the Open command, the Place command, and the drag-and-drop method. The method you choose to use depends on which file formats are available for saving the file in its original application and how you intend to use the imagery in Illustrator.

If you open a document from another drawing (vector) application using the **Open** command, a new Illustrator file will be created, and the acquired objects can be manipulated using any Illustrator tool, command, filter, or effect. If you open a document from a bitmap program other than Photoshop using the Open command, the image won't convert into workable paths; it will stay in its outlined box.

The **Place** command inserts imagery or text into an existing Illustrator document. For print output, the best formats to use for saving a file for placing into Illustrator are EPS and TIFF. Both formats preserve the color, detail, and resolution of the original image.

For Web output, the .psd (Photoshop) format works fine. If you place a layered .psd image, you can choose to make it appear as

new

a one-layer (flattened) object or as separate objects on separate layers in Illustrator. If you want to put the image on a template layer for tracing, check Template in the Place dialog box. The Template option can be turned on or off at any time.

A bitmap image that is acquired in Illustrator via the Open, Place, or drag-and-drop method can be moved, placed on a different layer, masked, modified using any transformation tool, or modified using any color or raster (bitmap) filter.

➤ If you reduce the scale of an opened or placed TIFF or EPS image, the resolution of that image will increase accordingly. Conversely, if you enlarge such an image, its resolution will decrease.

improved

Both the Open and Place commands preserve the resolution of the original image, regardless of whether the image is linked or embedded, with PICT files being the only exception. The resolution of a linked or embedded PICT will be changed to the multiple of 72 nearest to the resolution of the original image (e.g., a 180 ppi original will become 144, or 72 x 2).

Open and Place

File formats

File formats you can **Open** in Illustrator:

Native formats: Illustrator versions 1.0 through 9.0 (.ai).

Vector formats: CorelDRAW versions 5 through 8.

File formats you can **Open** or **Place** in Illustrator:

Native formats: EPS (.eps), Adobe PDF (.pdf).

Raster (bitmap) formats: EPS, Amiga IFF, BMP, FLM, GIF89a, JPEG, Kodak PhotoCD, PCX, PIXAR, PNG, Photoshop, RLE, TGA, and TIFF.

Graphics (vector) formats: CGM, DXF, DWG, FreeHand up to version 8, Macintosh PICT (from DeltaGraph or a CAD program), SVG, and WMF/EMF.

Text file formats: Plain text (ASCII), DOC, MS RTF, and MS Word (up to 2000).

Easy reopen

From the File menu > **Open Recent Files** sub-menu, you can choose from a list of up to 10 of the most recently opened files.

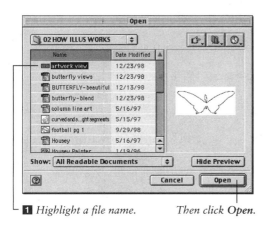

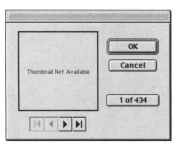

1 *Highlight a file name.*   *Then click* **Open***.*

2 *This* **Discard Profile** *prompt will appear if your Edit menu > Color Settings are set to* **Emulate Adobe Illustrator** *6 (Color Management off).*

3 *For a* **multi-page** *PDF, choose the page you want to open.*

A list of file formats that can be opened in Illustrator appears on the previous page.

To open a file from within Illustrator:

1. Choose File menu > Open (Command-O/ Ctrl-O).

2. Click the Show Preview button to display a thumbnail of the illustration, if it contains a preview that Illustrator can display. (Mac OS: QuickTime must be loaded for the preview to display.)

3. *Mac OS:* Choose Show: All Documents to list files in all formats or choose All Readable Documents to list only files in the formats Illustrator can read.

   Windows: Filter out files by choosing from the Format drop-down menu, or choose All Formats (the default setting) to display files of all formats.

4. Locate and highlight a file name, then click Open (Return/Enter) **1**.
   or
   Double-click a file name.

   Note: If you get a warning prompt about a linked file, see page 239. If you get the Discard Profile prompt **2**, see page 423.

5. If you're opening a multi-page PDF, another dialog box will open **3**. Click an arrow to locate the desired page (or click the "1 of [ ]" button, enter the desired page), then click OK.

   On the Layers palette, the image object will be listed within the currently active layer.

➤ If you Open an EPS that contains a clipping path, the image object will be nested within a group sublayer on the Layers palette (the word "<clipping path>" will appear directly above the image layer). If the clipping path is composed of several paths, it will be listed as "<compound clipping group>" instead. To select the clipping path, use the Layers palette; to move or reshape the path, use the Direct-selection tool.

new

To open a file from the Mac OS Finder or Windows Explorer:

Double-click an Illustrator file icon. Illustrator will launch if it is not already open **1**.

A placed image can be moved to a different *x/y* location; restacked within the same layer or to a different layer; masked; transformed; or modified using any raster filter. Its opacity and blending mode can also be changed. For a list of file formats that can be placed into Illustrator, see page 236.

To place an image from another application into an Illustrator document:

1. Open an Illustrator file. If your file contains more than one layer, activate a top-level layer.

2. Choose File menu > Place.

3. Locate and highlight the name of the file that you want to place, then click Place.
   or
   Double-click a file name **2**.

4. Check the Link box to place only a screen version of an image into Illustrator (the image must reside on your hard disk). The actual, original image will remain separate from the Illustrator file at its original resolution. If you modify and resave a linked image in its original application, it will automatically update in the Illustrator document (see pages 242–243).
   or
   Uncheck the Link box to embed (parse) the actual image into the Illustrator file. This increases a file's storage size.

   Read more about linking on pages 242–246.

5. *Optional:* Check the Template box to place a dimmed version of the image on a template layer for tracing.

6. Click Place (Return/Enter).

Place an Image

Replace one placed image with another

Check the **Replace** box before you click Place. Any transformations that were made to the original placed image will be applied automatically to the newly placed one.

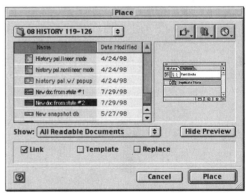

1 *Double-clicking an existing Illustrator file icon will cause the application to launch, if it isn't already open.*

2 *Double-click a bitmap or vector file in the **Place** dialog box.*

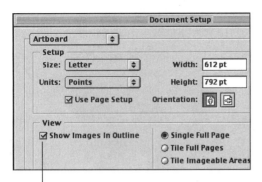

1 *Check the Show Images in Outline box in the Document Setup dialog box.*

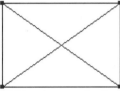

2 *Placed image, Outline view.*

3 *Placed image, Outline view, Show Images in Outline box checked.*

4 *Linked, placed image selected, Preview view. Notice the "X" across the outline box, designating this image as linked.*

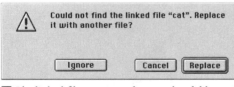

5 *If a linked file was **moved** to another folder or is otherwise **missing**, Illustrator will alert you with this dialog box when you open the illustration. To reestablish the link, click **Replace**, then locate the file.*

If a placed image was saved in its original application with a preview that Illustrator recognizes, it will render fully in Preview view, whether or not the "Show Images In Outline" box is checked in Document Setup. If you place an image that *doesn't* contain a preview that Illustrator recognizes, the image will display as an empty outlined box with an "x" through it in either view. Follow these instructions to have images display in black-and-white in their outlined box in Outline view.

To display a placed image in Outline view:

1. Choose File menu > Document Setup.
2. Choose Artboard from the drop-down menu.
3. Check the View: Show Images In Outline box **1**–**4**.
4. Click OK (Return/Enter).

Reopening a file that contains linked images

If the actual linked image is moved from its original location after the file into which it was placed was last saved, you will be prompted to re-link the image when you reopen the Illustrator file. Click **Replace 5**, relocate the same file or a different file, then click Replace again.

If you click **Ignore,** the linked image will not display, but a question mark icon will display for the file on the Links palette, and its bounding box will still be visible in the Illustrator file in Outline view or if Smart Guides is turned on. To completely break the link and prevent any alert prompts from appearing, delete this bounding box and save the file.

Display Place Image; Reopen File with Links

Photoshop to Illustrator *improved*

If you **drag-and-drop** a Photoshop selection or layer into Illustrator, the image will appear on the Layers palette in Illustrator as a "<group>" within the currently active layer, and a clipping path and the image will be nested within the group sublayer. The opacity of the selection or layer will become 100%; blending modes and any layer masks will be ignored. A generic clipping path will be created, and it will be sized to fit either the object or the width and height of the Photoshop file. Any clipping paths in the Photoshop file will be ignored, and the background of the image will be opaque white. All the effects filters can be applied to the image (the commands that appear below the horizontal black line on the Effect menu).

➤ A white background in an imported image can be removed using a blending mode in Illustrator. Change the Transparency percentage, or try Multiply, Color Burn, or Darken mode.

➤ You can use the Add-anchor-point tool to add points to a generic clipping path that was created for an imported image. The added points can be repositioned with the Direct-selection tool to follow the contour of the image more closely.

If you **place** a Photoshop image with the **Link** box checked in the Place dialog box, it will appear on the Layers palette as one image nested in the currently active layer—not a group—and no clipping path will be generated by Illustrator. Any Photoshop clipping path will remain in effect.

If you embed a Photoshop image as you place it (uncheck the Link box), the *new* Photoshop Import dialog box will open. You'll have a choice of two options for how the Photoshop layers will be treated. If you **open** a Photoshop image in Illustrator, the Photoshop Import dialog box will also open.

You can choose whether to have the Photoshop layers converted into objects or flattened into one layer. If you opt to **convert** Photoshop layers into objects, each object

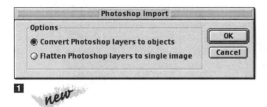

will appear on its own nested layer within an image sublayer. The sublayer will be nested within the currently active layer. All transparency, blending modes, and layer masks will be preserved. They will be listed as editable appearances (see pages 289–293), and they will be targeted to the appropriate image layer in Illustrator. Any clipping path saved with the Photoshop file will remain in effect, and it will be placed at the top of the stack of nested image layers within a group sublayer.

If you opt to **flatten** Photoshop layers into one image layer, that layer will be nested within an image sublayer within the current active layer. All transparency, blending modes, and layer masks effects will be preserved in the flattened image, but those attributes won't be listed as editable appearances in Illustrator. Any clipping path saved with the Photoshop file will be active and will be placed above the nested image within a group sublayer.

If a multi-layer Photoshop image is opened or placed into Illustrator with the Link box unchecked and the "Convert Photoshop layers to objects" button is clicked in the Photoshop Import dialog box **1**, the Background layer will become one of the separate nested layers within Illustrator, and it will be opaque. If you want to eliminate the background layer, you can either delete it in Photoshop before opening the image in Illustrator or delete it using the Layers palette in Illustrator after the image is opened or placed. You could also apply transparency to the Background layer.

➤ Each of the converted layers from the Photoshop image will be listed as a separate item on the Links palette.

Photoshop to Illustrator

Linking images

To keep file sizes down, you can link any imported EPS, GIF, JPEG, PICT, or TIFF image to an Illustrator file rather than embed it within the file. A copy of the image will act as a placeholder in your Illustrator document, but the actual image will remain separate from the Illustrator file. If you revise a linked image via the Edit Original button, the image will update in the Illustrator document (you can't do this with embedded images).

To link a file, use the File menu > Place command, and make sure the **Link** box is checked. Instructions for placing and linking images are on page 238. Illustrator's Links palette helps you and your service bureau or print shop keep track of linked files. It lists all the linked and embedded files in your Illustrator document and puts a number of useful controls at your fingertips **1**.

Raster filters can be applied to an embedded image, but not to a linked image. Effect menu filters can be applied to either type of image, and the effects are editable. To embed a linked image, see page 246. The Object menu > Rasterize command automatically embeds a linked image; the Effect menu > Rasterize command does not. A linked image can be transformed (moved, rotated, sheared, or reflected).

To edit a linked image in its original application:

1. Show the Links palette (Window menu > Show Links), then click the name of the image on the palette.

2. Click the Edit Original button at the bottom of the palette ▱ or choose Edit Original from the Links palette menu. The application in which the linked image was created will launch if it isn't already open, and the image will open. *Note:* Edit Original may not work in Windows, depending on the linked file's location.

3. Make your edits, save the file, and then return to Illustrator. If a warning prompt appears, click Yes (see the sidebar) **2**. The linked image will update.

Update options ~new~

To specify how linked images are updated when the original files are modifed, choose from the **Update Links** pop-up menu in Edit menu > Preferences > Files & Clipboard:

Automatically: Illustrator will update a linked image automatically whenever the original file is modified.

Manually: Linked images will remain unchanged when the original files are modified. You can always use the Links palette to update links.

Ask When Modified: A dialog box will appear if the original files are modified and you return to Illustrator or reopen the file (click Yes or No).

Modified linked image indicator. *Missing linked image indicator.*

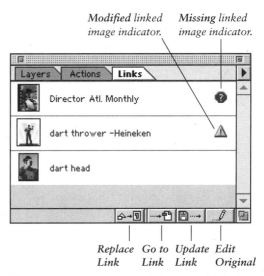

Replace Link *Go to Link* *Update Link* *Edit Original*

1 *The Links palette lets you keep track of linked images, link to new files, and convert linked images into embedded ones.*

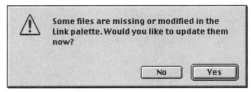

2 *This prompt will appear if you edit a link in its original application via the Edit Original button.*

Linked and embedded files

To a linked or embedded EPS file you can apply opacity and blending modes, the Feather command, and Effect menu filters. These attributes will become appearances on the image object. Filter menu color filters can also be applied to the embedded EPS. A linked EPS image will be listed on the Layers palette as a placed object within the currently active layer. Any clipping path in the file will be applied, but it won't be listed as a separate layer.

An embedded image in a non-EPS format will be listed on the Layers palette as a nested image object within a group sublayer, within the currently active layer. Any included clipping path will be applied and will be listed as a clipping path, nested within the group sublayer and stacked above the image object. *improved*

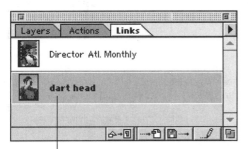

1 *Click on the name of the linked image that you want to replace, then click the Replace Link (first) button.*

2 *The linked image is replaced.*

If you replace one linked image with another, any transformations that were applied to the original image, such as scaling or rotating, will be applied to the new image.

To replace one linked image with another:

1. On the Links palette, click the name of the file that you want to replace **1**.

2. Click the Replace Link button at the bottom of the Links palette. or
   Choose Replace from the Links palette menu.

3. Locate the replacement file, then click Place **2**.

➤ To replace a linked image another way, click on the existing image in the document window, choose File menu > Place, check the Replace box, locate the replacement image, then click Place.

When you locate a linked image, it becomes selected in the document window.

To locate a linked image in an Illustrator file:

1. Open the illustration that contains the linked image.

2. Click the name of the linked image on the Links palette list.

3. Click the Go To Link (second) button at the bottom of the palette. or
   Choose Go To Link from the Links palette menu.

To view file information for a linked image:

1. Double-click an image thumbnail on the Links palette.

or

Click a file name on the Links palette, then choose Information from the palette menu.

A dialog box with the image's file format, location, size, modifications, and transform information will appear 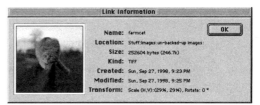.

2. Click OK (Return/Enter).

1 *The **Link Information** dialog shows the linked image's file format, location, size, and modifications.*

To choose Links palette display options:

To change the size of the **thumbnail** images that are displayed in the Links palette, choose **Palette Options** from the Links palette menu, click the preferred size, then click OK. To display just the file icon without a thumbnail, click None.

To change the order of links on the palette, from the Links palette menu choose **Sort by Name** (alphabetical order), **Sort by Kind** (file format) or **Sort by Status** (missing, then modified, then embedded, then fully linked) **2**–**3**. To sort only selected links, first click, then Shift-click consecutive names or Command-click/Ctrl-click non-consecutive names.

To control which type of links display on the palette, choose **Show All, Show Missing, Show Modified,** or **Show Embedded** from the Links palette menu.

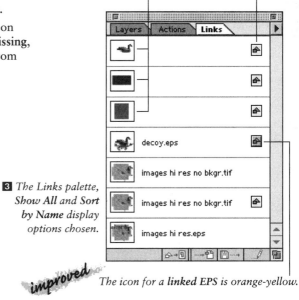

With the exception of TIFFs, embedded images have no name.

*The icon for an **embedded** image is gray.*

3 *The Links palette, Show All and Sort by Name display options chosen.*

improved

*The icon for a **linked EPS** is orange-yellow.*

1 *Modified image icon.*

An exclamation mark icon appearing to the right of a link on the Links palette list indicates that the original file has been modified and the link is outdated. Use the Update Link button to update it.

Note: If you edit a linked image via the Edit Original button, you will need to update it this way only if Manually is chosen in Edit menu > Preferences > Files & Clipboard > Update Links. Otherwise, you'll get a warning prompt or the image will be updated automatically, depending on the current Update Links setting. You can't update a missing linked image (indicated by a question mark). You can either physically move it back to its original location or replace it (see page 243).

To update a modified linked image:

1. Click on the name of the modified image on the Links palette list **1**.

2. Click the Update Link (third) button at the bottom of the palette. 🖫⋯
or
Choose Update Link from the Links palette menu.

Update Modified Linked Image

The Embed Image command will cause a file that's separate from, but linked to, your Illustrator document to become embedded into (part of) your Illustrator document. Beware! Embedding an image will cause the Illustrator file size to increase.

To convert a linked image to an embedded image:

1. On the Links palette list, click the name of the image that you want to embed **1**.

2. Choose Embed Image from the Links palette menu **2**.

   Note: There is no command to turn an embedded image into a linked image, but you can either Undo immediately or use the Replace command on the Links palette menu to replace the embedded image with a linked image.

➤ If a Filter menu filter is applied to a linked image, it will become embedded. If an Effect menu command is applied to a linked image, it won't become embedded.

1 *Click an image name on the Links palette, then choose* **Embed Image** *from the palette menu.*

2 *The* **embedded** *image icon appears. The file name is preserved for a TIFF image, even though the image is embedded.*

Drag-and-drop

A few pointers before you begin:

➤ Drag-and-drop does not use the Clipboard; whatever is currently on the Clipboard is preserved.

➤ If you drag-and-drop an image from Photoshop to Illustrator via Photoshop's Move tool, the image will be embedded as an RGB, in a ppi (pixels per inch) resolution that is the multiple of 72 nearest to the resolution of the original image (e.g., 220 ppi will become 216, or 72 x 3). Any opacity or blending modes for the Photoshop selection or layer will be lost in Illustrator. The dropped object will have an opaque white background (see pages 240–241). If you're going to print the image, use the following method instead: Convert the file to CMYK Color mode, save the Photoshop file as a TIFF or EPS, and then use the Place or Open command in Illustrator to acquire it.

improved

➤ You can drag-and-drop objects between Illustrator documents or between Illustrator and Adobe GoLive, Adobe InDesign, Adobe Acrobat, or any other drag-aware application. In our testing on Mac OS, we couldn't drag-and-drop a path from Photoshop to Illustrator. On Windows, select a path in Photoshop, then Ctrl-Alt drag the path into an Illustrator document window. We were able to copy from Photoshop and paste into Illustrator and then edit the pasted path in Illustrator.

➤ Currently, Windows supports drag-and-drop only between OLE-compliant applications. The dropped vector object will be rasterized in the receiving application.

To drag-and-drop an object:

1. Select the object you want to drag-and-drop in an Illustrator or Photoshop document. It can be any kind of object, even text. You can drag-and-drop a whole layer from the document window using Photoshop's Move tool.

Drag-and-Drop

2. Open the Illustrator or Photoshop file to which you want to copy the object.

3. Drag the object into the destination document window, and presto, a copy of the object will appear in the new location. The destination window will become active. In Photoshop, the object will become a new layer of pixels in the color mode and resolution of the Photoshop image.
or
Hold down Command/Ctrl when dragging a path object from Illustrator to Photoshop to preserve the object as a path in Photoshop.

➤ Hold down Shift after you start dragging into Photoshop to position the "dropped" pixels in the center of the Photoshop document window.

➤ If you drag an Illustrator object to the Desktop, a Picture Clipping file will be created in PICT format in Mac OS. This intermediate file can then be dragged into any drag-aware application.

➤ If you drag-and-drop a rasterized object (created without a mask), from Illustrator to Photoshop, the bounding area (background) of the object in Photoshop will become opaque white and will block pixels below it (even if you clicked Background: Transparent in the Rasterize dialog box in Illustrator). To make the non-pixel layer areas transparent, use Photoshop's Magic Wand tool to select the white background on that object's layer, then press Delete, or just click with the Magic Eraser tool.

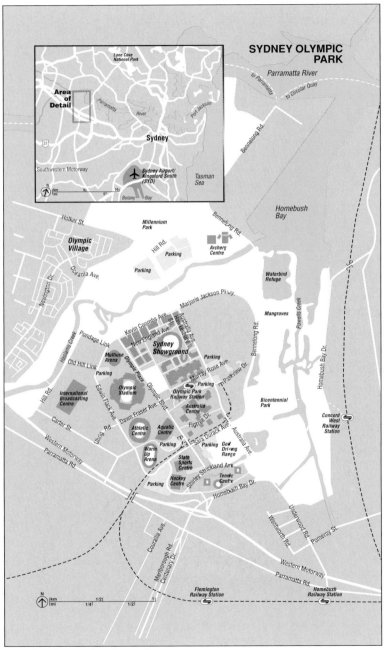

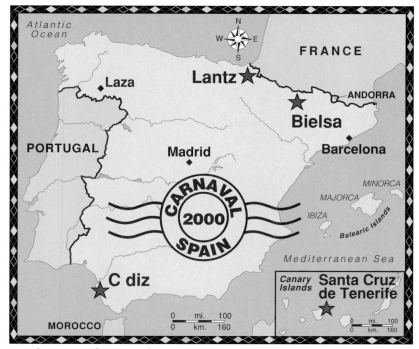

©*Mark Stein, Mark Stein Studios*

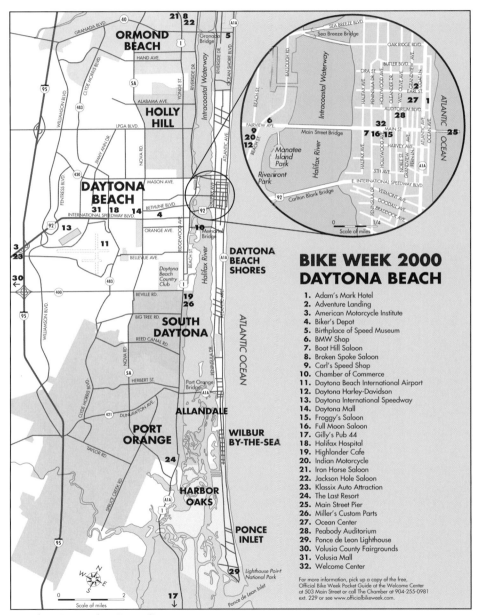

BIKE WEEK 2000
DAYTONA BEACH

1. Adam's Mark Hotel
2. Adventure Landing
3. American Motorcycle Institute
4. Biker's Depot
5. Birthplace of Speed Museum
6. BMW Shop
7. Boot Hill Saloon
8. Broken Spoke Saloon
9. Carl's Speed Shop
10. Chamber of Commerce
11. Daytona Beach International Airport
12. Daytona Harley-Davidson
13. Daytona International Speedway
14. Daytona Mall
15. Froggy's Saloon
16. Full Moon Saloon
17. Gilly's Pub 44
18. Halifax Hospital
19. Highlander Cafe
20. Indian Motorcycle
21. Iron Horse Saloon
22. Jackson Hole Saloon
23. Klassix Auto Attraction
24. The Last Resort
25. Main Street Pier
26. Miller's Custom Parts
27. Ocean Center
28. Peabody Auditorium
29. Ponce de Leon Lighthouse
30. Volusia County Fairgrounds
31. Volusia Mall
32. Welcome Center

For more information, pick up a copy of the free, Official Bike Week Pocket Guide at the Welcome Center at 503 Main Street or call The Chamber at 904-255-0981 ext. 229 or see www.officialbikeweek.com.

©*Mark Stein, Mark Stein Studios*

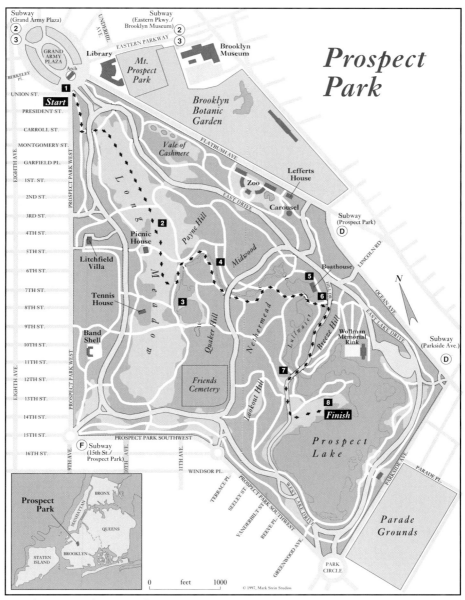

Prospect Park

©Mark Stein, Mark Stein Studios

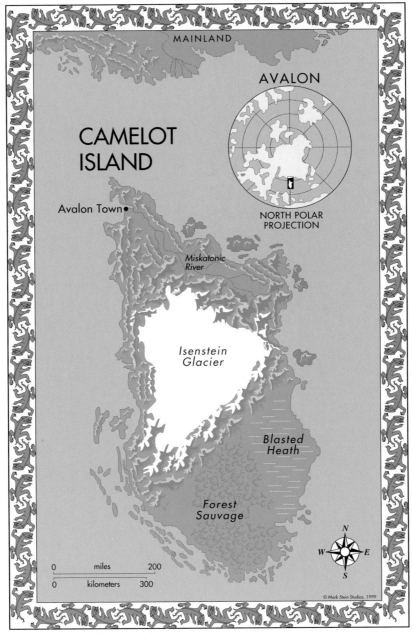

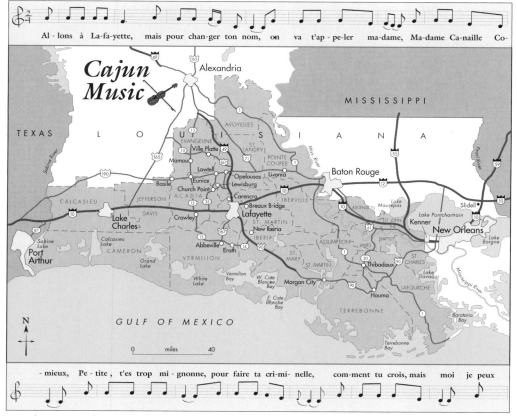

Al - lons à La-fa-yette, mais pour chan-ger ton nom, on va t'ap-pe-ler ma-dame, Ma-dame Ca-naille Co-

- mieux, Pe - tite, t'es trop mi - gnonne, pour faire ta cri-mi- nelle, com-ment tu crois, mais moi je peux

©Mark Stein, Mark Stein studios

©Jim Spiece

©Jim Spiece

Nancy Stahl

©Nancy Stahl, Big Dot

©Nancy Stahl, Café

©Nancy Stahl, Liner

©Daniel Pelavin, magazine cover for Publishers Weekly

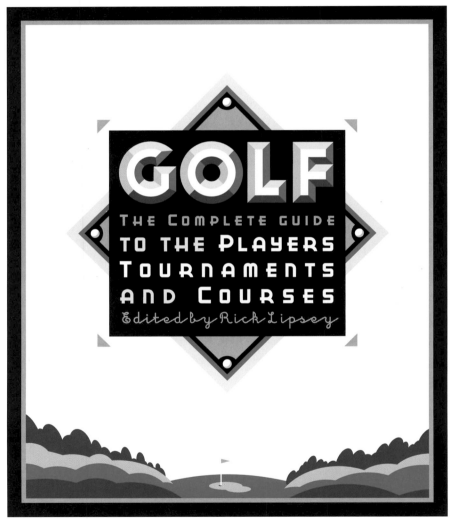

©Daniel Pelavin, book cover for Times Books

©Marti Shohet, illustration for CIO magazine

Led Pants

Led Pants

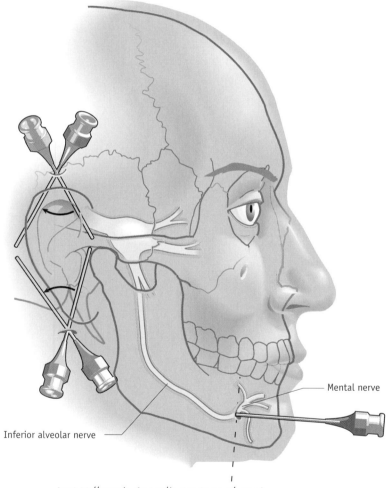

Mental nerve

Inferior alveolar nerve

Bart Vallecoccia (©Medic Art Research Inc.)

©Yoshinori Kaizu, Fish

©Yoshinori Kaizu, Cockatoo

©Yoshinori Kaizu, Flower

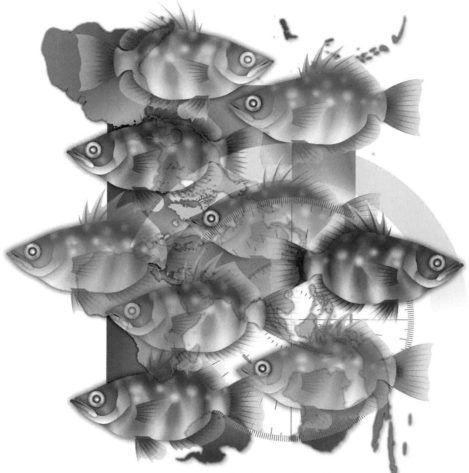

©Yoshinori Kaizu, Gradient Fish

BRUSHES 15

In this chapter you will learn about Illustrator's four types of brushes: calligraphic, scatter, art, and pattern. You will learn how to create and edit custom brushes; how to add, modify, or remove brushstrokes from existing paths; how to open or create brush libraries; and how to duplicate, move, or delete brushes from the Brushes palette.

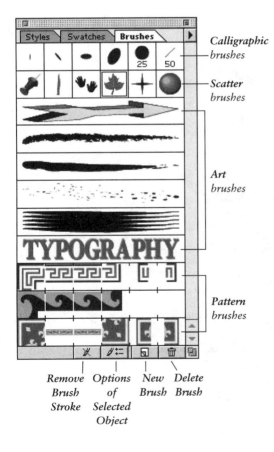

Calligraphic brushes

Scatter brushes

Art brushes

Pattern brushes

Remove Brush Stroke | Options of Selected Object | New Brush | Delete Brush

Using brushes

Illustrator's brushes are an illustrator's dream. They combine the ability to draw variable, freehand brushstrokes or apply a pattern or objects to a path with all the advantages of vector graphics—small file sizes, resizability, and crisp output.

There are two ways to work with the brushes: Choose the Paintbrush tool and a brush and draw a shape right off the bat with a brushstroke built in, or apply a brushstroke to an existing path.

To change the contour of a brushstroke, you can use any tool or command you'd normally use to reshape a path (Reshape, Pencil, Smooth, Erase, Add-anchor-point, Convert-anchor-point, etc.).

The brushes come in four flavors: **scatter**, **calligraphic**, **art**, and **pattern**, and they are stored on and accessed from the Brushes palette. The brushes that are currently on the Brushes palette save with the document. If you modify a brush that was applied to any existing paths in a document, you'll be given the option via an alert box to update those paths with the revised brush. You can also create your own brushes.

As an introduction to the brushes, grab the Paintbrush tool, click on a default brush on the Brushes palette, and draw (see the instructions on the following page).

249

Note: If you use a stylus and a pressure-sensitive tablet, the Paintbrush tool will respond to pressure. The harder you press on the tablet, the wider will be the shape.

To draw with the Paintbrush tool:

1. Choose the Paintbrush tool (B) **1**, and choose a fill of None.

2. Show the Brushes palette (Window menu > Show Brushes), then click a calligraphic, scatter, art, or pattern brush.

3. Draw with the Paintbrush tool to create an open path shape **2**–**3**. Drag, then Option-drag/Alt-drag to draw a closed path (release Option/Alt last).

   For quick reshaping, use the Pencil or Paintbrush tool (see page 111). For precise reshaping, use the Direct-selection tool.

Preferences you choose for the Paintbrush affect only future (not existing) brushstrokes. You'll learn how to choose options for individual brushes later on in this chapter.

To choose preferences for the Paintbrush:

1. Double-click the Paintbrush tool (or choose the tool and press Return/Enter).

2. Choose a Fidelity value (0.5–20) **4**. A Fidelity value below 5 produces a path very close to the way you drag the tool. A high setting produces a smoother path with fewer anchor points that only approximates the path you drag.

3. Choose a Smoothness value (0–100). The higher the Smoothness, the fewer the irregularities in the path.

4. *Do any of the following:*

   Check "Fill new brush strokes" to have new paths be filled with the current Foreground color.

   Check Keep Selected to keep the newly drawn path selected.

   Check Edit Selected Paths and choose a distance range (2–20 pixels) within which selected paths will be affected by the tool.

7. Click OK (Return/Enter).

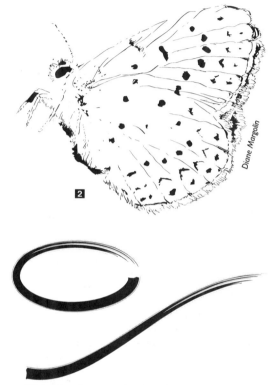

1 *Paintbrush tool.*

Diane Margolin

2

3 *Strokes drawn with an art brush.*

4 *Choose settings for the Paintbrush in its Preferences dialog box.*

Draw with Paintbrush; Paintbrush Options

improved

What's the difference?

On the surface, the pattern and scatter brushes may look similar, but they have different reasons for being. For a scatter brush, you can make the size, spacing, scatter, and rotation variables more or less random via the Brush Options dialog box. You can't do this with a pattern brush. They are not called scatter brushes for nothing. Pattern brushes, on the other hand, are made of up to five tiles: Side, Outer Corner, Inner Corner, Start, and End. Pattern brushes fit more tightly on a path than scatter brushes.

1 *Select a path.*

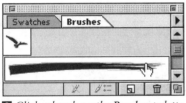

2 *Click a brush on the* **Brushes** *palette.*

3 *A* **calligraphic** *brushstroke is applied.*

Note: In Illustrator version 9.0 or later, you can apply a brushstroke to a type path. *improved*

To apply a brushstroke to an existing path:

1. Choose Window menu > Show Brushes, if the palette is not already displayed.

2. Click a brush on the brushes palette, then drag the selected brush onto an existing path (the path need not be selected first). Release the mouse when the hand pointer is directly over the edge of the object.
   or
   Select a path of any kind **1**, then click a brush on the Brushes palette **2**–**7**.

   Note: To create or modify a brush, see the instructions for the individual brush types starting on page 254.

➤ Choose Edit menu > Select > Brush Strokes to select all the brushstroked paths in an illustration.

➤ You can't use a brushstroked object in a compound path or a blend. Create the compound or blend first, then apply a brushstroke.

Apply Brushstroke to Existing Path

4 *An* **art** *brushstroke.*

Diane Margolin

6 *Another* **scatter** *brushstroke (made from five birds).*

5 *A* **scatter** *brushstroke.*

7 *A* **pattern** *brushstroke.*

After opening another brush library, you can apply a brush from that library directly to a path or you can move select brushes to the current document's Brushes palette. You can modify any brush from any library.

To add brushes from other libraries:

1. Choose a library name from the Window menu > Brush Libraries submenu.
   or
   To open a library that is not in the Brush Libraries folder, choose Window menu > Other Library, locate and highlight a custom library, then click Open.

2. Deselect all the objects in your illustration (Command-Shift-A/Ctrl-Shift-A).

3. Drag a brush from the library palette onto an object in your document (you don't have to select the object). The brush-stroke will appear on the object and the brush will appear on the Brushes palette.
   or
   Click a brush on the library palette. It will appear on the Brushes palette. To drag multiple brushes, Shift-click or Command-click/Ctrl-click them first **1**–**3**.
   or
   Select one or more brushes, then choose Add To Brushes from the library palette menu.

   Note: You can drag a library palette tab into another palette group, but it will only stay there until you relaunch Illustrator. To make a whole library palette open automatically when you re-launch Illustrator, choose Persistent from the library palette's menu. To save individual brushes with a document, add them to the brushes palette using any method in step 3, above.

➤ To delete brushes from the Brushes palette, see page 259.

➤ To close a library palette that's not in a palette group, click its close box. To close a palette in a group, drag its tab out of the palette group, then click its close box.

improved

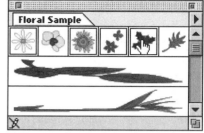

1 *To append multiple brushes, first **Shift-click** or **Command-click/Ctrl-click** them.*

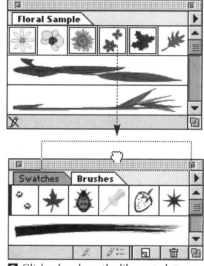

2 *Click a brush on the library palette or drag selected brushes to the Brushes palette.*

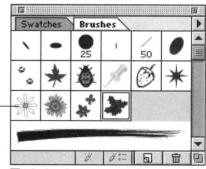

3 *The brushes appear on the current document's **Brushes** palette.*

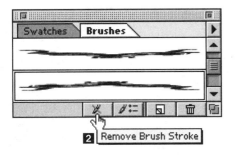

1 *The original object with a* **brushstroke***.*

2 Remove Brush Stroke

3 *The brushstroke is* **removed** *from the object.*

4 *The original* **brushstroke** *on an object.*

5 *The brushstroke is now an object,* **separate** *from the original path (they were ungrouped and moved away from each other for this illustration).*

When a brushstroke is removed from a path, you're left with a plain path.

To remove a brushstroke from an object:

1. Select the object or objects from which you want to remove the brushstroke **1**.

2. Click the Remove Brush Stroke button at the bottom of the Brushes palette **2**–**3**.
   or
   Click the Stroke box on the Toolbox, then click the None button ⊘.

If you expand a brushstroke, it will be converted into editable outlined paths that are no longer associated with the original brush. *Note:* If you edit the original brush that was applied to the object, you won't be able to update the brushstroke on the object—it no longer works like a brushstroke.

To convert a brushstroke into outlined paths:

1. Select the brushstroked object **4**.

2. Choose Object menu > Expand *improved* Appearance. The brushstroke is now a separate object or objects **5**. The outlined paths will be nested (or double or triple nested) under a group sublayer on the Layers palette.

Remove Brushstroke; Expand Brushstroke

To choose brush display options:

With View By Name checked on the Brushes palette menu, for each brush there will be a small thumbnail, the brush name, and an icon for the brush type (calligraphic, scatter, art, pattern) **1**. With View By Name unchecked, a large thumbnail for each brush will display, but no name or icon **2**.

To control which **brush types** (categories) display on the palette, choose a brush type from the palette menu to check or uncheck that option. A brush type that has no check mark won't display on the palette.

You can **drag** a brush to a different spot on the Brushes palette within its category. To move multiple brushes, select them first (click, then Shift-click a consecutive string or Command-click/Ctrl-click them individually).

Creating and modifying brushes

Scatter objects are placed evenly or randomly along the contour of a path. You *can* make a scatter brush from an open or closed path, text object, text outline, or compound path, but *not* from a pattern, gradient, gradient mesh, bitmap image (placed or rasterized), or clipping mask. As of Illustrator version 9.0, you can make a *blend* into a scatter brush. *improved*

To create or modify a scatter brush:

I. To create a new brush, select an object(s) **3** or a blend, click the New Brush button on the Brushes palette **5**, click New Scatter Brush, then click OK.
   or
   To modify an existing brush, deselect, then double-click the brush on the Brushes palette. Or click a brush, then choose Brush Options from the palette menu.

2. Enter a new name or modify the existing name (**1**, next page).

3. For an existing brush, check the Preview box. Changes will preview on any paths to which the brush is currently applied.

4. Each of the four brush properties (Size, Spacing, Scatter, and Rotation) can be set to the Fixed, Random, or Pressure variation via the pop-up menu next to

Dupe it

To create a **variation** of any type of brush (calligraphic, scatter, art, or pattern), either **drag** the brush over the **New Brush** button on the Brushes palette or click the brush and choose **Duplicate Brush** from the palette menu, then modify the duplicate.

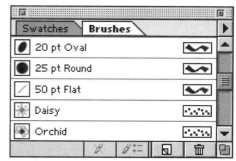

1 *With the* View By Name *option* checked *on the Brushes palette menu.*

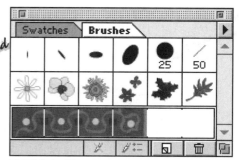

2 *With the* View By Name *option* unchecked *on the Brushes palette menu.*

3 *The original objects.*

254

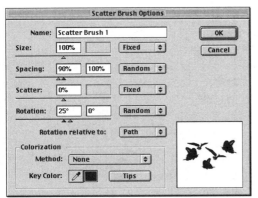

1 *The Scatter Brush Options dialog box.*

2 *The new scatter brush applied to a path.*

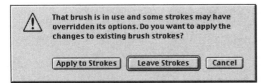

3 *The same scatter brush after moving the Size sliders apart (Random setting).*

4 *This prompt will appear if you modify a brush that is currently applied to objects in the file.*

each option. Choose **Fixed** to use a single, fixed value.

Choose **Random,** then move the sliders (or enter different values into the left and right fields) to define a range within which that property value can vary.

Choose **Pressure** and move the sliders (or enter different values in the left and right fields) to define a range within which that property can respond to stylus pressure. A light pressure will produce a brush property based on the minimum property value (left field); a heavy pressure will produce a brush property based on the maximum property value (right field). Pressure will be available only if you're using a graphics tablet.

Size controls the size of the scatter objects.

Spacing controls the spacing between the scatter objects.

Scatter controls the distance of the objects from either side of the path. When Scatter is set to Fixed, a positive value places all the objects on one side of the path; a negative value places all the objects on the opposite side of the path. The further the Scatter value is from 0%, the greater will be the distance from the path, and the less prominent will be the path shape.

Rotation adjusts the amount objects rotate relative to the page or the path. Choose **Page** or **Path** from the **Rotation relative to** pop-up menu for the axis the rotation will be based on.

5. For the Colorization options, see the sidebar on page 259.

6. Click OK or press Return/Enter **2**–**3**. If the brush was already applied to existing paths in the document, an alert box will appear. Click Apply to Strokes to change the existing strokes or click Leave Strokes to leave existing strokes unchanged **4**.

➤ You'll find scatter brushes in the Animal Sample, Arrow Sample, Floral Sample, and Object Sample libraries.

(Continued on the following page)

Create/Modify Scatter Brush

➤ Shift-drag a slider to move its counterpart gradually along with it. Option-drag/ Alt-drag a slider to move its counterpart apart or together the same distance.

➤ To make the scatter objects' orientation along a path uniform, set Scatter and Rotation to Fixed, set Scatter to 0°, and choose Rotation relative to: Path **1**–**2**.

➤ Make type into outlines before trying to drag it into the Brushes palette.

The calligraphic brushes create strokes that vary in thickness as you draw, like traditional calligraphy media.

To create or modify a calligraphic brush:

1. To create a new calligraphic brush, click the New Brush button on the Brushes palette **🔲**, click New Calligraphic Brush, then click OK.
   or
   To modify an existing brush **3**, double-click the brush on the Brushes palette **4**.

2. Enter a new name or modify the existing name **5**.

3. To preview an existing brush, check the Preview box. Changes will preview immediately on any paths to which the calligraphic brush is currently applied. Changes also update in the preview area of the dialog box.

4. The Angle, Roundness, and Diameter can be set to the Fixed, or Random, or Pressure variation via the pop-up menu next to each option.

   Choose **Fixed** to keep the value constant.

   Choose **Random** and move the Variation slider to define a range within which the specific brush attribute value can vary. A stroke can range between the set value (for angle, roundness, or diameter) plus or minus the Variation value (e.g., a 50° angle with a Random Variation value of 10 could have an angle anywhere between 40° and 60°).

1 *Illustrator's default "Fish"* **scatter** *brush applied to a path.*

2 *After choosing the Fixed option for Scatter and Rotation and setting Scatter to 0%.*

3 *Here's an existing object to which a* **calligraphic** *brush has been applied.*

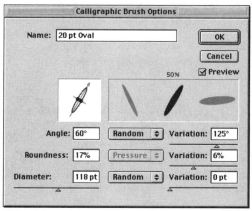

4 *Double-click a brush on the Brushes palette.*

5 *Modify the brush via the* **Calligraphic Brush Options** *dialog box.*

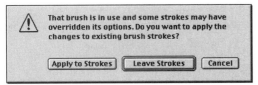

That brush is in use and some strokes may have overridden its options. Do you want to apply the changes to existing brush strokes?

[Apply to Strokes] [Leave Strokes] [Cancel]

1 *If you modify a brush that has been applied to objects in the file, this prompt will appear.*

2 *The Angle and Diameter were set to Random in the Calligraphic Brush Options dialog and Apply to Strokes was clicked when the prompt appeared. The brushstrokes* ***update*** *on the object.*

Choose **Pressure** and move the Variation slider to define a range within which the specific brush attribute value can respond to pressure from a stylus (available only with a graphics tablet). A light pressure will produce a brush attribute based on the set value for angle, roundness, or diameter minus the Variation value. A heavy pressure will produce a brush attribute based on the set value plus the Variation value.

5. Enter a value in the **Angle** field or drag the gray arrowhead in the preview box. The angle controls the thickness of the horizontals and verticals in the stroke. A 0° angle will produce a thin horizontal stroke and a thick vertical stroke. A 90° angle will produce the opposite effect. Other angles will produce different effects.

6. Enter a **Roundness** value or reshape the tip by dragging either black dot inward or outward on the ellipse.

7. Enter a value in the **Diameter** field or drag the slider for the size of the brush.

8. Click OK (Return/Enter). If the brush was already applied to existing paths in the document, an alert dialog will appear **1**. Click Apply to Strokes to update the existing strokes with the revised brush or click Leave Strokes to leave existing strokes unchanged **2**.

Create/Modify Calligraphic Brush

An art brush can be made from one or more objects, including a compound path, but not a gradient, gradient mesh, or mask. When it's applied to a path, an art brushstroke follows the shape of the path. If you reshape the path, the art brushstroke will stretch or bend to conform to the new path contour.

To create or modify an art brush:

1. To create a new brush, select one or more objects **1**, drag the object(s) onto the Brushes palette **2**, click New Art Brush **3**, then click OK (Return/Enter).
   or
   To modify an existing brush, double-click that brush on the Brushes palette. Or choose an art brush, then choose Brush Options from the palette menu.

2. For a new brush, enter a Name **4**.

3. For an existing brush, check the Preview box. Changes will preview immediately on any existing paths to which the art brush is currently applied.

4. Click a Direction button to control the orientation of the object on the path. The object will be drawn in the direction the arrow is pointing. The Direction will be more obvious for objects with a distinct directional orientation, like text outlines, a vase, or a leaf.

5. Enter a Size: Width to scale the brush. Check Proportional to preserve the proportions of the original object.

6. *Optional:* Check Flip Along to reverse the object on the path (left to right). Check Flip Across to reverse the object across the path (up and down).

7. Choose a Colorization option (see the sidebar on the next page).

8. Click OK (Return/Enter) **5**.

➤ You'll find art brushes in Illustrator's Animal Sample, Arrow Sample, Artistic Sample, Floral Sample, and Object Sample libraries.

Typeoutline

1 *To create a new art brush, select an object or objects. These objects are text outlines.*

2 *Drag the selected objects onto the Brushes palette.*

3 *Click New Art Brush.*

4 *Enter a Name for a new brush; change any of the settings to modify an existing brush.*

5 *The new art brush is applied to a path.*

The Colorization options

From the Colorization pop-up menu (available for all brush types except calligraphic), choose:

None, to leave the colors unchanged.

Tints, to change black areas in the brushstroke to the current stroke color at 100% and non-black areas to tints of the stroke color. White areas stay white. Use for grayscale or spot color.

Tints and Shades, to change non-black or white colors in the brushstroke to tints of the current stroke color. Black and white areas don't change. Use for grayscale.

Hue Shift, to apply the current stroke color to areas containing the most frequently used color on the object (the Key Color) and to change other colors in the brushstroke to related hues. Use for multicolored brushes.

If you're editing the brush itself (not a brush-stroke), you can click the **Key Color** eyedropper and then click on a color in the preview area of the dialog box to change the Key Color.

Click **Tips** in the Colorization Tips dialog box to learn more 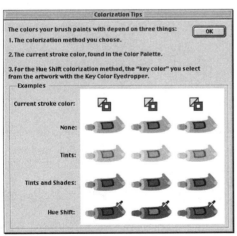.

1 *Click* Tips *in the Stroke Options dialog box to read these* Colorization Tips.

Beware! If you delete a brush from the Brushes palette that is currently applied to any objects in your illustration, you will have to choose whether to turn the brush-strokes into non-brushstroke objects or remove the brushstrokes from those objects.

To delete a brush from the Brushes palette:

1. Deselect all objects in your illustration.

2. Click the brush you want to delete.

3. Choose Delete Brush from the palette menu or click the Delete Brush button on the palette, then click Yes **2**.
   or
   Drag the selected brush over the Delete Brush button.
   or
   Option-click/Alt-click the Delete Brush button.

   Note: If the brush is currently applied to any objects in the current document, an alert dialog will appear **3**. Click Expand Strokes to turn the brushstrokes into non-brushstroke objects or click Remove Strokes to remove them from the objects.

➤ To restore the deleted brush to the palette, choose Undo immediately. Or, if the brush is from a library, you can add it again (see page 252).

➤ To delete all the brushes that are not being used in a file, choose Select All Unused from the Brushes palette menu, then use any method in step 2, above, to delete the selected brushes.

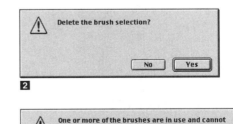

2

3

The pattern brush renders patterns along the edge of a closed or open path, and can be used to create custom frames, borders, or other decorative elements. You can use up to five different-shaped tile pieces when you create a path pattern: a Side tile, an Outer Corner tile, an Inner Corner tile, a Start tile, and an End tile. Each type of tile adapts to fit its assigned location on the path. Here's how to design your own tiles.

To create tiles for a pattern brush:

1. Draw closed path shapes for the side pattern tile. Try to limit the tile to about an inch wide, two inches at the most. You can resize it later via the Pattern Brush Options dialog box.

2. Since a pattern brush places side tiles perpendicular to the path, you should rotate any design that is taller than it is wide. To do this, choose the Selection tool, select the shapes for the side tile, double-click the Rotate tool, enter an Angle of 90°, then click OK.

3. Draw separate shapes for the corner, start, and end tiles **1**, if necessary, to complete the design. Corner tiles should be square, and they should be exactly the same height as the rotated side tile.

4. Choose the Selection tool, then select one of the tile shapes.

5. Drag the selection onto the Swatches palette **2**, then deselect the tile shape.

6. Double-click the new swatch. Enter a name in the Swatch Name field. Type words like "side," "outer," "start," and "end" after the tile name to help you remember the tile's placement. Click OK (Return/Enter) **3**.

7. Repeat steps 4 through 6 for the other tile shapes.

8. Follow the steps on the next page to make the new tiles that are now on the Swatches palette into a pattern brush **4**.

➤ You don't *have* to use a bounding rectangle behind the shapes when you a create pattern brush tile, but you *can* do so if

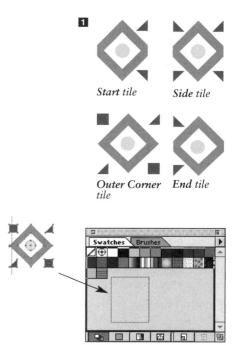

1

Start tile *Side tile*

Outer Corner tile *End tile*

2 *Drag the tile shape onto the Swatches palette.*

3 *Swatch Options dialog box.*

4 *The pattern tiles made into a pattern brush and then applied to a path.*

Tiles for a Pattern Brush

Side tile | Outer corner tile | Inner corner tile | Start tile | End tile

The Pattern Brush Options dialog box.

it helps you fit the tiles together. Apply a fill and stroke of None to the rectangle, and make sure none of the pattern shapes extend beyond it. The rectangle won't act as a cropping device as it would in a pattern fill.

➤ When they're applied to a path, corner tiles will be rotated 90° for each corner of the path, starting from the upper left corner.

➤ Apply global process fill and stroke colors to the tile shapes, and name the colors appropriately so they can be readily associated with the tile. The tiles can then be recolored easily by changing the global process colors.

➤ To make geometric shapes look more hand drawn, before making shapes into a pattern brush, apply Effect menu > Distort & Transform > Roughen at a low setting.

To create a pattern brush:

1. Create tiles for the pattern brush (instructions start on the previous page).

2. Click the New Brush button on the Brushes palette 🔲, click New Pattern Brush, then click OK.

3. Enter a Name.

4. Click a tile button (along the top) to assign the pattern to that part of a path, then click a pattern name on the scroll list ■. (The scroll list displays the tiles that are currently on the Swatches palette.) Repeat for the other tile buttons, if desired.

   Use the icons under the buttons to distinguish one type of tile from another. To assign no pattern for a position on the path, choose None. For a round object, you'll need to assign only a Side tile.

5. Click OK (Return/Enter). Apply the brush to a path, and then modify the path, or modify the brush by following the steps on the next page.

(Continued on the following page)

Create a Pattern Brush

➤ If you reshape a path that has a pattern brushstroke, the pattern will reshape along with the path. Corner and side tiles will be added or removed as needed.

➤ Effect menu commands can be applied to objects to be used in a pattern tile or to an object to which a pattern is applied.

➤ Illustrator's Border Sample library contains pattern brushes, and additional pattern brushes can be found in the Illustrator Extras > Pattern & Texture Libraries folder on the Adobe Illustrator 9 CD-ROM.

To modify a pattern brush:

1. Double-click the pattern brush you want to modify.
or
Click a pattern brush, then choose Brush Options from the palette menu.

2. Check the Preview box. Changes will preview on any existing paths to which the pattern is currently applied.

3. To change tiles, click a **tile** button, then click a pattern name on the scroll list **1**. Repeat for the other tile buttons, if desired. Use the icons under the buttons to distinguish one type of tile from another. To assign no pattern for a position on the path, choose None. For a round object, you need to assign only one tile. *Note:* To restore the settings for a selected tile button (from when the dialog box was opened), click Original on the scroll list.

4. Do any of the following:

Enter a new Size: **Scale** percentage for the pattern tiles.

To add blank space between pattern tiles, enter an amount in the Size: **Spacing** field.

To alter the pattern tile's orientation on the path, check the **Flip Along** and/or **Flip Across** box. Be sure to preview this—you may not like the results.

In the Fit area, click **Stretch to fit** to have Illustrator shorten or lengthen the tiles, where necessary, to fit on the path. Click

*A **pattern** brushstroke.*

Diane Margolin

1 *Reassign different tiles and choose other options in the **Pattern Brush Options** dialog.*

To create this pattern, Diane Margolin turned on the "Stretch to fit" option, and used Side, Outer Corner, and Inner Corner tile shapes.

Diane Margolin

Add space to fit to have Illustrator add blank space between tiles, where necessary, to fit the pattern along the path, factoring in the Spacing amount, if one was entered.

For a rectangular path, if you click **Approximate path**, the pattern tiles will be applied slightly inside or outside the path, rather than centered on the path, in order to produce even tiling.

5. For the **Colorization** option, see the sidebar on page 259.

6. Click OK (Return/Enter). If the pattern brush is currently applied to a path or paths in the file, an alert dialog will appear. Click Apply to Strokes to update the existing strokes or click Leave Strokes to leave them unchanged.

In addition to editing a brush via its Options dialog, you can also edit a brush by reshaping or recoloring it manually.

To edit a scatter, art, or pattern brush manually:

1. Drag the brush from the Brushes palette onto a blank area of the artboard (**1**–**2**, next page).

2. To recolor or transform the entire brush, select it using the Selection tool (**3**, next page). To recolor or transform individual objects within the brush or individual pattern brush tiles, select them using the Direct-selection tool or the Layers palette.

3. For a **scatter** or **art** brush:

Choose the Selection tool (V), and select the modified brush object or objects. Start dragging the objects onto the Brushes palette, hold down Option/Alt when you pass over the Brushes palette, then release the mouse when the pointer is over the original brush icon and the icon is highlighted. To save over the original brush, leave the name as is. To make the revised brush into a new brush, in addition to the original, enter a new name. Click OK (Return/ Enter).

(Continued on the following page)

Edit Brush Manually

For a **pattern** brush:

Drag each revised tile individually onto the Swatches palette, then deselect all the tiles on the artboard.

Double-click each new swatch on the Swatches palette, enter an appropriate name, then click OK.

Double-click the original pattern brush on the Brushes palette, reassign the new tiles to the appropriate tile buttons (see page 262), then click OK. If the brush is currently applied to paths in the document, an alert dialog box will appear. Click **Apply to Strokes** to update those paths with the revised brush or click **Leave Strokes** to leave the existing brushstrokes unchanged **4**–**5**.

or

Start dragging the new pattern tile shape, hold down Option/Alt as you pass over the Brushes palette, and release the mouse when the new tile is over a specific tile slot to replace only that highlighted tile. The Pattern Brush Options dialog box will open with the new tile in the chosen tile position. Click OK.

➤ The tile slots for a pattern brush on the Brushes palette are arranged, from left to right, in the following order: Outer Corner, Side, Inner Corner, Start, and End.

To create a new brush library:

1. Create brushes in an Illustrator file or move them to the current document's Brushes palette from other libraries.

2. Choose File menu > Save, and save the file in the Adobe Illustrator 9 > Brush Libraries folder. Use an appropriate name for the type of brushes.

3. Re-launch Illustrator. The new library will appear on the Window menu > Brush Libraries submenu.

➤ To make a brush library appear on the Brush Libraries submenu, you can also drag the saved Illustrator file into the Adobe Illustrator 9 > Brush Libraries folder, then re-launch Illustrator.

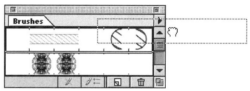

1 *The original pattern brushstroke.*

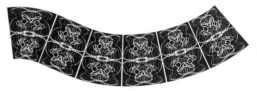

2 *Drag the brush onto the* **artboard**.

 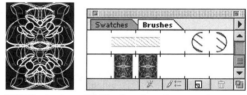

3 *Edit the pat-* **4** *The brush updates on the*
tern **manually**. *Brushes palette.*

5 *The* **edited** *pattern brushstroke.*

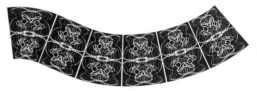

Create New Brush Library

1 *Select an object or objects to which a brush has been applied.*

2 *Choose* **Stroke Options** *for the brush.*

3 *The brushstroke is altered on the object.*

If you edit a brush, every object to which that brush has been applied will update to reflect the changes. Follow these instructions if you want to modify a brushstroke on a selected object or objects without editing the brush itself.

To change the stroke options for an individual object:

1. Select one or more objects to which the *same* brush is currently applied **1**.

2. If you want to recolor the brushstroke, choose a stroke color now.

3. Click the Options of Selected Object button on the Brushes palette ![icon].

4. Check the Preview box **2** (and **1**–**2**, next page).

5. For a scatter brushstroke, follow step 4 starting on page 254.

    For a calligraphic brushstroke, follow steps 4–7 starting on page 256.

    For an art brushstroke, follow steps 5–6 on page 258.

    For a pattern brushstroke, follow step 4 starting on page 262.

6. From the **Colorization** pop-up menu (this is *not* available for calligraphic brushes), choose:

    None to leave the colors unchanged.

    Tints to change black areas in the brushstroke to the stroke color at 100% and non-black areas to tints of the current stroke color. White areas stay white.

    Tints and Shades to change non-black or white colors in the brushstroke to tints of the current stroke color. Black and white areas stay as they are.

    Hue Shift to apply the current stroke color to areas containing the most frequently used color on the object (the Key Color) and to change other colors in the brushstroke to related hues.

    Note: If you're editing the brush itself (not a brushstroke), you can click the

(Continued on the following page)

Change Stroke Options for Individual Object

Key Color eyedropper and then click on a color in the brush or pattern tile preview area of the dialog box to change the Key Color.

7. *Optional:* Click Tips to see an illustration of the Colorization options.

8. Click OK (Return/Enter) (**3**, previous page). Only the selected object will change; the brush itself on the Brushes palette will not change.

➤ To restore the original brushstroke to the object, select the object, click a different brush on the Brushes palette, then click back on the original brush.

➤ If you've used the Options of Selected Object option to customize a brushstroke on a selected object and you now want to apply a different art brush with those new options to the same object, Option-click/Alt-click a different brush.

Here's a way to create a variation on an existing brush—a slimmer or fatter version, for example.

To duplicate a brush:

1. Click the brush you want to duplicate.

2. Choose Duplicate Brush from the palette menu.
   or
   Drag the selected brush over the New Brush button **3–4**.

   The word "copy" will be appended to name of the brush. To modify the brush, see the individual instructions for that brush type earlier in this chapter.

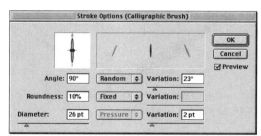

3 *To duplicate a brush, drag it over the New Brush button.*

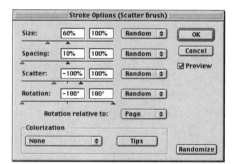

1 *Stroke Options for a calligraphic brush.*

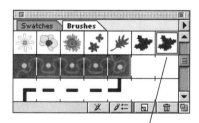

2 *Stroke Options for a scatter brush.*

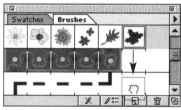

4 *The duplicate brush appears next to the original brush.*

Duplicate Brush

COMBINE PATHS | 16

In this chapter, you will learn to create a compound path using the Compound Path > Make command or the Minus Front command, to release a compound path, and to recolor parts of a compound path.

You will also learn about the Pathfinder commands, which are applied via the Pathfinder palette. The Pathfinders create a new, closed object by uniting, splitting, cropping, intersecting, etc.

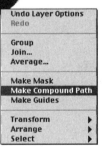

1 *Place smaller objects on top of a larger object and make sure all the objects are selected.*

2 *Then Control-click/ Right-click and choose* **Make Compound Path** *from the context menu.*

Compounds

The compound path command joins two or more objects into one object—until or unless the compound path is released. Where the original objects overlapped, a transparent hole is created, through which shapes or patterns behind the object are revealed. Regardless of their original paint attributes, all the objects in a compound path are painted with the attributes of the backmost object, and they become one unit.

To create a compound path:

1. Arrange the objects you want to see through in front of a larger shape **1**. Closed paths work best. As of Illustrator 9, you can make a compound out of a path that has a brushstroke. *improved*

2. Choose the Selection tool (V), then marquee or Shift-click all the objects.
   or
   Choose the Lasso tool (Y), then drag around all the objects.

3. Choose Object menu > Compound Path > Make (Command-8/Ctrl-8).
   or
   If the objects aren't grouped, you can Control-click/Right-click on the artboard and choose Make Compound Path from the context menu **2**.

(Continued on the following page)

Create Compound Path

The frontmost objects will cut through the backmost object like a cookie cutter . The words "<compound path>" will appear on the Layers palette. Any areas where the frontmost objects originally overlapped each other or any parts of the frontmost objects that originally extended beyond the edge of the backmost object will be painted with the color of the backmost object .

If the holes don't happen, see page 270.

➤ Regardless of which layers the objects were on originally, the compound path will be placed on the frontmost object's layer.

➤ The Minus Front command on the Pathfinder palette also creates a compound if all the objects are completely on top of (don't hang over the edge of) the bottommost object. See page 272.

➤ Don't overdo it. Too many compound paths in the same illustration or a compound path that is made up of very complex shapes could cause a printing error.

To add an object to a compound path:

1. Using the Selection tool or the Lasso tool, select both the compound path and the object you want to add to it.

2. Choose Object menu > Compound Paths > Make (Command-8/Ctrl-8).

Working with compounds

➤ Use the Selection tool to select or move a whole compound path.

➤ Use the Direct-selection tool to select or move part of a compound path.

➤ Option-click/Alt-click with the Direct-selection tool to select a subpath within a compound.

➤ You can reshape any path within a compound by the usual means (e.g., add points, delete points, use the Scissors).

➤ Only one fill color can be applied to a compound path at a time.

➤ Effects, transparency, and blending modes can be applied to a compound path. *new*

1 *The objects are converted into a compound path.*

2 *A background object is placed behind the compound path (and a white stroke is applied).*

1 *Click on the compound path.*

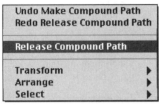

2 *Choose Release Compound Path from the context menu.*

3 *The compound path is released. The buttonholes are no longer transparent.*

4 *Type outlines (a compound path).*

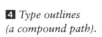

5 *The compound path is released into separate objects. (We moved the counter of the "P.")*

You can release a compound path back into its individual objects at any time.

To release a compound path:

1. Choose the Selection tool.
2. Click on the compound path **1**.
3. Choose Object menu > Compound Path > Release (Command-Option-8/ Ctrl-Alt-8) **2**.
   or
   Control-click/Right-click on the artboard and choose Release Compound Path from the context menu.

   All the objects will be selected and they will be painted with the attributes, effects, and appearances from the compound path, not their original, pre-compound colors **3**. Use Smart Guides to figure out which shape is what.

➤ The objects will all be nested within the same layer or sublayer, regardless of which layer they were on when the compound was created.

➤ A compound path is created automatically when the Create Outlines command is used on a type character that has a counter (interior shape). If you release this type of compound path, the counter will become a separate shape with the same paint attributes and appearances as the outer part of the letterform **4**–**5**.

➤ To remove an object from a compound path: without releasing the whole compound, select the object with the Direct-selection tool, then press Delete/Backspace. Or cut and paste the object if you want to save it (and then move or recolor it).

Release Compound Path

You can remove the fill color of any shape in a compound and make the object transparent, or vice versa, by flicking the Reverse Path Direction switch on the Attributes palette.

To reverse an object's fill in a compound path:

1. Deselect the compound path (Command-Shift-A/Ctrl-Shift-A).

2. Choose the Direct-selection tool (A).

3. Click the object in the compound path whose color you want to reverse .

4. Display the Attributes palette (Window menu > Show Attributes).

5. Click the Reverse Path Direction Off button or the Reverse Path Direction On button—whichever button isn't currently highlighted **2**–**4**.

➤ If neither of the Reverse Path Direction buttons is highlighted, you have selected the whole compound path. Select only one path in the compound and try again.

➤ If any effects have been applied to the compound, clicking either Reverse Path Direction button will have no effect.

1 *Click an object in a compound path.*

2 *Reverse Path Direction Off button*   **3** *Reverse Path Direction On button*

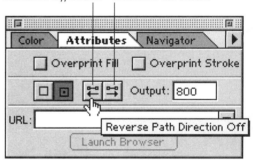

4 *The color of two of the buttonholes is reversed.*

Reverse Object Fill in Compound Path

Repeat yourself

To repeat the last-applied Pathfinder command, choose **Repeat** [command name] from the Pathfinder palette menu (Command-4/Ctrl-4).

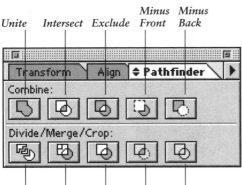

Unite   Intersect   Exclude   Minus Front   Minus Back

Divide   Trim   Merge   Crop   Outline

1 *The original objects.* **2** *Unite.*

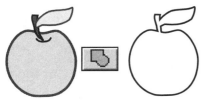

3 *The original objects.*

4 *Intersect. Only areas that originally overlapped other objects remain.*

5 *The original objects.*

6 *Exclude. Two paths were turned into four.*

Pathfinders

Most of Illustrator's powerful and useful Pathfinder commands create a new, closed path or a compound path (a group of two or more closed shapes) from two or more selected and overlapping objects by joining, splitting, or cropping them. The Pathfinder commands fall into four general categories: combining, dividing, color mixing, and trapping. They are applied via the **Pathfinder palette** (shown at left). First, a few pointers:

➤ For the best results, apply Pathfinders to filled, **closed** paths with no strokes. If a Pathfinder is applied to an open path, Illustrator closes the path before performing the command. If you want to control how a path is closed, apply Object menu > Path > Outline Stroke before applying a Pathfinder (see page 274).

➤ As of Illustrator 9.0, Pathfinders can be applied to a gradient mesh, a pattern fill, and a path with a brushstroke. *improved*

➤ To read about Pathfinders and effects, see page 310. The Mix commands are discussed on page 336, the Trap command on page 438.

➤ To use type as path shapes, convert it into outlines first.

Combining commands

Unite: Joins the outer edges of selected objects into one compound path object. Interior objects are deleted. The paint attributes and appearances of the frontmost object are applied to the new object **1**–**2** (see also page 119). Unite can be used to close an open path.

Intersect: Deletes any non-overlapping areas from overlapping, selected objects. The paint attributes and appearances of the frontmost object are applied to the new object **3**–**4**. The selected objects must partially—not completely—overlap to apply this command.

Exclude: Areas where an even number of selected objects overlap become transparent; areas where an odd number of objects overlap are filled. The paint attributes and appearances of the frontmost object are applied to the new object **5**–**6**.

Unite; Intersect; Exclude

271

Minus Front: Subtracts the frontmost selected objects from the backmost object. The paint attributes and appearances of the backmost object, including any stroke, are preserved. This command works like the Make Compound Paths command if the original frontmost objects do not extend beyond the edge of the backmost object **1**–**2**.

Note: If you want the backmost object to be divided into separate objects and *not* become a compound path, make sure the edges of the frontmost objects extend beyond the edge of the backmost object before clicking Minus Front **3**–**4**. Overhanging areas will be deleted.

Minus Back: Subtracts the backmost selected objects from the frontmost object. Parts of objects that overlap the frontmost object are deleted. The paint attributes and appearances of the frontmost object are applied to the new path **5**–**6**. The selected objects must at least partially overlap for this command to produce an effect.

Dividing commands

These commands divide overlapping areas of selected paths into separate, non-overlapping closed paths or lines. Objects with effects may product different results than objects without them.

Note: If the "Divide & Outline will remove unpainted artwork" box is checked in the Pathfinder Options dialog box (open from the palette menu), any non-overlapping areas of paths that originally had a fill of None will be deleted after the Divide or Outline command is applied.

Divide: The new objects will keep their original fill and stroke colors **7**–**8**.

➤ After applying the Divide command, click away from all objects to deselect them, choose the Direct-selection tool, click any of the objects, and apply new fill colors; or apply a fill of None to make an object see-through; or apply transparency. Or remove individual objects to create cutouts.

1 *The frontmost object doesn't go beyond the edge of the black square.*

2 *Minus Front turns it into a compound path.*

3 *In this case, the lines go beyond the box.*

4 *After clicking* **Minus Front**, *the box is divided into three separate, grouped objects, and it doesn't become a compound path.*

5 *The original objects.*

6 *Minus Back works like an upside-down cookie cutter.*

7 *The original objects.*

8 *Divide. (We recolored the resulting shapes.).*

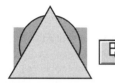

1 *The original objects.*

2 *Trim (pulled apart afterwards).*

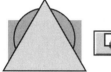

3 *The original objects.*

4 *Merge (pulled apart afterwards).*

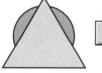

5 *The original objects.*

6 *Crop.*

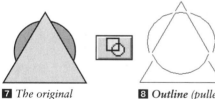

7 *The original objects.*

8 *Outline (pulled apart afterwards).*

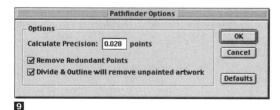

9

Trim: The frontmost object shape is preserved; parts of objects that are behind it and overlap it are deleted. Adjacent or overlapping objects of the same color or shade remain separate (unlike the Merge command). Objects keep their original solid or gradient fill colors and appearances; stroke colors are deleted (except if effects have been applied) **1**–**2**.

Merge: The frontmost object shape is preserved; adjacent or overlapping objects with the same fill attributes are combined. Objects retain their original solid or gradient fill colors and appearances; stroke colors are deleted (except if effects have been applied) **3**–**4**.

Crop: The frontmost object "trims" away areas of selected objects that extend beyond its borders. The remaining non-overlapping objects retain only their fill colors; stroke colors are removed (except if effects have been applied). The frontmost object is also removed **5**–**6**. Unlike a mask, the original objects can't be restored, unless you Undo immediately.

Outline: Objects turn into stroked line segments **7**–**8**. The fill colors of the original objects become the stroke colors (transparency settings are preserved), and fill colors are removed. Use this command to create strokes on individual sides of a copy of objects that originally had a stroke of None.

The Pathfinder Options are preferences for all the Pathfinder commands.

To choose Pathfinder options:

1. Choose Pathfinder Options from the Pathfinder palette menu.

2. Change any of the following **9**:

    The higher the **Calculate Precision** value, the more precisely a Pathfinder command is applied, but the longer it takes to process.

    With **Remove Redundant Points** checked, any anchor points that have a duplicate in the exact same location are deleted when the Pathfinder command is applied.

    For the Divide & Outline option, see the Note on the previous page.

Trim; Merge; Crop; Outline; Pathfinder Options

Outline Stroke

If you're going to apply a Pathfinder command to an open path, you can use the Outline Stroke (formerly called "Outline Path") command first to turn the stroke into a filled object instead of letting the Pathfinder command close it automatically. Another reason for using this command is to convert a line or a stroke into a closed path so it can be filled with a gradient or prepared more easily for trapping. *Note:* The Object menu > Expand command with just the Stroke box checked produces the same effect.

To turn a stroke or an open path into a filled object:

1. Select an object that has a stroke color ▉.

2. Choose Object menu > Path > Outline Stroke. The width of the new filled object will be the same thickness as the original stroke ▉.

Outline Stroke tips

➤ The Outline Stroke command produces the most predictable results when applied to an object that has wide curves. It may produce odd corner shapes when applied to an object that has sharp corners. You can use the Unite button on the Pathfinder palette to eliminate odd corner shapes that may result.

➤ If you apply the Outline Stroke command to a closed path to which fill and stroke colors have been applied, you'll end up with two separate objects: a fill object and a compound stroke object.

▉ *Select an object that has a stroke. To produce the button shown below, a gradient fill and a stroke were applied to the object before applying the* **Outline Stroke** *command.*

▉ *The* **Outline Stroke** *command converted the stroke into a compound path. To produce this button, the compound path (outer ring) was selected with the Selection tool and a gradient fill was applied to it. Then the Gradient tool was dragged downward across it to make it contrast with the gradient fill in the inner circle. To modify the gradient in the inner circle, we clicked its selection area on the Layers palette.*

GRADIENTS 17

A gradient fill is a gradual blend between two or more colors. In this chapter you will learn how to fill an object or objects with a gradient, how to create and save gradients, how to edit a gradient using the Gradient palette, and how to change the way a gradient fills an object or objects using the Gradient tool.

You will also learn how to use the Gradient Mesh tool and the Gradient Mesh command to create painterly gradient mesh objects, and how to modify mesh objects by adding, moving, deleting, or recoloring mesh points and lines.

Chris Spollen, **New York Retro**

Gradient basics

Gradients are used to create volume in realistic objects or to soften abstract shapes. The simplest gradient fill consists of a starting color and an ending color, with the point where the colors are equally mixed together located midway between them. A gradient can be **linear** (side-to-side) or **radial** (out-from-center). You can apply a gradient fill to one object or across several objects. A set of predefined gradients is supplied with Illustrator, but you can also create your own gradients using the **Gradient palette**.

Once an object is filled with a gradient, you can use the **Gradient tool** to modify how the fill is distributed within the object. You can change the direction of the gradient or change how quickly one color blends into another. You can also change the location of the center of a radial gradient fill.

Note: Open the Color, Gradient, and Swatches palettes for the instructions in this chapter.

Follow these instructions to apply an existing gradient to an object. You can use a gradient that's supplied with Illustrator, but you're more than likely going to want or need to create your own. To create your own gradient, follow the instructions that begin on the next page.

To fill an object with a gradient:

1. Select an object, then click a gradient swatch on the Swatches palette **1**–**2**.
   or
   Drag a gradient swatch from the Swatches palette or the Gradient Fill box from the Gradient palette over a selected or unselected object.

2. *Optional:* For a Linear gradient, enter a different Angle on the Gradient palette.

➤ If an object now has a solid color or pattern fill, but it previously had a gradient fill, click the Gradient Fill box on the Gradient palette **3** or click the Gradient button on the Toolbox (. [period]) to reapply the gradient.

➤ To apply a gradient to a stroke, first apply Object menu > Path > Outline Stroke to convert the stroke into a closed object (see page 274).

➤ To fill type with a gradient, first convert it into outlines (Type menu > Create Outlines). Or select the type, click Fill on the Appearance palette, then click a gradient swatch.

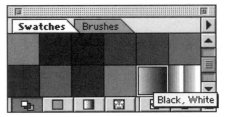

1 *A gradient is selected on the Swatches palette.*

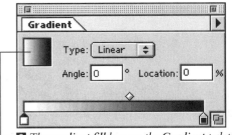

2 *An object filled with a radial gradient.*

3 *The gradient fill box on the Gradient palette.*

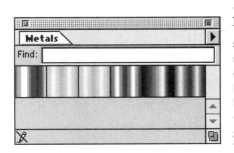

More gradients

To access the other gradient libraries that are supplied with Illustrator, choose Window menu > Swatch Libraries > Other Library, open the Adobe Illustrator 9 > Other Libraries > Gradients folder, highlight the library you want to open, then click Open. Click on swatches on the library palette to get them into your file's Swatches palette.

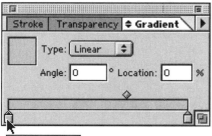

1 First click the **Gradient Fill** box here...

2 ...or on the Toolbox.

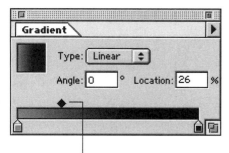

3 Choose a color for the left and right gradient sliders.

4 Move the **midpoint diamond** to adjust the amount of each color.

A gradient can be composed of all CMYK colors or all RGB process colors, tints of the same spot color, or multiple spot colors. *improved*

To create and save a two-color gradient:

1. Display the full Gradient palette, with its options panel.

2. Click the Gradient Fill box on the Gradient palette **1**.
   or
   Click the Gradient (middle) button on the Toolbox **2**.

3. Drag a swatch from the Swatches palette over the left gradient slider on the Gradient palette **3**.
   or
   Click the left gradient slider on the Gradient palette. Then use the Color palette to mix a color; or Option-click/ Alt-click a swatch on the Swatches palette; or Shift-click a color anywhere in the document window using the Eyedropper tool.

4. Repeat the previous step to choose a color for the right gradient slider.

5. From the Type pop-up menu on the Gradient palette, choose Linear or Radial.

6. *Optional:* Move the midpoint diamond to the right to produce more of the starting color than the ending color or to the left to produce more of the ending color than the starting color **4**.

7. *Optional:* For a Linear gradient, you can change the Angle.

8. If you select another object or swatch now, the new gradient will be lost— unless you save it. To save the gradient:

   Drag the Gradient Fill box from the Gradient palette onto the Swatches palette.
   or
   Click the Gradient Fill box on the Gradient palette, then click the New Swatch button at the bottom of the Swatches palette. **⬗**
   or

   (Continued on the following page)

(Continued on the following page)

Create Two-Color Gradient

To type a name for the gradient as you save it, Option-click/Alt-click the New Swatch button, enter a name, then click OK.

➤ To use an existing gradient as a starting point for a new gradient, click a gradient swatch on the Swatches palette, choose Duplicate Swatch from the palette menu, then edit the gradient.

➤ To swap the starting and ending colors (or any other two colors) in a radial or linear gradient, Option-drag/Alt-drag one slider over the other.

➤ To delete a gradient swatch from the Swatches palette, drag it over the Delete (trash) button.

➤ If you're going to color separate a gradient that contains more than one spot color, talk to your prepress specialist. You can assign a different screen angle to each color using File menu > Separation Setup (uncheck the Convert to Process box). See page 432. You can also convert each spot color to process by clicking the spot color slider, then choosing a process color model from the Color palette menu.

It's hard to tell whether a gradient looks right until it's been applied to an object. Luckily, editing a gradient is easy.

To edit colors in an existing gradient:

1. Choose the Selection tool. Click an object that contains the gradient you want to edit. (For type, click the type, then click the Fill attribute on the Appearance palette that has a gradient icon.)
   or
   Click the gradient swatch on the Swatches palette that you want to edit.

2. On the Gradient palette, click the gradient slider that you want to change, then choose a color from the Color palette.
   or
   Drag a swatch from the Swatches palette over a gradient slider.

➤ To copy a gradient slider color, Option-drag/Alt-drag the slider.

Color to white

To color separate a gradient that changes from a spot color to white on one piece of film (one plate), create a gradient with the spot color as the starting color and 0% tint of the **same** color as the ending color.

Edit a Gradient

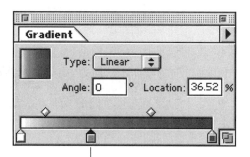

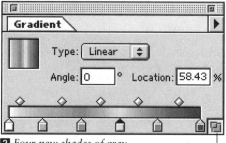

1 *Click below the gradient bar to add a new slider, then choose a color.*

2 *Four new shades of gray were added to this gradient.* *You can drag the resize box to widen the palette if your gradient contains a lot of colors.*

A gradient can contain over 100 colors. The colors can be changed and the number of sliders can be adjusted at any time. *improved*

To add colors to a gradient:

1. Follow the steps on the previous two pages to produce a two-color gradient.
or
On the Swatches palette, click an existing gradient swatch.

2. On the Gradient palette, click below the gradient bar to add a gradient slider **1**. Then use the Color palette to mix a color or Option/Alt click a swatch on the Swatches palette.
or
Drag a swatch from the Swatches palette to the gradient bar on the Gradient palette. A new slider will be created automatically.

3. *Do any of the following optional steps:*

Move a slider to the left or to the right to change how abruptly that color spreads into its adjacent colors.

Move the midpoint diamond located above the gradient bar to the left or right of the new color to adjust the amount of that color.

To remove a slider, drag it downward out of the Gradient palette.

Repeat step 2 to add more colors **2**–**3**.

4. If you edited a gradient from the Swatches palette and you want to keep the modified version, you have to save it as a new swatch (see step 8 on page 277).

➤ To make a gradient appear in every new Illustrator document, save it to either or both of the two Illustrator Startup files (see page 381).

3 *Multi-colored gradients.*

You've already learned how to edit a gradient swatch. Now you'll learn to adjust how a gradient looks in a particular object. Using the Gradient tool, you can manually change the direction of a linear fill or change the location of the center of a radial gradient fill. On the next page, you'll learn how to apply a gradient across a series of objects.

To use the Gradient tool:

1. Apply a gradient fill to an object, and keep the object selected.

2. Choose the Gradient tool (G) **1**.

3. Drag across the object in any direction (e.g., right-to-left or diagonally):

   To blend the colors abruptly, drag a short distance (as in **3**–**4**). To blend the colors more gradually across a wider span, drag a longer distance.

   To reverse the order of the fill colors, drag in the opposite direction.

   For a radial gradient, position the pointer where you want the center of the fill to be, then click or drag **5**–**6**.

   You can start to drag or finish dragging outside the object. In this case, the colors at the beginning or end of the gradient fill won't appear in the object.

4. If you don't like the results, drag in a different direction. Keep trying until you're happy with the results.

1 *Gradient* tool.

2 *The original linear gradient fill.*

3 *Dragging a short distance with the **Gradient** tool.*

4 *After using the Gradient tool, as shown in the previous figure).*

5 *The original radial gradient fill.*

6 *After dragging using the Gradient tool. The center of the gradient was moved.*

To spread a gradient across multiple objects:

1. Select several objects, and fill them all with the same gradient **1**.

2. Choose the Gradient tool (G).

3. Drag across all the objects **2**. Shift-drag to constrain the angle to a multiple of 45° (actually, to a multiple of the current Constrain Angle in Edit menu > Preferences > General).

➤ Once multiple objects are filled with the same gradient, don't combine them into a compound path. The resulting object may be too complex to print.

1 *The original gradient fill. The gradient starts anew in each object.*

2 *After dragging across all the objects using the **Gradient tool** in the direction shown by the arrow. The gradient starts in the first type outline and ends in the last type outline.*

Gradient meshes

What is a gradient mesh?

A gradient mesh is an object that contains multiple gradients in various directions and locations with seamless transitions between them . Using the gradient mesh features, you'll be able to easily render and modify photorealistic or painterly objects and complex modeled surfaces, such as skin tones, objects of nature, machinery, etc.

Both the **Gradient Mesh tool** and the **Create Gradient Mesh command** convert a standard object into a mesh object with lines and intersecting points. A gradient mesh can be produced from any path object or bitmapped image, even a radial or linear blend, but not from a compound path, text object, or linked image (it must be rasterized first).

After you create a mesh object, you'll assign colors to mesh points or mesh patches. Then you'll manipulate the points and lines to push colors around in the object—sharpen or soften color transitions, or add or delete gradient colors. It's like a watercolor or airbrush drawing with a flexible armature above it. Reconfigure the armature, and the colors beneath the armature will shift right along with it.

Mesh building blocks

A mesh object consists of anchor points, mesh points, mesh lines, and mesh patches **2**. A gradient mesh can be reshaped by manipulating its anchor or mesh points or mesh lines.

- **Anchor points** on the bounding box appear as square points in the mesh. They are the standard Illustrator anchor points that can be added, deleted, or moved in order to reshape the overall object.

- **Mesh points** are diamond shaped (called "anchor points" by Smart Guides). They are used for assigning colors to gradients, and they can be added, deleted, or moved.

- **Mesh lines** crisscross the object to connect the mesh points. They act as guides for placing and moving points.

- A **mesh patch** is an area that is defined by four mesh points.

1 *Illustrator's* **gradient mesh** *features are ideal for rendering natural forms.*

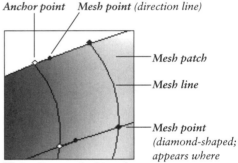

Anchor point   Mesh point (direction line)

Mesh patch

Mesh line

Mesh point (diamond-shaped; appears where two mesh lines intersect)

2 *Gradient mesh objects have anchor points, mesh points, mesh lines, and mesh patches. (This is a closeup.)*

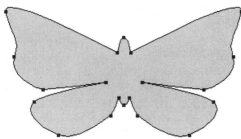

1 *Select an object that has a fill.*

2 *Gradient Mesh tool.*

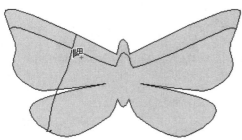

3 *Click on the object—it will convert immediately into a* ***gradient mesh*** *object.*

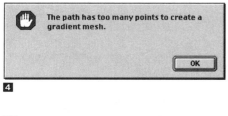

4

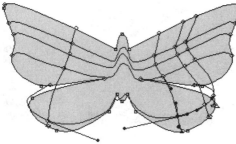

5 *Continue to click to create additional sets of mesh lines.*

Note: If you're converting a complex object into a gradient mesh, it's best to use the Create Gradient Mesh command. If you're converting simple objects, on the other hand, you can use either the Create Gradient Mesh command or the Gradient Mesh tool, whichever you prefer. The Gradient Mesh command creates more regularly spaced mesh points and lines than does the Gradient Mesh tool.

Beware! A mesh object cannot be converted back to a path object (except using Undo).

To convert an object into a gradient mesh using the Gradient Mesh tool:

1. Select an object (*not* a text object, compound path, or linked image), and apply a solid color fill to the object if it doesn't have one already **1**. The object can have an applied brushstroke, but the brushstroke will be removed. You can use a bitmap image. Copy the object if you want to preserve a non-gradient mesh version of it.

2. Choose the Gradient Mesh tool (U) **2**.

3. Click on the object to place a mesh point. The object will be converted immediately into a mesh object with the minimum number of mesh lines **3**.

    If you get an alert box **4**, it means you must remove points from the path before you can convert it into a gradient mesh. You can do this using the Delete-anchor-point tool or the Smooth tool.

4. Click to create other sets of mesh lines **5**. Now proceed to page 285 to learn how to apply colors to the mesh.

Create Gradient Mesh

The path has too many points to create a gradient mesh.

OK

Note: Complex gradient meshes increase file size and require a significant amount of computation, so keep them as simple as possible. You'll be less likely to get a printing error if you build a drawing from a few mesh objects than from one large, complex one.

To convert an object into a gradient mesh using a command:

1. Choose the Selection tool, select an object (*not* a text object, compound path, or linked image), and apply a solid color fill to the object if it doesn't have one already. The object can have an applied brushstroke, but the brushstroke will be removed. You can use a bitmap image. Copy the object if you want to preserve a non-gradient mesh version of it.

2. Choose Object menu > Create Gradient Mesh.

3. Click the Preview box **1**.

4. Enter the number of horizontal Rows and vertical Columns for the mesh grid. The greater the number of Rows and Columns, the more complex the mesh.

5. From the Appearance pop-up menu, choose Flat for a uniform surface with no highlight; To Center for a highlight at the center of the object; or To Edge for a highlight at the object's edges.

6. If you chose the To Center or To Edge Appearance option, enter an intensity percentage for the white Highlight.

7. Click OK (Return/Enter) **2**–**4**. Now recolor the gradient mesh (instructions on the next page).

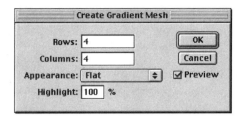

1 *The Create Gradient Mesh dialog box.*

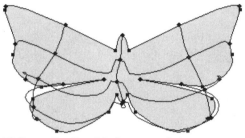

2 *Create Gradient Mesh command, Appearance: Flat.*

3 *Create Gradient Mesh command, Appearance: To Center.*

4 *Create Gradient Mesh command, Appearance: To Edge (shown here on a dark background so you can see the highlight on the edge).*

284

Create Gradient Mesh

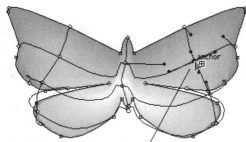

1 *Click an existing mesh point.*

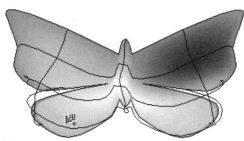

2 *The point is recolored.*

3 *Or click inside a mesh patch.*

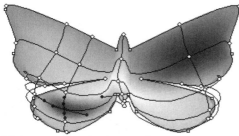

4 *A new mesh point is created.*

Each mesh point or mesh patch can be assigned a different color, and each color will blend into its surrounding colors. Click a mesh point to assign a color to a small area; click a mesh patch to assign a color to a wider area.

To recolor a gradient mesh:

1. Zoom in on a mesh object (you should still see the entire object in the document window, though), and **deselect** it!

2. Choose the Gradient Mesh tool (U) or the Direct-selection tool (A), click a mesh point **1**, then choose a fill color from the Color or Swatches palette **2**. You can use Smart Guides to help you locate mesh points (turn on Smart Guides from the View menu and check the Text Label Hints box in Edit menu > Preferences > Smart Guides).
   or
   Choose the Direct-selection tool (A), click the mesh object, then drag a color from the Color or Swatches palette over a mesh point or mesh patch.
   or
   Choose a fill color from the Color or Swatches palette, choose the Gradient Mesh tool (U), then click inside a mesh patch **3**–**4**. A new point with connecting mesh lines will be created in the fill color you chose.
   or
   Choose the Direct-selection tool (A), click a mesh patch, then choose a fill color from the Color or Swatches palette. The Direct-selection tool will not create a new point, but all four mesh points that surround the patch will be recolored.

➤ Read about other ways to recolor a mesh object on the next page.

Recolor Gradient Mesh

To add mesh points or lines:

1. Choose the Gradient Mesh tool (U).

2. Click anywhere on the mesh object. A new point and connecting mesh lines will appear, and the current fill color will be applied to that point.

   or

   Shift-click a mesh line to add a mesh point without applying the current fill color.

   or

   Click an existing mesh line to add a new line perpendicular to it **1**–**2**.

3. *Optional:* To recolor the new mesh point with a color from another part of the object, keep the point selected, choose the Eyedropper tool (I), then Shift-click a color in the object.

➤ You can also recolor a gradient mesh using Filter menu > Colors > Adjust Colors, Convert to CMYK (or Convert to RGB), Invert, or Saturate.

Follow these instructions to add or remove square-shaped (not diamond-shaped) anchor points from a mesh object. These points are used to reshape the edge of the overall mesh object—not to push colors around on the mesh. To add diamond-shaped mesh points with their connecting mesh lines, follow the previous set of instructions instead.

To add or remove square points:

1. Select a mesh object, and zoom in on it, if necessary.

2. To add an anchor point, choose the Add-anchor-point tool (+), then click the outer edge of the mesh object or click a mesh line inside the object **3**.

   or

   To delete an anchor point, choose the Delete-anchor-point tool (-), then click the anchor point you want to delete **4**.

improved

More color controls

To select and recolor multiple instances of the same color, choose the Direct-selection tool, click on a mesh point that contains the color you want to change, choose Edit menu > Select > **Same Fill Color**, then choose a new color from the Color palette or the Swatches palette.

To make a color area **smaller**, add more mesh lines around it in a different color. To **spread** a color, delete mesh points around it or assign the same color to adjacent mesh points.

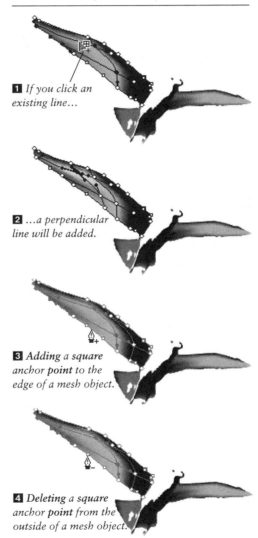

1 *If you click an existing line…*

2 *…a perpendicular line will be added.*

3 *Adding a square anchor* **point** *to the edge of a mesh object.*

4 *Deleting a square anchor* **point** *from the outside of a mesh object.*

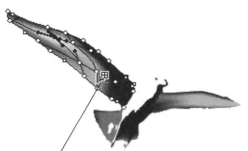

1 *Option-click/Alt-click a mesh point to delete it.*

2 *The point is deleted.*

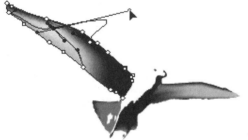

3 *Drag a direction line.*

To delete a mesh point:

1. Choose the Gradient Mesh tool (U).

2. Option-click/Alt-click on the point you want to delete (a minus sign will appear next to the pointer). The mesh lines that cross through that point will also be deleted **1**–**2**.

To reshape mesh lines:

1. Choose the Direct-selection tool (A), then click the gradient mesh object to select it.

2. Click a mesh point or an anchor point.

3. Lengthen or rotate either of the point's direction lines to reshape its adjacent mesh lines **3**. Shift-drag a direction line to constrain the angle of the line to a multiple of 45° or the current Constrain Angle (Edit menu > Preferences > General).
   or
   Drag a mesh point **4**. You can drag a point outside the object. This is an easy way to move mesh colors.
   or
   Drag a mesh patch **5**. This is like electronic sculpting. You can also drag a patch outside the object.
   or
   With the Gradient Mesh tool, Shift-drag a mesh point to drag it along an existing mesh line.

➤ To convert a point into a corner point with direction lines that move independently of each other, choose the Convert-direction-point tool (Shift-C), click the point, then drag a direction line.

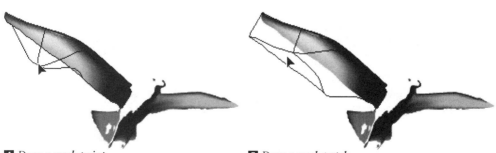

4 *Drag a mesh point.*

5 *Drag a mesh patch.*

Delete Mesh Points; Reshape Mesh Lines

To expand a standard gradient into separate objects:

1. Select the object that contains a gradient (not a gradient mesh) .

2. Choose Object menu > Expand.

3. Click Expand Gradient To: Specify, then enter the desired number of objects to be created **2**. To print a gradient successfully, you'll need to enter a number that's high enough to produce smooth color transitions.

4. Click OK (Return/Enter) **3**.

   Note: The resulting number of objects may not match the specified number of objects if there were minimal color changes in the original gradient.

➤ You could also use the Expand command to simplify a gradient fill that won't print.

➤ Option/Alt choose Object menu > Expand to expand a gradient using the last-used "Specify [ ] Objects" setting.

Here is another, albeit less useful, method for creating a mesh object.

To expand a radial or linear gradient into a gradient mesh:

1. Select an object that contains a radial or linear gradient **1**.

2. Choose Object menu > Expand.

3. Click Expand Gradient To: Gradient Mesh.

4. Click OK (Return/Enter) **4**. The resulting expanded objects can be a little confusing. You'll have a mask object that limits the gradient color area, with the gradient mesh object on top of it. Use the Layers palette to view the nested groups, clipping paths, and mesh.

Bird by Diane Margolin

1 *The original object contains a* **linear** *gradient.*

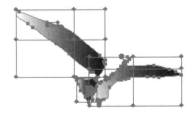

3 *After applying the* **Expand** *command, the gradient is converted into a series of separate rectangles, grouped with a clipping mask. Each rectangle is a different shade.*

4 *This is the original object after expanding it into a* **gradient mesh**.

Expand Command

APPEARANCES/STYLES 18

In this chapter you will learn how to create, apply, and modify appearance attributes. You will learn to save appearance attributes as styles, which are used to quickly apply sets of appearance attributes to an object, group, or layer. And you will also learn how to use live effects, which also change the appearance of an object without actually changing its underlying path.

This whole chapter is brand new!

1 *The **Appearance** palette is used to apply, restack, and remove **appearance attributes** from layers, sublayers, groups, objects, and styles. This screenshot illustrates the appearance attributes for an **object.***

Using appearances

Appearances, which make their debut in Illustrator 9, provide a whole new approach to object editing. Before appearances, you could apply only one stroke and fill to an object. With appearances, you can now apply multiple fills and strokes to the same object, and to each stroke or fill you can apply a different opacity level, blending mode, and Effect menu command. Furthermore, appearance attributes change how an object looks, but they don't actually alter the path's underlying shape. Appearances add flexibility—and complexity—to object editing.

Since appearance attributes only change an object's appearance, not its actual underlying path, you can save, close, and reopen an illustration and you'll still be able to re-edit or remove the appearance attributes in the saved file. When an object is selected, its appearance attributes are listed on the Appearance palette. This palette is also used to re-edit, restack, and remove appearance attributes.

➤ Copy an object, then experiment with different appearance attributes for each copy. No commitment, no obligation. Create a handful of variations on a basic shape, and then gradually hone in until you achieve a combination or combinations of appearance attributes that you're satisfied with.

Appearances and layers

If attributes other than just the basic stroke and fill have been applied to a layer, sub-layer, or object, those additional attributes are called **appearance attributes**, and a gray **target circle** will appear for that layer, sub-layer, or object on the Layers palette **1**.

Instead of applying appearance attributes to individual objects one by one, you can target a whole top-level layer or group for appearances. In this case, the appearance attributes that you choose will apply to all the objects nested within the targeted layer or group. For example, if you target a layer and then modify its opacity or blending mode, all objects nested within that layer will have the same opacity or blending mode, and those attributes can be re-edited quickly by re-targeting the layer.

These are the basic techniques:

➤ To **select** an object, group, or layer, click the **selection area** on the Layers palette.

➤ To **target** an object, group, or layer for **appearance attributes**, click the **target** circle on the Layers palette.

➤ To **view** and **modify** the existing **appearance attributes** for an object, group, or layer, click the **gray** target circle; Shift-click the gray circle to deselect the object, group, or layer.

To target appearances to a group or layer:

To target appearance attributes to a whole group or top-level layer, click its target circle on the Layers palette. A ring will appear around the circle, indicting an active target, and all the objects in that group or on that layer will become selected in the illustration. (Shift-click the ring to un-target.)

Selecting isn't targeting!

Even though selecting and targeting both cause objects to become selected in your illustration, they are not interchangeable operations, especially when you're working with whole layers or groups. If you **target** a layer or group by clicking its target circle and then apply appearance attributes (e.g., fill color, Effect menu command, Transparency palette values), those attributes will be applied to, and will be listed on the Appearance palette for, the layer as a **whole**.

If you click the **selection** area for a layer or a group instead of the target circle and then apply appearances, those attributes will be applied separately to each object in that layer instead of to the layer as a whole. In this case, you won't see an itemized list of appearance attributes on the Appearance palette—you'll just see the generic words "mixed attributes" at the top of the palette, nor will they be listed if you subsequently target the layer.

*This layer is **active**, but **not targeted**, and it doesn't contain appearances.*

1 *This path object contains appearances, but it's not currently targeted.*

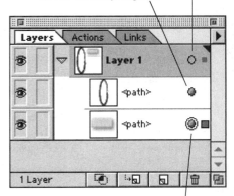

*This object is **targeted**, and it already contains appearances.*

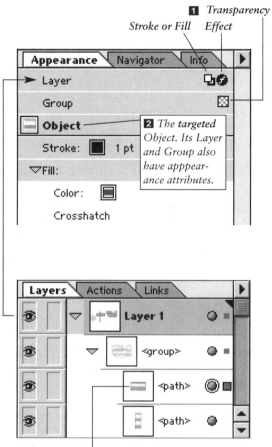

1 *Transparency*
Stroke or Fill *Effect*

2 *The targeted Object. Its Layer and Group also have apppearance attributes.*

3 *A targeted object nested within a group and a layer. They all have appearance attributes.*

Understanding the icons

One of three icons may display in the upper portion of the Appearance palette to the right of the word "Layer" or "Group" **1**:

➤ ◻ means a stroke or fill is applied to a layer or group.

➤ ◉ means an effect is applied to a layer or group.

➤ ▨ means transparency is applied to a layer or group.

The generic name for the currently targeted item—"Layer," "Group," or "Object"— is listed in boldface at the top of the Appearance palette. If an object is targeted, and that object is nested within a layer and/or group to which appearance attributes have been applied, the words "Layer" and/or "Group" will appear above the word "Object" at the top of the palette to indicate its position in the stacking order **2**–**3**.

To copy or move appearance attributes via the Layers palette:

To copy appearance attributes, Option-drag/ Alt-drag the target circle for the item from which you want to copy onto the target circle for another layer, group, or object.
or
To move appearance attributes from one item to another, drag a target circle from one layer, group, or object to another without holding down any keys **4**. The appearance attributes will be removed from the original layer, group, or object.

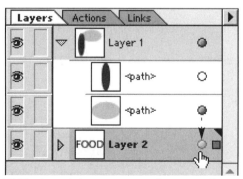

4 *Moving existing appearances from a <path> to a layer (Layer 2).*

Copy or Move Appearances

When you apply appearance attributes, your object will have a totally new look that can be modified or removed at any time, even after the file is saved, closed, and reopened.

To apply appearance attributes:

1. In the document window, select the object whose appearance attributes you want to modify.
   or
   On the Layers palette, click the gray circle for a layer, group, or object to target that item for appearance changes.

2. Choose Window > Show Appearance.

3. On the Appearance palette, do any of the following **1**:

   Double-click Stroke to select the Stroke square on the Color palette, then modify the stroke color and/or stroke width via the Stroke palette.

   Click Fill to select the Fill square on the Color palette, then modify the fill color.

   Double-click Default Transparency (or the current transparency appearance attribute) to show the Transparency palette, then modify the Opacity value and/or change the blending mode.

   Choose a command from a submenu on the Effect menu (for starters, try an effect from the Distort & Transform or Stylize submenu), modify the dialog box settings, then click OK. The Effect command will be listed at the top of the attributes area of the palette. (Read more about effects on pages 308–314.)

   Note: Remember to choose appearance commands from the Effect menu, not the Filter menu. Filter menu commands will permanently rasterize an object. Effect menu commands, on the other hand, since they are vector effects, can be re-edited or removed at any time without permanently changing the object. Some of the vector filters, for which there are Effect menu equivalents, are illustrated on pages 339–341.

Working with attributes

If a layer or group is targeted, the word **Contents** will appear on the attributes list on the Appearance palette. If an individual text object is targeted, you'll see the word **Text**. If an object with gradient mesh fill is targeted, you'll see the words **Mesh Points**.

Moving any attribute up or down on the palette changes the order and appearance of that attribute on the actual item.

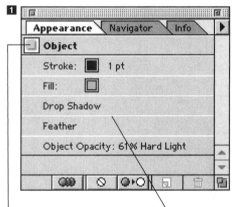

The item the appearance attributes are being targeted to is listed at the top of the palette: Layer, Group, or Object.

*The actual **appearance attributes** are listed in this part of the palette.*

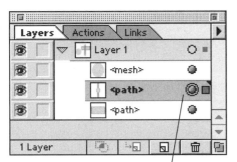

1 *A path is* **targeted** *on the Layers palette.*

2 *The* **Fill** *appearance attribute is clicked.*

3 *Various attributes are applied, and then the* **Fill** *list is expanded.*

Aside from just listing appearance attributes, the Appearance palette can also be used to open palettes and other dialog boxes (e.g., Effect menu, Stroke) for previously applied appearance attributes in order to edit them.

To edit or restack appearance attributes:

1. In the document window, select the object whose appearance attributes you want to modify.
   or
   On the Layers palette, click the gray circle for a layer, group, or object to target that item for appearance changes.

2. On the Appearance palette, double-click any appearance attribute to open its dialog box or show its palette, and make modifications.
   and/or
   Drag any appearance attribute (except Object Opacity) upward or downward on the list. Not only will its location change on the list, but its appearance on the actual object will change because of its new stacking position. For example, if you drag a stroke below a fill attribute and then lower the opacity of the fill attribute, the stroke will then show through the fill.

To edit a stroke or fill appearance attribute:

1. Target a layer, sublayer, group, or object **1**.

2. On the Appearance palette, click Stroke or Fill **2**.

3. On the Transparency palette, change the opacity or blending mode and/or apply an Effect menu command. These attributes will apply only to the selected Stroke or Fill—not to the object as a whole.

   Click the triangle for the Stroke or Fill list to see its nested attributes **3**; click the triangle again to collapse the list.

   A brush can be applied to a stroke. The brush name will appear next to the Stroke attribute on the Appearance palette. Double-click the brush name to open the Stroke Options dialog box.

Edit, Restack Appearances

To remove a brushstroke from a stroke attribute:

1. Target a layer, group, or object.

2. Show the Brushes palette, then click the Remove Brush Stroke button at the bottom of the palette.
   or
   Click the Stroke attribute on the Appearance palette, then click the Delete Selected Item (trash) button at the bottom of the palette. The stroke becomes None.

To apply multiple stroke or fill attributes:

1. Target a layer, group, or object **1**.

2. Choose Add New Stroke or Add New Fill from the Appearance palette menu.
   or
   Click Stroke or Fill on the Appearance palette, then click the Duplicate Selected Item button at the bottom of the palette **2**.
   or
   Drag Stroke or Fill over the Duplicate Selected Item button at the bottom of the Appearance palette.

3. A new Stroke or Fill attribute will appear on the palette **3**–**4**. Now modify its attributes.

➤ Make sure narrower strokes are stacked above wider strokes on the palette list. If the narrower strokes are on the bottom, you won't see them. Similarly, apply opacity and blending modes to the upper fill attributes, not lower ones.

➤ If a layer, group, or object has multiple Fills or Strokes, be careful about clicking the attribute you want to modify. If you want to target the whole item, on the other hand, click the word "Object," "Group," or "Layer" at the top of the Appearance palette.

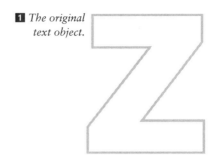

1 *The original text object.*

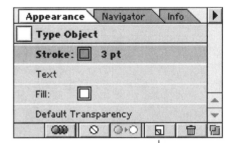

2 *Click the attribute you want to duplicate, then click the **Duplicate Selected Item** button.*

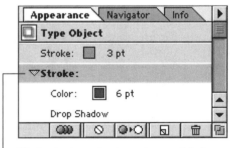

3 *The duplicate Stroke is then modified.*

4 *After duplicating the Stroke, widening the duplicate, and applying the Drop Shadow effect to it.*

Remove Brushstroke; Apply Multiple Appearances

To duplicate an appearance attribute:

1. Target a layer, group, or object.

2. Choose Duplicate Item from the Appearance palette menu.
   or
   Click an attribute, then click the Duplicate Selected Item button at the bottom of the palette. Or drag an attribute over that button.

To remove an appearance attribute:

1. Target a layer, group, or object.

2. On the Appearance palette, click the attribute you want to remove.

3. Choose Remove Item from the palette menu.
   or
   Click the Delete Selected Item (trash) button at the bottom of the palette, or drag the attribute over that button.

➤ The last remaining stroke and fill appearance attribute cannot be removed. Clicking the Delete Selected Item (trash) button for this appearance attribute will produce a stroke or fill of None.

To remove all appearance attributes from an item:

1. Select an object or target a layer, sublayer, group, or object.

2. Click the Clear Appearance button at the bottom of the Appearance palette to remove all of its appearance attributes and apply a stroke and fill of None.
or
Click Reduce to Basic Appearance button at the bottom of the Appearance palette to remove all the object's appearance attributes and apply the bottommost stroke and fill to the object **1**–**2**.

To choose appearance options for new objects:

If the **New Art Has Basic Appearance** command on the Appearance palette menu has a check mark or you click the **New Art Maintains Appearance** button at the bottom of the palette, newly created objects will have only one fill and one stroke. With this option unchecked in either location, the current appearance attributes will apply automatically to all new objects.

If the **Layer/Group Overrides Color** command on the Appearance palette menu has a check mark and specific stroke and fill color appearance attributes are attached to the current layer or group, those color attributes will also be applied automatically to all new or existing objects nested within that layer or group. With Layer/Group Overrides Color unchecked, objects will keep their existing stroke and fill colors if color appearance attributes are created for its layer or group.

1 *Target a layer, group, or object, then click the **Reduce to Basic Appearance** button at the bottom of the Appearance palette.*

2 *All appearance attributes are **removed** from the Layer.*

1 *The **Drop Shadow** effect was applied to the bottom horse, but not to the top one. The drop shadow gradually fades.*

Blends and appearances

If you blend objects that contain different appearance attributes (e.g., effects, fills, or strokes), the appearance attribute will be in full force in the original object and have sequentially less intensity in the blend steps **1**. Blend objects are nested on the Layers palette onto one blend object layer.

If you blend objects containing different blending modes, the blending mode for the topmost object will be applied to all the intemediate blend steps. The blend object layer will have a gray target circle on the Layers palette. This indicates that an appearance attribute is applied to the object, and the appearance attribute is the Knockout Group transparency option, which is turned on. This option is checked by default to prevent the blend steps from showing through each other. Uncheck Knockout Group if you want the blend steps to show through each other. Regardless of whether Knockout Group is on or off, objects below the blend will always show through when blend objects are less than 100% opaque.

To attach appearance attributes to, and view the Transparency palette options for, an entire blend, first click the blend layer circle on the Layers palette to target the entire blend. Don't select the blend with the Selection tool or click on the selection area for the blend layer if you want to work with appearances for an entire blend. (Read more about transparency in the next chapter.)

Blends and Appearances

Using styles

Styles, introduced in Illustrator 9, are used to apply sets of attributes. Any kind of appearance attribute can be saved in a style, such as color, gradient, or pattern (stroke and fill); stroke attributes (weight, dash pattern, etc.); blending mode; transparency; or live effect. Even Attribute palette overprint options can be saved to a style. In short, any appearance attribute that can be applied to an object can also be saved as a style.

Styles are created, saved, and applied via the Styles palette **1**. Each style's individual attributes, however, are listed on the Appearance palette, and the Appearance palette is also used to create or modify those attributes.

There are three main advantages to working with styles:

➤ By applying a style, you can apply many attributes at once with the click of a button. This saves you time and your employer or client money.

➤ Like an appearance attribute, a style changes the way an object looks, but doesn't actually change the underlying object. This means a style can be turned on or off easily, and a different style can be applied at any time.

➤ If you edit a style, the style will update on any objects to which that style is already linked. This streamlines object editing and ensures consistency from object to object.

Illustrator styles differ in one significant way from styles in a layout or word processing program. If you modify an attribute directly on an object to which an Illustrator style is already applied, that modification breaks the link between the selected object and the style. The object's style attributes won't be removed, but if you subsequently edit the style, that object's appearance won't change because it is no longer associated with that style. This "local styling" has no effect on the original style, nor any other objects that may be linked to that style.

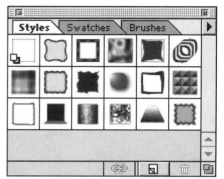

1 *Illustrator's default Styles palette.*

Cast Shadow

Rough Steel

Rainbow Plaid

Black Red Dashes

2 *A few of Illustrator's default styles applied to an editable text object.*

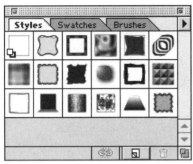

1 *Styles palette: Swatch View.*

2 *Styles palette: Small List View.*

3 *Styles palette: Large List View.*

As always, we'd like you to learn a few ground rules first:

➤ A style can be applied to a layer, sublayer, group, or object. A style will be associated with all the objects in a layer or group, as well as any new objects that are added to a layer or group after the style is applied.

➤ Only one style can be associated with a layer, sublayer, group, or object at a time.

➤ If you close and reopen a file that contains styles, those styles will remain associated with the objects to which they were applied.

➤ For more dramatic results on a placed image or rasterized object, apply a style that contains raster effects (from the lower portion of the Effect menu).

To warm up, start by getting acquainted with the Styles palette.

To choose a view for the Styles palette:

1. Show the Styles palette (Window menu > Show Styles).

2. From the palette menu, choose one of the following:

Swatch View to display style thumbnails only **1**.

Small List View to display style names with smaller thumbnails **2**.

Large List View to display style names with larger thumbnails **3**.

Styles Palette Views

To apply a style to an object:

1. Choose the Selection tool (V), then select an object or objects in the document window.
   or
   On the Layers palette, click the target circle for an object **1**–**2**.

   Remember, selecting and targeting are two different things! See page 290.

2. Click a style name or thumbnail on the Styles palette **3**–**4**.
   or
   Drag a style name or thumbnail from the Styles palette over a group or object in the illustration window. The object doesn't have to be selected.

➤ To access other Illustrator style libraries, choose from the Window menu > Style Libraries submenu.

➤ The name of the currently applied style will be listed at the top of the Appearance palette.

If you apply a style to a layer or a group, that style will be applied to all current and subsequently created objects on that layer, sublayer, or group.

To apply a style to a layer, sublayer, or group:

1. On the Layers palette, click the target circle for a layer, sublayer, or group.

2. Click a style name or thumbnail on the Styles palette **5**.

1 *The original text object.*

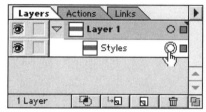

2 *The text object is **targeted** for an appearance change on the **Layers** palette.*

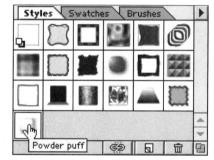

3 *Our custom Powder puff swatch is clicked.*

4 *The style appears on the **object**.*

5 *Here, the same style is also applied to a **group**.*

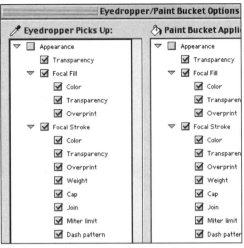

1 Choose appearance attributes for the Eyedropper tool in *Eyedropper/Paint Bucket Options*.

2 An object is clicked on with the **Eyedropper** tool.

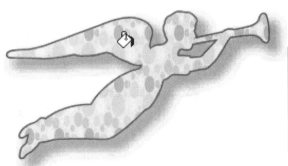

3 An object is clicked on with the **Paint Bucket** tool. The style from the text object is applied to the angel.

To copy a style or an appearance attribute from one object to another:
(Method 1)

1. Double-click the Eyedropper tool (I).

2. Check the Appearance box to activate all appearance options.
   or
   Click the triangle for Appearance, if that list isn't already expanded, then uncheck any attributes you don't want the Eyedropper to pick up.

3. Click OK (Return/Enter) **1**.

4. Click with the Eyedropper on the object whose style or appearance attributes you want to copy **2**.

5. Choose the Paint Bucket tool (K) or hold down Option/Alt to toggle to the Paint Bucket tool **3**.

6. Click the object or objects to which you want to apply the copied style.

(Method 2)

1. Choose the Selection tool (V), then click an object whose style or appearance attribute you want to copy.

2. Drag the icon from the top left corner of the Appearance palette over an unselected object **4**.

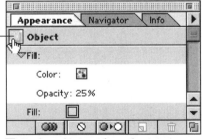

4 Or drag this icon from the Appearance palette over an object.

Copy Style

To break the link between a style and a layer, sublayer, group, or object:

1. Choose the Selection tool (V), then select an object or objects in the illustration window, or click the target circle for an object on the Layers palette.

   or

   If the style was applied to a group or layer, click the target circle for a layer, sublayer, or group on the Layers palette.

2. Click the Break Link to Style button at the bottom of the Styles palette **1**.

   or

   Change any appearance attribute for the selected item (e.g., apply a different fill color, stroke color, pattern, gradient, or effect).

   The style name will no longer be listed on the Appearance palette for the selected item.

Next, we offer two methods for creating a new style. In the first set of instructions, you will create a style based on an object. This method will probably feel the most natural and intuitive, especially if you're going to experiment with various settings for the new style. If you already have a good idea of what attributes you want the new style to have, follow the instructions on the next page instead.

To create a new style using an object:

1. Target an object, then use the Appearance palette to create attributes you want the style to have **2**.

2. From the Styles palette menu, choose New Style, enter a name for the style, then click OK **3**. The new style will appear at the bottom of the list or below the existing swatches on the Styles palette **4**.

   or

   Drag the icon next to the Object name from the top of the Appearance palette onto the Styles palette. Double-click the new style swatch, then type a name for the style, then click OK (Return/Enter).

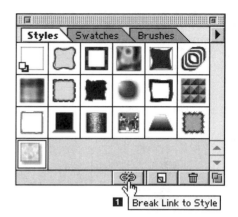

1 Break Link to Style

2 *Click the object whose attributes you want to save as a style.*

Style Options

Style Name: Powder puff   OK   Cancel

3 *Give the new style a* **name**.

Styles | Swatches | Brushes

Froth

Endorific

Bristly

Powder puff

4 *The new style swatch appears at the bottom of the* **Styles** *palette.*

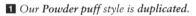

1 *Our Powder puff style is duplicated.*

2 *The duplicate style is renamed, and then its attributes are edited via the Appearance palette. The style name is listed at the top of the palette.*

3 *After replacing the old style with the new.*

To create a new style using a duplicate of an existing style:

1. On the Styles palette, click the style you want to copy.

2. Click the New Style button or drag the swatch over the New Style button. The number "1" will be added to the existing style name **1**.
   or
   Choose Duplicate Style from the Styles palette menu, type a name for the style, then click OK.

3. Click the duplicate style swatch or name, then use the Appearance palette to edit the style so it contains the desired attributes **2**.

4. Option-drag/Alt-drag the object icon from the top left corner of the Appearance palette over the new swatch on the Styles palette **3**.
   or
   Choose Replace "[style name]" from the Appearance palette menu.

Create a Style

Beware! If you edit a style, that style will update on any objects that were linked to it prior to its being modified. If you don't want this to happen, just duplicate the style and edit the duplicate (see the previous page).

To edit a style:

1. In order to "preview" your changes, apply the style you want to edit to an object **1**.

2. Via the Appearance palette, edit or restack the existing appearance attributes or add new attributes **2**.

3. Choose Replace "[style name]" from the Appearance palette menu.
   or
   Option-drag/Alt-drag the object icon from the top left corner of the Appearance palette over the original style swatch on the Styles palette.

   With either method, the style swatch will update to reflect the modifications **3** and any objects to which the style is currently applied will also update **4**.

➤ While editing a style, don't click on other styled objects or style swatches, or you'll lose your current appearance attributes settings.

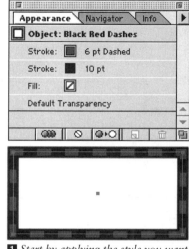

1 *Start by applying the style you want to edit to an object.*

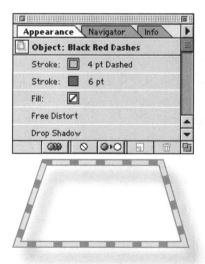

2 *The style is edited on the object via the Appearance palette.*

3 *The style is replaced on the Styles palette.*

4 *The style also updates on other objects to which it was previously applied.*

What stays; what goes

Attributes are listed on the Appearance palette in the order in which they are applied. The order of fills in the list of attributes on the Appearance palette is controlled by the order of swatches that were originally selected on the Styles palette. The fill of the selected style listed closest to the top of the Styles palette (in list view or swatch view) will be listed above any and all other fills in the merged style. If you merge styles that contain solid fills, only the topmost fill will be visible.

To change the list order (and thus the applied order) of the fills, edit the existing fills' opacity or blending modes and/or drag a fill attribute on the Appearance palette list.

If you have two styles whose attributes you want to combine into one style, you can merge them into one new style. The original swatches won't be altered. See the sidebar at left.

To merge styles:

1. Command-click/Ctrl-click two or more style swatches or names on the Styles palette.

2. Choose Merge Styles from the Styles palette menu **1**.

3. Enter a name for the merged style, then click OK **2**. A new style swatch will appear at the bottom of the list of names or below the existing swatches, depending on the current palette View **3**.

To delete a style from the Styles palette:

1. On the Styles palette, click the style that you want to remove.

2. Click the Delete Style (trash) button on the palette.
   or
   Choose Delete Style from the Styles palette menu.

3. Click Yes to delete the style.

➤ You can Undo a style deletion.

➤ If you delete a style that is linked to objects, the appearance of those objects will remain. They will become unlinked to the style, however, since it no longer exists.

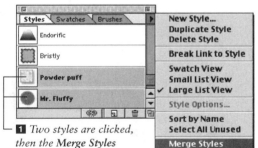

1 *Two styles are clicked, then the* **Merge Styles** *command is chosen.*

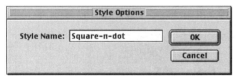

2 *The merged style is given a new* **name**.

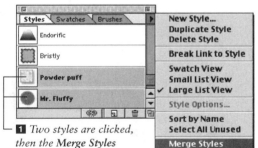

3 *The* **merged** *style appears on the* **Styles** *palette.*

Merge Styles; Delete Styles

Styles from Illustrator's predefined style files or any other Illustrator 9 files can be imported into the current document's Styles palette using the Style Libraries command. Style libraries are stored in the Adobe Illustrator 9.0 > Style Libraries folder. The styles in a Style library can't be deleted or edited. A library style that is copied into the current document can be edited.

To add a style from an existing library or from another document to the Styles palette:

1. Open the Styles palette.

2. If the style library you want to add is already in the Adobe Illustrator 9.0 > Style Libraries folder (such as a predefined style library), choose Window menu > Style Libraries > [style library name], then open the library **1**–**4**.
   or
   If the style library is in a location other than the Adobe Illustrator 9.0 > Style Libraries folder, choose Window > Style Libraries > Other Library, then locate and open the library. You can use this command to open any Illustrator 9 file, and then use that file's Styles palette as a library.

3. To add a style, select an object, then click a style swatch in the library. Or drag a style swatch from the library over a selected or unselected object. The new style will appear on the Styles palette.
   or
   To add a style to the Styles palette without using an object, click a library style swatch.
   or
   Shift-click consecutive styles or Command-click/Ctrl-click individual styles on the library palette, then drag the selected styles onto the Styles palette.

➤ To make an Illustrator file appear as a library choice on the Style Libraries submenu, drag the file from the Desktop into the Adobe Illustrator 9.0 > Style Libraries folder, then relaunch Illustrator.

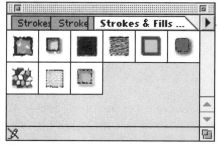

1 *Illustrator's Strokes & Fills (RGB) style library.*

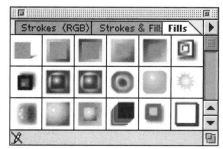

2 *Illustrator's Fills style library.*

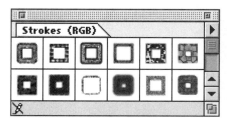

3 *Illustrator's Strokes (RGB) style library.*

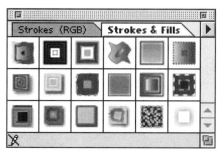

4 *Illustrator's Strokes & Fills style library.*

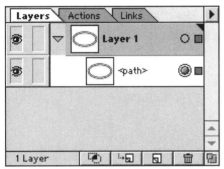

1 *An object to which a style is applied is selected.*

2 *The Layers palette **before** choosing the* **Expand Appearance** *command. The <path> object is targeted.*

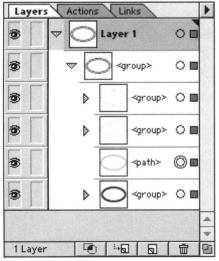

3 *The Layers palette **after** choosing the* **Expand Appearance** *command.*

To create a style library:

1. In a new Illustrator document, create objects with the desired appearance attributes, and save those appearances as styles on the Styles palette.

2. *Optional:* To remove all styles from the Styles palette that are not currently applied to objects in the document, choose Select All Unused from the Styles palette menu, click the Delete Style button on the palette, then click Yes.

3. Choose File menu > Save, enter a name for the library file, and choose the Adobe Illustrator document format.

4. Locate and open the Style Libraries folder inside the Adobe Illustrator 9.0 folder, then click Save.

5. Quit/Exit Illustrator, then relaunch. The new style library will be listed on the Window menu > Style Libraries submenu.

➤ Any Brush shape that is used in a style in the style library, but isn't present on the document's Brushes palette, will be added to the document's Brushes palette if the library style is applied to an object in the document.

➤ To restore the default style swatches to the Styles palette, choose Window menu > Style Libraries > Default_RGB or Default_CMYK, then add the needed swatches.

When you use the Expand Appearance command, a new group sublayer will replace the original object layer on the Layers palette, and effects and appearance attributes will be listed as separate objects or an image within that group.

To expand an appearance into its attributes:

1. Select an object that has the appearances (or style) you want to expand **1**–**2**.

2. Choose Object menu > Expand Appearance **3**.

Using effects

Illustrator 9 also debuts the **Effect menu** commands, which include the vector commands that you're already familiar with from the Filter menu, like Drop Shadow and Roughen, as well as some new commands that are not found on the Filter menu, such as Feather, Inner Glow, Outer Glow, and Convert to Shape **1**. In addition, all the bitmap filters on the Filter menu now have counterparts on the Effect menu.

Effects change only the appearance of an object, not its underlying path. Unlike the Filter menu commands, which change the underlying object and are not re-editable, Effect menu commands don't change the object and are re-editable. Effects lend themselves to experimentation, because an effect can be re-edited or deleted at any time without affecting the object or any other effects or appearance attributes currently applied to that object. What's more, the underlying object's path can be reshaped at any time, and the effects will adjust accordingly (they're **live!**).

Effects can also be applied to any kind of object, including editable text (it doesn't have to be converted into outlines first), and the text stays editable. In fact, the Outline Object effect itself converts text into outlines, yet the underlying text is still editable, (providing the font is available to the system).

Like object attributes, applied effects are listed on the Appearance palette for each selected object. If an effect is applied to a targeted layer, sublayer, or group, that effect will be applied to all existing and future objects on that layer, sublayer, or group.

Furthermore, since effects display on the Appearance palette along with other attributes, they can also be saved in a style, and you can re-edit any effect that is contained in a style at any time.

Where to find it

Effect	Page
General instructions for applying effects	309–310
Convert to Shape	311
Outline Object	312
Inner Glow/ Outer Glow	313
Pathfinder	310
Add Arrowheads	314
Raster filter	342–353
Drop Shadow	334

1 *Like the Filter menu, the* Effect *menu is divided into two sections.*

1 *The original* **targeted** *object.*

2 *A value is chosen in the effect dialog box.*

3 *The Feather effect is applied.*

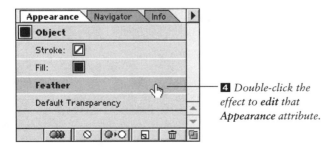

4 *Double-click the effect to edit that* **Appearance** *attribute.*

In these instructions, you will apply an effect directly to a layer, sublayer, group, or object. In the instructions on the following page, you will add to, or edit an effect in, a style.

To apply an effect:

1. On the Layers palette, target a layer, sublayer, group, or object **1**.

   Note: To limit an effect to only an object's stroke or fill, select the object, then click the Stroke or Fill attribute on the Appearance palette.

2. Choose an effect from a submenu on the Effect menu.

3. Check the Preview box, if there is one, to preview the effect as you choose options, then choose options **2**.

4. Click OK (Return/Enter) **3**. (If you applied the effect to only a stroke or fill, the effect name will be nested below the Stroke or Fill attribute on the Appearance palette. Expand the attribute list, if necessary, to see the effect list.)

To edit an effect:

1. On the Layers palette, target the layer, sublayer, group, or object to which the effect you want to edit is applied. If the effect was applied to only an object's stroke or fill, select the object, then expand the Stroke or Fill attribute on the Appearance palette.

2. Double-click the effect on the Appearance palette **4**.

3. Make the desired adjustments, then click OK (Return/Enter).

Apply Effect; Edit Effect

309

To add to, or edit an effect in, a style:

1. Click the style name or swatch on the Styles palette 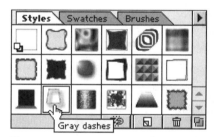. The style name will appear at the top of the Appearance palette.

2. To add an effect, choose an effect from a submenu on the Effect menu, check the Preview box, if there is one, to preview the effect as you choose options, then choose options.
   or
   To edit an existing effect, double-click the effect name on the Appearance palette **2**.

4. Click OK (Return/Enter).

5. Choose Replace "[style name]" from the Appearance palette menu to update the style.

Easy come, easy go.

To remove an effect from a layer, object, or style:

1. On the Layers palette, target the layer, sublayer, group, or object that contains the effect to be removed.
   or
   On the Styles palette, click the style name or swatch that contains the effect to be removed.

2. On the Appearance palette, click the effect name.

3. Click on, or drag the effect name to the Delete Selected Item (trash) button on the Appearance palette.

4. If you're removing an effect from a style, choose Replace "[style name]" from the Appearance palette menu to update the style.

Pathfinder effects

The Pathfinder commands that are available on the Pathfinder palette are also available as effects (Effect menu > **Pathfinder** submenu), except the Pathfinder effects don't affect the actual objects; they only affect their appearance. You can delete a Pathfinder appearance attribute at any time without affecting the actual objects. Before applying a Pathfinder effect, collect the objects to which you want to apply the effect into a sublayer or group, then target that sublayer or group (target—not select).

The Divide, Trim, and Merge effects don't break up objects' overlapping areas into separate objects for recoloring or repositioning, as their counterparts on the Pathfinder palette do; the Outline Stroke effect only changes the appearance of an object's stroke; the stroke won't be editable as a separate object.

1 *A style is clicked on the* Styles *palette.*

2 *To edit an existing style, double-click the style name on the* Appearance *palette.*

1 *The original object.*

2 *Shape and scale options are chosen in the Shape effect dialog box.*

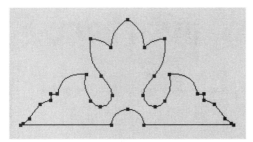

3 *A rectangular shape appearance attribute is added to the object; the underlying path is unchanged.*

In these instructions, you'll use the Convert to Shape effects, which are found only on the Effects menu and are new to Illustrator. Like all effects, they change an object's shape without changing the actual underlying path.

To apply a Convert to Shape effect:

1. Select/target an object or objects in the document window or via the Layers palette **1**.

2. Choose Effect menu > Convert to Shape submenu > Rectangle, Rounded Rectangle, or Ellipse. *Note:* Any of these three options can also be chosen from the Shape pop-up menu once the dialog box is open **2**.

3. Click Absolute, then enter the total desired Width and Height values for the shape appearance.
   or
   Click Relative, then enter the Extra Width or Extra Height that you want added to or subtracted from the object's current shape. Enter a positive value to expand the shape or a negative value to contract the shape.

4. *Optional:* For the Rounded Rectangle shape, you can change the Corner Radius value.

5. Click OK (Return/Enter) **3**–**4**.

➤ Try also using Effect menu > Stylize > Round Corners to change the appearance of an object's shape.

4 *The word "Rectangle" displays on the Appearance palette.*

Convert to Shape

Now we'll show you how to use the much heralded "live" aspect of effects.

To use live shapes with text:

1. Select/target a type block in the document window or using the Layers palette .

2. On the Appearance palette, click the Fill attribute. *Note:* Initially, a type object contains stroke and fill attributes of None. The default (or user-defined) fill or stroke color will be displayed if "Text" is clicked on the Appearance palette.

3. If the Fill attribute is None, click the Last Color button on the Color palette.

4. Click the Duplicate Selected Item button at the bottom of the Appearance palette.

5. Click the lower Fill attribute on the Appearance palette, then choose a different color for it .

6. Apply an Effect menu > Convert to Shape effect to the new Fill attribute, using the Relative option (see steps 2–3 on the previous page) 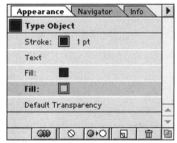.

7. To see how the live effect works, add or delete some type. The new fill shape will resize accordingly .

Outline Object for text

If you open an Illustrator file containing a font that is not currently active in the system, the Font Problem alert box will open (click Open to have Illustrator substitute a font). If Effect menu > Path > Outline Object was applied to any of the type using a now inactive font, that type will display and print properly—but it can't be edited. If the font used in the Outline Object text *is* active in system when the document is reopened, the text will be editable in Illustrator and in any other program that reads Illustrator objects.

Unlike the Create Outlines command on the Type menu, Outline Object creates outlined text that remains fully editable as text. You can't reshape a text character's paths using this effect, however, as you can using Type menu > Create Outlines. The Outline Object effect is better suited for large text than for small text.

1 *The original text.*

2 *A new **Fill** attribute is created, and a different color is chosen for it.*

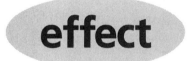

3 *After applying the **Convert to Shape** effect to the new Fill (Shape: Ellipse; Relative: Extra Width 13 pt, Extra Height 3 pt).*

4 *When more characters are **added** to the text, the **shape enlarges** to accommodate it.*

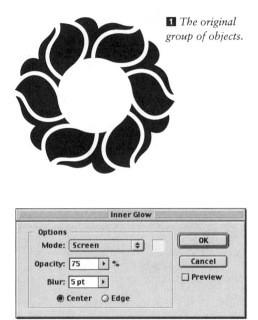

1 *The original group of objects.*

The Inner Glow effect applies a color glow that spreads from the edge of an object toward its center. The Outer Glow effect applies a color glow that spreads from the edge of an object outward.

To apply the Feather effect, see page 331. To apply the Drop Shadow effect, see page 334.

To apply the Inner Glow or Outer Glow effect:

1. Select/target a layer, sublayer, group, or object **1**.

2. Choose Effect menu > Stylize > Inner Glow or Outer Glow.

3. Check the Preview box **2**.

4. Do any of the following:

   Click the Color square, then choose a different glow color.

   Choose a blending mode for the glow color from the pop-up menu.

   Change the Opacity for the glow color.

   Move the Blur slider to adjust the distance the glow extends inward or outward from edge of object. The higher the Blur value, the wider the glow.

   For Inner Glow, click Center to have the glow spread outward from the object's center or click Edge to have the glow spread inward from the object's edge to its center.

5. Click OK (Return/Enter) **3**–**5**.

2 *Options in the* **Inner Glow** *effect dialog box are chosen.*

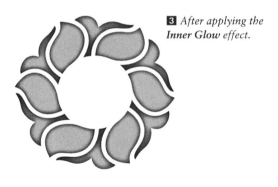

3 *After applying the* **Inner Glow** *effect.*

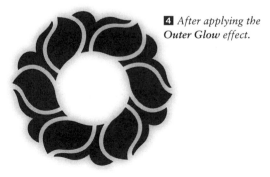

4 *After applying the* **Outer Glow** *effect.*

5 *Both Glow effects applied.*

Inner Glow; Outer Glow

An advantage to using the Effect menu version of Add Arrowheads over the Filter menu version is that it has a preview option.

To apply the Add Arrowheads effect:

1. Select an open path.

2. Choose Effect menu (or Filter menu) > Stylize > Add Arrowheads.

3. Click the Start left or right arrow to choose from the various head designs **1**. Click until no style appears if you don't want an arrow head or tail at the start of the path.

4. Click the End left or right arrow to choose from the various head designs. Click until no style appears if you don't want an arrow head or tail at the end of the path.

5. *Optional:* Choose a Scale percentage for the Start and End styles (hard to do without a preview, huh?). To choose a different Scale percentage for the Start and End styles, apply the effect or filter in two separate passes.

6. Click OK (Return/Enter). If you used the Filter command, the arrowhead can be reshaped or moved like any other path (use the Direct-selection tool) **2**–**4**.

➤ If a Filter menu arrowhead or tail winds up on the wrong end of the path, undo it or delete it, then redo it (use Command-E/Ctrl-E to reopen the last-used filter dialog box). To redo an Effect menu arrowhead or tail, double-click the Add Arrowheads appearance attribute on the Appearance palette to reopen the Add Arrowheads dialog box.

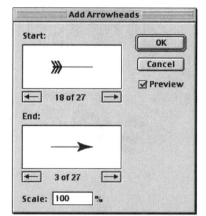

1 *Choose a style, a location (Start, End, or Both Ends), and a Scale in the Add Arrowheads dialog box (Effect menu).*

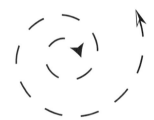

2 *Arrowheads on a spiral.*

3 *Arrowhead and tail on a Pencil line.*

4 *Arrowhead on a brushstroke.*

Add Arrowheads

MASKS/TRANSPARENCY

In this chapter you will learn how to create clipping masks; how to restack, select, copy, lock, or add masked objects; how to unmask one object; and how to release a mask.

You will also learn how to use Illustrator's powerful new Transparency palette to apply opacity levels and blending modes to a layer, group, or object; how to restrict those effects to specific objects; how to use the Transparency Grid; how to create opacity masks; how to apply the Feather command; how to use the improved Drop Shadow command; and how to apply the Hard Mix and Soft Mix commands.

The entire section on Transparency is brand new! (pages 321–333)

Daniel Pelavin (icon appears courtesy DFS Group, Ltd.)

The **masking** object.   A **masked** object.

*The same image in **Outline** view.*

Standard masks

In Illustrator, a clipping mask works like a picture frame or mat. While it is in effect, it hides (clips) parts of an illustration that fall outside its borders. Only parts of objects within the confines of the masking object will be visible. Masked objects can be moved, restacked, reshaped, or repainted.

To mask objects:

1. Arrange the objects to be masked **1**. The masking object ("clipping path") can be an open or closed path. You can use a brushstroke object, but remember that the object's path shape will be used as the clipping path. You can use type as a clipping path without having to convert it to outlines. Try not to use very intricate objects—they may not print.

2. Make sure the clipping path is in front of the objects it will be masking. If you need to restack it, on the Layers palette, drag its name upward on the list.

3. Choose the Selection tool (V).

4. Select the clipping path and the objects to be masked.

5. Choose Object menu > Clipping Mask > Make (Command-7/Ctrl-7) **2**. The clipping path will now have a stroke and fill of None and all the objects will be selected. The clipping path layer will be the underlined name "<clipping path>" on the Layers palette (unless it's text, in which case the text character(s) will be underlined instead). The clipping path and the masked objects will be moved from their former layers into a group within the clipping path's original top-level layer.

   Note: To restroke or refill the clipping path, see page 320. To move a masked object individually, use the Direct-selection tool.

➤ To use a group of objects as a clipping path, you have to convert them into a compound path first (choose Object menu > Compound Path > Make).

Using the button *new*

The **Make Clipping Mask** button at the bottom of the Layers palette clips the objects and/or groups that are nested within the currrently active or selected layer or group—not objects from other layers. This button doesn't create a separate group.

1 *The original objects: A normal type character and a placed bitmap image.*

2 *After selecting both objects and applying the Clipping Mask command.*

1 *The object to be added (the star) is moved over the clipping path (the banner shape) to the desired x/y location.*

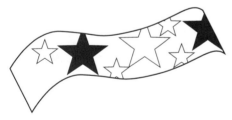

2 *A path is moved downward into the clipping path group.*

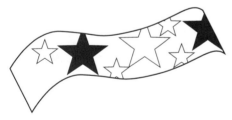

3 *The object is now being masked.*

To select the clipping path and masked objects in a mask group:

Click the clipping path or a masked object with the Selection tool.
or
Option-double-click/Alt-double-click any of the objects with the Direct-selection tool.
or
Click the selection area for the clipping path group or layer on the Layers palette.

To select only the clipping path:

Click the selection area for the clipping path layer on the Layers palette. *Note:* Unless you apply a fill or stroke color to the clipping path, it will be invisible in Preview view.
or
Turn on View menu > Smart Guides and check the Object Highlighting box in Edit menu > Preferences > Smart Guides. Move the pointer over the edge of the clipping path, then click when you see its Smart Guide.

To select all the clipping paths in your illustration:

Deselect all objects, then choose Edit menu > Select > Masks. (With the Selection tool, Shift-click the edge of any masking object you don't want selected.) This is buggy in Windows.

To add an object to a mask:

1. Choose the Selection tool (V).
2. Select the object to be added.
3. Move the object over the clipping group to the desired x/y location **1**.
4. On the Layers palette, expand the clipping group list.
5. Drag the object layer upward or downward into the group list **2**. Release when the object is in the desired stacking position **3**. The stacking order for any object in a mask group can be changed using the Layers palette.

➤ To convert a gradient or a pattern into a grouped set of masked objects, select an object that contains a gradient or pattern fill, then use Object menu > Expand (Fill).

new

Select Mask Objects; Add Object to Mask

317

Basic stacking techniques are explained on pages 176–177.

To restack a masked object within its group:

1. *Optional:* On the Layers palette, click in the selection area for the object you want to restack **1**. Or choose the Direct-selection tool (A), then click the object to be restacked in the illustration window.

2. On the Layers palette, drag the object's layer upward or downward to a new position within the group **2**–**4**.

To copy a masked object:

1. On the Layers palette, click the object's selection area.

2. Option-drag/Alt-drag the selection square upward or downward. The copy will be a member of the same clipping group. (Click its selection square twice to force a screen redraw.) *Note:* If you drag outside the clipping group or layer, the copy will be independent of the mask.

Using the Layers palette, you can lock any object within a mask group or lock the entire group to prevent it from being moved.

To lock one masked object or an entire clipping group:

1. Expand the clipping group or layer list on the Layers palette.

2. To lock one object, click its blank box in the second column.
   or
   To lock the whole clipping group or layer, click the blank box in the second column for the group or layer.

   Note: To unlock a layer, group, or object, click its padlock icon.

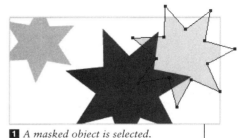

1 *A masked object is selected.*

The **mask**.

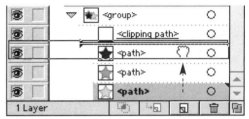

2 *The selected objects layer is moved upward.*

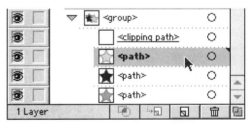

3 *The lightest star is now at the topmost level within its* **clipping group**.

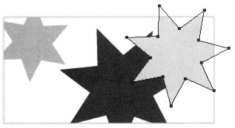

4 *The object is now on top of the other masked objects.*

improved

new

Restack, Copy, Lock Masked Object

Learn from the masters

Once you've mastered the basics, we highly recommend Sharon Steuer's four-color **The Illustrator 9 Wow! Book** (Peachpit Press), which features advanced tips and techniques from Illustrator pros.

1 *The mask is released.*

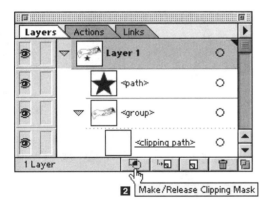

2 Make/Release Clipping Mask

If you release a clipping group or layer, the complete objects will redisplay and the former clipping path will be listed as a standard path layer on the Layers palette.

After using method 1, below, the objects will no longer be nested within the group sub-layer. After using method 2, the clipping group will be released, but the objects will still be nested within any existing group.

To release a mask:

(Method 1)

1. Choose the Selection tool (V).

2. Click on any part of the mask group.

3. Choose Object menu > Clipping Mask > Release (Command-Option-7/ Ctrl-Alt-7) **1**.

➤ If no fill or stroke was applied to the clipping path, that object won't display in Preview view. It will display as a Smart Guide object when the pointer is over it if the Object Highlighting box is checked in Edit menu > Preferences > Smart Guides.

(Method 2)

1. Click the clipping group name (<group>) or layer name on the Layers palette.

2. Click the Make/Release Clipping Mask button at the bottom of the palette **2**. *new*

   Note: The Make/Release Clipping Mask button may cause a pattern or gradient fill to become black. If this occurs, Undo and use the Object menu > Clipping Mask > Release command instead.

Release Mask

It's easy to unmask an object. All you gotta do is drag its layer outside the clipping group or layer on the Layers palette.

To unmask one object:

1. Expand the clipping group list on the Layers palette.

2. *Optional:* For the object you want to unmask, click the object layer name on the Layers palette. Or choose the Direct-selection tool, then click the object in the illustration window **1**.

3. On the Layers palette, drag the nested object layer upward or downward out of the group or layer **2**.

➤ To simultaneously unmask an object and delete it from the illustration, select it, then press Delete/Backspace.

To recolor a clipping path:

1. Select the clipping path by clicking in its selection area on the Layers palette.

2. Apply color as you would to any object **3**–**6**. The fill and stroke will belong to the clipping path layer. The fill will appear behind the masked objects, whereas the stroke will appear in front of them.

new

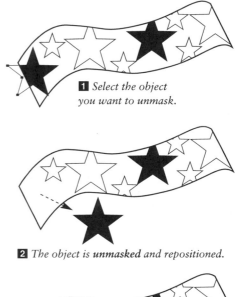

1 *Select the object you want to unmask.*

2 *The object is **unmasked** and repositioned.*

3 *The original clipping mask, before filling.*

4 *A black **fill** was applied to the clipping mask object and the masked objects were **recolored**.*

5 *The original clipping mask object (the zebra) and masked objects (the stripes).*

6 *The **recolored** clipping mask object and masked objects.*

Exporting transparency

Exporting a file that contains transparency to another application involves choosing from new options in the File menu > Export dialog boxes and the Document Setup dialog box. Read about these new options in chapter 24.

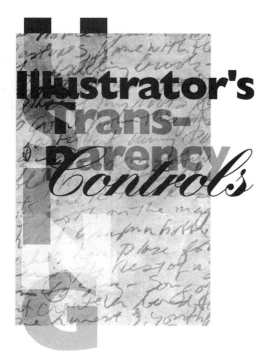

1 *Various opacities and blending modes were applied to some of these objects.*

Transparency *new*

Adobe Illustrator users have long wished for the ability to add a touch of realism to their drawings. Study a real object on your desk for a minute (e.g., a lamp or your keyboard if it's in one of the jelly colors). When a lamp is on, the shade looks semi-transparent rather than solid. You might say "The shade is white" when you describe it, but in reality it's not a dense, solid white, especially when a light bulb is projecting light through it. Objects in real life have different densities, depending on what they're made of. If you have the capacity to render light filtering through various materials, you can create a sense of realism.

Until now, artists have cleverly built their styles around Adobe Illustrator's lack of transparency controls, skillfully choosing colors for areas where objects overlap to make them appear semi-transparent. But somehow, even with Illustrator's gradient features, everything still had a flat, hard-edged look.

With the transparency and feathering controls introduced in Illustrator 9.0, artists will have a whole new bag of tricks to work with. If you draw a window, for example, you can then draw a tinted, semi-sheer, diaphanous curtain on top of it. If you draw a vase on a table, you can create a realistic shadow for the vase that feathers softly into the table color. You can even adjust the transparency of editable type objects. Object opacity can be readjusted at any time.

Furthermore, you can also choose a blending mode for any object (the standard line-up from Photoshop) to control how it blends with objects below it in the stacking order. And you can turn any object into an opacity mask whose fill color values control the transparency of the objects it masks.

Where Illustrator 8.0 was hard, Illustrator 9.0 is soft **1**.

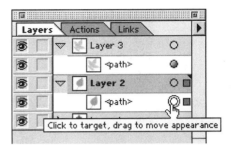

new The Opacity slider controls the transparency of each object. The blending modes control how an object's color is affected by the colors in underlying objects. When a group or layer is targeted, the transparency settings affect the entire group or layer. Any objects that are added to a group or layer take the group or layer's transparency settings.

1 *Click the* **target** *button for an object, group, or layer.*

To change the opacity or blending mode of an object, group, or layer:

1. Show the Layers palette, then select, or click the target circle for, an object whose opacity or blending mode you want to change **1**. For an imported image, target the <image> or <placed> layer. You must click a group or layer's target circle to edit the appearance of all the objects on that group or layer.
   or
   Select type characters with a type tool.

2. Show the Transparency palette (Window menu > Transparency). The thumbnail for the selected layer, group, or object will display on the palette.

3. Move the Opacity slider (0–100%) **2**–**3**.
   and/or
   Choose a different blending mode from the pop-up menu (see "The blending modes" beginning on the next page).

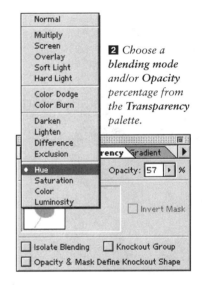

2 *Choose a* **blending mode** *and/or* **Opacity** *percentage from the* **Transparency** *palette.*

new ### To change the opacity or blending mode of only an object's fill or stroke:

1. Click the target circle for an object on the Layers palette.

2. On the Appearance palette, click Fill or Stroke. (For a text object, click Text to change the whole object; click Fill or Stroke to change just that attribute.

3. On the Transparency palette, move the Opacity slider **4**.
   and/or
   Choose a different blending mode.

   Attribute changes will be nested under the targeted object's Fill or Stroke attribute on the Appearance palette.

3 *The Opacity of the* **entire** *type character is lowered to 29%*

4 *The type* **Fill** *Opacity is lowered to 29%; the Stroke Opacity is left at 100%.*

Think ahead

To ensure consistency, target a group or layer, then choose a blending mode. That mode will apply to all existing and future objects that may be nested within that group or layer.

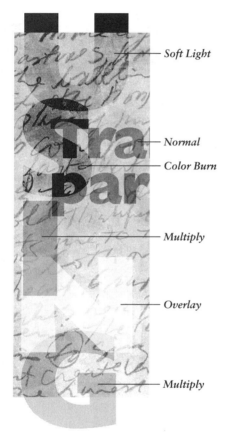

The text is in front of the image object.

Soft Light — Normal — Color Burn — Multiply — Overlay — Multiply

The blending modes *new*

You can choose from 16 blending modes on the Transparency palette—the very same modes that you see in Photoshop. The mode you choose for an object (the "blend layer") affects how that object modifies underlying pixels (the "base color").

NORMAL
All base colors are modified equally. At 100% opacity, the blend layer color will be opaque.

MULTIPLY
A dark blend layer color removes the lighter parts of the base color to produce a darker base color. A light blend layer color darkens the base color less. Good for creating semi-transparent shadow effects.

SCREEN
A light blend layer color removes the darker parts of the base color to produce a lighter, bleached base color. A dark blend layer lightens the base color less.

OVERLAY
Multiplies (darkens) dark areas and screens (lightens) light base colors. Preserves luminosity (light and dark) values. Black and white are not changed, so details are preserved.

SOFT LIGHT
Lightens the base color if the blend layer color is light. Darkens the base color if the blend layer color is dark. Preserves luminosity values in the base color. Creates a soft, subtle lighting effect.

HARD LIGHT
Screens (lightens) the base color if the blend layer color is light. Multiplies (darkens) the base color if the blend layer color is dark. Greater contrast is created in the base color and layer color. Good for creating glowing highlights and composite effects.

COLOR DODGE
Lightens the base color where the blend layer color is light. A dark blend layer color tints the base color slightly.

(Continued on the following page)

Blending Modes

new

COLOR BURN
A dark blend layer color darkens the base color. A light blend layer color tints the base color slightly.

DARKEN
Base colors that are lighter than the blend layer color are modified, base colors that are darker than the blend layer color are not. Use with a blend layer color that is darker than the base colors you want to modify.

LIGHTEN
Base colors that are darker than the blend layer color are modified, base colors that are lighter than the blend layer color are not. Use with a blend layer color that is lighter than the base colors you want to modify.

DIFFERENCE
Creates a color negative effect on the base color. When the blend layer color is light, the negative (or invert) effect is more pronounced. Produces marked color changes.

EXCLUSION
Grays out the base color where the blend layer color is dark. Inverts the base color where the blend layer color is light.

HUE
The blend color's hue is applied. Saturation and luminosity values are not modified in the base color.

SATURATION
The blend color's saturation is applied. Hue and luminosity values are not modified in the base color.

COLOR
The blend color's saturation and hue are applied. The base color's light and dark (luminosity) values aren't changed, so detail is maintained. Good for tinting.

LUMINOSITY
The base color's luminosity values are replaced by tonal (luminosity) values from the blend layer color. Hue and saturation are not modified in the base color.

1 *The original objects: an image and a group of squares. Each square has a different blending mode and opacity that interacts with all underlying layers.*

2 *Isolate Blending is turned on for the group of nested squares. Now the blending modes are only in effect within that group, though transparency to the image below it remains in effect.*

If you apply a blending mode to multiple *new* selected objects, that mode will become an appearance for each selected object, and the objects will blend with one another and with underlying objects below them. In some circumstances, you might want to "seal" a collection of objects so blending modes will only affect its own members. Opacity settings within the nested objects, group, or layer are not affected by the Isolate Blending option, and underlying objects will still show through objects of lower opacity.

To restrict a blending mode effect to specific objects:

1. On the Layers palette, click the target circle for a group or layer that contains nested objects to which a blending mode or modes are applied **1**.

2. Check the Isolate Blending box on the Transparency palette **2**. Nested objects within the group or layer will blend with each other, but those objects won't blend with any underlying objects outside the layer or group.

   (Re-target the group or layer and uncheck Isolate Blending to remove that option.)

➤ To change the mode for any individual object, first target that object.

➤ Isolate Blending can also be used on individual objects that have overlapping strokes and/or fills. Each object can have a different blending mode.

➤ When Illustrator's Isolated Blending box is checked for object layers, they look the same in relation to one another as they would if they were exported to Photoshop with both the layers and nested layers options chosen in the Export dialog box (see page 404).

Knockout Group

new The Knockout Group option on the Transparency palette controls whether objects nested in a group or layer show through each other (knock out) where they overlap. To see the knockout effect, objects must have an opacity or blending mode other than 100% or Normal. Only objects inside the targeted group or layer will be affected by this option.

To knock out objects:

1. Arrange objects nested in the same group or layer so they partially overlap each other. Apply the same or different blending modes to some or all of the nested objects.

2. On the Layers palette, target the group or layer the objects are nested within **1**.

3. On the Transparency palette, keep clicking the Knockout Group box until a check mark displays **2**. When the Knockout Group check box is checked, objects won't show through each other, but they will be transparent to objects below them.

➤ If both the Knockout Group and Isolate Blending options are checked, nested objects will look like they have a blending mode of Normal.

➤ The Knockout Group option can also be applied to an object or editable text that has a stroke with transparency applied only to the stroke. Click the top ("Object") line on the Appearance palette to target the whole object, then check the Knockout Group box. The stroke will no longer be transparent to the object's Fill **3**–**4**.

new
To turn off the Knockout Group option:

1. Target the group or layer to which the option is applied.

2. On the Transparency palette, keep clicking the Knockout Group check box until the ckeck mark disappears.

When to put it in neutral

Objects will show through each other, whether the Knockout Group box is unchecked or dashed (neutral). Choose the neutral setting if you want a smaller group of nested objects to be independent of the Knockout Group setting for the larger group, of which that smaller group is a part.

1 *The original group of nested objects on top of an image, with* **Knockout Group** *turned off.*

2 *Knockout Group turned on.*

3 *Knockout Group off. The stroke is transparent to the object fill.*   **4** *Knockout Group on. The stroke knocks out the object fill.*

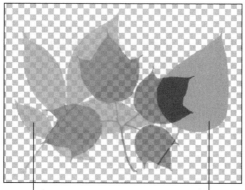

Semi-transparent object.   Light-colored,
                                  opaque object.

1 *With the **transparency grid** showing, you can easily see which objects are opaque and which are not.*

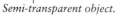

2 *Choose preferences for the transparency grid in Document Setup.*

Once you start working with semi-transparent objects, it may be hard to distinguish between objects that have a light, but solid, tint and those that are semi-transparent. With the transparency grid turned on, you'll be able to see the gray and white checkerboard behind any object whose opacity is less than 100%.

To show/hide the transparency grid:
Choose View menu > Show Transparency Grid (Command-Shift-D/Ctrl-Shift-D) **1**. To turn this feature off, choose View menu > Hide Transparency Grid or use the shortcut again.

You can change the transparency grid colors or size to make the grid contrast better with colors in your artwork.

To choose preferences for the transparency grid:
1. Choose File menu > Document Setup **2**.
2. Choose Transparency from the first pop-up menu.
3. Choose the desired Grid Size.
4. Choose Grid Colors:

    From the pop-up menu, choose the Light, Medium, or Dark grayscale grid or choose a color.
    or
    To choose custom colors, click the top color swatch (this color will also be the Artboard color when no transparency grid is showing), choose a color from the color picker, then click OK. Then click the second swatch, click a second color, and click OK again.

5. *Optional:* Check the Simulate Colored Paper box if you want objects and placed images in the illustration to look as if they're printed on colored paper. The object color will blend with the "colored paper" (the paper color being the color chosen in the top color swatch).

6. Click OK (Enter/Return).

Transparency Grid

327

new Like the Pathfinder commands, the Flatten Transparency command turns areas where selected paths overlap into separate, non-overlapping objects. Strokes are converted into thin, non-overlapping objects; fills will look the same, but their transparency will no longer be editable. (Read about printing and exporting transparency on page 415.)

To flatten objects and maintain the look of transparency:

1. *Optional:* The results from Flatten Transparency will be permanent as soon as you save your file, so we recommend you do a Save As first.

2. Choose the Selection tool (V).

3. Select the objects you want to flatten **1**.

4. Choose Object menu > Flatten Transparency.

5. Check the Preview box **2**.

6. Choose a Quality/Speed. As you move the slider to the right, watch the preview in the illustration window to see how the objects are divided.

7. Choose a Rasterization Resolution. For Web output, choose 72 dpi. For print output, choose between 150 and 300 dpi. Print resolution is usually 1.5 to 2 times the screen resolution of the final printing device (see page 416).

8. Click OK (Return/Enter) **3**–**4**. If you change your mind, Undo right away.

➤ Flatten Transparency has other uses. For one, you can use it to control the flattening of transparent appearances before saving a file to an older version of Illustrator. And for another, you can use Flatten Transparency to prepare a file for export to programs that don't support transparency (at this time, that includes most programs except Photoshop).

1 *Two objects are selected. One has a stroke, the other doesn't.*

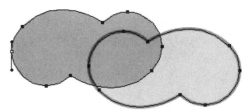

2 *Move the **Quality/Speed** slider in the **Flatten Transparency** dialog box.*

3 *After applying the **Flatten Transparency** command, the paths now total five instead of two. (We pulled the paths apart for this figure.)*

Quality/Speed:
Lower/Faster — Higher/Slower

This will be faster and smaller than rasterizing the entire image. But there is the potential for seaming problems so it is ideal for low quality previews when there are transparent objects in a small area only.

Quality/Speed:
Lower/Faster — Higher/Slower

The entire illustration will be printed as vectors with the exception of complex areas, which will be rasterized. This is a trade-off between rasterization and vector printing.

Quality/Speed:
Lower/Faster — Higher/Slower

Most of the illustration will be printed as vectors. There may be rasterization of areas with many complex objects. This produces high quality output that is generally resolution independent.

4 *We've included these screenshots from the Document Setup > Transparency dialog box so you can read the information for various **Quality/Speed** settings.*

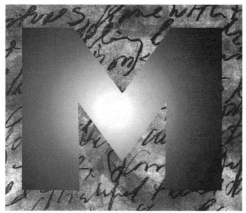

1 *Two objects are selected: A normal type object containing a radial fill and a placed bitmap image.*

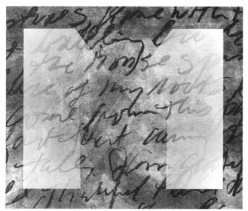

2 *After applying the Make Opacity Mask command.*

3 *Mask thumbnail.*

Opacity masks *new*

An opacity mask is an object whose shape and fill controls the opacity (transparency) of the objects it masks. The topmost object in a selection of objects works as the opacity mask. The masking is controlled by the value level, or grayscale equivalent, of the top object's fill. In the mask, black or dark values will make underlying masked objects totally transparent (see-through); white or very light values will make underlying masked objects opaque; and shades of gray (mid-range color values) will make underlying masked objects partially transparent.

To create an opacity mask:

1. Arrange the object to be used as the mask and the object or objects to be masked, then select them all **1**. You can use editable text, a placed (linked or embedded) image, a pattern, a gradient, or a gradient mesh as the mask, among other things.

2. Choose Make Opacity Mask from the Transparency palette menu **2**. On the Transparency palette, a thumbnail for the mask will appear next to the thumbnail of the object(s) being masked **3**. The Make Opacity Mask command links the object(s) and mask (note the link icon between the thumbnails on the palette).

   (See also figures **1** and **2** on the following page.)

   If you used two objects, the objects will be combined into a new layer or sublayer; if you used more than two objects, the objects will be combined into a group with nested object layers. The new layer name or group name will have a dashed line underneath it to indicate the presence of an opacity mask.

➤ The object-mask combo can be transformed, recolored, or assigned transparency attributes, effects, or styles—like any other object.

Make Opacity Mask

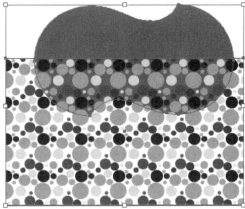

1 *A rectangle with a **pattern** fill is positioned on top of an irregular shape with a **solid gray** fill.*

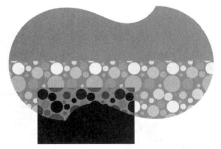

2 *After choosing the **Make Opacity Mask** command, the value levels in the pattern mask out areas in the underlying object. We put a black rectangle behind the other objects to demonstrate how the whites are transparent.*

new

Unlike a clipping mask, an opacity mask normally won't clip parts of objects that extend beyond its edges. Its job is to change the transparency of a masked object's fill—not its shape. With the Invert Mask box checked on the Transparency palette, however, not only are the value levels in the masking object reversed, the masked objects are also clipped to the opacity mask's shape.

To invert an opacity mask:

1. Choose a selection tool, then select the opacity mask object.
2. Check the Invert Mask box on the Transparency palette **3**. (Uncheck the box to un-invert the mask.)

3 *Figure 2 from the previous page, after clicking the **Invert Mask** button on the Transparency palette.*

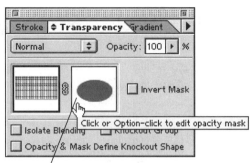

 Opacity mask thumbnail.

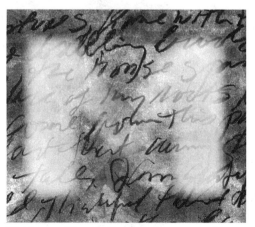

2 *We applied the Scribbly style to this masking object to produce an interesting contour.*

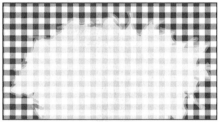

4 *After applying the Feather effect to a masking object (the "M"—the opacity mask).*

Follow these instructions to edit a masking object independent of the masked objects. *new*

To reshape or edit an opacity masking object:

1. Choose a selection tool, then select the opacity mask object.

2. Click the mask thumbnail on the Transparency palette **1**.

3. Do any of the following: Use any usual path reshaping tool to change the contour of the mask; transform the object; change its color, pattern, or gradient fill; change its opacity; or apply an effect or style to it **2**.

4. When you're done, click the object thumbnail on the Transparency palette!

➤ Option-click/Alt-click the opacity mask thumbnail on the Transparency palette to view the masking object in the document window and hide the masked objects.

➤ When the opacity mask thumbnail is selected, the Layers palette displays only the <opacity mask> layer with a nested path (or paths) layer. Either layer can be targeted for changing appearances. To redisplay the normal layers on the Layers palette, click the object thumbnail on the Transparency palette.

Stylize > Feather is only one of the many Effect menu commands that can be applied to a masking object.

To feather the edge of a mask object: *new*

1. Target an opacity mask object using the Layers palette.

2. Click the mask thumbnail on the Transparency palette.

3. Choose Effect menu > Stylize > Feather.

4. Check the Preview box, then choose a Feather Radius value for the width of the feathered area **3**.

5. Adjust the Feather Radius, if desired, then click OK (Return/Enter) **4**.

Reshape Opacity Mask

new If you want to reposition the masking object relative to the masked object(s), you first have to unlink the mask.

To move mask objects independently:

1. Choose a selection tool, then select the opacity mask object.

2. On the Transparency palette, click the link icon between the object thumbnail and the mask thumbnail **1**. (Or choose Unlink Opacity Mask from the Transparency palette menu.)

3. Select and reposition any of the objects individually **2**–**3**.

4. Make sure the object thumbnail is selected, then click again between the thumbnails to re-link the mask. (The link icon is accessable only when the object thumbnail is selected.)

new **To temporarily disable a mask:**

1. Choose a selection tool, then select the opacity mask object.

2. Shift-click the mask thumbnail on the Transparency palette.
   or
   Choose Disable Opacity Mask from the Transparency palette menu.

   A red "X" will appear over the thumbnail and the mask effect will disappear.

3. Shift-click the mask thumbnail again to reinstate the mask.

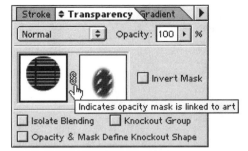

1 *Click the link icon to unlink (not unmask!) the masking and masked objects.*

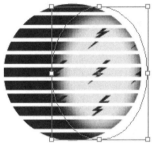

2 *The masking object is selected...*

3 *...and then it's moved.*

1 *The original object, with an opacity mask.*

2 *After releasing the mask.*

To release an opacity mask:

1. Choose a selection tool, then select the opacity mask object **1**.

2. From the Transparency palette menu, choose Release Opacity Mask **2**. The masked object(s) and the masking object will become separate objects, complete with their original appearances, as well as any modifications that were made to the mask. The opacity mask thumbnail will disappear from the Transparency palette.

If you have enabled the Knockout Group option for a group or layer and that group or layer also contains an opacity mask, the Knockout Group option will prevent the opacity mask from displaying any nested group or layer objects through the mask transparency. To regain the display of nested objects underneath the opacity mask, do as follows.

To use an opacity mask within a knockout group or layer:

1. On the Layers palette, target a group or sublayer that contains an opacity mask as well as other nested objects below the mask. Make sure the Knockout Group option is checked for the group or sublayer.

2. Target the opacity mask object.

3. On the Transparency palette, check the Opacity & Mask Define Knockout Shape box **3**–**4**. Other objects within the same nested group that are underneath the opacity mask object will now show through areas of transparency in the opacity mask.

➤ Regardless of the current Opacity & Mask Define Knockout Shape setting, objects on lower layers will always show through areas of transparency in the opacity mask.

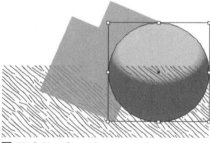

3 *With Knockout Group on, the opacity mask does not reveal shapes nested in the same layer.*

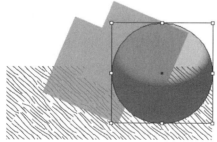

4 *After turning on Opacity & Mask Define Knockout Shape, shapes nested in the same layer are revealed through the opacity mask.*

new

new

Release Opacity Mask; Mask in Knockout

improved The Drop Shadow dialog box is markedly improved. Using its blending mode, opacity, offset, blur (softness), color, and darkness options, you can create soft, naturalistic shadows. A Drop Shadow can be applied as a filter or as an effect.

The Drop Shadow filter creates a new shadow object on its own object layer, separate from the original object. The filter dialog box also offers a Create Separate Shadows option that nests the object and the shadow into a new group on the Layers palette. This is advantageous because the shadow object can then be transformed, reshaped, repositioned by dragging, or recolored via the Adjust Colors filter—independent from the object. Furthermore, the shadow object can be deleted at any time without affecting the object.

Unlike the filter, the Drop Shadow effect becomes an appearance on the original object. You can double-click the Drop Shadow effect attribute on the Appearance palette to reopen its dialog box and edit its settings, including its color; also, the shadow appearance can be removed at any time. However, unlike the Drop Shadow filter, the Drop Shadow effect cannot be transformed, reshaped, or moved via dragging independent from the object. For this reason, we tend to favor the filter over the effect.

To create a drop shadow:

1. Select one or more objects. The Drop Shadow filter can be applied to editable type—it doesn't have to be converted into outlines.

2. Choose Filter menu > or Effect menu > Stylize > Drop Shadow. If you chose the command from the Effect menu, check the Preview box.

3. Choose a blending Mode **1**.

4. Choose an Opacity for the shadow.

5. Enter a number in the X Offset field (the horizontal distance between the object and the shadow) and a number in the Y Offset field (the vertical distance).

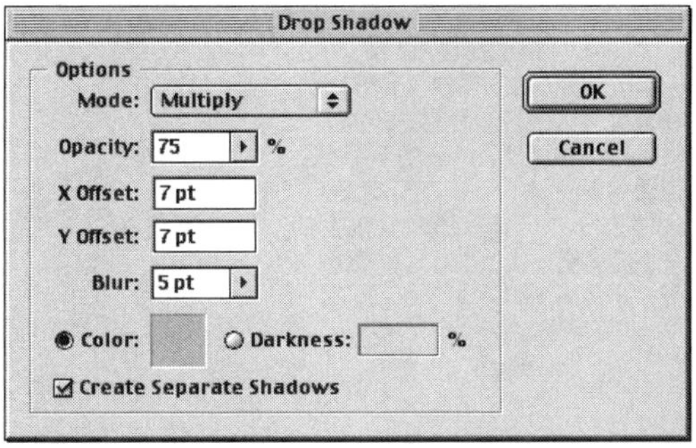

1

Drop Shadow *(side tab)*

1 *After applying the* **Drop Shadow** *effect, default settings.*

2 *After applying the* **Drop Shadow** *filter.*

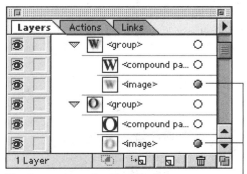

3 *After applying the* **Drop Shadow** *filter with the* **Create Separate Shadows** *box checked. Each shadow is stacked directly below its matching object.*

Shadows

6. Enter a Blur amount for the width of the shadow.

7. *Optional:* Click Color, click the color square, then choose a different color from the Color Picker. Or click Darkness, then enter the percentage of black to be added to the shadow.

8. *Optional:* If you're using the Drop Shadow filter, check the Create Separate Shadows box to group the object with its shadow. If this option is checked, each shadow will be nested directly below its matching object in a new group. If this option is unchecked, the whole shadow object will be placed below all the nested objects in the same group or layer. We recommend checking this option.

9. Click OK (Return/Enter) **1**–**3**.

➤ With the current value highlighted in the Opacity or Blur field, you can press the up or down arrow on the keyboard to increase or decrease it.

To apply the Hard Mix and Soft Mix commands:

We covered most of the Pathfinders in Chapter 16, but we're covering the Hard Mix and Soft Mix commands in this chapter because we want you to see how they differ from the Opacity controls.

Until "real" transparency controls were added to Illustrator, the Mix commands were the only tools illustrators had for simulating transparency. These commands lack the adjustability of the blending mode and opacity features that the Transparency palette now offers. And while the flattening feature of the Soft Mix command can be used to simplify complex shapes and simulate transparency for export, the Flatten Transparency feature on the Object menu and in the Document Setup dialog box offer superior controls for simplifying shapes and their appearances.

(Continued on the following page)

That said, there's no harm in playing with the Hard Mix or Soft Mix commands. Here are the facts:

➤ To apply either command, select two or more objects that overlap at least partially, then click either button on the Pathfinder palette. (If the color mixing commands aren't visible on the Pathfinder palette, choose Show Options from the palette menu.)

➤ Both Mix commands convert areas where objects overlap into separate objects. Their fill colors will be changed to a mixture of their formerly overlapping colors.

➤ The Mix commands remove all stroke colors.

➤ When the Mix commands are applied to a mixture of global or non-global process colors and spot colors, all the colors will be converted to non-global process colors in the current document color mode.

HARD MIX

Simulates overprinting. The highest C, M, Y, and K, or R, G, and B values from each of the original objects are mixed in areas where they overlap. The greater the difference between the original colors, the more marked will be the resulting effect **1**–**2**.

SOFT MIX

Creates an illusion of partial transparency. The higher the Mixing Rate specified in the Pathfinder Soft Mix dialog box, the more transparent and altered the color of the frontmost object will become **3**–**5**.

➤ To create a painterly effect, try layering three objects of different colors, then apply Soft Mix at around 75–85% **6**.

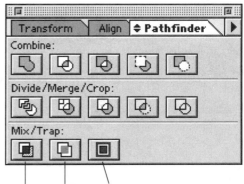

Hard Mix Soft Mix Trap

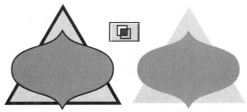

1 *The original objects.*   **2** *Hard Mix.*

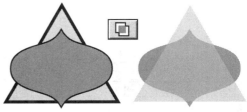

3 *The original objects.*   **4** *Soft Mix (50%).*

5 *Enter a **Mixing Rate** for the Soft Mix command.*

6 *The circle on top had a white fill, and we used a Mixing Rate of 80%.*

(left margin) **Soft Mix/Hard Mix**

Illustrator's object-reshaping and raster image-enhancing filters are powerful, but easy to use. This chapter includes a how-to section for applying filters, specific instructions for applying a few of the vector filters, a section on applying filters to bitmap images, a compendium of all the raster filters, and instructions for applying the two Pen and Ink filters (Hatch Effects and Photo Crosshatch).

Hatch lines created using Illustrator's **Hatch Effects** filter.

Filter
Apply Crystallize	⌘E
Crystallize...	⌥⌘E

Colors	▶
Create	▶
Distort	▶
Pen and Ink	▶
Stylize	▶

— *Mostly **Vector** filters for path objects (except Photo Crosshatch, Object Mosaic).*

Artistic	▶
Blur	▶
Brush Strokes	▶
Distort	▶
Pixelate	▶
Sharpen	▶
Sketch	▶
Stylize	▶
Texture	▶
Video	▶

— ***Raster** filters for placed images or RGB color mode bitmap objects.*

1 *The **Filter** menu.*

Filter basics

Some of Illustrator's filters are designed primarily for use with **vector** (path) objects, and they are grouped in five submenu categories: Colors, Create, Distort, Pen and Ink, and Stylize **1**. Several of these filters are discussed in the pages that follow.

Other Illustrator filters are designed for use with **bitmap** images or rasterized objects, and they are grouped in ten submenu categories at the bottom of the Filter menu: Artistic, Blur, Brush Strokes, Distort, Pixelate, Sharpen, Sketch, Stylize, Texture, and Video. If you're a Photoshop user, you may already be familiar with these. The raster filters are discussed and illustrated in the latter part of this chapter. *Note:* Some raster filters work on RGB or Grayscale images, but not on CMYK or 1-bit Bitmap images.

You can also apply **Photoshop-compatible** filters to placed images and to objects that are rasterized in Illustrator. To make them accessible in Illustrator, copy the filters (or aliases of the filters) into the Photoshop Filters folder inside Illustrator's Plug-ins folder, then relaunch Illustrator.

In Illustrator 9.0 or later, you have two methods for applying the same filters: via the **Filter** menu or via the **Effects** menu. Via the Filter menu, the filter changes the actual objects. Via the Effects menu, the filter only affects the appearance of the image or object, and the effect can be re-edited at any

(Continued on the following page)

Filter Basics

time (we prefer this method). Settings used for a Filter menu command become the settings for the matching command on the Effect menu, and vice versa.

As for the actual mechanics of the application, some filters are applied simply by selecting the filter name from a submenu. Other filters are applied via a dialog box in which special options are chosen. You'll probably want to memorize the shortcuts listed in the sidebar at right.

➤ Some filters are memory-intensive, but using lower or different settings in a filter dialog box can help speed things up.

Many vector filter dialog boxes have a **Preview box** ■. Check it to preview the filter effect in your illustration while the dialog box is open. Press Tab to preview after entering a new amount in a field.

Raster filter dialog boxes have a **preview window** inside the dialog box ■. You can drag in most preview windows to move the image inside it. Click the + button to zoom in on the image in the preview window or click the – button to zoom out. A flashing line below the preview percentage indicates the preview is taking a moment to render.

➤ In a raster filter dialog box, you can hold down Option/Alt and click Reset to reset the slider settings to what they were when the dialog box was opened.

Note: Some Illustrator filters are covered in other chapters. Look up the filter name under "Filters" in the index for page locations.

Quick reapply

Reapply last-used filter using the same settings	Command-E/ Ctrl-E
Open last-used filter dialog to choose new settings	Command-Option-E/ Ctrl-Alt-E
Reapply last-used effect	Command-Shift-E/ Ctrl-Shift-E
Last-used effects dialog box	Command-Option-Shift-E/ Ctrl-Alt-Shift-E

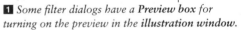

■ *Some filter dialogs have a **Preview box** for turning on the preview in the **illustration window.***

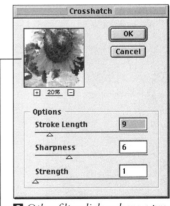

■ *Other filter dialogs have a **preview window** inside the **dialog box.***

Filter Basics

1 *The Scribble and Tweak dialog box.*

A few vector filters
To scribble or tweak:
1. Select a path object or objects.
2. Choose Filter menu > Distort > Scribble and Tweak.
3. Check the Preview box and move the dialog box out of the way, if necessary **1**.
4. Choose Horizontal and Vertical percentages to control how much anchor points can be moved in either direction.
5. Click Relative to move points by percentages of the size of the object or click Absolute to move points by a specific amount. *new*
6. *Optional:* Check Anchor Points if you want anchor points to move; check "In" Control Points to change the segments that extend to anchor points; check "Out" Control Points to change the segments that extend from anchor points. Or leave Anchor Points unchecked to preserve more of the object's original shape.
7. Click OK (Return/Enter) **2–3**. Corner points will automatically be converted into points with direction lines. How direction lines are moved depends on whether you chose either or both of the "In" or "Out" options.
➤ The greater the number of anchor points on the path, the stronger the Scribble and Tweak effect. To intensify the filter's effect, apply Object menu > Path > Add Anchor Points before applying the filter.

2 *The original object.*

3 *After applying the Scribble and Tweak filter (Horizontal 14.5, Vertical 19.5, "In" and "Out" boxes checked).*

Scribble and Tweak Filter

The Roughen filter makes an object look more hand drawn by adding anchor points and then moving them.

To rough up a shape:

1. Select a path object or objects, and choose View menu > Hide Edges (Command-H/Ctrl-H), if you like, to make previewing easier.

2. Choose Filter menu > Distort > Roughen.

3. Check the Preview box **1**.

4. Choose a Size percentage to specify how far points can be moved. Try a very low percentage first to preserve the object's basic shape.

5. Click Relative to move points by percentages of the size of the object or click Absolute to move points by a specific amount.

6. Choose a Detail amount for the number of points to be added to each inch of the path segments.

7. Click Smooth to produce soft edges or click Corner to produce pointy edges.

8. Click OK (Return/Enter) **2**–**3**.

To twirl path points around an object's center (dialog box method):

1. Select a path object or objects **4**. If two or more objects are selected, they will be twirled together.

2. Choose Filter menu > Distort > Twirl (in the upper part of the menu).

3. Enter an Angle (-3600–3600). A positive number will twirl the path(s) clockwise; a negative number will twirl it counter-clockwise.

4. Click OK (Return/Enter) **5**–**6**. Now try using the Twirl tool for comparison (instructions on the next page).

➤ To add points to a path and heighten the Twirl filter effect, choose Object menu > Path > Add Anchor Points before applying the Twirl filter.

Roughen Filter; Twirl Filter

new

1 *The Roughen dialog box.*

2 *The original object.*

3 *After applying the Roughen filter (or seeing a dog).*

4 *The original objects.*

5 *The objects twirled together, Angle 1000°.*

6 *The Twirl filter applied to* **5**, *Angle 3000°.*

1 *The Twirl tool.*

2 *The original objects.*

3 *After twirling.*

gothic horror

4 *The original type outlines. Effect menu > Punk & Bloat can be applied to editable text!*

5 *After applying the Punk part of the filter.*

6 *The original object.*

7 *After applying the Bloat filter.*

Like the Twirl filter, the Twirl tool twirls points around an object's center, but its effect is usually more subtle.

To twirl points around an object's center (mouse method):

1. Select a path object.

2. Choose the Twirl tool on the Rotate tool pop-out menu **1**.

3. *Optional:* Click to establish a different location for the center of the twirl than the object's center.

4. Move the mouse slightly away from the center point (if one was established), then drag clockwise or counterclockwise. Repeat to tighten the twirl effect **2**–**3**.

➤ To open the Twirl dialog box to enter an angle, Option/Alt click in the document window with the Twirl tool.

➤ Neither the Twirl tool nor the Twirl filter affect a pattern or a gradient fill; they only twirl the object's outer shape. To twirl a pattern or gradient fill, apply the Object menu > Expand command to the object first (check the Fill box), and select all the shapes before twirling. The monster that results won't print easily, though.

To punk or bloat an object:

1. Select an object or objects **4** and **6**.

2. Choose Filter menu > Distort > Punk & Bloat.

3. Check the Preview box.

4. Move the slider to the left to Punk (anchor points move outward and curve segments move inward) **5** or move the slider to the right to Bloat (anchor points move inward and curve segments move outward) **7**.

5. Click OK.

➤ To add points to the path and intensify the Punk or Bloat effect, choose Object menu > Path > Add Anchor Points before applying the filter. See also Figures 1–3 on page 108.

➤ For fun, try punking or bloating an object that contains a pattern or gradient fill.

Twirl Tool; Punk & Bloat Filter

Raster (bitmap) filters

All the raster filters are available for a raster-ized object or a placed bitmap image in RGB or Grayscale color mode; only the Blur, Sharpen, and Pixelate filters are available for an image in CMYK color mode; no raster fil-ters are available for an image in Bitmap color mode. **No raster filters are available for a linked image**; it has to be embedded.

Some of these filters introduce an element of randomness or distortion that would be diffi-cult to achieve by hand. Others, like the Artistic, Brush Strokes, Sketch, and Texture filters, are designed to make an image look a little less machine-made, more hand-ren-dered. When a raster filter is applied to a large, high resolution bitmap image, a progress bar may display while the filter is processing. Click Stop or press Return/Enter to cancel a filter in progress.

In some filter dialog boxes, like Rough Pastels or Grain, there is a Texture or Grain Type option. To use this option, choose a texture type from the Texture or Grain Type pop-up menu **1**–**2**, move the Scaling slider to enlarge or reduce the size of the texture pattern, and move the Relief slider, if there is one, to adjust the depth and prominence of the texture on the image's surface. In some dialog boxes you'll also have the option to load in a bitmap image saved in Photoshop format (files with the ".psd" extension) to use instead of a preset texture. To do this, choose Load Texture from the Texture pop-up menu, highlight the name of the bitmap file you want to use, then click Open.

In addition to the raster filters, other filters you can apply to a raster image include Colors submenu > Adjust Colors, Convert to Grayscale, Convert to CMYK or Convert to RGB (depending on the current document color mode), Invert Colors, and Saturate and also the Photo Crosshatch filter under the Pen and Ink submenu.

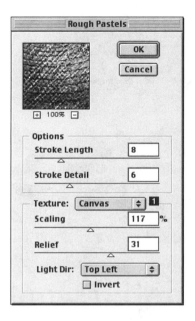

2 *Rough Pastels filter, Burlap* **Texture.**

Raster Filters

Transparent versus clipping mask

Both the Background: Transparent and Create Clipping Mask options remove an object's background. Unlike Create Clipping Mask, the Transparent option creates an alpha channel to remove the background, and the resulting image stays as a single layer. Any blending mode or opacity settings are removed, but the object retains the appearance of transparency. Blending modes and opacity can be applied to the targeted image layer at any time.

The Create Clipping Mask option, on the other hand, creates a nested group composed of a clipping path and the image. The clipping path retains any transparency appearances. Blending modes and opacity for the object can be adjusted on the targeted image layer (not the clipping path layer).

Note: Before experimenting with the raster filters, you should learn about Illustrator's Rasterize command, which converts a vector (path) object into a pixel object. You can apply any raster (bitmap) filter to a rasterized object.

To rasterize a path object: *improved*

1. Select a path object or objects.

2. Choose Object menu > Rasterize.

3. Choose a Color Model for the image: RGB for video or on-screen display (all raster filters available) or CMYK for print output (only the Blur, Sharpen, and Pixelate raster filters available), depending on the current document color mode; Grayscale for shades of black and white (all raster filters available); or Bitmap for only black-and-white (no raster filters available) **1**.

4. Click a Resolution setting or enter a resolution value in the Other field. Choose Screen for Web output; choose High for imagesetter output.

5. Click Background: White to make the object's background opaque white or click Transparent to make the background transparent (see the sidebar).

6. *Optional:* Check Anti-Alias to have Illustrator add pixels to soften the edge of the rasterized shape. This option may make text or thin lines look blurry.

7. *Optional:* Check Create Clipping Mask to have Illustrator generate a clipping mask for the shape so its background will be transparent (see the sidebar).

8. *Optional:* To have Illustrator add pixels around the object for padding (the bounding box becomes larger), enter a value in the "Add ___ Around Object" field.

9. Click OK (Return/Enter). A bounding box will surround the path object (**1**–**4**, next page).

➤ If a solid color object is rasterized with Create Clipping Mask checked, then

(Continued on the following page)

Rasterize an Object

the object color can be changed after rasterizing. To recolor the object, first select only the clipping path layer that's nested within the group on the Layers palette.

➤ If you rasterize an object that contains a pattern fill, the pattern color and line weight may change somewhat, especially if the Anti-Alias option is on. If the object originally had a pattern fill with a transparent background, the transparent background will be retained if you click Background: Transparent.

1 *A rasterized object **with a clipping mask** after applying the Glass filter. The mask limits the filter effect to the object shape.*

2 *A rasterized object **without a clipping mask** after applying the Glass filter. The filter effect extends beyond the object's original edge.*

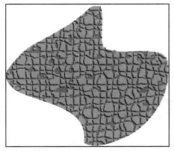

3 *A rasterized object **with a clipping mask** after applying the Mosaic Tile filter. The mask limits the filter effect to the object shape.*

4 *A rasterized object **without a clipping mask** after applying the Mosaic Tile filter. The filter effect extends beyond the object's original edge.*

Rasterize an Object

1 *The original image.*

*The **Object Mosaic** dialog box.*

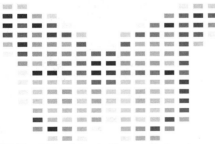

3 *The **Object Mosaic** filter applied.*

The Object Mosaic filter breaks up a raster image into a grid of little squares. Each of the squares is a separate object that can be moved or recolored individually.

To apply the Object Mosaic filter:

1. Click on a rasterized object or an embedded bitmap image **1**.

2. Choose Filter menu > Create > Object Mosaic.

3. *Optional:*

   The Current Size field displays the width and height of the image in points. Enter new numbers in the New Size: Width and/or Height fields **2**. (If you want to enter the dimensions in percentages relative to the original, first check the Resize using Percentages box.)
   or
   Enter a New Size: Width (or Height), click Constrain Ratio: Width (or Height) to lock in that dimension, then click Use Ratio (right side of the dialog box) to have Illustrator automatically calculate the opposite dimension proportionate to the object's original dimensions.

4. Enter the Number of Tiles to fill the width and height dimensions. If you clicked Use Ratio, the Number of Tiles will be calculated automatically.

5. *Optional:* To add space between each tile, enter numbers in the Tile Spacing: Width and Height fields.

6. *Optional:* When it's applied to a bitmap image, the Object Mosaic filter affects a copy of the image that's made automatically, and the original is left unchanged. Check the Delete Raster box if you want the original image to be deleted.

7. Click Result: Color or Gray.

8. Click OK (Return/Enter) **3**–**4**.

➤ The mosaic object is listed as a group on the Layers palette.

4 *The **Object Mosaic** filter applied to the original image with spacing between the tiles.*

The raster filters illustrated
Artistic filters

Original image

Colored Pencil

Cutout

Dry Brush

Film Grain

Fresco

Neon Glow

Paint Daubs

Palette Knife

Artistic Filters

Artistic filters

Original image

Plastic Wrap

Poster Edges

Rough Pastels

Smudge Stick

Sponge

Underpainting

Watercolor

CHAPTER 20

Blur filters

Original image

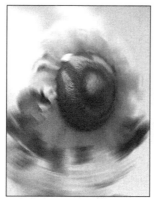

Radial Blur

Gaussian Blur

Brush Strokes filters

Original image

Accented Edges

Angled Strokes

Crosshatch

Dark Strokes

Ink Outlines

Brush Strokes filters

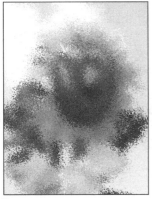

Spatter

Sprayed Strokes

Sumi-e

Distort filters

Original image

Diffuse Glow

Glass (Blocks)

Ocean Ripple

Pixelate filters

Original image

Color Halftone

Crystallize

Mezzotint (Short Strokes)

Mezzotint (Medium Dots)

Pointillize

For the Unsharp Mask filter, see our Visual QuickStart Guide on Photoshop!

Stylize filter

Original image

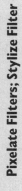

Glowing Edges

Sketch filters

Original image

Bas Relief

Chalk & Charcoal

Charcoal

Chrome

Conté Crayon

Graphic Pen

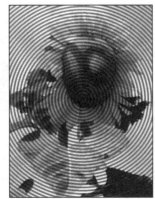

Halftone Pattern (Circle)

Halftone Pattern (Dot)

Sketch Filters

Sketch filters

Original image

Note Paper

Photocopy

Plaster

Reticulation

Stamp

Torn Edges

Water Paper

Texture filters

Original image

Craquelure

Grain (Enlarged)

Grain (Horizontal)

Mosaic Tiles

Patchwork

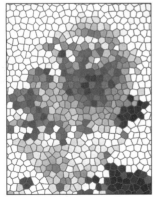

Stained Glass

Texturizer

353

The Pen and Ink filters

In this section, we discuss the Hatch Effects filter and the Photo Crosshatch filter. The Hatch Effects filter creates an amazing assortment of line work patterns by turning a path object into a mask and then creating a fill of linework shapes behind the mask. You can choose from 26 preset pen patterns—called hatch styles—that you can use as is or further modify using a wide variety of options. You can also create a new hatch from scratch from an Illustrator object.

To apply the Pen and Ink filter:

1. Select a path object.

2. Choose Filter menu > Pen and Ink > Hatch Effects.

3. Check the Preview box or leave it unchecked to speed processing.

4. Choose a predefined effect from the Hatch Effect pop-up menu 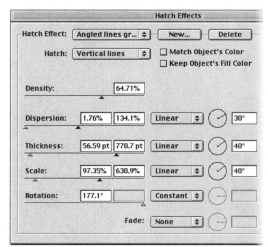.

    If you're satisfied with the pattern, click OK. To further modify it, follow any of the remaining steps.

5. Choose another predefined hatch from the Hatch pop-up menu to use with the current effect.

6. Move the **Density** slider to adjust the number of hatch shapes in the fill. Or to adjust the density a different way, click a different gray on the vertical grayscale bar next to the preview window 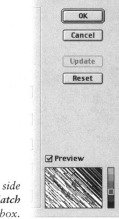.

7. For any of the following options, choose a setting other than None from its corresponding pop-up menu (read the sidebar on the next page), and move one or both of the sliders.

    Dispersion controls the spacing between hatch shapes.

    Thickness controls the line thickness of the hatch shapes. This property is available only for hatch styles that are composed of lines (Cross, Crosshatch 1, Vertical lines, and Worm).

    Scale controls the size of the hatch shapes.

    Rotation controls the angle of the hatch shapes.

Big hairy monster?

Pen and Ink fills can be quite complex, and their direction lines and line endpoints may extend way beyond the edge of the original object. To prevent inadvertent selection of a Pen and Ink fill, put the Pen and Ink object on its own layer and then lock that layer.

If your Pen and Ink fill doesn't print, try reducing the object's Output resolution (see page 400). Also, don't apply the Pen and Ink filter to an object that already contains a Pen and Ink fill—it will demand too much from your output device.

1 *The left side of the Hatch Effects dialog box.*

2 *The right side of the Hatch Effects dialog box.*

Hatch Effect pop-up menu options

None: No effect.

Constant: Effect repeats without changing across the entire shape.

Linear: Effect intensifies in a progression from one side of the fill shape to the other.

Reflect: Effect varies from the center of the fill shape outward.

Symmetric: Like Linear, but more proportionate and even. Hatch shading looks like shading on a cylindrical object.

Random: Effect changes in a random, haphazard fashion across the fill shape.

The Linear, Reflect, Symmetric, and Random options have two sliders each, and their position controls the range of choices for that option. The wider the distance between a pair of sliders, the wider the range of possibilities for that option. Enter a value in the Angle box or drag the angle dial to specify an axis for the change.

1 *Enter a **name** for the new hatch. (In Windows, this dialog box is called "New Settings" if you click New in the Hatch Effects dialog box.)*

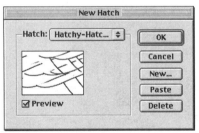

2 *The new hatch previews.*

8. Check the **Match Object's Color** box to make the hatch match the object's fill color. Check the **Keep Object's Fill Color** box to make the hatch black and leave the object color unchanged.

9. From the **Fade** pop-up menu, choose whether the hatch style will fade To White or To Black across the fill shape. If the object's fill was a gradient, choose Use Gradient to color the hatch shapes with the gradient. You can enter an angle for the axis along which the fade will occur.

10. Click OK (Return/Enter).

➤ To **save** any current property option changes to a custom Hatch Effect variation, click New at the top of the dialog box, enter a Name, then click OK.

➤ To **delete** the current Hatch Effect variation, click Delete, then click Yes. *Warning:* This can't be undone by pressing Cancel in the Hatch Effects dialog box or by using the Undo command.

➤ Click **Update** to save the current property options to the current Hatch Effect variant. *Warning:* Update overwrites the existing Hatch Effect variant. Click **Reset** to remove any property variations from the current Hatch Effect. If you click Update now, the current Hatch Effect will be overwritten.

The hatch is the underlying pattern tile that is used by the Pen and Ink filter.

To create a new hatch pattern:

1. Create a small object or objects to use as the hatch pattern.

2. Select the object or objects.

3. Choose Filter menu > Pen and Ink > New Hatch.

4. Click New, type a Name for the hatch **1**, then click OK.

5. Check the Preview box to display the new pattern in the preview window **2**. Click OK (Return/Enter) to close the New Hatch dialog box. The hatch will be saved in the currently open hatch library.

To modify an existing hatch:

1. Scroll to a blank area of the artboard, and deselect all objects.

2. Choose Filter menu > Pen and Ink > New Hatch.

3. Choose the pattern you want to edit from the Hatch drop-down menu.

4. Click Paste.

5. Click OK (Return/Enter). The hatch pattern objects will be selected.

6. Zoom in, and modify the hatch pattern.

7. Reselect the hatch pattern object(s).

8. Follow steps 3–5 in the previous set of instructions.

➤ Click Delete to remove the currently chosen hatch style from the Hatch pop-up menu. This can't be undone.

The default Hatch Sets library opens automatically when Illustrator is launched.

To save a hatch library:

1. Create your own custom Hatch Effect variations.

2. Choose Filter menu > Pen and Ink > Library Save As.

3. Enter a new name for the library, open the Adobe Illustrator 9 > Plug-ins > Illustrator Filters > Pen and Ink folder, where the default Hatch Sets library is located, then click Save. *Note:* If you don't change the file name from the default name "Hatch Sets," and you then click Save, you will be asked to cancel or replace the existing file. Click Replace if you want to edit the default library.

To open a hatch library:

1. Choose Filter menu > Pen and Ink > Library Open.

2. Locate and highlight the name of a pre-saved library, then click Open.

Fanya, Diane Margolin.

Taj Mahal, Diane Margolin.

1 *The original grayscale photo.*

2 *The Photo Crosshatch filter applied using these settings: Two Layers, Density 3.5 pt., Dispersion Noise 0, Thickness .4 pt., Max. Line Length 24 pt., Rotation Noise 2°, Rotation Variance 100°, and Top angle 40°. The image below is a close-up.*

The Photo Crosshatch filter translates a rasterized, photographic image into a crosshatch pattern. When applied at the appropriate density, the crosshatches look like hand-drawn shading—as in an artist's pen drawing.

To convert a continuous-tone image into a crosshatch image:

1. Place a photographic image, without a saved clipping path, into an Illustrator document **1**. The filter won't be available for a linked bitmap image or any kind of EPS image. To use a PSD image, flatten it down to a single image when placing.
or
Select an image in your illustration, then choose Embed Image from the Links palette menu.

2. Choose Filter menu > Pen and Ink > Photo Crosshatch.

3. Choose the number of Hatch Layers (1–8). This is similar to choosing levels of posterization. The greater the number of hatch layers, the more levels of shading will be produced in the image. (Don't get confused here. The layers won't appear as separate layers in the document.)

4. *Optional:* Move the sliders under the histogram to determine how different lightness levels in the original image will be rendered by line patterns. Move the rightmost slider to the right to create more line patterning in the image highlights and lessen areas of absolute white, or move the rightmost slider to the left to decrease line patterning in the highlights and increase areas of absolute white. Move the middle slider to increase or decrease line patterning in the midtones. Move the leftmost slider to the right to decrease line patterning in the shadows.

5. Move the sliders on the left side of the dialog box to control the hatch lines (**1**, next page):

   The **Density** slider controls the number of hatch lines used. A low Density will produce a very dense collection of hatch

(Continued on the following page)

Photo Crosshatch Filter

lines. A high image resolution may affect the density of the hatch lines.

The **Dispersion Noise** slider controls the spacing between hatch line segments. 0% Dispersion Noise produces line segments that align perfectly end to end to form a long, straight-line texture. A value greater than 0% produces line segments that don't align end to end, and thus no long straight lines. A low Dispersion Noise creates a hand-drawn look; a high Dispersion Noise produces more obvious patterning and less obvious shading.

The **Thickness** slider controls the stroke weight of the line segments.

The **Max. Line Length** slider controls the length of the line segments.

The **Rotation Noise** slider controls the amount of arbitrary rotation given to individual line segments on each hatch layer. The higher the Rotation Noise setting, the more obvious the patterning and the less obvious the shading.

The **Rotation Variance** slider controls how much each hatch layer is rotated relative to the previous layer. High values distinguish each layer more, but make shading less smooth.

The **Top Angle** is the angle along which hatch lines are drawn in the topmost hatch layer.

6. Click OK (Return/Enter) (**2**, previous page, and **2**, this page). To produce shading, hatch lines start on the edge of an image's highlights and continue into the midtones or all the way into the shadows, while other hatch lines start in the midtones and continue into the shadows. Still other hatch lines are drawn only in the shadows.

➤ The Photo Crosshatch filter converts the original rasterized image. Make a copy first to retain the original image.

➤ To darken selected areas in the resulting crosshatch, lasso some line segments using the Direct-select Lasso tool, then increase their stroke weight.

1 *The Photo Crosshatch dialog box.*

2 *The Photo Crosshatch filter applied to the original image on the previous page using these settings: Two Layers, Density 3.5, Dispersion Noise 15%, Thickness .5, Max. Line Length 24, Rotation Noise 18°, Rotation Variance 90%, Top angle 40°. In this image, the higher Dispersion Noise, Rotation Noise, and Rotation Variance values create a more hand-drawn look, as compared with the image on the previous page. The image below is a close-up.*

There are many tools you can use to position or move objects with exact precision. In this chapter you will learn how to use rulers, guides, and grids to align and position objects. How to move an object a specified distance via the Move dialog box. How to use the Measure tool to calculate distances between objects. How to use the Transform palette to reposition, resize, rotate, or shear objects. And how to use the Align palette to align or distribute objects.

Smart Guides are precision tools, too, but they're so helpful and so easy to use, we discussed them early in the book (see pages 76–77, 85, and 158). The Transform Each command is discussed on page 93, Transform Effect on page 94.

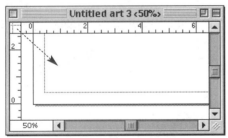

1 Drag diagonally away from the intersection of the rulers.

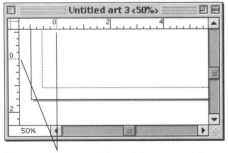

2 Note the new position of the zeros on the rulers after you change the **ruler origin**.

Ruler guides and object guides

The rulers are located at the top and left edges of the document window. Location measurements (e.g., the X and Y readouts on the Transform and Info palettes) are read from the ruler origin, which is the point where the zeros of both rulers meet. By default, the **ruler origin** is positioned at the lower left corner of the page, but it can be moved to a different location for any individual document to help you measure or position objects. The current pointer location is indicated by a mark on each ruler.

To move the ruler origin:

1. Make sure the rulers are displayed. To do this, choose View menu > Show Rulers; or use the Command-R/Ctrl-R shortcut; or make sure nothing is selected in the illustration window, then Control-click/ Right-click on the artboard and choose Show Rulers from the context menu.

2. Drag the square where the two rulers intersect to a new position **1**–**2**. The ruler origin will stay in the new location even if you close and reopen the file.

➤ If you move the ruler origin, pattern fills in any existing objects may shift position.

To restore the ruler origin to its default location:

Double-click where the two rulers intersect at the upper left corner of the document window.

➤ Control-click/Right-click either ruler to open a context menu from which you can choose a different unit of measure for the document. This setting will supercede the units setting in Edit menu > Preferences > Units & Undo.

For most purposes, Smart Guides work adequately for arranging objects (see page 76). If you need guides that stay on the screen, however, you'll need to create them using either method described on this page. Ruler guides don't print.

If View menu > **Snap to Point** is turned on, as you drag an object near a guide, the black pointer will turn white and the part of the object that's under the pointer will snap to the guide. The **Snapping Tolerance** (the distance within which an object will snap to a guide) can be changed in Edit menu > Preferences > Smart Guides.

To show/hide guides:

Choose View menu > Guides > Hide Guides or Show Guides (Command-;/Ctrl-;).

To create a ruler guide:

1. *Optional:* Create a new layer expressly for the guides.

2. If the rulers are not displayed, choose View menu > Show Rulers.

3. Drag a guide from the horizontal or vertical ruler onto your page **1**. If View menu > **Snap to Grid** is on, as you create or move the guide, it will snap to the nearest ruler tick mark. The newly created guide will be locked and it will be listed on the Layers palette as an object nested in the active layer.

➤ Option-drag/Alt-drag from the horizontal ruler to create a vertical guide, and vice versa.

snap to pixel *new*

If View menu > **Pixel Preview** is turned on, the Snap to Grid feature becomes **Snap to Pixel**. With Snap to Pixel on, any new objects that you create or any existing objects that you drag will snap to the pixel grid and anti-aliasing will be removed from any horizontal or vertical edges on those objects. To use this option, make sure **Use Preview Bounds** is turned **off** in Edit menu > Preferences > General.

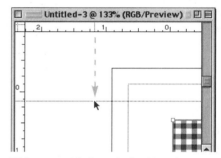

1 *Drag a guide from the horizontal or vertical ruler.*

1 *An object is selected.*

2 *Make Guides is chosen from the context menu.*

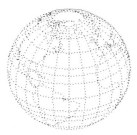

3 *The object is now a guide. The former "path" object will now be listed as "guide" on the Layers palette.*

So far we've shown you how to work with two kinds of guides: ruler guides and smart guides. Now you'll learn how to create guides from standard Illustrator paths. Best of all, the conversion is reversible; an object guide can be converted back into a standard object at any time.

Note: If the object you turn into a guide is part of a group, the guide will also be part of that group.

To turn an object into a guide:

1. Select an object, a group of objects, or an object within a group **1**. Copy the object and work off the copy, if desired.

2. Choose View menu > Guides > Make Guides (Command-5/Ctrl-5).
   or
   Control-click/Right-click and choose Make Guides from the context menu (this may not be available for some types of objects) **2**–**3**.

➤ You can transform or reshape a guide object, as long as it isn't locked. Relock guides when you're done editing them.

Back we go.

To turn all object guides back into objects:

1. If guides are locked, Control-click/Right-click and choose Lock Guides from the context menu to uncheck that option.

2. Choose the Selection tool (V).

3. Select one guide or marquee or Shift-click multiple guides.

4. Choose View menu > Guides > Release Guides (Command-Option-5/Ctrl-Alt-5).
   or
   Control-click/Right-click and choose Release Guides from the context menu. The guide will revert to an object, with its former fill and stroke.

To turn one guide back into an object:

Command-Shift-double-click/ Ctrl-Shift-double-click the edge of the guide.

To select or move guides, standard or object, they must first be unlocked. By default, the Lock Guides command is turned on.

To lock or unlock all guides:

Choose View menu > Guides > Lock Guides (Command-Option-;/Ctrl-Alt-;) to check or uncheck the command.

or

Make sure no objects are selected, then Control-click/Right-click the artboard and choose Lock Guides from the context menu.

If you don't want all of your guides to be locked, you can unlock them all, and then lock any guide individually. (See the sidebar!)

To lock one guide:

1. Unlock all guides.
2. Click the guide you want to lock.
3. Choose Object menu > Lock.

To remove one guide:

1. Make sure either all guides are unlocked or the guide you want to remove is unlocked.
2. Choose the Selection tool (V), then select the guide.
3. Mac OS: Press Delete/Windows: Press Backspace or Del.
4. Re-lock the remaining guides, if desired (View menu > Guides > Lock Guides).

To clear all guides:

Choose View menu > Guides > Clear Guides.

Guide control **new**

Each guide is listed as a separate layer on the Layers palette, and you can hide/show or lock/unlock each individual **guide layer**.

If you like, after the guides are created, you can drag guide layers into one top-level layer. Then if you hide/show or lock/unlock that top-level layer, all the guides nested in that layer will be affected simultaneously.

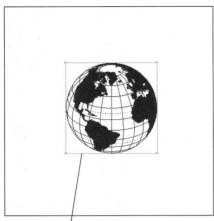

1 *A rectangle is drawn around the globe to define the guide area.*

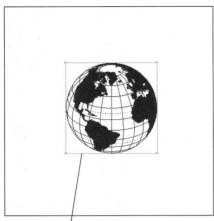

2 *The Rows & Columns dialog box.*

To place guides around an object or create evenly spaced guides:

1. Choose the Selection tool (V), then select an existing rectangle. Make sure the rectangle is on the printable page. *Warning!* If you use a non-rectangular shape, the shape will revert to a rectangle!
or
Choose the Rectangle tool, then drag a rectangle to define the guide area **1**.

2. Make sure the ruler origin is in the default location.

3. Choose Type menu > Rows & Columns.

4. Check Add Guides and Preview **2**.

5. To encircle the object with guides without dividing it, leave both the Columns and Rows Numbers as 1. To create a set of evenly spaced guides, enter a Rows: Number, Height, and Gutter width and a Columns: Number, Width, and Gutter width.

6. Click OK (Return/Enter) **3**.

7. On the Layers palette, Shift-click the rectangular path object(s) to deselect it so it's not affected by the next step.

8. With only the lines selected, choose View menu > Guides > Make Guides (Command-5/Ctrl-5) **4**. The guides will be listed as a group on the Layers palette. If you like, you can delete the rectangle that was used to create the guides.

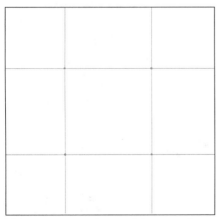

3 *Lines are created around the rectangle.*

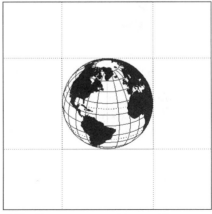

4 *The lines are converted into guides.*

Row and Column Guides

Using the Grid

The grid is like non-printing graph paper. You can use it as a framework to help you arrange objects, either by eye or using the Snap to Grid function.

You can change the grid style (lines or dots), color, or spacing in Edit menu > Preferences > **Guides & Grid** (see page 386). Check the Grids In Back box in Guides & Grid Preferences to force the grid to appear in back of objects rather than in front of objects.

To turn on the snap to grid function:

Choose View menu > Snap to Grid (Command-Shift-"/Ctrl-Shift-"). This snap function works even when the grid isn't displayed.

To hide/show the grid:

Choose View menu > Show Grid or Hide Grid (Command-"/Ctrl-") **1**.
or
Deselect, then Control-click/Right-click and choose Show Grid or Hide Grid from the context menu.

The default Constrain Angle is 0°—the horizontal/vertical *(x/y)* axes. When you change the Constrain Angle, any new object that you draw in any new or *existing* document will rest on the new axes, and any new object that you move or transform with Shift held down will snap to the new axes.

To change the Constrain Angle:

Choose Edit menu > Preferences > General, enter a new number in the Tool Behavior: Constrain Angle field, then click OK (Return/Enter) **2**.

➤ To establish a Constrain Angle based on an existing object, select the object, and use the Angle readout from the Info palette as the new Constrain Angle.

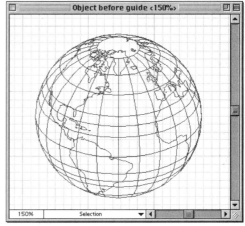

1 *The Grid displayed.*

What the Constrain Angle affects

➤ Text objects

➤ Rectangle, Ellipse, and Graph tools

➤ Transformation tools (Scale, Reflect, and Shear, but not Rotate or Blend)

➤ Gradient tool and Pen tool when used with Shift held down

➤ Moving objects with Shift held down or using the arrow keys

➤ Grid

➤ Smart Guides

➤ Info palette readouts

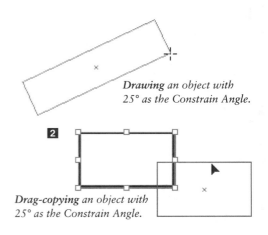

Drawing an object with 25° as the Constrain Angle.

2

Drag-copying an object with 25° as the Constrain Angle.

Shifting patterns

If you move an object that contains a pattern fill manually or using the Move dialog box and the Patterns box is unchecked in the Move dialog box, the object will move, but not the pattern. If the Patterns box is checked but the Objects box is not and you use the Move command, only the pattern position will shift—not the object.

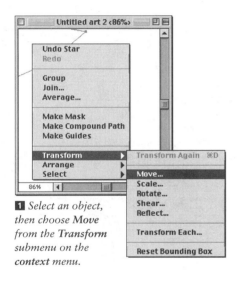

1 *Select an object, then choose Move from the Transform submenu on the context menu.*

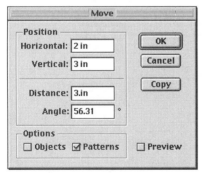

2 *In the Move dialog box, enter numbers in the Horizontal and Vertical fields or enter the Distance and Angle you want the object to move.*

Transforming using numbers

You can precisely reposition an object by entering values in the Move dialog box. Move dialog box settings remain the same until you change them, move an object using the mouse, or use the Measure tool, so you can repeat the same move as many times as you like using the Transform Again shortcut (Command-D/Ctrl-D).

To move an object a specified distance:

1. *Optional:* Choose a lower view percentage for your illustration so the object won't disappear from view when it's moved.

2. Choose the Selection tool (V).

3. Select the object you want to move.

4. Double-click the Selection tool.
   or
   Press Return/Enter.
   or
   Control-click/Right-click and choose Move from the Transform submenu on the context menu **1**.
   or
   Choose Object menu > Transform > Move (Command-Shift-M/Ctrl-Shift-M).

5. Check the Preview box.

6. Press Tab to preview these changes:
   Enter a positive number in the Horizontal and Vertical fields to move the object to the right and upward, respectively. Enter negative numbers to move the object to the left or downward **2**. Enter 0 in either field to prevent the object from moving along that axis. You can use any of these units of measure: "p," "pt," "in," "mm," "q," or "cm."
   or
   Enter a positive Distance and a positive Angle between 0 and 180 to move the object upward. Enter a positive Distance and a negative Angle between 0 and –180 to move the object downward. The other fields will change automatically.

7. *Optional:* Click Copy to close the dialog box and move a copy of the object (not the object itself).

8. Click OK (Return/Enter).

Move Using Numbers

Transform Palette

Use the Transform palette to reposition, resize, rotate, or shear an object or objects based on exact values or percentages. To apply a transformation as an easily removable effect, see page 94.

To reposition, resize, rotate, or shear an object using the Transform palette:

1. If the Transform palette isn't open, choose Window menu > Show Transform.

2. Select an object or objects.

3. Choose the reference point from which you want the transformation to be measured by clicking one of the nine square Reference Point handles on the left side of the palette ■.

4. From the Transform palette menu, choose Transform Object Only, Transform Pattern Only, or Transform Both (to transform objects and patterns).

5. If you're going to scale the object(s), turn Scale Strokes & Effects on or off from the palette menu. With this option on, the object's stroke and appearances will scale proportionally. Scale Strokes & Effects can also be turned on and off in Edit menu > Preferences > General.

6. To apply any of the following values, use a shortcut from the sidebar:

   To **move** the object horizontally, enter a new X position. (Enter a higher value to move the object to the right.)

   To **move** the object vertically, enter a new Y position. (Enter a higher value to move the object upward.)

   To change the object's **width** and/or **height**, enter new W and/or H values. You can enter a percentage. To force the other field (W or H) to change proportionately, press Command-Return/Ctrl-Return.

   Enter or choose a positive Rotate value to **rotate** the object counterclockwise or a negative value to rotate it clockwise.

   To **shear** an object to the right, enter or choose a positive Shear value. To shear

Applying Transform palette values

Return/Enter	Exit the palette
Tab	Apply a value entered in a field and highlight the next field
Shift-Return/ Shift-Enter	Apply a value and re-highlight the same field
Option-Return/ Alt-Return	Clone the object and exit the palette
Option-Tab	Clone the object and highlight the next field
Repeat last transformation	Command-D/Ctrl-D

The x and y axes location of the currently selected reference point. Enter new values to position the object's reference point at that value on the x or y axis.

The selected object's Height.

The selected object's Width.

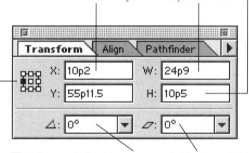

■ *Reference Point (the part of the object from which Transform palette values are calculated).*

Rotate field for rotating the object.

Shear field for shearing the object.

Let the palette do the math

In the W or H field on the Transform palette, you can perform simple math to resize an object. After the current number, type an asterisk and then a percentage value. For example, to reduce the current size value by half, click to the right of the current value and type "*50%" (e.g., 4p becomes 2p). Or replace the entire field with "50%". Or type "75%" to reduce the W or H to three-quarters of its current value (e.g., 4p becomes 3p).

Or enter a positive or negative number to the right of the current number, like "+2" or "-2", to increase or decrease, respectively, the current value by that amount. Press Tab to apply the math and advance to the next field, or press Return/Enter to exit the palette.

an object to the left, enter or choose a negative Shear value.

7. From the palette menu, you can also choose Flip Horizontal or Flip Vertical.

➤ If the Use Preview Bounds box is checked in Edit menu > Preferences > General, the full dimensions of an object, including its stroke, will display on the Width and Height fields on the Transform and Info palettes.

Transform Palette

Aligning and distributing

Buttons, point type blocks, anything that's lined up in a row or column will require aligning and distributing in order to look neat and tidy. With the Align palette, it's easy to do. Illustrator 9.0 introduces several new Align palette features. One feature that's particularly hard to ignore is Key Object.

To align or distribute objects:

1. To align, select two or more objects or groups. To distribute, select three or more objects. Show the Align palette.

2. Choose **Use Preview Bounds** from the Align palette menu to have Illustrator factor in an object's stroke weight when calculating alignment or distribution. Turn this option off to have Illustrator ignore the stroke weight. The stroke straddles the edge of the path, halfway inside and halfway outside. *new*

3. *For occasional use:* Choose **Align To Artboard** from the palette menu to align the objects along the top, right, bottom, or left edge of the artboard, depending on which Align Objects button is clicked. If Align to Artboard is turned on and then objects are distributed vertically, the topmost object will move to the top edge of the artboard, the bottommost object will move to the bottom edge of the artboard, and the remaining objects will be distributed between them. With this option on, the horizontal distribute buttons will align objects between the leftmost and rightmost edges of the artboard. *new*

4. *Optional:* By default (with Align To Artboard turned off), the topmost, bottommost, leftmost, or rightmost object will remain stationary, depending on which Align button you click. To choose a non-default object to remain stationary, click that object now (that is, after all the objects are selected and before you click an align button). To go back to the default object, choose **Cancel Key Object** from the palette menu. *new*

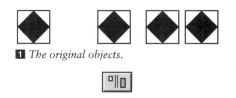

1 *The original objects.*

Horizontal distribute space.

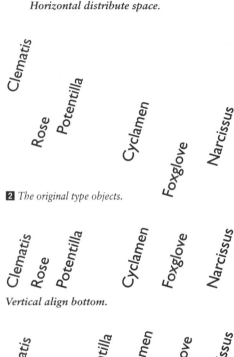

2 *The original type objects.*

Vertical align bottom.

Horizontal distribute center. The Align commands have no effect on paragraph alignment.

5. Click an **Align Objects** button (▮1▮–▮2▮, previous page; ▮1▮–▮2▮, this page).
and/or
Click a **Distribute Objects** button. Or for **Distribute Spacing,** choose Auto from the pop-up menu to keep the two objects that are farthest apart stationary (topmost and bottommost or leftmost and right-most) and redistribute the remaining objects evenly between them or enter the desired distance between objects (the outermost objects will probably move); then click a Distribute Spacing button.

➤ To apply a different align or distribute option, first Undo the last one.

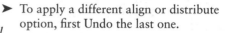

Horizontal align center *Horizontal align right* *Vertical align top* *Vertical align center*

Horizontal align left ▮1▮ *Vertical align bottom*

Align Objects:

Vertical distribute top **Distribute Objects:** *Horizontal distribute right*

Vertical distribute center *Vertical distribute bottom* *Horizontal distribute left* *Horizontal distribute center*

Note: To display this bottom panel, click the arrows on the Align tab.

Distribute Spacing: *new* Auto

Vertical distribute space *Horizontal distribute space* *Either choose* **Auto** *to keep the out-ermost objects stationary or enter the desired distance between objects.*

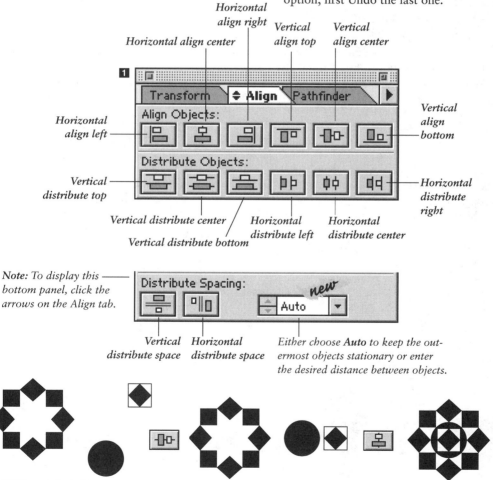

▮2▮ *The original objects.* *Vertical align center.* *Horizontal align center.*

You can use the Measure tool to calculate the distance and angle between two points in an illustration. When you use the Measure tool, the amounts it calculates are displayed on the Info palette, which opens automatically when the tool is used.

The distance and angle calculated using the Measure tool also become the current values in the Move dialog box, which means you can use the Measure tool as a guide to mark a distance and direction, then use the Transform Again shortcut to move any selected object.

To measure a distance using the Measure tool:

1. Choose the Measure tool on the Hand tool pop-out menu **1**.

2. Click the starting point and then the ending point that span the distance and angle you want to measure **2**–**3**.

   or

   Drag from the first point to the second point.

   The distance (D) and angle readouts will display on the Info palette **4**.

3. *Optional:* To move any object the distance and angle you just measured (until those values are changed), select the object, then press Command-D/Ctrl-D.

➤ Shift-click or Shift-drag with the Measure tool to constrain the tool to a multiple of 45°.

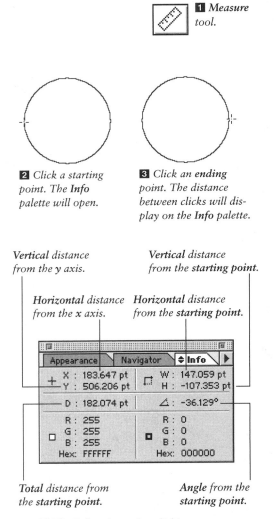

1 *Measure tool.*

2 *Click a starting point. The **Info** palette will open.*

3 *Click an ending point. The distance between clicks will display on the **Info** palette.*

Vertical distance from the y axis.

*Vertical distance from the **starting point**.*

Horizontal distance from the x axis.

*Horizontal distance from the **starting point**.*

*Total distance from the **starting point**.*

*Angle from the **starting point**.*

4 *The **Info** palette after clicking a starting and ending point with the **Measure** tool. The X and Y positions are measured from the ruler origin.*

Measure

ACTIONS 22

In this chapter you will learn how to record a sequence of edits in an action, edit the action using various methods, and replay the action on one document or a batch of documents.

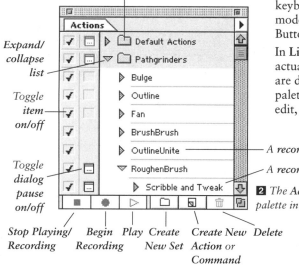

1 *The Actions palette in Button mode.*

An actions set

Expand/ collapse list

Toggle item on/off

Toggle dialog pause on/off

Stop Playing/ Recording *Begin Recording* *Play* *Create New Set* *Create New Action or Command* *Delete*

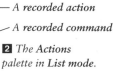

A recorded action

A recorded command

2 *The Actions palette in List mode.*

Actions and the Actions palette

An action is a recorded sequence of tool and menu events. When an action is replayed, the same series of commands is executed in exactly the same sequence it was recorded in. Actions can be simple (as short as a single command) or complex—whatever your work demands. And they can be replayed on any document. What's more, actions can be edited, reorganized, included in other actions, and traded around among Illustrator users.

Actions are recorded, played back, edited, saved, and deleted using the Actions palette. The Actions palette has two modes: Button and List (choose either one from the palette menu). **Button mode** is used only for playback, since in this mode only the action name is listed **1**. Actions can be assigned keyboard shortcuts for fast access in Button mode. To turn Button mode on or off, choose Button Mode from the Actions palette menu.

In **List mode** (Button mode turned off), the actual commands that the action contains are displayed in sequential order on the palette **2**. This mode is used to record, play, edit, save, and load actions.

Actions Palette

371

Note: For the instructions in this chapter, put your Actions palette into List mode.

Actions are organized in sets, which are represented as folder icons on the Actions palette.

To create a new actions set:

1. Click the Create New Set button at the bottom of the Actions palette **1**.
   or
   Choose New Set from the Actions palette menu.
2. Enter a Set Name **2**.
3. Click OK (Return/Enter). A new folder icon and set name will appear on the palette **3**. (To save the set, see page 379.)

Note: Until you become familiar with using actions, you should practice recording on a duplicate file. Figure out beforehand what the action is supposed to accomplish, and run through the command sequence a few times before you actually record it.

To record an action:

1. Open an existing file or create a new one.
2. On the Actions palette, click the name of the action set you want the new action to belong to. (To create a new set, follow the previous set of instructions on this page).
3. Click the Create New Action button at the bottom of the Actions palette **4**.
4. Enter a name for the action **5**.
5. *Optional:* Choose a keyboard shortcut for the action from the Function Key pop-up menu, and click the Shift and/or Command/Control box. Choose a color for the action name in Button mode from the Color pop-up menu.
6. Click Record (Return/Enter).
7. Create and edit objects as you normally would. Any tool and menu commands that are recordable will appear on the action command list.
8. Click the Stop button to end recording **6**.
➤ You can combine smaller actions or parts of actions into one action (see page 378).

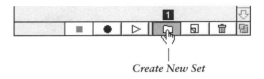

Create New Set

Create New Action

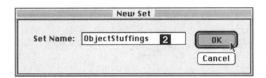

Create New Action

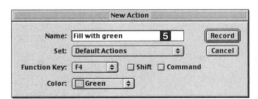

Use the **New Action** dialog box to change an action name, keyboard shortcut, or button display color for Button mode.

Stop

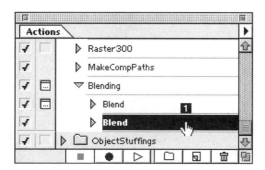

You may find that an action needs to be enhanced or modified from its original recorded version. There are several techniques you can use to edit actions.

To insert a menu item into an action's command list:

1. Put the Actions palette in List mode (turn off the Button Mode option).

2. If the list for the action into which you want to insert the menu item isn't expanded, click the right-pointing triangle.

3. To add a menu command to an action, click the command on the action list that you want the new command to follow █.

4. Choose Insert Menu Item from the Actions palette menu.

5. Choose the desired menu command from the menu bar (the command name will appear in the Find field automatically) █.
or
Type the command name into the Find Field, then click the Find button.

6. Click OK (Return/Enter). When the action is played back, a pause will occur at any menu command that includes a dialog box.

➤ Object menu > Transform commands can be recorded for a selected object. Or use the Selection tool on the handles of the object's bounding box.

Insert Menu Item

If you insert a stop into an action, the action will pause during playback to allow you to perform a manual operation, such as entering type or selecting an object. When you're finished with the manual operation, you can resume the action playback.

To insert a stop in an existing action:

1. Put the Actions palette in List mode, and expand the action into which you want to insert a stop.

2. Click the command after which you want the stop to be inserted **1**.

3. Choose Insert Stop from the Actions palette menu.

4. Type an instructional message in the Record Stop dialog box to tell the user which operations to perform during the stop. At the end of the message, tell the user to click the Play button on the Actions palette when they're ready to resume playback (e.g., "Click the Play button to resume") **2**–**3**.

5. *Optional:* Check the Allow Continue box to permit the user to bypass the pause.

6. Click OK (Return/Enter).

➤ To insert a pause while you're recording an action, choose Insert Stop from the Actions palette menu, follow steps 4–6 on this page, then click the Play button to continue recording.

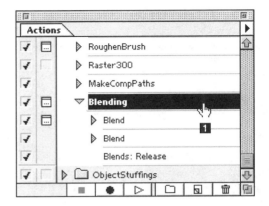

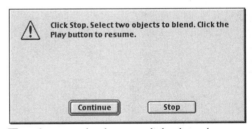

3 *In this example of a* **pause** *dialog box, the user is instructed to press* **Stop***, select two objects for blending, and then click the Play button on the Actions palette to resume the action playback. If the two objects are already selected, the user can click* **Continue** *instead of Stop.*

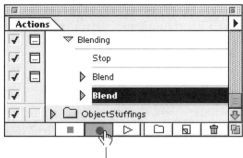

 Record

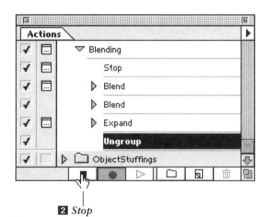

2 *Stop*

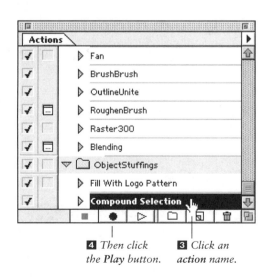

4 *Then click
the Play button.* **3** *Click an
action name.*

In much the same manner as you would insert a menu command, you can record additional commands into an existing action.

To record commands into an existing action:

1. Put the Actions palette in List mode, and expand the action into which you want to insert a command or commands.

2. Choose the command you want the new command(s) to follow.

3. Click the Record (round) button **1**.

4. Make modifications to the file as you would normally, using the commands you want inserted in the action. Any recordable tool or menu command that you use now will be added to the action (see the sidebar on page 380).

5. Click the square Stop button to stop recording **2**. The command(s) you just recorded will be listed below the chosen insertion point on the Actions palette.

Note: The first time you play back an action, do it on a duplicate file or on a file that you don't care about.

To replay an action on an image:

1. Open the Illustrator file on which you want to play the action, and select any objects, if necessary.

2. If the Actions palette is in List mode, make sure the check mark is present for the action you want to play back. Click the name of the action you want to play back **3**, then click the Play button at the bottom of the palette **4**.
   or
   If the palette is in Button mode, just click an action name. *Note:* If the action name is dark (unavailable), go back to List mode and click in the leftmost column for that action to make a check mark appear.

Add to Action; Replay Action

If you find that you've got the right action for the job, but it contains more commands than you need, you can temporarily exclude the ones you don't need from playback.

To exclude or include a command from a playback:

1. Put the Actions palette into List mode.

2. Click the right-pointing triangle to expand the command list of the action you want to play back 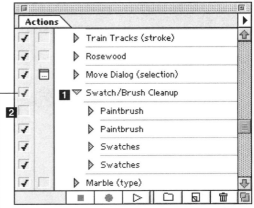.

3. Click the check mark (√) in the leftmost column to disable that command ☑ or click in the blank spot to restore the check mark and enable that command.

*A **red check mark** signifies that at least one of the commands in that action is turned off.*

For any command or tool that uses a dialog box that requires pressing Return/Enter (also known as a "modal control"), you can insert a pause to enable the user to change any of the dialog settings during playback. To insert this type of pause, you simply click a button on the Actions palette.

To turn on a command's dialog pause:

If a recorded command has a dialog box associated with it, it will have either a pause icon ☑ or a blank space in the same spot for toggling the icon on ☑. Click the icon to disable the dialog pause and use the pre-recorded input instead. Or click the blank space to enable the command's dialog pause and allow user input.

To rerecord a dialog:

1. Put the Actions palette into List mode.

2. Click the right-pointing triangle to expand the action's command list ☑.

3. Select an object in your illustration, then double-click the command you want to rerecord. It must have a dialog box icon (or a blank box for the icon) ☑.

4. Change any of the dialog settings, then click OK. The next time this action is played back, the new parameters will be used.

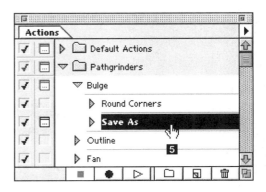

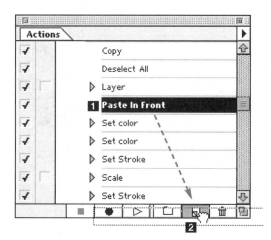

Note: Before you go ahead and wreck all the good work you've done so far, save the actions set you're working on! (See page 379.)

To move a command:

In List mode, click the action command you want to move, then drag it upward or downward to a new location in the same action or into another action (it will appear at the bottom of that list).

To copy a command:

1. In List mode, click the action command you want to copy **1**.

2. Option-drag/Alt-drag the command upward or downward in the same action or into another action list. If you move it to a new list, it will appear at the bottom of that list.
   or
   Drag the command name over the Create New Action button at the bottom of the Actions palette **2**, then drag the duplicate command to another location.

Follow these instructions if you want an action to be included in more than one set.

To copy an action from one set to another:

1. In List mode, click the action you want to duplicate.

2. Drag the action over the New Action button.
   or
   Choose Duplicate from the Actions palette menu.

3. Drag the duplicate action into another set.

4. *Optional:* To rename the new action, double-click it.

To delete an action or a command:

Click the action or command you want to delete, click the Delete button at the bottom of the Actions palette **3**, then click Yes.
or
To bypass the prompt, drag the action or command over the Delete button.

Move, Copy Command; Copy, Delete Action

Another way to combine actions is to prompt an action from one set to play back from within another set. You can build a complex action from simpler, smaller actions this way, without having to actually duplicate and move them.

To include one action in another action:

1. If you want to insert a Play Action command as you're recording an action, skip to step 3.
   or
   If you want to insert a Play Action command into an existing, completed action, click the command after which you want the Play Action to occur, then click the Record button **1**.

2. Click the action you want to include **2**.

3. Click the Play button **3**. The secondary action will play through. When it has completed, it will be listed on the action's command action list as "Play Action."

4. If you're in the middle of recording an action, continue recording.
   or
   If you're inserting the Play Action into an existing action, click Stop to finish.

   Note: If you expand the Play Action command list, you'll see the name of the secondary action to be played and the name of the set that that action belongs to **4**.

➤ If the action or set that the Play Action is calling for has been deleted or if its name has been changed, an alert dialog will appear during playback **5**.

➤ Watch out for any commands in a Play Action that could conflict with the main action. For example, a Deselect command in the Play Action could have an adverse effect on the main action playback.

Actions storeroom

Instead of starting from scratch each time you create a new action, create a set of simple utility actions that you can include in larger actions. Save them in a utility set that you can draw from (see the next page). Remember to supply the utility set along with the main action.

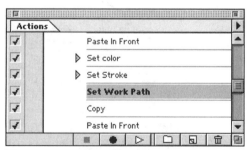

1 *Enter a name in the Save Set To field. Note: In Windows, the actions set file name must have the ".aia" extension.*

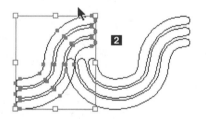

3 *"Set Work Path" appears on the Actions palette.*

One of the handiest things about actions is that you can share them with other Illustrator users. To do this, you must save them as sets. Try to keep your actions and sets well organized—and back up frequently!

To save an actions set:

1. Click on the actions set you want to save.
2. Choose Save Actions from the Actions palette menu.
3. Enter a name in the Name: field **1**, and choose a location in which to save the set. You can save it in the Action Sets folder inside the Illustrator 9 folder.
4. Click Save (Return/Enter).

To load an actions set:

1. Choose Load Actions from the Actions palette menu.
2. Locate and click the actions set you want to load, then click Open. The action will appear on the palette.

If you want a path shape to be part of an action, it has to be inserted as a pre-drawn path.

To record paths for insertion:

1. Have the path(s) you want to insert into the action ready to be selected.
2. Start recording an action.
   or
   To insert the path(s) into an existing action, choose the command after which you want it to appear.
3. Select the paths you want to insert **2**. You can use up to ten paths at a time. You can't use a path that's masked or that's part of a group, blend, compound, or clipping mask. *Note:* To apply stroke and fill attributes to an inserted path, those steps must be recorded separately.
4. Choose Insert Select Path from the Actions palette menu. "Set Work Path" will appear on the action's command list **3**. It cannot be renamed.
5. Click the Stop button, if you're recording.

Workaround for non-recordable tools

Many tools and commands can't be recorded, such as painting tools, tool options, effects, view menu commands, and preferences. However, for some tools that aren't recordable, their menu equivalents can be recorded as commands in an action.

For example, to make a blend part of an action, use Blend submenu commands instead of the Blend tool. Start recording an action, select the two objects you want to blend, choose Object menu > Blend > Blend Options, choose a Spacing value **1**, and click OK. Then choose Object menu > Blend > Make. The two separate blend steps will appear with the same name on the action's command list, but if you expand the command lists, you'll see the differences between the two steps **2**. Continue recording the action or stop recording.

Important note: Back up all your actions sets using the Save Actions command before performing any of the remaining instructions.

To reset actions to the default set:

1. Choose Reset Actions from the Actions palette menu.

2. If you want the default set to **replace all** the actions on the palette, click OK.
   or
   If you want to **append** the original default set to the current actions set list **3**, click Append, then rename the appended set.

To clear all actions sets from the palette:

Choose Clear Actions from the Actions palette menu, then click Yes.

To replace all current actions sets:

1. Choose Replace Actions from the Actions palette menu.

2. Locate and highlight the replacement actions set.

3. Click Open.

What's recordable?

Operations performed by these tools are **recordable**: Ellipse, Rectangle, Rotate, Scale, Reflect. Fill and stroke commands are also recordable.

Operations performed by these tools are **not recordable**: Selection, Direct-selection, Lasso, Direct-select lasso, Pen, Add-anchor-point, Delete-anchor-point, Convert-anchor-point, Type (all varieties), Paintbrush, Pencil, Free Transform, Blend, Graph, Gradient Mesh, Gradient, Eyedropper, Scissors, Hand, Zoom.

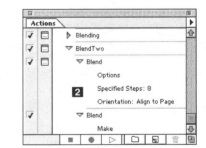

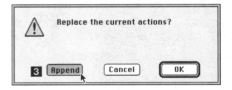

PREFERENCES 23

In this chapter you will learn to choose default settings for commands, tools, and palettes. First you will learn how to create a custom startup file. Then you will learn how to use the Edit menu > Preferences dialog boxes to set tool behavior, keyboard increments, units, undos, guides, grid, hyphenation, scratch disk, and many other preferences for current and future documents.

The startup files *new*

The startup files are stored in the Plug-ins folder in the Adobe Illustrator 9.0 application folder.

Mac OS: Adobe Illustrator Startup_CMYK or Adobe Illustrator Startup_RGB

Windows: Adobe Illustrator Startup_CMYK.ai or Adobe Illustrator Startup_RGB.ai

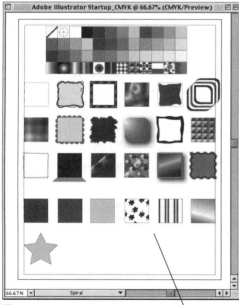

1 *An Adobe Illustrator **Startup** file.*

Custom colors, patterns, gradient, and brush shape in the bottom two rows.

You can create a custom CMYK and/or RGB startup file containing the colors, patterns, gradients, and document settings that you work with regularly so those elements will automatically be part of every new document.

To create a custom startup file:

1. For safekeeping, duplicate the existing startup file, and move the copy to a different folder (see the sidebar).
2. Double-click one of the default Adobe Illustrator Startup file icons.
3. Do any of the following **1**:

   Create new colors, patterns, or gradients, and add these new items to the Swatches palette. For a visual reminder, apply swatches to separate objects in the file.

   Drag-copy swatches from other swatch libraries to the Swatches palette—spot color libraries or files from the Other Libraries folder in the Illustrator folder.

   Create custom brushes or new styles, and apply them to objects as a visual reminder.

   Choose Document Setup or Page Setup options.

   Choose ruler and page origins.

   Choose a view size, document window size, and scroll positions, or create new view settings.
4. To help Illustrator launch quickly, delete whatever you don't need in the startup file (e.g., brushes from the Brushes palette).
5. Save the file in the Plug-ins folder using the same name (as listed in the sidebar).

General Preferences *improved*

Choose Edit menu > Preferences > General

Keyboard Increment
The distance a selected object moves when an arrow is pressed on the keyboard.

Constrain Angle
The angle for the *x* and *y* axes. The default setting is 0° (parallel to the edges of the document window). Tool operations, dialog box measurements, and the grid are calculated relative to the current Constrain Angle (see page 364).

Corner Radius
The amount of curvature in the corners of objects drawn with the Rounded Rectangle tool. 0 produces a right angle. Changing this number updates the same value in the Rectangle dialog box, and vice versa.

Use Area Select
When checked, clicking with a selection tool on an object's fill when an illustration is in Preview view selects the whole object.

Use Precise Cursors
The drawing and editing tool pointers display as a crosshair icon. To turn this option on temporarily when the preference is turned off, press Caps Lock.

Disable Warnings
Check this box to prevent Illustrator from displaying an alert dialog box when a tool is used incorrectly.

Show Tool Tips
Check this box to see an on-screen display of the name of the tool or button currently under the pointer.

Anti-aliased Artwork
Makes the edges of existing and subsequently created objects look smoother on screen. It doesn't affect placed graphics; it does affect artwork that's rasterized in Illustrator.

Select Same Tint Percentage *new*
When checked, Edit menu > Select > Same Fill Color or Same Stroke Color will select only colors with the same tint percentage (spot color percentage) as the selected object.

(Continued on the following page)

General Preferences

Preferences

General

Keyboard Increment: 0p1.008
Constrain Angle: 0 °
Corner Radius: 5p0.59

OK
Cancel
Previous
Next

☑ Use Area Select   ☐ Disable Auto Add/Delete
☐ Use Precise Cursors   ☐ Japanese Crop Marks
☑ Disable Warnings   ☐ Transform Pattern Tiles
☑ Show Tool Tips   ☐ Scale Strokes & Effects
☑ Anti-aliased Artwork ☑ Use Preview Bounds
☐ Select Same Tint Percentage

Reset All Warning Dialogs

Fast track to the Preferences

Use the shortcut that opens the General Preferences dialog box (**Command-K/Ctrl-K**), then choose a preferences dialog box from the pop-up menu.

Disable Auto Add/Delete

Disables the Pen tool's ability to change to the Add-anchor-point tool when the pointer passes over a path segment or to the Delete-anchor point-tool when the pointer passes over an anchor point.

Japanese Crop Marks

Check this box to use Japanese style crop-marks when printing separations. Preview this style in the Separation Setup dialog box.

Transform Pattern Tiles

When checked, if you use a transformation tool on an object that contains a pattern fill, the pattern will also transform. You can also turn this option on or off for an individual transformation tool in its own dialog box, in the Move dialog box, or on the Transform palette.

Scale Strokes & Effects

Check this box to scale an object's stroke weight and appearances when you use the bounding box, the Scale tool, the Free Transform tool, or the Effect menu > Distort & Transform > Transform > Transform Effect command to scale an object. This option can also be turned on or off in the Scale dialog box.

Use Preview Bounds *new*

Factors in an object's stroke weight when an object's height and width dimensions are calculated. This option changes the dimensions of the bounding box.

For the Pencil tool preferences, see page 68.

General Preferences

Type & Auto Tracing Preferences

*Choose Edit menu > Preferences > Type &
Auto Tracing*

Type Options

Size/Leading, Baseline Shift, Tracking
The increment by which selected text is
altered each time a keyboard shortcut is
executed for the respective command.

Greeking
The point size at or below which type displays on the screen as gray bars rather than
as readable characters. Greeking speeds
up screen redraw. It has no effect on how
a document prints.

Type Area Select
When checked, you can select type by clicking with a selection tool anywhere within
a type character's bounding box. When
unchecked, you'll have to click right on the
type outline.

Show Font Names in English
When checked, two-byte font names display
in English on the font pop-up menu. When
unchecked, these font names display in a
two-byte script.

Auto Trace Options

Auto Trace Tolerance
The value (0–10) that controls how closely
the Auto Trace tool follows the original path.
Enter a low value to have the tool follow
the path closely; enter a high Auto Trace
Tolerance to have the tool ignore minor
irregularities on the path's contour.

Tracing Gap
The exactness with which the Auto Trace
tool traces the contour of a bitmap image
(0–2). The tool will ignore gaps that are
equal to or less than the specified number of
pixels. The smaller the gap, the more closely
an image will be traced, and the more anchor
points will be created.

Type & Auto Tracing Preferences

Resetting preferences

To restore all the default Illustrator preferences, trash the Adobe Illustrator 9.0 preferences file. On Mac OS, it's stored in the System Folder > Preferences > Adobe Illustrator 9 folder. In Windows, it's stored in Windows > Application Data/Adobe/Adobe Illustrator 9 > AIPrefs. Whatever you do, don't delete the whole Preferences folder! You need everything else that's in there to run other applications and utilities.

```
┌─────────────────── Preferences ──────────────────┐
│  ┌──────────────────┐                             │
│  │ Units & Undo  [▲▼]│                            │
│  ┌─Units──────────────────────────────────────┐  │
│  │  General: [ Inches          [▲▼]]          │  │
│  │   Stroke: [ Inches          [▲▼]]          │  │
│  │     Type: [ Points          [▲▼]]          │  │
│  │        ☐ Numbers Without Units Are Points  │  │
│  └────────────────────────────────────────────┘  │
│  ┌─Undo───────────────────────────────────────┐  │
│  │  Minimum Undo Levels: [ 21 ]               │  │
│  │                                            │  │
│  └────────────────────────────────────────────┘  │
└───────────────────────────────────────────────────┘
```

Units & Undo Preferences

Choose Edit menu > Preferences > Units & Undo

Units

General
The unit of measure for the rulers and all dialog boxes for the current document and all new documents. If you choose different Units in the Document Setup dialog box, those new Units will override the Units & Undo setting only for the current document (see page 25).

Stroke
The unit of measure used on the Stroke palette.

Type
The unit of measure used on the Character and Paragraph palettes. We use Points.

Numbers Without Units Are Points
If the Numbers Without Units Are Points option is checked with Picas chosen as the General Units and you enter a points value in a field, the value won't be converted into picas (e.g., if you enter "99," it won't be converted into "8p3").

Undo

Minimum Undo Levels
Normally, you can undo/redo up to 200 operations in a row, depending on available memory. If additional RAM is required to perform illustration edits, the number of undos will be reduced to the specified Minimum number of Undo Levels.

Guides & Grid Preferences

Choose Edit menu > Preferences > Guides & Grid

Guides

Color

The guide color. Choose a color from the Color pop-up menu. Or choose Other or double-click the color square to open the System color picker and mix your own color.

Style

The guide Style. To help differentiate between guide lines and grid lines, choose the Dots style for guides.

Grid

Color

The grid color. Choose a color from the Color pop-up menu. Or choose Other or double-click the color square to open the System color picker and mix your own color.

Style

The grid style. Subdivision lines won't display if the Dot style is chosen.

Gridline every

The distance between the more prominent grid lines.

Subdivision

The number of subdivision lines to be drawn between the major grid lines when the Line Style is chosen for the grid.

Grids in Back

Check the Grids In Back box to have the grid display behind all objects. With the grid in back, you can easily tell which objects have a fill of None, because the grid will be visible underneath them.

➤ Guides will snap to grid lines if View menu > Snap to Grid is turned on.

➤ If Snap to Grid and Snap to Point (or Snap to Pixel) are both turned on, it can be hard to tell whether an object is snapping to the grid or to a guide, particularly if the grid isn't displayed.

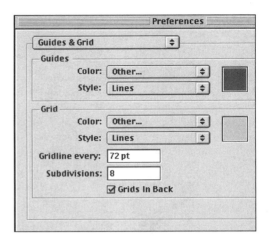

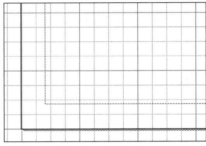

*Grid lines with **four** subdivisions.*

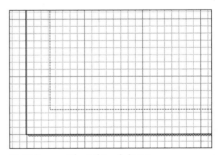

*Grid lines with **eight** subdivisions.*

Smart Guides Preferences

Choose Edit menu > Preferences > Smart Guides

Note: To turn on smart guides, choose View menu > Smart Guides (Command-U/Ctrl-U).

Display Options

Text Label Hints
Labels display as you pass the pointer over an object, an anchor point, etc.

Construction Guides
As you draw or drag an object, angle lines will display **1**. Choose or create an angles set in the Angles area of the dialog box. *improved*

Transform Tools
Angle lines display as you transform an object using an individual transformation tool **2**. Choose or create an angle set in the Angles area of the dialog box.

Object Highlighting
An object's path displays as you pass the pointer over it **3**. This is helpful for locating unpainted paths (like clipping masks) or paths that are behind other paths. Hidden paths (eye icon off on the Layers palette) won't highlight.

Angles

When Smart Guides are turned on, angle lines will temporarily display relative to other objects in the illustration as you drag an object or move the pointer. You can choose a preset angle set from the Angles drop-down menu or enter your own angles in any of the text fields. If you enter custom angles, "Custom Angles" will appear on the pop-up menu. If you switch from Custom Angles to a predefined set and then later switch back to Custom Angles, the last-used custom settings will reappear in the text fields.

Snapping Tolerance
The length of time our kids can whine before we snap. Actually, the Snapping Tolerance is the distance within which the pointer must be from an object for Smart Guides to display. 4 is the default.

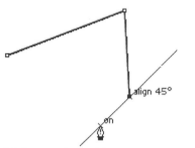

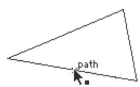

1 *Construction guide.*

2 *Transform tool guide.*

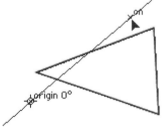

3 *Object Highlight guide.*

Smart Guides Preferences

Hyphenation Options Preferences

Choose Edit menu > Preferences >
Hyphenation Options

Default Language

Choose the language dictionary Illustrator
will use when inserting hyphen breaks. You
can choose a different hyphenation language
dictionary just for the current document
from the Language pop-up menu on the
Character palette.

Exceptions

Enter words that you want to be hyphenated
in a particular way. Type the word in the
New Entry field, inserting hyphens where you
would want them to appear. Enter a word
with no hyphens to prevent Illustrator from
hyphenating it. Click Add. To remove a word
from the list, highlight it, then click Delete.

Plug-ins & Scratch Disk Preferences

Choose Edit menu > Preferences > Plug-ins & Scratch Disk

Plug-ins folder

Note: For changes made in this dialog box to take effect, you must quit/exit and relaunch Illustrator.

Folder

Illustrator comes with core and add-on plug-in files that provide additional functionality to the main application. These and other plug-in files are placed in the Plug-ins folder in the Adobe Illustrator 9 folder. If for some reason you need to move the Plug-ins folder, you must use this Preferences dialog box to tell Illustrator the new location of the folder.

The current Plug-ins folder location is listed after the word "Folder." To change the plug-ins location, click Choose, locate and highlight the desired folder name, then click "Select [folder name]" at the bottom of the dialog box. The new location will now be listed.

➤ Plug-ins use a lotta RAM, so store only the ones you use regularly in the Adobe Illustrator 9 > Plug-ins folder.

Scratch Disks

Primary

The Primary (and optional Secondary) Scratch Disk is used as virtual memory when available RAM is insufficient for image processing. Choose an available hard drive, preferably your largest and fastest, from the Primary pop-up menu. Startup (Mac OS)/ C:\ (Windows) is the default.

Secondary

As an optional step, choose an alternate Secondary hard drive to be used as extra work space, when needed. If you have only one hard drive, of course you'll have only one scratch disk.

➤ To see how much of Illustrator's memory allotment is currently available, choose Free Memory from the status line pop-up menu at the bottom of the document/ application window and read the readout.

Plug-ins & Scratch Disk Preferences

389

Files & Clipboard Preferences *new*

Choose Edit menu > Preferences > Files & Clipboard

Files

Mac OS only: Choose **Append Extension:** Always or Ask When Saving to have Illustrator append the file extension when a file is saved for the first time. Check the Lower Case box to have the extension appear in lowercase characters. When exporting files, extensions are a must.

To specify how linked images are updated when the original files are modifed, from the **Update Links** pop-up menu, choose:

Automatically to have Illustrator update a linked image automatically whenever the original file is modified.

Manually to leave linked images unchanged when the original files are modified. You can always use the Links palette to update links.

Ask When Modified to display a dialog box when the original files are modifed. (In the dialog box, click Yes to update the linked image or click No to leave it unchanged.)

Clipboard

The Clipboard can be used to transfer selections between Illustrator and other Adobe programs (e.g., Photoshop, GoLive, LiveMotion, and Premiere). When a selection is copied to the Clipboard, it is copied as a PICT and as PDF and/or AICB, depending on which of those options you choose. Copied artwork is pasted as PICT in most programs.

Choose either or both of these options for copying files to other applications:

The **PDF** format to preserve transparency information in the selection. PDF is really a format for Adobe InDesign, Photoshop 6, and future Adobe applications.

AICB (a PostScript format) to have Illustrator break the selections into smaller opaque objects, and thus preserve the appearance of transparency through flattening. Choose this option to copy to and from Photoshop. Check the **Preserve Paths** box to copy the selection as a set of paths or check the **Preserve Appearance** box to preserve the appearance of the selection.

Note: If you check both options, the receiving application will choose its preferred format, but this will slow down the copying time and use more memory.

➤ If you're unable to paste a file format into Illustrator, try using the drag-and-drop feature instead (and vice versa).

OUTPUT/EXPORT 24

Illustrator objects are described and stored as mathematical commands. But when they are printed, they are rendered as dots. The higher the resolution of the output device, the more smoothly and sharply lines, curves, gradients, and continuous-tone images are rendered. In this chapter you will learn to print an illustration on a PostScript black-and-white or composite color printer, to create crop or trim marks, to print an oversized illustration, and to optimize print performance. You'll also learn how to save a file in a variety of formats for export to other applications, how to output transparency, and how to manage color using the Color Settings dialog box. To produce color separations, see Chapter 25. For Web output, see Chapter 26.

Charles, *Nancy Stahl*

Norah, *Nancy Stahl*

Outputting files

To print on a black-and-white or color PostScript printer:

1. Choose File menu > Document Color mode > CMYK, if necessary, before outputting to a color printer.

2. *Mac OS:* Open the Chooser (Apple menu), click the desired printer driver, then close the Chooser.

3. *Mac OS:* Choose File menu > Page Setup (Command-Shift-P) **1**.

   Win: Choose File menu > Print Setup (Ctrl-Shift-P), then select a printer.

4. Choose a size from the Paper pop-up menu, make sure the correct Orientation icon is selected (to print vertically or horizontally on the paper), then click OK.

5. Choose File menu > Print (Command-P/Ctrl-P).

6. *Mac OS:* Choose Adobe Illustrator 9.0 from the pop-up menu **2**.

   Mac OS and Win: Choose PostScript®: Level 2 or 3 (depending on your printer and printer driver) **3**.

If you don't know about profiles and Color Settings, read pages 420–428 first.

7. Choose a Print Space profile from the Profile pop-up menu **4**:

   Use Same As Source only when a profile has already been set for the document (via the Edit menu > Assign Profile command). This profile name will display in the source space area.
   or
   Choose an appropriate profile for your type of output printer.

   ➤ The profile you chose in Color Settings for Working Spaces: CMYK is probably a good print profile choice.

8. Leave the Intent: menu option on the default Relative Colorimetric option unless you or your output specialist have a reason to change it. See page 426 for more on intents.

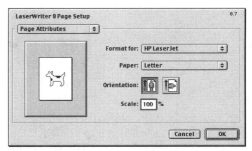

1 *In the* **Page Setup** *dialog box for a* **black-and-white** *printer, choose a paper size from the* **Paper** *pop-up menu.*

2 *In Mac OS, choose* **Adobe Illustrator 9.0.**

3 *Choose PostScript®:* **Level 2 or Level 3.**

4 *Choose a* **Print Space** *profile from the* **Profile** *pop-up menu.*

1 *In the* **Print** *dialog box, enter a number of* **Copies** *and which* **Pages** *you want to print.*

9. *Mac OS:* Choose Color Matching from the pop-up menu used in step 6. Choose Print Color: Color/Grayscale. For a color printer, choose the appropriate color options.

   Win: Accept the default setting for your printer. If necessary, click the Properties button, click the Page Setup tab, then choose a Color Appearance. For a color printer, choose the appropriate color options.

10. *Mac OS:* Choose General from the pop-up menu. *Mac OS and Win:* Enter the desired number of Copies **1**.

11. To print a single full-page document or a Tile imageable areas document, on Mac OS, leave the Pages: All button selected; in Windows, leave the Print Range: All button selected.
    or
    To print select tiled pages, enter starting and ending page numbers in the From and To fields.

12. *Mac OS:* Click Print. *Win:* Click OK.

Print

Crop marks are short perpendicular lines around the edge of a page that a print shop uses as guides to trim the paper. Illustrator's Crop Marks command creates crop marks around a rectangle that you draw, and they become part of your illustration.

To create crop marks:

1. Choose the Rectangle tool (M) .

2. Carefully draw a rectangle to encompass some or all of the objects in the illustration .

3. With the rectangle still selected, choose Object menu > Crop Marks > Make . The rectangle will disappear, and crop marks will appear where the corners of the rectangle were.

➤ If you don't create a rectangle before choosing Object menu > Crop Marks > Make, crop marks will be placed around the artboard.

➤ Only one set of crops can be created per illustration using the Crop Marks command. If you apply Object menu > Crop Marks > Make a second time, new marks will replace the existing ones. To create more than one set of crop marks in an illustration, use the Trim Marks filter (see page 395).

1 *Rectangle tool.*

2 *A rectangle is drawn.*

3 *After choosing the Make Crop Marks command.*

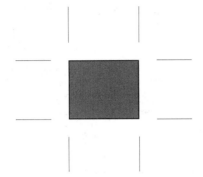

1 *After applying the **Trim Marks** filter.*

To remove crop marks created with the Crop Marks command:

Choose Object menu > Crop Marks > Release. The selected rectangle will reappear, with a fill and stroke of None. Toggle to Outline view or use Smart Guides (with Object Highlighting option checked in Smart Guides Preferences) to locate it. You can recolor it or delete it.

➤ If crop marks were created for the entire page, the released rectangle will have the same dimensions as the artboard.

➤ To quickly set crop marks for the entire page, make the artboard the same size as the printable page.

The Trim Marks filter places eight trim marks around a selected object or objects. You can create more than one set of Trim Marks in an illustration.

To create trim marks:

1. Select the object or objects to be trimmed.

2. Choose Filter menu > Create > Trim Marks. Trim marks will surround the smallest rectangle that could be drawn around the selection **1**.

➤ Group the trim marks with the objects they surround so you can move them in unison. Trim marks are listed as nested objects within a group on the Layers palette.

➤ To move or delete trim marks, select them first with the Selection tool or using the Layers palette.

Remove Crop Marks; Create Trim Marks

To print (tile) an illustration that is larger than the paper size:

1. Choose File menu > Document Setup (Option-Shift-P/Alt-Shift-P) 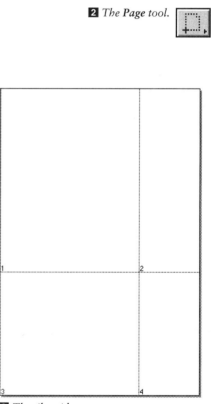.

2. For the illustration's artboard dimensions, make sure Artboard is chosen from the topmost pop-up menu. Then choose a preset size from the Size drop-down menu, or choose a unit of measure from the Units pop-up menu and enter custom Width and Height dimensions.

3. Click Tile Imageable Areas.

4. *Optional:* To change the tile orientation, click Page Setup/Print Setup, and then click the unselected Orientation button.

5. Click OK (Return/Enter).

6. Double-click the Hand tool to display the entire artboard.

7. *Optional:* Choose the Page tool ▓, then drag the tile grid so it divides the illustration into better tiling breaks. The grid will redraw ▓.

8. Follow steps 5–12 on page 392–393 to print.

➤ On a document that's set to Tile Imageable Areas, only tile pages with objects on them will print. If a direction line from a curved anchor point extends onto a blank tile, that page will also print.

▓ *In File menu > Document Setup, choose or enter the appropriate Artboard dimensions and click Tile Imageable Areas.*

▓ *The Page tool.*

▓ *The tile grid.*

1 *Delete-anchor-point tool.*

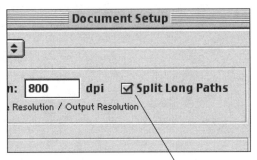

2 *Check the Split long paths box in File menu > Document Setup.*

Solving printing problems

If things don't go as smoothly as you'd like...

Patterns

➤ By default, patterns preview and print. If a document containing patterns doesn't print, place the objects that contain patterns on a new layer, uncheck the Print option for that layer, then try printing again. If the document prints, the patterns were the likely culprit.

➤ Try to limit the number of pattern fills in an illustration.

➤ Make the original bounding rectangle for the pattern tile no larger than one-inch square (see page 152).

➤ Use a PostScript Level 2 or Level 3 printer when printing elaborate patterns.

➤ Don't use a blend, a gradient fill, or type as a pattern fill on a compound path.

Complex paths

Sometimes a file containing complex paths with many anchor points won't print (a limitcheck or virtual memory error message may appear in the print progress window). To help prevent a limitcheck error, limit the number of complex objects in your illustration. If you do get such a message, delete excess anchor points from long paths using the Delete-anchor-point tool, then try printing again **1**.

If that doesn't work, check the Split Long Paths box in File menu > Document Setup > Printing & Export **2** and try printing yet again. Complex closed paths will be split into two or more separate paths, but their overall path shapes won't change. The Split Long Paths option does not affect stroked paths, compound paths, or clipping masks. You can also split a stroked path manually using the Scissors tool. (To preserve a copy of a document with its non-split paths, before checking the Split Long Paths box, save the document under a new name using File menu > Save As.) To rejoin split paths, select them and then click the Unite button on the Pathfinder palette.

(Continued on the following page)

Solving Printing Problems

More troubleshooting tips

➤ Clipping masks may cause printing problems, particularly if they're produced from compound paths. In fact, a file containing multiple masks may not print at all. For a complex mask, consider using the Knife tool to cut all the shapes in half—including the mask object itself—before creating the mask. Select and mask each half separately, then move them together.

➤ Choose Object menu > Path > Cleanup to delete any Stray Points (inadvertent clicks on the artboard with the Pen tool), Unpainted Objects, or Empty Text Paths ∎.

➤ If you get a VM error, try reducing the number of fonts used in the file or convert large type into outlines (Type menu > Create Outlines) so fewer fonts will need to be downloaded.

➤ Use a Pathfinder command—like Divide or Minus Front—to produce the same effect as a compound.

➤ To improve gradient fill printing on an older PostScript imagesetter or some PostScript clone printers, check the Compatible Gradient and Gradient Mesh Printing box in File menu > Document Setup > Printing & Export, then re-save the file. A mesh object will be converted to JPEG format. Don't check this option if your gradients are printing well, as it may slow printing.

➤ If you're using complex elements like compounds, masks, or patterns in a document and the *document* doesn't print, place a complex object on its own layer, uncheck the print option for that layer, and try printing again. And by the same token, if an *object* doesn't print, double-click the name of the layer the object is on and make sure the Print box is checked.

➤ If a pattern doesn't print, simplify it.

➤ As a last resort you can lower the output resolution of individual objects to facilitate printing (see page 400).

∎

Smoother halftones

If your printer has halftone enhancing software,

Mac OS: Choose File menu > Print, choose Imaging Options from the second pop-up menu, choose PhotoGrade and/or FinePrint or whatever your particular printer imaging options are, then click OK.

Windows: Choose File menu > Print Setup, choose Properties, turn on the enhancement option under the Graphics tab or the Device Options tab (on NT, click the Advanced tab), then click OK.

Next, make sure the Use Printer's Default Screen box is checked in File menu > Document Setup > Printing & Export (this is the default setting) to enable the printer's halftone method and disable Illustrator's built-in halftone method.

Smoother blends

When printing gradients and blends, consider the relationship between the printer's lines per inch setting and the number of gray levels the printer is capable of producing. The higher the lines per inch (also known as screen frequency), the fewer the printable levels of gray. For the smoothest printing of gradients and blends, use a printer that's capable of outputting 256 levels of gray.

If you—and not the print shop—are supervising the color separation process, first ask your print shop what screen frequency (lpi) you will need to specify when imagesetting your file and what resolution (dpi) to use for imagesetting. Some imagesetters can achieve resolutions above 3000 dpi.

The blend or gradient length

To ensure that a gradient fill or a blend does not band into visible color strips:

➤ Use the correct lines per inch setting for the printer to output 256 levels of gray.

➤ Make sure at least one color component (R, G, or B, or C, M, Y, or K) in the starting color of the gradient or blend differs by at least 50% from the same component in the ending color.

➤ Keep the blend or gradient length to a maximum of 7½ inches. If you need a longer blend or gradient, create it in Photoshop, then place it in Illustrator, or rasterize the blend or gradient object in Illustrator.

Illustrator chooses the number of steps in a gradient or a blend based on the largest difference in percentage between gradient color components. The greater the percentage difference, the greater the potential number of steps, and thus the longer the blend can be. At 256 steps, for example, the blend can be up to 7½ inches long. Here's the formula for calculating the optimal number of blend steps:

Number of steps = Number of gray levels from the printer ✕ The largest color percentage difference

Use the chart on page 372 of the Adobe Illustrator 9.0 User Guide to calculate the maximum blend length based on the number of blend steps.

Smooth Blends

Object Output Resolution

The precision with which Illustrator renders an object is determined by the object's output resolution. Different objects in the same illustration can be rendered at different resolutions. If a complex object doesn't print, try lowering its output resolution and then print the document again. But first, read the sidebar at right.

To lower an object's output resolution to facilitate printing:

1. Select the object that did not print or that you anticipate may not print.

2. Show the Attributes palette.

3. Enter a lower number in the Output field **1**, then try printing the file again. If the object prints, but with noticeable jaggedness on its curve segments, its output resolution is too low. Raise the Output value, and try printing again.

➤ To reset the Output resolution for all future objects in the same document, choose File menu > Document Setup > Printing & Export, then change the Output Resolution. 800 dpi is the default Output resolution for path objects.

The flatness equation

The Output resolution controls the degree of flatness in an object's curve segments. Flatness equals the printing device resolution divided by the object's output resolution. For any given printer, lowering the output resolution raises the flatness value. The lower the output resolution (or the higher the flatness value), the less precisely an object's curve segments will print.

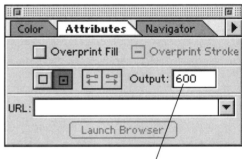

1 *Change the **Output** resolution for an individual object using the **Attributes** palette.*

Potential gray levels at various output resolutions and screen frequencies

	Output Resolution (DPI)	Screen Frequency (LPI)					
		60	**85**	**100**	**133**	**150**	**180**
Laser printers	**300**	26	13				
	600	101	51	37	21		
Image-setters	**1270**	256	224	162	92	72	
	2540		256	256	256	256	
	3000			256	256	256	256

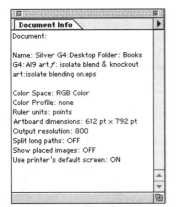

1 *The Document Info palette, with Document information displayed. This information is always available—whether the Selection Only option is on or off.*

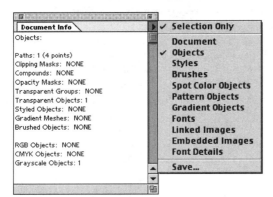

2 *The Document Info palette with the Objects and Selection Only options checked on the palette menu.*

To display information about an object or an entire document: *improved*

1. *Optional:* Select the object (or objects) about which you want to read info.

2. Choose File menu > Document Info to show the Document Info palette **1**.

3. To display information about a selected object (step 1, above), make sure Selection Only on the palette menu has a checkmark **2**.
   or
   To display information pertaining to all the objects in the illustration, uncheck the Selection Only option.

4. Choose Objects from the palette menu to make the palette list the number of paths, clipping masks, compounds, opacity masks, transparent groups, transparent objects, styled objects, gradient meshes, brushed objects, and color, font and linking info in the selection.
   or
   Choose another category from the palette menu to see a listing of styles, brushes, spot color objects, pattern objects, gradient objects, fonts, linked images, embedded images, or font details (PostScript name, font file name, language, etc.) for a selection or for the entire document.

5. *Optional:* If the Selection Only option is checked on the palette menu, you can click on other objects in the document to see info for that object in the currently chosen category.

6. *Optional:* Choose Save from the palette menu to save the currently displayed information as a text document. Choose a location in which to save the text file, rename the file, if desired, then click Save. Use the system's default text editor to open the text document. You can print this file and refer to it when you prepare your document for imagesetting.

Document Info palette

401

Exporting files

Choose File menu > Save As to save another version of your file with a location, name, or file format. Choose File menu > Save a Copy to save a copy of your file with the word "Copy" after the file name. If you use this command, your original file will remain as the active file on screen.

In order to open an Illustrator file in other graphics programs that won't recognize the Illustrator 9.0 file format, you may need to save it in an earlier Illustrator format. While you won't be able to preserve effects that are new to Illustrator 9.0 (e.g., transparency), in some situations, this might be your only option.

To save as an earlier version of Illustrator:

improved

1. Choose File menu > Save As or Save a Copy.

2. Mac OS: Choose Adobe Illustrator Document from the Format pop-up menu, then click Save.

   Windows: Choose Illustrator (*.ai) from the Save as Type drop-down menu, then click Save.

3. In the Illustrator Native Format Options dialog box, choose an earlier version of Illustrator **1**.

4. Click "Preserve Paths (discard transparency)" to preserve your objects' paths and eliminate any transparency effects altogether.
   or
   Click "Preserve Appearance (flatten transparency)" to preserve the appearance of transparency.

5. Click OK.

What about AI, EPS, and PDF?

To learn how to save a file in **Illustrator** format, see pages 42–43. For **Illustrator EPS** format, see pages 44–46, and for **Adobe PDF** format, see pages 47–49.

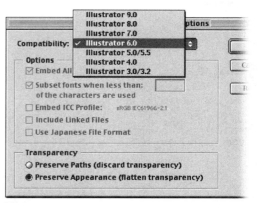

1 *Choose an earlier version of Illustrator from the **Compatibility** pop-up menu in the **Illustrator Native Format Options** dialog box.*

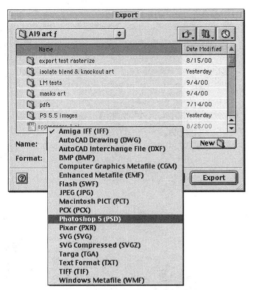

1 *Mac OS: Choose from the **Format** pop-up menu.*

2 *Windows: Choose from the **Save as type** drop-down menu.*

It doesn't all end here. An Illustrator file can be saved in a variety of file formats for export into other applications. Some of these formats are discussed on the following ten pages.

To export a file: *improved*

1. With the file open, choose File menu > Export.

2. If you don't want to use the original file name, enter a new name in the Name field *(Mac)* or File Name field *(Windows)*.

   Windows: When saving a file, Illustrator automatically appends the proper file extension to the name (e.g., .ai, .eps, .tif) based on the chosen file format.

   Mac OS: Extensions will be appended if Preferences > Files & Clipboard's Append Extensions is set to Always.

3. Choose from the Format pop-up menu *(Mac OS)* **1** or Save as Type drop-down menu *(Win)* **2**.

4. Choose a location in which to save the new version.

   Optional: To create a new folder for the file,

   Mac OS: Click New, enter a name, then click Create.

   Win: Click Create New Folder, enter a name, then click Create.

5. Click Export (Return/Enter). Choose the desired settings from any secondary dialog box, then click OK. Some of these dialogs are discussed on pages 404–407.

➤ *Mac OS:* If Append Extensions is set to Never in Preferences > Files & Clipboard and you don't change the file name in the Export dialog box, when you click Save, a warning prompt will appear. Click Replace to save over the original file or click Cancel to return to the Export dialog box.

Export

Secondary export dialog boxes

Raster

If you choose a raster (bitmap) file format, such as Amiga IFF, BMP, PCX, Pixar, or Targa, the Rasterize dialog box will open **1**. Choose a Color Model for the resulting file color. For file Resolution, choose Screen (72 dpi), Medium (150 dpi), or High (300 dpi), or enter a custom resolution (Other). Check the Anti-Alias box to smooth the edges of objects (pixels will be added along object edges).

Amiga (IFF) format

The Amiga Interchange File Format is intended for use with Video Toaster and for working with the Commodore Amiga system. For some paint programs, such as Deluxe-Paint from Electronic Arts, IFF is the best format to use.

Bitmap (BMP) format

BMP is the standard bitmap image format on Windows and DOS computers. If you choose this format, you will also need to select Windows or OS/2 format for use with those operating systems, specify a bit depth, and choose whether you want to include RLE compression.

PCX format

The PCX format was created by Z-Soft for use with its PC Paintbrush program.

PIXAR format (PXR)

The PIXAR format is used for exchanging files with high-end PIXAR workstations. These workstations are designed for such applications as three-dimensional animation.

Photoshop 5

Exporting to Photoshop is a good idea if you want to preserve transparency effects. If you choose the Photoshop 5 file format, the Photoshop Options dialog box will open **2**. Choose a Color Model, a Resolution (preset or custom), and turn the Anti-Alias option on or off. To export Illustrator layers to Photoshop, check the Write Layers box. If this option is unchecked, Illustrator will flatten layers and the illustration will appear as one layer in Photoshop. The Write Layers

Layers and layers

If you keep layers intact when you export files to Photoshop, you'll then have the opportunity to apply Photoshop filters to those individual layers. You can also drop a native Photoshop PSD file containing Illustrator layers into Adobe's ImageReady application, where you can convert the layers to animations. ImageReady is designed specifically for creating and optimizing raster graphics, rollovers, and animations for the Web.

Photoshop and Illustrator *improved*

Illustrator 9.0 boasts improved compatibility with Photoshop. When you open a Photoshop file in Illustrator, you can preserve the file's blending modes, transparency, and clipping masks, and convert layers to separate Illustrator objects. When you export an Illustrator file to Photoshop 5.5 format, you can keep its blending modes, transparency, opacity masks, layers, and editable type. Layer masks from Photoshop convert to opacity masks in Illustrator, while opacity masks from Illustrator convert to layer masks in Photoshop.

option preserves the visual stacking of objects and groups nested within a layer, but only the top-level layers will become layers in Photoshop. You also have the option to Write Nested Layers to export layers and sublayers ("nested layers") as separate layers to Photoshop. The sublayers may be stacked below the top-level layer on Photoshop's Layers palette, but you can rearrange them.

You can also check Editable Text to keep Illustrator text editable in Photoshop. Text must be stacked as individual objects nested in a top-level layer.

If you have hidden layers you wish to include, check the Include Hidden Layers box. You can also choose to embed an ICC profile in the Photoshop document, assuming you have assigned one to your Illustrator file.

You must use the Photoshop 5 format to place an illustration that contains gradient mesh objects into Photoshop. (Neither Copy/Paste nor drag-and-drop will correctly import a gradient mesh object.)

Tagged-Image File Format (TIFF)

TIFF is a bitmap image format that is supported by virtually all paint, image-editing, and page-layout applications. It supports RGB, CMYK, and grayscale color schemes, and it support the lossless LZW compression model. You can specify a color space and resolution when you create TIFF files.

If you choose the TIFF file format, the TIFF Options dialog box will open **1**. Choose a Color Model. Choose a Resolution: Screen (72 dpi), Medium (150 dpi), or High (300 dpi), or type in a custom resolution. And turn the Anti-Alias option on or off. Check the LZW Compression box to compress the file. This type of compression is lossless, which means it doesn't cause loss or degradation of image data. Choose your target operating platform in the Byte Order area. Embed an ICC profile if you have assigned one to your file.

(Continued on the following page)

TIFF

JPEG

JPEG format is a good choice if you want to compress files that contain placed, continuous-tone, bitmap images, or objects with gradient fills. JPEG is also used for viewing 24-bit images via the Web. (The JPEG format for Web output is discussed on pages 442 and 451).

When you choose an Image Quality, keep in mind that there's a tradeoff between image quality and the amount of compression. The greater the compression, the greater the loss of image data and the lower the image quality. To experiment, export multiple copies of a file and use a different compression setting for each copy, and then view the results in the target application. Or use Illustrator's Export for Web option to preview different compression settings (see page 450).

If you choose the JPEG file format the JPEG Options dialog box will open **1**:

1. Choose an Image Quality. Enter a numerical value (0–10); or move the slider; or choose Low, Medium, High, or Maximum from the pop-up menu.

2. Choose a Color model: RGB, CMYK or Grayscale.

3. Choose a Format Method: Baseline ("Standard"); Baseline Optimized, which lets you adjust the color quality of the image; or Progressive. A Progressive JPEG displays at increasingly higher resolutions as the file downloads from the Web. Choose the number of scans (iterations) you want displayed before the final image is available. (This type of JPEG is not supported by all Web browsers and requires more RAM to view.)

4. Choose a Resolution Depth: Screen, Medium, or High. Or choose Custom and enter a Custom resolution (dpi).

5. In the Options section:

   Check the Anti-Alias box if you want your image to have smooth edges.

   If you have linked objects in your file to URLs, check Imagemap and choose

1 *The JPEG Options export dialog lets you tailor your image for a number of uses, whether it's optimizing it for fast downloading on the Web or preserving enough resolution to output a crisp print.*

JPEG

More about SVG

To learn more about SVG, review the files in the SVG Sample Files folder on the Adobe Illustrator 9 CD. It's best to open the .html, .svg and .js files in a browser.

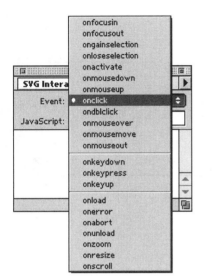

1 *Choose from the Event pop-up menu on the SVG Interactivity palette.*

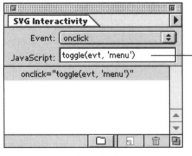

2 *Then enter a JavaScript action.*

Client-side or Server-side. For Client-side, Illustrator saves the JPEG file with an accompanying HTML file that holds the link information; both files are required by your Web-creation application in order to interpret the links correctly. For Server-side, Illustrator saves the file for use on a Web server. Check Embed ICC Profile to embed the file's Color Settings profile.

The SVG (Scalable Vector Graphics) format allows you to incorporate interactivity into an image. Currently, Web surfers must download an SVG plug-in to view graphics in this format. Keep in mind that many people won't bother to do this and will miss out on your artwork. Using SVG, you can add Javascript interactivity right in Illustrator and then export the result using the Export dialog box. For example, you can create a Javascript action that will trigger an action if a Web user moves the cursor over part of the image.

If you choose SVGZ in the Export dialog box, your file will be compressed.

new **To add interactivity to SVG artwork:**

1. Select an object.

2. Choose Window: Show SVG Interactivity.

3. Choose an event from the Event pop-up menu **1**. This will determine when your action will take place. For example, if you choose "onclick," your action will occur when the user clicks on that object.

4. In the JavaScript text window, write a JavaScript action **2**. To learn more about JavaScript, we recommend *Java for the World Wide Web: Visual QuickStart Guide*, by Dori Smith (Peachpit Press).

5. Click the Add Event and Function button or press Return/Enter. The event will now have a script routine that will run when the event occurs in a browser. You can later delete the event by highlighting it and clicking the trash button or choosing Delete Event from the SVG Interactivity palette menu.

SVG

407

To export an SVG or SVGZ file:

1. Choose File menu > Export.

2. Choose a location and file name for the graphic.

3. In the Export dialog box, choose SVG or SVGZ, then click Export.

4. In the SVG Options dialog box , choose a Font Subsetting option to embed the specific characters of the fonts you used in your document. All Glyphs includes every font character, including non-Roman characters; Common English or Common Roman includes only English or Roman characters.

5. Choose an Embedded Font Location. You can embed the font sets in the document or link the document to subsetted fonts from the Illustrator file.

6. Choose a Raster Image Location option to embed rasterized images in the exported file or link the file to JPEG images from the Illustrator file.

7. Choose how precise the vectors will be in your exported file by selecting a value between 1 and 7 Decimal Places. A higher value produces a more precise image (and a larger file size).

8. Choose an Encoding option: ASCII or UFT format. ISO 8859 is an ASCII character format; UTF-8 is an 8-bit format; UTF-16 is a 16-bit format.

9. Use the CSS [Cascading Style Sheet] Property Location option to choose a method of attaching style attributes to your document. Style Attributes (Entity Reference) will yield a smaller file; Style Attributes will result in a larger file, but is useful if the SVG code includes Extensible Stylesheet Language Transformation (XSLT); Style Element should be used if the file will be interacting with an HTML document, but it will make your SVG file render more slowly.

10. Click OK.

Don't know much about JavaScript?

You can create interactivity on a Web page without knowing JavaScript. Adobe LiveMotion does a super job of importing Illustrator objects for use in Web animation and interactivity. In fact, we wrote a book about LiveMotion entitled *LiveMotion for Windows and Macintosh: Visual QuickStart Guide*, Peachpit Press, 2000.

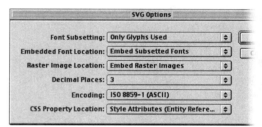

1 *The SVG Options dialog box for SVG export.*

1 *The Flash (SWF) Format Options dialog box for Flash export.*

The Macromedia Flash (SWF) format is another vector graphics format for the Web. This format is commonly used for animations, as it is compact and scales very well. Adobe LiveMotion imports (using the Load Movie Behavior) and exports SWF format files. Using Illustrator, you can create frames for an animation on separate layers and then export the layers to an animated Flash file.

Keep in mind that the Flash format does not support such transparency appearances as blending modes and opacity masks. Also, gradients that encompass a wide range of color will appear as rasterized shapes. Patterns will also be rasterized.

And finally, Flash supports only some kinds of joins. For example, beveled or square joins and caps will be converted to rounded joins.

To export a Flash file:

1. Choose File menu > Export.

2. Choose a location and type a name for your file.

3. In the Export dialog box, choose Flash as your file type, then click Export.

4. Choose from the Export Options, Export As pop-up menu **1**: AI file to SWF File exports your entire Illustrator file as one Flash frame; AI Layers to SWF Frames exports each layer in your Illustrator file to a separate Flash frame within a Flash document; AI Layers to SWF Files exports each Illustrator layer to a separate Flash file composed of one frame.

5. Choose the Frame Rate (in frames per second) for your Flash file if you have chosen AI Layers to SWF Frames.

6. Check the Auto-create Symbols box if you want a symbol to be created for each object in the file. If you later open the file in Flash, these symbols will appear in your Symbol Library. Check this option if you think you might edit your Flash file later. However, keep in mind that if you select this option, your Flash file will contain a duplicate of every frame in

(Continued on the following page)

Flash

your animation, which you should later delete.

7. Check the Read Only box if you do not want users to modify the Flash file.

8. Check the Clip to Artboard Size box to export only the artwork that is inside the artboard.

9. Use the Curve Quality slider to determine how accurate the bézier curves will appear in your Flash file. A higher number produces a more accurate curve (although the file size will also increase).

10. Choose an Image Format. Lossless is useful for images with large solid areas of color or for images that are to be edited later; Lossy (JPEG) is useful for bitmapped images, but it decreases the image quality.

11. If you chose the Lossy (JPEG) format option, choose a JPEG Quality to determine the amount of compression in your placed bitmaps. As quality increases, so does file size.
and
Choose Method: Baseline (Standard) or Baseline Optimized for your JPEGs.

12. Enter a Resolution value between 72 ppi and 2400 ppi to for your bitmap images. Higher resolutions will increase your file size.

If you plan to export rasterized images and scale them up in Flash, choose a resolution above 72 ppi so the scaled images won't appear pixelated.

➤ Choose Release to Layers from the Layers palette menu to put nested objects onto their own layers before exporting them to Flash format.

Targa (TGA)

The TGA format is designed for use on systems with the Truevision video board. You can specify a resolution and color depth for this format. If you choose the Targa file format and then click OK in the Rasterize dialog box, the Targa Options dialog box will open. Choose a Resolution (bit depth) for the amount of color/shade information each pixel is capable of storing.

Text (TXT)

You can export any text in your Illustrator file to a text file. Choose File > Export, choose Text as your file format, enter a file name, then click Save. Only editable text objects will be saved to the resulting file.

Other file formats

AutoCAD Drawing (DWG) and AutoCAD Interchange File (DXF)

DWG is AutoCAD's standard file format. DXF is a tagged data representation of the information contained in an AutoCAD drawing file. If you export either of these files, you will also need to choose an AutoCAD version, the number of colors you wish to include, and a raster file format.

Metafile formats

A metafile describes a file that functions as a list of commands to draw a graphic. Typically, a metafile is made up of commands to draw objects such as lines, polygons and text and commands to control the style of these objects.

Computer Graphics Metafile (CGM)

CGM, a vector-based metafile format, is used mostly for the exchange of graphical images, in particular, complex engineering or architectural images. This format does not work well for artwork that contains text. However, it is considered a platform-independent format.

Windows Metafile (WMF)

WMF is a 16-bit metafile format used by Windows platforms.

Enhanced metafile (EMF)

EMF is a 32-bit metafile format used by Windows platforms. It can contain a broader variety of commands than a WMF file.

PostScript file format (PS)

PostScript is a language that describes images for output to printers and other printing systems. PostScript Level 1, which Illustrator 9 does not support for export to EPS, represents grayscale vector graphics and grayscale bitmap images. Level 2 adds support for RGB, CMYK, and CIE color, and supports compression techniques for bitmap images. Level 3 adds the ability to print gradient mesh objects to a PostScript 3 printer. You can't save files as PS files directly in Illustrator 9, but you can use the Print-to-File option in the Print dialog box to create a PS file if you are using a PostScript printer.

Pasting out of Illustrator

You can use the Clipboard (Copy and Paste commands) to paste an Illustrator object into a document in another Adobe application.

Mac OS: If you copy and paste an object from Illustrator into Photoshop using the AICB Clipboard format, the **Paste** dialog box will open **1**. Click Paste As Pixels (check or uncheck the Anti-Alias box) or click Paste As Paths. To preserve blending modes and opacity settings for an object pasted into InDesign or Photoshop 6, use the PDF Clipboard format. To choose Clipboard data format options, see page 390.

➤ If you drag-and-drop a path object from Illustrator into Photoshop, it will appear as pixels on its own layer. Hold down Command/Ctrl while dragging to keep the path object as a path in Photoshop 5.5 or later.

1

new To export an Illustrator file to Adobe LiveMotion:

1. Before placing a file into LiveMotion, ungroup all groups, then, for each top-level layer, choose Layers palette menu > Release to Layers. *Note:* When the Illustrator file is placed, all objects will initially be one composite object. Use LiveMotion's Convert Layers Into command to convert the object into separate objects or a sequence.

If the Illustrator file contains effects and/or appearances, use Object menu > Expand Appearance, ungroup, then release to layers. This seems to work best when there is more than one top-level layer in the Illustrator file. Now do the first technique in step 2 (save, then Place).

2. Save a copy of the file in Adobe Illustrator version 8 format, then place the file using the File menu > Place command in LiveMotion. Yes, you read that correctly. Illustrator version 9 files cannot yet be placed into LiveMotion 1.0.
or
Select an object or objects in an Illustrator 9 document window, then copy/paste or drag-and-drop them into a LiveMotion document window. If you use the drag-and-drop method, arrange and resize both the Illustrator and LiveMotion windows so there is a minimum of overlap. You can also drag-and-drop an Illustrator file icon from the Desktop into a LiveMotion window.

➤ Whenever possible, bring Photoshop images directly into LiveMotion from Photoshop (not through Illustrator), and use LiveMotion's commands, such as its Photoshop filters, to modify the image. You can set opacity, color changes (Color, Brightness, Contrast, Saturation, etc.), edge softness, 3D effects such as Emboss and Shadow, and other effects within LiveMotion.

(Continued on the following page)

Export to LiveMotion

➤ Any opacity and blending mode appearances in the Illustrator file will be removed by LiveMotion. To preserve the look of opacity or blending mode appearances between two or more objects or images, you can either copy those objects together as one selection into LiveMotion or copy the objects separately and then apply opacity levels to the objects in LiveMotion.

➤ Illustrator's scatter brushes contain groups. To place a path that has a scatter brushstroke, apply the Object menu > Expand Appearance command; Ungroup; then release to layers so you'll be able to place the scatter brush path; then, in LiveMotion, convert it into separate objects. Some scatter brush objects contain a lot of separate paths that are grouped together. If this is the case, it will be easier to just copy the grouped object used in the scatter brush, paste it into LiveMotion, and then duplicate, transform, and reposition it in LiveMotion.

➤ LiveMotion's Edit Original command will open a copy of the imported Illustrator object's file in Illustrator. The original Illustrator file won't be changed. You can edit the Illustrator object (say, its shape), save the file, return to LiveMotion, and the imported object will update to reflect the change. Just make sure you don't change the name of the copy of the file that Illustrator generates. Using the Edit Original command, Illustrator can really be used as LiveMotion's "drawing" tool.

Animation

To animate a transition from one shape into another, use Illustrator's Blend tool to create intermediate steps between two objects. In the Blend Options dialog box, use a specified number of steps (say around 10 or 15) to limit the number of layers that will be created in LiveMotion. Expand the blend, ungroup, then release to layers. Finally, place the file into LiveMotion, and use Convert Layers Into and choose Sequence (to have LiveMotion automatically create a sequence of frames) or Objects (to let you manually sequence the objects in the LiveMotion Timeline window).

Don't stop here

The information contained in this section is explained in greater depth in the **AI9printwhitepaper.pdf file**. It's in the Adobe Technical Info > White Papers folder on the Illustrator 9 CD.

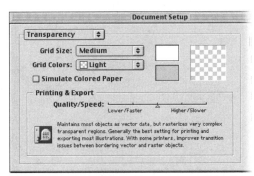

1 *The Document Setup > Transparency dialog box.*

Printing and exporting transparency *new*

Transparency settings (non-default blending modes and opacity levels) in objects, groups or layers are preserved when a document is saved in either of the native Illustrator formats: Adobe Illustrator (version 9) or Adobe PDF 1.4 (Acrobat 5).

When a file that contains Transparency palette settings is printed, or saved and exported, in a non-native format, Illustrator uses the settings in the Document Setup dialog box to determine how objects will be flattened and rasterized to preserve the look of those settings.

Illustrator flattens overlapping objects that contain transparency. It does this by breaking the overlapping objects into separate shapes for the non-overlapping area, along with a shape for the overlap area. Adobe calls these resulting, non-overlapping, non-transparent shapes the "flattened" components.

In order to represent the look of transparency, Illustrator usually keeps flattened shapes as vector objects. If the look of transparency settings cannot be preserved in a flattened shape as a vector object, Illustrator will rasterize the shape instead. This would happen, for example, if two gradient objects with non-default transparency settings overlap. The resulting flattened shape would be rasterized in order to keep this complex area of transparency.

Vector shapes print with cleaner, higher quality color and edges as compared to rasterized shapes. The Document Setup dialog box is used to control the percentage of flattened shapes that remain vectors versus the percentage of shapes that will be rasterized. Choose File menu > **Document Setup**, then choose **Transparency** from the pop-up menu **1**. Move the Quality/Speed slider to control whether flattened shapes remain as vectors or are rasterized. The Quality/Speed settings only apply to flattened shapes that represent transparency. As you move the slider, the info description under the slider updates to inform you what result that

Print and Export Transparency

slider position will produce vis-à-vis the rasterization of flattened shapes.

The higher positions (to the right) produce a higher percentage of flattened shapes as vectors, though complex flattened areas may be rasterized. A higher percentage of vector shapes will result in higher quality output, but at the expense of slower, more memory-demanding output processing.

The lowest position (to the left) won't necessarily produce poor output quality. If the illustration is very complex with lots of transparency effects, this may be the only setting that produces adequate output. Low settings are usually used to produce fast output at a low resolution.

The rasterization process requires a resolution setting to determine output quality. To set the resolution for areas that are rasterized, choose **Printing & Export** from the pop-up menu in File menu > Document Setup. The value in the **Rasterization Resolution** field is used for rasterizing flattened objects. The default value is 300 ppi. As a rule of thumb, the resolution should equal twice the output device's line screen (lpi). For type, at least 600 ppi is required for good quality output.

➤ To control the flattening of a current selection in the document, the Quality/Speed slider and Rasterization Resolution field that we discussed above are also found in Object menu > Flatten Transparency. Use the info descriptions found in the Document Setup dialog box to help you decide which position to use for the Flatten Transparency slider.

new Rasterization settings for effects

Some Effect menu commands must be rasterized when printed or exported. The default resolution setting is 72 ppi, a rather low setting that is suitable only for on-screen output.

To choose a higher resolution, choose Effect menu > Rasterize > **Raster Effects Settings** ▮. Click another resolution option, or click Other and enter a custom resolution setting. The higher the resolution, the slower the output processing time.

What gets rasterized

The Effect menu effects that will **rasterize** on export or output include all the effects below the line on the menu: Artistic, Blur, Brush Strokes, Distort, Pixelate, Sharpen, Sketch, Stylize, Texture, and Video. These effects on the Stylize submenu will also rasterize: Drop Shadow (if the Blur value is greater than 0), Inner Glow, Outer Glow, and Feather.

▮ *The **Raster Effects Settings** dialog box.*

Print and Export Transparency

➤ Leave the resolution for effects at the default 72 ppi while working on an illustration, and then increase the resolution before printing or exporting the file. A new resolution setting will affect all objects with applied effects that will rasterize as well as resolution-dependent filters such as Crystallize and Pointillize.

Color stitching

When an output file contains rasterized flattened shapes next to vector flattened shapes, a visible discrepancy in shared color areas may occur. An example of this is when a large area of solid color has a smaller complex transparent object overlapping it that must be rasterized when flattened. The solid color in the flattened vector shapes that represent the large solid color object may not perfectly match the background color of the flattened rasterized shape that represents the transparent object. This is called "color stitching," and it is most likely to occur when the Quality/Speed slider in Document Setup > Transparency is at position 2 (from the left). Positions 3, 4 and 5 progressively diminish the likelihood of stitching being visible. At position 1 (all the way left), the entire document is rasterized, so no color stitching occurs.

If you use the Layers palette to flatten (a copy of) your Illustrator file, you may see an on-screen version of color stitching when anti-aliasing is on, but this screen anomaly won't print. To gain a more accurate preview of a flattened file, choose Preferences > General, then uncheck Anti-aliased Artwork.

Flattening different types of objects

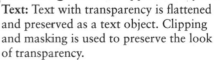

Text: Text with transparency is flattened and preserved as a text object. Clipping and masking is used to preserve the look of transparency.

Text that is stroked, filled with a pattern, or used as a clipping mask will be converted to outlines. When strokes are converted to outlines, the filled "strokes" may be wider than the original stroke by 1 or 2 pixels. To prevent this thickening, set the Quality/Speed slider to position 5 (far right) or position 1 (far left, where all objects will be rasterized). Or enter a Rasterization Resolution value (Document Setup dialog box) of 600 ppi or higher.

Gradient mesh objects: When printed to a PostScript level 3 printer, gradient mesh objects print as vectors. When gradient mesh objects are printed to a PostScript level 2 printer or saved to an EPS format that is PostScript Level 2 compatible, both vector data and rasterized data are saved in the file. This way the output device can choose which set of data to use. Specify the resolution for the rasterized mesh object in the Mesh field in File menu > Document Setup > Printing & Export 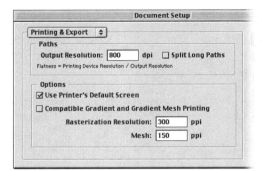.

Placed or embedded images: Illustrator rasterizes placed images at the resolution specified in the Rasterization Resolution field in File menu > Document Setup > Printing & Export dialog box when the Quality/Speed slider is at position 3, 4, or 5. At position 2, Illustrator will use the Rasterization Resolution value only for any portion of the image that overlaps an object with transparency. The remainder of the image will print at the image's original resolution. To keep things simple, always choose a Rasterization Resolution that's equal to or higher than the original resolution of the placed image.

For an EPS image that overlaps an object with transparency, embed the image into the Illustrator document via the Embed Image command on the Links palette menu. This will ensure an accurate printout of the image and the transparency effect.

Strokes: Strokes are converted into filled objects. The width of the object will equal the weight of the original stroke.

A Quality/Speed position of 1 will cause all strokes (and all objects, for that matter) to be rasterized. A high Rasterization Resolution will ensure good quality output.

A Quality/Speed position of 2 or 3 will cause any strokes that overlap an object with transparency to be converted to a filled

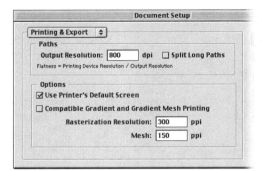

1 *The Document Setup > Printing & Export dialog box.*

object. Very thin strokes may thicken a bit and look different from the portion of the strokes that don't overlap the transparency.

A Quality/Speed position of 4 or 5 causes all strokes to be converted to filled objects, regardless of whether the strokes interact with transparency. This preserves a stroke's look for its entire length, but results in a larger number of paths in the file.

Exporting Illustrator files: a summary

new

The best way to save and export an Illustrator 9 file is by saving it in the Illustrator EPS format. On Mac OS, choose Compatibility: Illustrator 9. In Windows: choose Compatibility: Version 9. A file in this format can be reopened in Illustrator 9 at any time, and it can be edited and resaved with no loss of object data. Choose the EPS format for export to Adobe InDesign 1.5, Adobe PageMaker, and QuarkXPress.

For export to Adobe GoLive 5, use the native Adobe Illustrator document format, Compatibility: Illustrator 9/Version 9.

To export to Adobe LiveMotion 1.0, Premiere 5, or After Effects 4.1, one option is to choose the native Adobe Illustrator document format, Compatibility: Illustrator 8/Version 8. A second option is to copy/paste from Illustrator. Before copying and pasting, in Edit menu > Preferences > Files & Clipboard, check the AICB option and check the Preserve Appearances option to maintain the look of transparency.

Summary

improved

Managing color

Problems with color can creep up on you when various hardware devices and software packages you use treat color differently. For example, if you open a graphic in several different imaging programs and in a Web browser, the colors in your image might look completely different in each case. And none of those programs may match the color of the picture you originally scanned in on your scanner. Print out the image, and you will probably find that your results are different again. In some cases, you might find these differences slight and unobjectionable. But in other circumstances, such color changes can wreak havoc with your design and turn a project into a disaster.

A color management system can solve most of these problems by acting as a color interpreter. A good system knows how each device and program understands color, and it can help you move your graphics between them all by adjusting color so that it appears the same in every program and device.

A color profile is a mathematical description of a device's color space. Illustrator 9.0 uses ICC (International Color Consortium) profiles to tell your color management system how particular devices use color.

You can find most of Illustrator's color management controls in the Color Settings dialog box under the Edit menu. This dialog box includes a list of predefined management options for various publishing situations, including prepress output and Web output.

Illustrator 9 also supports color management policies for RGB and CMYK color files. In the case that you, for example, import a graphic into an Illustrator document and that graphic does or does not have a color profile attached, these color management policies govern how Illustrator deals with color in such graphics.

➤ Consult with your prepress service provider, if you are using one, about color management. Make sure your color management workflows will work together.

Learn it now

Illustrator's new color management features will probably seem complex to you at first. But it's well worth the investment of time to learn about them, because those features will be adopted by other Adobe programs (such as Photoshop) in upcoming versions.

new

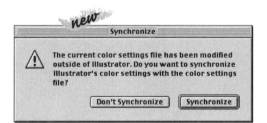

*The **Synchronize** alert box may open when Illustrator 9 is launched if the current color settings have been modified in another Adobe program (e.g., Photoshop 6). Click Synchronize to have Illustrator's Color Settings match the Color Settings from the other program.*

420

The Adobe Gamma dialog box after choosing the Control Panel option.

➤ If you plan on using the same graphics for different purposes, such as for the Web and for printed material, you may benefit from using color management.

Calibration

The first step toward achieving color consistency is to calibrate your monitor. In this procedure, you will define the RGB color space your monitor can display using the Adobe Gamma control panel, which is installed automatically with Illustrator and some other Adobe applications. You will adjust the contrast and brightness, gamma, color balance, and white point of your monitor.

The Adobe Gamma Control Panel creates an ICC profile, which Illustrator can use as its working RGB space to display the colors in your artwork accurately.

Note: You have to calibrate your monitor and save the settings as an ICC profile only once for all applications.

To calibrate your monitor:

1. Give the monitor 30 minutes to warm up so the display is stabilized, and establish a level of room lighting that will remain constant.

2. Set the desktop pattern to light gray.

3. *Mac OS:* Choose Apple menu > Control Panels > Adobe Gamma.

   Windows: Choose Program Files > Common Files > Adobe > Calibration > Adobe Gamma.

4. Click Step by Step (Assistant), which will walk you through the process.
   or
   Click Control Panel to choose settings from a single dialog box with no explanation ■. (If the Adobe Gamma dialog opens directly, you can skip this step.)

   Note: Click Next. If you're using the Assistant, click Next between dialogs.

5. Leave the default monitor ICC profile.
   or

(Continued on the following page)

Calibration

Click Load and select a profile that more closely matches your monitor.

6. Turn up your monitor's brightness and contrast settings; leave the contrast at maximum; and adjust the brightness to make the alternating gray squares in the top bar as dark as possible, but not black, while keeping the lower bar bright white.

7. For Phosphors, choose your monitor type or choose Custom and enter the Red, Green, and Blue chromaticity coordinates specified by your monitor manufacturer.

The gray square represents a combined grayscale reading of your monitor. Adjust the gamma using this slider until the smaller solid-color box matches the outer, stripey box. It helps to squint. You might find it easier to deselect the View Single Gamma Only box and make separate adjustments based on the readings for Red, Green, and Blue.

For Desired, select the default for your system: 1.8 (Mac) or 2.2 (Windows), if this option is available.

For Hardware, select the white point the monitor manufacturer specifies, or click Measure and follow the instructions.

For Adjusted, choose Same as Hardware. Or if you know the color temperature at which your image will ultimately be viewed, you can choose it from the pop-up menu or choose Custom and enter it. *Note:* This option is not available for all monitors.

8. Close the Adobe Gamma window and save the profile. *Mac OS:* Save it in the System Folder > ColorSync Profiles folder. *Windows:* Save it in Windows > System > Color (extension, .icm). Illustrator can use this profile as its working RGB space in the Color Settings dialog box (see the next page).

Note: If you change your monitor's brightness and contrast settings or change the room lighting, you should recalibrate your monitor. Also keep in

Point and learn!

The Color Settings dialog box provides a Description area **2** that displays valuable information on options the mouse is currently over. Make use of this great feature!

1 *The **Color Settings** dialog box with the **Web Graphics Defaults** setting chosen.*

mind that this procedure is just a beginning. Professional calibration requires more precise monitor measurement using expensive hardware devices such as colorimeters and spectrophotometers.

To choose a predefined color management setting:

1. Choose Edit menu > Color Settings.
2. Choose a configuration Option from the Settings pop-up menu **1**:

   Emulate Adobe Illustrator 6.0 uses the same color workflow used by Illustrator versions 6.0 and earlier. This option does not recognize or save color profiles.

   Color Management Off emulates the behavior of applications that do not support color management. This is a good choice for projects destined for video or onscreen presentation.

   U.S. Prepress Defaults manages color using settings based on common press conditions in the U.S. In the European or Japanese Prepress option, the CMYK Work Space is changed to a press standard for that region.

   Web Graphics Defaults manages color for content that will be published on the Web.

   ColorSync Workflow (Mac OS only) manages color using the ColorSync 3.0 color management system. Profiles are based on those in the ColorSync control panel (including the monitor profile you may have created using the Adobe Gamma).

3. Click OK (Return/Enter).

Choosing individual work space settings

You can choose color working spaces, which define how RGB and CMYK color will be treated in your document. For CMYK settings, you should check with your service provider. The following choices are available for **RGB** settings:

(Continued on the following page)

423

Adobe RGB (1998)

This color space produces a wide range of colors, and is useful if you will be converting RGB images to CMYK images. This is not a good choice for Web work.

sRGB IEC61966-2.1

This is a good choice for Web work, as it reflects the settings on the average computer monitor. Many hardware and software manufacturers are using it as the default space for scanners, low-end printers, and software. sRGB IEC61966-2.1 should not be used for prepress work—Apple RGB or ColorMatch RGB should be used instead.

Apple RGB

This space is useful for files that you plan to display on Mac monitors, as it reflects the characteristics of the older Standard Apple 13-inch monitors. It also is a good choice for working with older desktop publishing files, such as Adobe Photoshop 4.0 and earlier.

ColorMatch RGB

This space produces a smaller range of color than the Adobe RGB (1998) model, but it matches the color space of Radius Pressview monitors and is useful for print production work.

Monitor RGB

This choice sets the RGB working space to your monitor's profile. This is a useful setting if you know that other applications you will be using for your project do not support color management. Keep in mind that if you share this configuration with another user, the configuration will use that user's monitor profile as the RGB working space and color consistency may be lost.

ColorSync RGB (Mac only)

Use this color space to match Illustrator's RGB space to the space specified in the Apple ColorSync 3.0 (or later) control panel. This can be the profile you created using Adobe Gamma. If you share this configuration with another user, it will utilize the ColorSync space specified by that user.

1 *Color Management Policies options are chosen from the middle portion of the Color Settings dialog box.*

You can choose a customized color management policy that will tell Illustrator how to deal with artwork that doesn't match your current color settings. *new*

To customize your color management policies:

1. Choose Edit menu > Color Settings.

2. Choose any predefined setting from the Settings pop-up menu other than Emulate Adobe Illustrator 6.

3. Choose a color management policy:

   If you choose **Off**, Illustrator will not color-manage imported or opened color files.

   Choose **Preserve Embedded Profiles** if you think you're going to be working with both color-managed and non-color-managed documents. This will tie each color file's profile to the individual file.

   Choose **Convert to Working Space** if you want all your documents to reflect the same color working space. This is usually the best choice for Web work.

   For Profile Mismatches, check **Ask When Opening** to have Illustrator display a message when the color profile in a file you are opening does not match your selected working space. If you choose this option, you can override your color management policy when opening documents.

   Check **Ask When Pasting** to have Illustrator display a message when color profile mismatches occur as you paste color data into your document. If you choose this option, you can override your color management policy when pasting.

4. Click OK (Return/Enter).

new

To customize your conversion options:

1. Choose Edit menu > Color Settings.

2. Check the Advanced Mode box ◼.

3. Under Conversion Options, choose a color management **Engine** that will be used to convert colors between color spaces: **Adobe (ACE)** uses Adobe's color management system and color engine; **Apple ColorSync** or **Apple CMM** uses Apple's color management system; and **Microsoft ICM** uses the system provided in the Windows 98 and Windows 2000 systems. Other CMMs can be chosen to fit into color workflows that use specific output devices.

4. Choose a rendering **Intent** to determine how colors will be changed as they are moved from one color space to another:

   Perceptual changes colors in a way that seems natural to the human eye, even though the color values actually do change; good for continuous tone images.

   Saturation changes colors with the intent of preserving vivid colors, although it compromises the accuracy of the color; good for charts and business graphics.

   Absolute Colorimetric keeps colors that are inside the destination color gamut unchanged, but the relationships between colors outside this gamut are changed in an attempt to preserve a color.

   Relative Colorimetric, the default intent for all predefined settings options, is the same as Absolute Colorimetric, except it compares the white point, or extreme highlight, of the source color space to the destination color space and shifts all colors accordingly. The accuracy of this intent depends on the accuracy of white point information in an image's profile.

   Note: Differences between rendering intents are visible only on a printout or a conversion to a different working space.

   Check **Use Black Point Compensation** if you would like to adjust for differences in black points between color spaces. When this option is chosen, the full dynamic

Save your settings

To save your custom settings for later use, click **Save** in the Color Settings dialog box. If you want your custom file to display on the Settings pop-up menu, save it in the Settings folder, in the default location: deeply nested in the System Folder (Mac OS)/Program Files folder (Win). When you're ready to reuse the saved settings, click **Load** in the Custom Settings dialog box, then locate your settings file.

◼ *When the **Advanced Mode** box is checked in the **Color Settings** dialog box, the **Conversion Options** become available.*

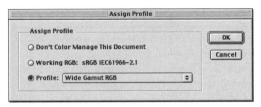

1 *The Assign Profile dialog box. The assigned profile is listed as the Source Space in the Adobe Illustrator 9 section of the File menu > Print dialog box.*

range of the source color space is mapped into the full dynamic range of the destination color space. If you don't select this option, your blacks may appear as grays.

We recommend you check Use Black Point Compensation for RGB to CMYK or CMYK to CMYK conversions.

5. Click OK (Return/Enter).

➤ When you save a file in a format that supports embedded profiles (e.g., the native Illustrator formats), you can check the Embed ICC Profile option to save the profile in the document.

If you decide later that you want to change the color profile of a document or remove a profile, you can use the Assign Profile command. For example, you may want to prepare a document for a specific output purpose, and you may need to adjust the profile accordingly. You also may want to use this option if you change your mind about your color management settings. *new*

To change a document's color profile:

1. Choose Edit menu > Assign Profile **1**.

2. Click Don't Color Manage This Document to remove the color profile.
or
Click Working [plus the document color mode and name of the working space you are using] to assign that particular working space to a document that uses no profile or that uses a profile that is different from the working space.
or
Click Profile to reassign a different profile to a color-managed document. Choose a profile from the pop-up menu.

3. Click OK (Return/Enter).

➤ When you save a file in (or export a file to) a format that supports embedded profiles, you have the choice to select or deselect the Embed ICC Profile option. You should keep this option chosen unless you have a specific reason not to.

AssignProfile

Specifying a color management setup is all well and good, but sometimes all you want is to know how a document will look when it is printed out or viewed on a Windows or Mac monitor as part of a Web page. To do this, you can soft-proof your colors. While this method is less accurate than actually making a print or viewing your Web artwork on different monitors, it can give you a general idea of how your work will look in different settings.

new

To proof your colors:

1. From the View menu > Proof Setup submenu, choose which type of output display you want to simulate.

   Custom will allow you to create a proofing model for a specific output device using the Proof Setup dialog box. To do this, choose the color profile for your desired output device from the Profile pop-up menu, then check or uncheck Preserve Color Numbers. If you check this option, Illustrator will simulate how the colors will appear if they're not converted to the proofing space. If you uncheck this option, Illustrator will simulate how the colors will appear if they are converted, and you will need to specify a rendering intent as described on page 426 ("Customize your conversion options").
   or
   Choose **Macintosh RGB** or **Windows RGB** to soft-proof colors using a Mac or Windows monitor profile as the proof space you wish to simulate.
   or
   Choose **Monitor RGB** to use your monitor profile as the space for proofing.

2. View menu > **Proof Color** will be checked automatically so the soft-proof can be previewed. Uncheck this option to turn off proofing.

If Preserve Color Numbers is gray

The **Preserve Color Numbers** option is available only when the color mode of the current file is the same as that of the output device profile currently chosen in the Proof Setup dialog box. For example, if the document color mode is RGB and the chosen proofing profile is an RGB profile, then the Preserve Color Numbers option will be available.

Proof Setup

SEPARATIONS 25

You can produce color separations directly from Illustrator. This chapter contains a brief introduction to Illustrator's Separation Setup dialog box and an introduction to trapping, which helps to compensate for color misregistration on press.

©Chris Spollen

Color separation setup

Trapping and color separations are usually handled by a prepress provider—either a service bureau or a print shop. Talk with your print shop before producing color separations or building traps. They'll tell you what settings to use. Don't guess—this isn't the time to "wing it."

To print an illustration on press, unless your print shop uses direct-to-plate technology, you need to supply them with or have them produce film output (color separations) from your Illustrator file—one sheet per process or spot color. Your print shop will use the film separations to produce plates to use on the press—one plate for each color.

In **process color** printing, four ink colors, Cyan (C), Magenta (M), Yellow (Y), and Black (K), are used to produce a multitude of colors. A document that contains color photographs or other continuous-tone images must be output as a four-color process job.

In **spot color** printing, a separate plate is produced for each spot color. PANTONE inks are the most commonly used spot color inks, at least in the U.S. Using Illustrator's Separation Setup, you can control which spot colors are converted into process colors and which will remain as spot colors, and you can specify which colors will output.

To prepare a file for separations:

1. Calibrate your monitor (see pages 421–422).

2. Choose File menu > Document Color Mode > CMYK Color.

3. Decide which colors in the illustration are to be overprinted (see "Overprinting," below).

4. Create traps, if needed (see pages 435–438).

5. Place any objects that you don't want to appear on the color separations on a separate layer and uncheck the Print option for that layer, or hide the layer altogether.

6. Create crop marks, if needed (see page 433).

Overprinting

Normally, Illustrator automatically knocks out any color under an object so the object color won't mix with the color beneath it on press. If you check the **Overprint Fill** or **Overprint Stroke** box on the Attributes palette, the fill or stroke color will overprint colors underneath it instead—the inks will mix on press. Where colors overlap, a combination color will be produced. Turn the Overprint option on if you're building traps. Colors will overprint on a printing press, but not on a PostScript color composite printer.

Illustrator can show you how spot color objects, with the Overprint Fill or Overprint Stroke option checked (Attributes palette, see page 435), will overprint underlying objects. To view overprinting, choose View menu > Overprint Preview **1**–**2**. "Overprint Preview" is listed in the document window title bar when this option is checked. Also, any traps created with the Pathfinder Trap command will preview (see page 438). Now proceed with the instructions on the following page.

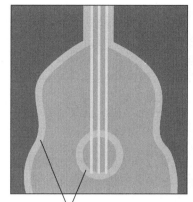

1 *Two objects with their strokes set to overprint.*

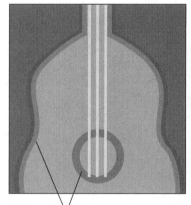

2 *With* **Overprint Preview** *checked, the overprint strokes simulate ink mixing with objects below.*

To use Separation Setup:

1. With your file in CMYK Color mode, choose File menu > Separation Setup.

2. You'll see a file preview window on the left and separation settings on the right. The dialog box will be grayed out until a PPD file is opened (the next step).

3. To open or change the current PPD file, click Open PPD on the right side of the dialog box, locate and highlight the PPD file specified by your service bureau for your target printer or imagesetter, then click Open 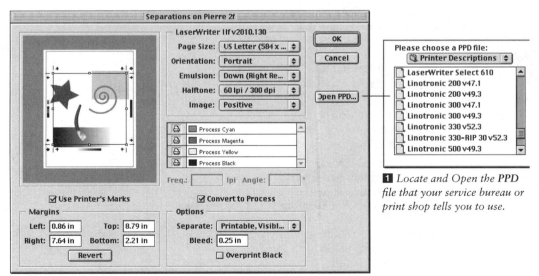 **1**. The PPD files should be located in the Printer Descriptions folder in the Macintosh Systems folder > Extensions folder (Mac OS)/Windows > System subdirectory (Win).

4. *Optional:* The white (or black) area in the preview window represents the page size. Separation Setup will automatically choose the default page size for the chosen printer definition. Choose a new size from the Page Size pop-up menu if your print shop requests that you do so.

For steps 5–8, ask your print shop for advice.

5. From the Orientation pop-up menu, choose Portrait to position the image vertically inside the imageable area of the separation **2**.
   or
   Choose Landscape to position the image horizontally inside the imageable area of the separation. The orientation of the image on the page will change; the orientation of the page on the film will not.

6. Choose Up (Right Reading) or Down (Right Reading) from the Emulsion pop-up menu.

7. Choose a combined Halftone screen ruling (lpi)/Device resolution (dpi) from the Halftone pop-up menu.

8. Choose Positive or Negative from the Image pop-up menu.

9. You can click OK at any time to save the current Separation Setup settings and you can reopen the dialog box at a later time to make further changes. When you save your document, the separation settings will save with the document. Continue with the instructions on the next page.

Separation Setup

1 *Locate and Open the PPD file that your service bureau or print shop tells you to use.*

2 *The illustration will preview on the left side of the Separations dialog box. Choose the settings your print shop specifies from the right side of the dialog box.*

By default, Illustrator will create and print a separation for each process and spot color used in an illustration. Using the Separation Setup dialog box, you can turn printing on or off for individual colors or convert individual spot colors into process colors.

Choosing colors to print and/or convert to process

1. Choose File menu > Separation Setup if that dialog box isn't already open.

2. In the scroll window, you will see a listing for each color used in the illustration **1**. For each process color you don't want to print, click the printer icon next to the color name to hide the icon. (Click again to show the icon.)

3. Check the Convert to Process box to convert all spot colors in the document into process colors. This is the default setting.

   or

   Uncheck the Convert to Process box, then:

   Click in the box next to the spot color name until a four-color process icon appears for each spot color you want to convert into a process color and print.
   or
   Keep clicking until a printer icon appears to keep the color as a spot color and print it.
   or
   Keep clicking until the printer icon disappears to prevent a spot color from printing.

➤ Don't change the Freq. (Frequency) or Angle settings unless you're advised to do so by your print shop.

➤ Check the Overprint Black box if you want black fills and strokes to overprint background colors. You don't need to mix a process black (a black made from a mixture of C, M, Y, and K) to use this option. An alert box will appear, instructing you to use the Colors > Overprint Black filter when the file contains transparency (see page 437).

Proof it

There are several reasons to proof your computer artwork before it's printed. First, the RGB colors that you see on your computer screen won't match the printed CMYK colors unless your monitor is properly calibrated. Obtaining a proof will give you an opportunity to correct the color balance or brightness of a picture, or to catch output problems like banding in a gradient. And most print shops need a proof to refer to so they know what the printed piece is supposed to look like. **Digital** (direct-from-disk) **color proofs**—like IRIS or 3M prints—are inexpensive, but they're not perfectly reliable. An advantage of using an IRIS print, though, is that you can color correct your original electronic file and run another IRIS print before you order film.

A more accurate but more expensive proof is a **Chromalin** or **Matchprint**, which is produced from the actual film (color separations). Matchprint colors may be slightly more saturated than final print colors, though. The most reliable color proof—and the most expensive—is a **press proof**, which is produced in the print shop from your film negatives on the final paper stock.

Four-color process icon: This spot color will convert to process and print.   *Printer icon: This color will print as a separate plate.*

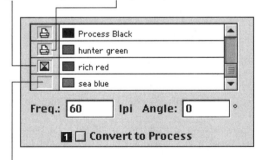

*A **blank** space (no icon): This color **won't print**.*

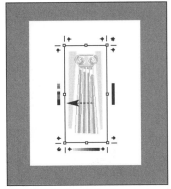

1 *Move the image in its printing bounding box.*

Creating crop marks for separations

If you haven't created crop marks for your document in Illustrator, the Separation Setup feature will, by default, create crop marks at the edge of the illustration's bounding box, which is the smallest rectangle that can encompass all the objects and direction lines in the illustration. It displays as a black rectangle in the preview window. Adobe recommends setting crop marks in Illustrator using Object menu > Crop Marks > Make rather than using Separation Setup to set crop marks so you can control more precisely the exact printable area of your illustration.

Separation Setup regards crop marks created using the Trim Marks filter as artwork. If your document contains Trim Marks, you can uncheck Use Printer's Marks to remove the default cropmarks. Unfortunately, this will also remove all printer's marks (crop marks, registration marks, and color bars). Check this box to restore printer's marks.

The printing bounding box defines the printable area around which Separation Setup places crop marks. You can resize the printing bounding box in the preview window so it surrounds a different part of the illustration, though it usually does not need to be adjusted. If you move or resize this printing bounding box, Separation Setup crop marks will move with the bounding box. You might need to move the image and/or resize the bounding box if the illustration contains objects that are outside the artboard and there are no Illustrator-generated crop marks, because Separation Setup will include off-the-page objects as part of the image to be printed. Follow the instructions below if you want to resize the printing bounding box (and thus re-crop the illustration).

Re-cropping the illustration in the printing bounding box

In the Separation Setup dialog box:

To move the illustration relative to the printing bounding box, position the pointer over the image in the preview window, then drag **1**.

or

To move the black line printing bounding box and the image, position the pointer over any non-handle part of the line and drag the box **1**.

or

To resize the printing bounding box (the black line), drag any of its four corner or side handles **2**.

➤ To restore the default printing bounding box, click Revert. The original values will be reentered into the Left, Right, Top, and Bottom fields.

Specifying which layers in the illustration will separate

Choose one of these options from the Separate pop-up menu in the Separation Setup dialog box to control which layers will be color separated **3**:

Printable, Visible Layers, to separate only those visible layers for which the Print option was turned on. To use this option effectively, place any objects you don't want separated on a special non-printing layer. Separation Setup will place the crop marks correctly.

Visible Layers, to separate only those layers that aren't hidden.

All Layers, to separate all layers.

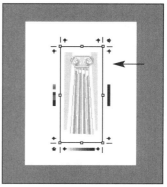

1 *Drag any part of the line except a handle to move the printing bounding box and the illustration together.*

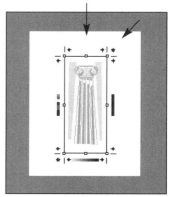

2 *Drag a side or corner handle to reshape the printing bounding box.*

Options	
Separate:	✓ Printable, Visible Layers
Bleed:	Visible Layers
	All Layers
	☐ Overprint Black

3 *The Separate pop-up menu in the Separation Setup dialog box.*

Separation Setup

Scale, then trap

If you apply automatic trapping and then change an object's size, the trap width will change. You should apply trapping **after** you finalize the objects' dimensions.

Avoid the trap!

If all your colors have at least one component color in common (Cyan, Magenta, Yellow, or Black), you won't need to trap!

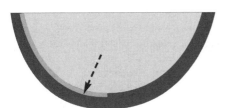

1 *Spread a lighter-colored foreground object.*

2 *Choke a darker-colored foreground object.*

The trap shrinks the darker-colored object.

3 *Overprint Stroke*

The Attributes palette.

Trapping

Trapping is the slight enlargement of a color area so it overlaps another color. The purpose of trapping is to compensate for gaps that might appear between printed colors due to misregistration on press.

There are two basic kinds of traps. A **spread** trap extends a lighter-colored object over a darker background color **1**. A **choke** trap extends a lighter background color over a darker-colored object **2**. In either case, the extending color overprints the object or background color, and a combination color is produced where they overlap.

In Illustrator, you can build traps automatically or you can build them manually by specifying your own stroke width percentages. To turn on automatic trapping, see page 438.

Note: Ask your print shop for advice before building traps into your illustration.

To create a spread trap manually:

1. With your file in CMYK Color mode, select the lighter colored foreground object.

2. Apply a stroke in the same color as the object's fill. The stroke weight should be **twice** the trap width that your print shop recommends for this object.

3. Open the Attributes palette, and check the Overprint Stroke box **3**. The foreground object will overlap the background object by half the thickness of the new stroke. The new stroke will blend with the background color via the Overprint option, and it will extend halfway inside and halfway outside the edge of the object.

   Note: You'll be able to see the trap effect if you study the high-end output closely. To "proof" the overprinting effect on screen, use View menu > Overprint Preview.

Trapping

435

To create a choke trap manually:

1. Select the darker-colored foreground object.

2. Apply a stroke in the same color as the lighter background object's fill, in a weight that's twice the trap width your print shop recommends for this object.

3. Check the Overprint Stroke box on the Attributes palette. The lighter background color will now overlap the darker foreground object by half the width of the new stroke.

➤ A choke trap reduces the area of a darker object by half the stroke weight. Be careful when choking small type!

To trap a line manually:

1. Apply a stroke color and weight.

2. Choose Object menu > Path > Outline Stroke. The line becomes a filled object, the same width as the original stroke.

3. Apply a stroke to the modified line. If the line is lighter than the background color, apply the same color as the fill of the line. Otherwise, apply the lighter background color. Choose a stroke weight that is twice the trap width your print shop recommends for this object.

4. Check the Overprint Stroke box on the Attributes palette. The line will now overlap the background color by half the width of the new stroke ■. The stroke will blend with the background color when it overprints.

➤ If you're going to apply a choke trap to the line (where the stroke created in step 3 takes on the background color), the original outlined path will be reduced by the stroke weight. The stroke will reduce the path by half the stroke weight on each side of the path. To counteract this, create a stroked line (step 1) in a weight that is equal to the desired line weight plus the needed trap weight. For example, let's say you have a 1 pt. line that needs a .2 pt. trap: Create a line with a 1.2 pt. weight stroke for step 1.

Strokes where you need 'em

You can use the **Pathfinder Outline** command to create trap strokes only where they're needed. To do this, create a new layer, then select the objects to be trapped. On the Layers palette, Option-drag/Alt-drag each layer's selection square up to the new layer to copy the objects in their exact same x/y location on the new layer. Position the copies in the proper stacking order, then hide the original layer. Select the copied objects, click the Outline button on the Pathfinder palette to create strokes from those objects, then set the resulting strokes to overprint. Finally, using the Direct-selection tool, select and delete any stroke segments that you don't need, such as any strokes on a blank white background, then apply a stroke weight that's twice the trap amount your print shop specifies.

Why the Overprint Black filter?

Normally, in PostScript color separations, objects on top knock out the color of objects underneath them so their ink colors don't intermix on press. When a color overprints, on the other hand, it prints right on top of the color beneath it and mixes with that color. Black is sometimes printed this way to eliminate the need for trapping. Using the **Overprint Black** filter, you can turn on overprinting or prevent overprinting in individual objects by exact percentages of black. (Using the Separation Setup dialog box to specify overprinting instead would cause all black areas to overprint.)

Trapping type

Try not to use process colors on small type. Any misregistration on press will make the small type difficult to read. To trap type, make a copy of the type, choose Paste in Back, create a stroke for the copy, and set the stroke to overprint. Type can also be converted into outlines. The resulting outline objects can be trapped like any other object.

1 *The Overprint Black* dialog box.

Before using this feature, read the sidebar at left and consult with your print shop.

To overprint a specified percentage of black:

1. Select an object(s) that contains black.

2. Choose Filter menu > Colors > Overprint Black.

3. Choose Add Black from the pop-up menu to turn the Overprint option on for the specified percentage you will enter **1**.
   or
   Choose Remove Black to turn the Overprint option off for the specified percentage you will enter.

4. Enter a Percentage value. Objects containing this black percentage will overprint or not overprint, depending on your choice for step 3.

5. Check Apply To: Fill to overprint black fills; check Stroke to overprint black strokes.

6. Check Options: Include Blacks with CMY to overprint any CMYK mixture containing the specified percentage of black.

   Check Options: Include Spot Blacks to overprint any spot color containing the specified percentage of black.

   Note: To overprint a spot color, you must check both Options boxes.

7. Click OK (Return/Enter).

➤ If you select more than one black object and then apply the Overprint Black filter, the filter will affect only those objects containing the specified percentage of black. The objects that are affected will remain selected after the filter is applied.

Trapping

The Trap command creates traps automatically by determining which color object is lighter, and then spreading that color into the darker object. *Note:* The Trap command won't trap a placed image or any object that contains a gradient or pattern fill.

To create traps automatically:

1. With your document in CMYK Color mode, select two or more objects.

2. Click the Trap button on the Pathfinder palette **1**. (Choose Show Options from the palette menu to expand the palette.)

3. Enter the Thickness value your print shop specifies for the trap **2**.

Ask your print shop about optional steps 4–7.

4. Enter a Height/Width percentage to compensate for paper stretch on press (see the sidebar at right).

5. Enter a Tint Reduction percentage to prevent trap areas between light colors from printing too darkly.

6. Check Traps with Process Color to convert spot color traps in the selected objects into process colors, and thus prevent the creation of a separate plate just for traps.

7. Check Reverse Traps to trap darker colors into lighter colors.

8. Click OK (Return/Enter). The trap shapes will become a new group on the currently active layer on the Layers palette.

The Trap filter doesn't always take the stroke color of a selected object into consideration. To overcome this limitation, convert the stroke into a filled object.

To create a trap on top of a fill and a stroke (a workaround):

1. Select an object that has a fill and a stroke, then choose Object menu > Path > Outline Stroke.

2. Deselect, choose the Direct-selection tool, click the outermost object (the "stroke"), then click the Unite button on the Pathfinder palette to remove any excess points from the outline path object (the "stroke").

3. Apply the Trap command (see above).

Adjust trap height and width

Using the Trap command, you can adjust a trap to compensate for horizontal or vertical stretching of the paper on press. Enter a Height/Width percentage above 100% to widen the trap thickness for horizontal lines, or enter a Height/Width percentage below 100% to narrow the trap thickness for horizontal lines. Leave the percentage at 100 to have the same trap width apply to both horizontals and verticals.

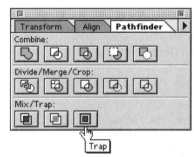

1 *Click the* **Trap** *button on the Pathfinder palette.*

2 *Choose the trap* **Thickness** *and other options in the Pathfinder Trap dialog box.*

WEB 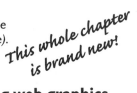 26

This chapter covers the preparation of Illustrator images for use in multimedia (on screen) and on the World Wide Web (online). This whole chapter is brand new!

Illustrator's Save for Web

The file optimization features in Illustrator 9 are combined in the File menu > **Save for Web** dialog box ◼. There you'll find Original, Optimized, 2-Up, and 4-Up preview tabs at the top of main window; a Color Table palette; and format, matte, quality, and other options. You'll also find Preview and Preview in [browser] menus in this dialog box.

◼ *Illustrator's Save for Web dialog box.*

Exporting web graphics

Illustrator excels at creating crisp, tidy graphics—the kind of graphics that are perfect for the Web. Thankfully, the latest version of the program boasts a number of tools that make preparing Web graphics much easier.

The basic formula for outputting an image for on-line viewing may seem straightforward: Design the image in RGB color mode and export it in GIF or JPEG format, which is the file format used by Web servers and browsers (the applications that combine text, images, and HTML code into a viewable page on the World Wide Web). However, when you load and view an image via a Web browser, you may be disappointed to find that not all colors or blends display well on the Web. And an illustration with a large, placed image may take an unacceptably long time to download and render, due to its large storage size. If an image looks overly dithered (grainy and dotty), or was subject to unexpected color substitutions, or takes too long to view on a Web page, it means your design is not outputting well. Some of the key issues that you'll need to address for on-line output are discussed on the remaining pages of this chapter.

When you are preparing Web graphics, there are four important issues you'll need to address for on-line output: The pixel size of the image, the color palette, the color depth, and the file format (GIF, JPEG, PNG, Flash, or SVG).

(Continued on the following page)

Image size

In order to calculate the appropriate image size, you must know the monitor size and the modem speed of your intended viewers beforehand. In most cases, you should be designing your image for a 800 x 600-pixel viewing area, the most common monitor size, and a 56 Kbps modem, the most common modem speed (at least for the moment).

The Web browser window will display within these parameters, so your maximum image size will occupy only a portion of the browser window—about 8 inches high (570 pixels) by 7 inches wide (500 pixels). The image resolution needs to be only as high as the standard monitor resolution.

Saving a file in the GIF or JPEG file format reduces its storage size significantly, because these formats have built-in compression schemes.

To determine a file's actual storage size:

Windows: Right-click the file in Windows Explorer and choose Properties from the pop-up menu.

Mac OS: Highlight the file name in the Finder, then choose File menu > Get Info.

If you know the exact size of the compressed image, you can then calculate how long it will take to transmit over the Web. If you use the Save for Web dialog box, you can find out exactly how big your JPEG, GIF, PNG-8, or PNG-24 is, and how long it will take to download **1**. Click the preview menu arrow in the upper right to change the modem speed used to calculate the download time.

The degree to which the GIF or JPEG file format compresses depends on how compressible the image is **2**. Both formats cause a small reduction in image quality, but it's worth the size-reduction tradeoff, because your image will download faster on the Web. A file size of about 50K traveling on a 28.8 Kbps modem will take about 18 seconds to download, and half that time for a 56 Kbps modem. (No, this isn't a test question!)

Image Size (margin)

Create a browser window layer

Take a screen shot of your browser window, open the file in Illustrator, and paste it into a document as your bottommost layer. Now you can design your layout for that specific browser window's dimensions.

1 *The current file's size and download time display in the Info annotation area in the lower left corner of the Save for Web dialog box.*

20K GIF, from a 5-level posterized image.

120K GIF, from a continuous-tone image.

2 *A size comparison of GIFs.*

*GIF is a suitable optimization format for this image, because it has **flat** color shapes.*

*GIF optimization is also a good choice for this **hybrid** image, which contains both sharp-edged (type) and continuous-tone elements (the ducky).*

A document with a flat background color and a few flat-color shapes will compress a great deal (expect a file size in the range of 20 to 50K). A large document (over 100K) with many color areas, textures, or patterns won't compress nearly as much. Continuous-tone, photographic images may compress less than flat-color images when you use the GIF format. If you posterize a continuous-tone image down to somewhere between four and eight levels, the resulting file size will be similar to that of a flat-color image, but you will have lost the continuous color transitions in the bargain. JPEG is a better format choice for a photographic-type image.

To summarize, if an image must be large (500 x 400 pixels or larger), ideally it should contain only a handful of large, flat-color shapes. If you want the image to be more intricate in color and shape, restrict its size to only a portion of the Web browser window. (Patterned imagery that completely fills the background of the browser window is usually created using a tiling method in a Web-page design program or using HTML code.)

Also keep in mind that many Web designers will slice larger images into smaller ones so that they will load faster. While Illustrator does not have a slicing command, other applications, such as Adobe Photoshop 6 and ImageReady 3, do.

GIF

GIF is an 8-bit file format, which means a GIF image can contain a maximum of 256 colors. GIF is the standard format, though, because a majority of Web users have 8-bit monitors which can display a maximum of 256 colors—not the thousands or millions of colors that make images look pleasing to the eye. It's a good choice for images that contain flat-color areas and shapes with well-defined edges, such as type.

To save an image in the GIF format and to see how it will actually look when it's viewed via the browser, use File menu > Save for Web (we'll show you how in this chapter).

(Continued on the following page)

GIF

Your color choices for a GIF image should be based on what a Web browser palette can realistically display. Most browser palettes are 8-bit, which means they can display only 256 colors. Colors that aren't on the palette are simulated by dithering, a display technique that intermixes color pixels to simulate other colors.

To prevent unexpected dithering, consider optimizing your image using the Web palette in the Save for Web dialog box. Or Web Snap 30–50 percent of the colors in the image using Save for Web and manually Web-shift the critical areas of flat color. (You'll read more about these methods later.) Color substitutions will be particularly noticeable in flat-color areas.

➤ If you want to apply a gradient fill to a large area of an image and you're going to use the GIF format, create a top-to-bottom gradient. Top-to-bottom gradients produce smaller file sizes than left-to-right or diagonal gradients.

Color depth

If you lower an image's color depth, you will reduce the actual number of colors it contains, which will in turn reduce its file size and speed up its download time on the Web. Color reduction may produce dithered edges and duller colors, but you'll get the reduction in file size that you need.

You can reduce the number of colors in an 8-bit image to fewer than the 256 colors it originally contained using Illustrator's Save for Web dialog box.

➤ Always preview an image at 100% view to evaluate its color quality.

JPEG

The JPEG format may be a better choice for preserving color fidelity if your image is continuous tone (contains gradations of color or is photographic) and your viewers have 24-bit monitors, which have the capacity to display millions of colors **1**.

A JPEG plus: It can take a 24-bit image and make it as small as the GIF format can make an 8-bit image.

Color depth

Number of colors	Bit depth
256	8
128	7
64	6
32	5
16	4
8	3
4	2
2	1

1 *JPEG optimization is suitable for continuous-tone images.*

JPEG isn't a great choice for optimizing sharp-edged imagery. Note the artifacts around the type.

The word "duck" looks crisper in this GIF.

JPEG shortcomings: First, a JPEG file has to be decompressed when it's downloaded for viewing on a Web page, which takes time.

Second, JPEG is not a good choice for flat-color images or type, because its compression methods tend to produce artifacts along the well defined edges of these kinds of images.

And third, not all Web viewers use 24-bit monitors. A JPEG image will be dithered on an 8-bit monitor, though dithering in a con-tinuous-tone image will be less noticeable than in an image that contains flat colors. You can lower your monitor's setting to 8-bit to preview what the image will look like in an 8-bit setting, or choose Browser Dither from the Preview menu in the Save for Web dialog box. If it doesn't contain type or objects with sharp edges, the JPEG image will probably survive the conversion to 8-bit.

JPEG format files can now be optimized as Progressive JPEG, which is supported by both the Netscape Navigator and Internet Explorer browsers (versions 4 and up). A Progressive JPEG displays in increasing detail as it downloads onto a Web page.

If you choose JPEG as your output format, you can experiment in Illustrator's Save for Web dialog box by optimizing an image, then using the 4–Up option to preview sev-eral versions of the image in varying degrees of compression. Decide which degree of compression is acceptable by weighing the file size versus diminished image quality. In Illustrator, you can save the optimized file separately and leave the original file intact to reserve it for potential future revision.

Each time an image is optimized using the JPEG format, some image data is lost. The greater the degree of compression, the greater the data loss. To prevent this data loss, use Illustrator's Save for Web feature to save an optimized version of the file. Then if you need to make changes later, go back to your original Illustrator file.

(Continued on the following page)

JPEG

Dithering

Dithering is the intermixing of two palette colors to create the impression of a third color. It's used to make images that contain a limited number of colors (256 or fewer) appear to have a greater range of colors and shades. Dithering is usually applied to continuous-tone images to increase their tonal range, but—argh, life is full of compromises—it can also make them look a bit dotty.

Dithering usually doesn't produce aesthetically pleasing results in flat-color images. This is because the browser palette will dither pixels to recreate any color that the palette doesn't contain. For a flat-color image, it's better to create colors using the Web Safe RGB model on the Color palette with its Web Safe color ramp. Existing flat-color areas should also be selected and Web-shifted to make them Web-safe.

Continuous-tone imagery is, in a way, already dithered. Some continuous-tone imagery looks fine on a Web page with no dithering and 256 colors. However, color banding will result if you lower both the number of colors in the palette and the amount of dithering when an image is optimized. A Dither value is chosen in Illustrator's Save for Web dialog box. The higher the Dither value, the more seamless the color transitions will appear, but the more dotty the image may also appear. You can decide which of these two evils appears lesser to your eye.

One more consideration: Dithering adds noise and additional colors to the file, so compression is less effective when dithering is turned on than when it's off. So, with dithering enabled, you may not be able to achieve your desired degree of file compression. As is the case with most Web output, you'll have to strike an acceptable balance between aesthetics and file size.

Alias versus anti-alias

Anti-aliasing blends the edge of an object with its background. It achieves this blending by adding pixels with progressively less opacity along an object's edge. When imagery is composited or montaged, anti-aliasing helps

*A closeup of an image with a **small** amount of dithering.*

*The same image with a **lot** of **dithering**.*

Dress down your bitmaps

Use an image-editing program such as Photoshop to reduce the number of pixels and lessen the color complexity in a bitmap image before placing it. And lower the image resolution to 72 ppi.

You can also use Illustrator's Rasterize command to reduce the pixel resolution of a placed image (check the Anti-Alias option).

To reduce color complexity, try posterizing a continuous-tone image down to somewhere between four and eight levels in Photoshop, then place the image. The result will be a smaller file size—albeit with noticeable color transitions.

to smooth the transitions between shapes. With anti-aliasing turned off, the edge of an object will look sharp because no extra pixels will have been added.

If you create an object, save it for the Web, and later place it against a colored background, an unattractive fringe of pixels, sometimes called a halo, may be visible. To avoid halos, follow the instructions for creating a background matting for the GIF, PNG, and JPEG formats. This will determine how partially transparent pixels (the kind of pixels that are created by anti-aliasing) are treated.

PNG-8 and PNG-24

The two PNG formats can save partially transparent pixels (e.g., soft, feathered edges) using a method called alpha transparency. With alpha transparency, a pixel can have any one of 256 levels of opacity, ranging from totally transparent to totally opaque. The PNG-8 format is limited to a maximum of 256 colors in the optimized image, and is similar to the GIF format. The PNG-24 format allows for millions of colors in the optimized image and is similar to the JPEG format. The PNG formats use a lossless compression method (no data is lost).

Are there any drawbacks to using PNG? For one thing, animation cannot be done in the PNG format (animation can be done in the GIF format) and PNG-24 files are larger in size than equivalent JPEGs. More important, PNG is not supported by all major Web browsers. As of this writing, Internet Explorer versions 4.0 and later directly support PNG. But earlier versions of Explorer and Netscape Navigator 2.0 or later require a plug-in, like PNG Live, in order to display this format. What's wrong with a plug-in? Viewers may be reluctant to spend time downloading a plug-in, but your site won't display at its full potential without it.

Optimizing images for the Web

Optimization is the process by which file format, storage size, and color parameters are chosen for an image in order to maximize its quality, yet still enable it to download quickly on the Web. Illustrator provides a variety of choices and options for optimization. In this section you will learn the basic steps. Your overall goal is to reduce the file size until the image quality reaches its reduction limit (starts to degrade). Keep this goal in mind as you adjust the various palette options.

GIF and JPEG are the two most commonly used file formats for displaying graphics on the Web. GIF is recommended for images that contain elements with sharp edges, such as flat-color areas, line art, and text. The PNG-8 format, which is similar to GIF, uses the same Optimize palette options, and the optimize results are practically the same. An optimized GIF or PNG-8 file can contain up to 256 colors. You can view the color table for GIF and PNG-8 files and manipulate individual colors in the optimized image.

If you know that your artwork is destined for the Web, then it's best to choose the RGB Color mode when you start a new document, as this is the color space you will eventually be using. You can change this later by using the File menu > Document Color Mode submenu.

The other thing to keep in mind is that while you're working in Illustrator, your vector drawings will appear crisp and smooth. But when your artwork is displayed on the Web as a GIF or JPEG, it will be rasterized. That is to say, your images will be mapped to a 72 ppi grid, making some of your edges appear jagged or blurry due to the anti-aliasing process.

But you can preview how your images will look in a Web browser using the Pixel Preview command. Your artwork will display as if it had already been rasterized, allowing you to see the effect of anti-aliasing. With Snap to Pixel selected, any artwork you create while you are in Pixel Preview

Web color palette

If you've ever created an image with millions of colors, and then viewed your image on a monitor that can only display thousands—or even hundreds—of colors, then you have some idea what Web-safe colors are all about.

No matter how few—or how many—colors a monitor can display, all monitors with at least eight bits of color can render 216 specific colors without dithering. This is because eight bits of color can be expressed as two to the eighth power, or 256 (each bit has one of two possible values). Subtract 40 for the colors that Mac and Windows systems reserve for other uses, and you're left with 216 colors that you can use with confidence in your Web graphics.

But keep in mind that not even these 216 colors will display in the same way on every machine. Windows and Mac systems use different color gamma values, and each monitor may be calibrated somewhat differently. Since the Windows operating system uses a higher gamma value than the Macintosh operating system, an image created on the Mac will appear darker on a Windows system than on a Mac.

1 *View menu > Pixel Preview unchecked (off).*

2 *View menu > Pixel Preview checked (on).*

mode will automatically snap to a pixel grid that will prevent any horizontal and vertical edges in your artwork from being anti-aliased.

To work in **Pixel Preview** mode, choose View menu > Pixel Preview **1**–**2**. Also choose View menu > Snap to Pixel—or deselect it if you desire.

Transparent GIFs and JPEGs cannot show soft-edged shapes against transparency. If you want your image to fade into a flat-color background (as in a Drop Shadow effect, Outer Glow effect, or opacity mask), create two layers in your Illustrator document: a lower layer that contains a flat color filled with the Web-safe color that will be used on the full Web page; and an upper layer that contains the image element with a soft, feathered edge or an effect such as Drop Shadow that overlaps the color on the lower layer.

For a hybrid image that contains flat areas of color or type combined with photographic imagery, the best choice may be the GIF format using the Perceptual, Selective, or Adaptive palette (not the Web palette). This combination will strike a good balance between keeping the flat-color areas Web-safe and rendering the continuous-tone areas reasonably well.

Pixel Preview

To optimize an image in the GIF or PNG-8 format:

1. Save your image, then choose File menu > Save for Web.

2. Click the 2-Up tab at the top of the image window to display both the original and optimized previews of the image simultaneously.

3. Choose a named, preset combination of optimize settings from the Settings pop-up menu **1**, leave the preset as is, click OK, then save your file with a new name.
   or
   Follow the remaining steps to customize your optimization settings (**1**, next page).

4. Choose GIF or PNG-8 from the File Format pop-up menu.

5. For GIF only, drag the Lossy slider or enter a value to allow the compression scheme to eliminate pixels from the image, thus reducing file size. Note that you cannot use the Lossy option with the Interlaced option, or with Noise or Pattern Dither algorithms.

6. Choose a palette option (color reduction algorithm) from the next pop-up menu (see the sidebar on the next page). The GIF and PNG-8 formats permit a maximum of only 256 colors. Perceptual, Selective, and Adaptive render the optimized image using colors from the original image. Web shifts all the image colors to Web-safe colors. Web is not generally the best choice if the image contains continuous-tone areas, blends, or gradients. Custom optimizes image color based on a palette that you previously saved.

7. If you want to choose a specific number of colors, choose a number from the Colors drop-down menu; or enter a value in the field; or use the arrows to change the number of colors.

8. From the next pop-up menu, choose a Dither method: No Dither, Diffusion, Pattern, or Noise. Choose a dither value using the slider.

Transparency

When creating GIF or PNG-8 files, you can create a hard-edged transparency effect. This will cause all pixels that are more than 50% transparent to be fully transparent. Pixels less than 50% transparent will be fully opaque. This type of transparency will eliminate the halo effect that can occur when the matte color is different from the image's original background color.

To create hard-edged transparency:

1. Open an image that contains transparency.

2. Choose File menu > Save for Web, then choose GIF or PNG-8.

3. Check Transparency.

4. Choose None from the Matte pop-up menu.

5. Click OK to save the file.

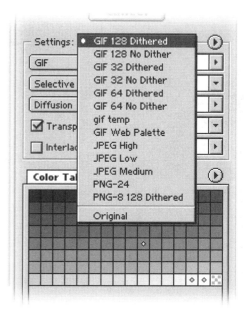

1 *Choose a preset combination of optimization settings from the* **Settings** *pop-up menu in the* **Save for Web** *dialog box.*

Four of the GIF color palettes

Perceptual

Generates a color table based on the colors currently in the image, with particular attention to how people actually perceive colors. This table's strength is in preserving overall color integrity.

Selective

Generates a color table based on the colors currently in the image. The Perceptual and Selective options are similar, but the Selective option leans more toward preserving flat colors and Web-safe colors.

Adaptive

Generates a color table based on the part of the color spectrum that represents most of the color in the image. This choice produces a slightly larger optimized file.

➤ If you switch among the Perceptual, Selective, or Adaptive options, any Web-safe colors that are currently on the Color Table palette are preserved.

Web

Generates a color table by shifting image colors to colors that are available in the standard Web-safe palette. This choice produces the least number of colors and thus the smallest file size, but not necessarily the best image quality.

1 *Using the* **Optimize** *panel to choose custom settings for a GIF export.*

9. If the image contains transparency that you want to preserve, check the Transparency box. This will preserve fully transparent pixels as transparent. Partially transparent pixels will be filled with the Matte color or will be converted to fully transparent or fully opaque pixels, depending on which Matte option you choose.

   If you don't check Transparency, both fully and partially transparent pixels will be filled with the Matte color.

10. To control how partially transparent pixels along the edge of an image blend with the background of a Web page (as on the edges of anti-aliased or rasterized elements), choose a Matte option.

    Choose Other to set the Matte color to the color of the Web page background, if you happen to know what that color is. If the backgound color is unknown, set Matte to None (this will result in a hard, jagged edge). Both options eliminate halo effects along the edge of an image when it's displayed on the Web. Any soft-edged effect (such as Drop Shadow or Feather) on top of transparency will be filled with the current Matte color.

11. Check the Interlaced box to have the GIF or PNG image display in successively greater detail as it downloads on the Web page.

12. To automatically shift colors to their closest Web palette equivalents, drag the Web Snap slider or enter a value. A higher value will cause more colors to be shifted.

13. Click OK. The current file format extension will be appended to the file name. Change the name, if desired, then click Save.

To use the Save for Web previews:

Click the 4-Up tab on the main window to see an original view and three previews simultaneously. Illustrator will use the current Optimize panel settings to generate the first preview, and then automatically generate ("autopopulate") the two other previews as variations based on the current optimization settings. You can click on any preview and change the Optimize panel settings for just that preview. The optimized preview(s) will update every time a value or setting is changed on the Optimize panel.

You can choose to repopulate your 4-up view. This will create new optimized versions in each panel based on the changes you make in the optimization settings. To do this, choose an optimized version of the image, make changes, click the arrow to the right of the Settings pop-up menu, and choose Repopulate Views. The original file and your selected optimization won't be affected, but Illustrator will generate smaller optimized versions for the other previews. If you're not happy with any particular optimization, choose Original from the Settings pop-up menu and the Original image will appear in that preview.

You can save your settings so that you can apply them to other images.

To save your Save for Web settings:

1. In the Save for Web dialog box, click the small arrow to display the Optimize menu (to the right of the Settings pop-up menu).

2. Choose Save Settings, then name the settings. By default, they are saved in the Adobe Illustrator 9 > Settings > Optimize folder.

3. Click Save. Your new settings will appear on the Settings pop-up menu, if they were saved in the default location.

1 *The **Optimize** panel with settings chosen for a JPEG export.*

JPEGs and Web-safe colors

JPEG compression adds compression artifacts to an image. Because of this, Web-safe colors in a JPEG image are rendered non-Web-safe after compression. This is acceptable because the JPEG format is usually used to optimize continuous-tone images, and on these types of images, browser dither isn't objectionable. Don't try to match a color area in a JPEG file to a color area in a GIF file or on the background of a Web page, though, because the JPEG color will shift and dither when the image is compressed.

JPEG is the format of choice for optimizing continuous-tone imagery for display on the Web (photographs, paintings, gradients, and blends). If you optimize to JPEG, the file's 24-bit color depth will be preserved, and these colors will be seen and enjoyed by any Web viewer whose monitor is set to millions of colors (24-bit depth). Keep in mind, however, that JPEGs are optimized using a compression method that is lossy, which means it causes image data to be eliminated.

The PNG-24 format is similar to JPEG, except that PNG allows for multiple levels of transparency along edges and employs a lossless method of compression. PNG-24 files are larger than equivalent JPEGs.

To optimize an image in the JPEG format:

1. Open the original Illustrator file, choose File menu > Save for Web, then choose one of the JPEG settings from the Settings pop-up menu or choose JPEG from the File Format pop-up menu **1**.

2. Click the 2-Up or 4-Up tab at the top of the main window to display the original and optimized previews of the image simultaneously.

3. Specify image quality by dragging the quality slider or by entering a value in the Quality box.
   or
   Choose Low, Medium, High, or Maximum from the pop-up menu to

(Continued on the following page)

Optimize as JPEG

the left. A higher setting preserves more color information, but makes the file size larger. Experiment with this setting to find the best balance between file size and file quality.

4. Check Progressive to create an image that displays in stages in browsers. This feature isn't supported in all browsers, but where it is, users will see a low-resolution version of your image before the highest resolution loads.

5. Increase the Blur value to lessen the visibility of JPEG artifacts that arise from JPEG's compression method and also reduce the file size. Be careful not to over-blur the image, though, or your details will soften too much. The Blur setting can be lowered later in order to reclaim image sharpness.

6. *Optional:* Check the ICC Profile box to embed an ICC Profile in the optimized image. To utilize this option, the illustration must have had a profile assigned to it in Illustrator (see the sidebar on this page).

7. Choose a Matte color to be used for areas of transparency found in the original image. If you choose "None," transparent areas will appear as white.

Note: The JPEG format doesn't support transparency. To have the Matte color simulate transparency, choose Other and use the same solid color as the background of the Web page, if that color is known. Now soft edges will fade into the Web background color.

8. *Optional:* Check the Optimized box to produce the smallest file size. Beware: Older browsers (version 3.0 or earlier) may not be able to read a JPEG that's saved with this option.

9. Click OK. The current file format extension will be appended to the file name. Change the name, if desired, then click Save.

Check your profiles

An embedded profile will slightly increase a file's size. As of this writing, Internet Explorer for Mac versions 4.01 and later support profiles. On the Mac, ColorSync makes sure the browser and the operating system know the viewer's monitor profile. This helps to ensure consistent color between the monitor and JPEG files. As color management support and profile automation improve, and as soon as Navigator supports embedded profiles, embedded profiles will become standard. Windows has a bit of catching up to do in this area. For the moment, use your own judgment.

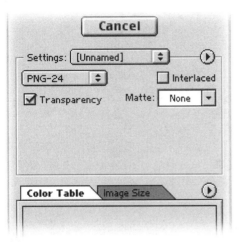

1 *The Optimize panel with settings chosen for a PNG-24 export.*

2 *The Color Table panel in the Save for Web dialog box, with a color swatch highlighted.*

Highlighted swatch

Web Shift button

You can preserve multiple levels of transparency in PNG-24 images using a feature called alpha transparency. When the PNG is displayed in a browser that has a plug-in supporting alpha transparency, the PNG can display up to 256 levels of transparency.

To preserve multi-level transparency in PNG-24 images:

1. Open the Illustrator file, then choose File menu > Save for Web.

2. Choose PNG-24 from the File Format pop-up menu **1**.

3. Check Interlaced to have the PNG image display in successively greater detail as it downloads on the Web page. File size will increase.

4. Check Transparency to preserve transparent pixels.
   or
   Uncheck Transparency to fill transparent pixels with the Matte color.

5. Click OK to save your file.

Let's say you have an image that you're going to optimize in the GIF format using the Perceptual, Selective, or Adaptive palette, but the image has flat-color areas that aren't Web safe. Before outputting the image online, you can make the flat-color areas Web safe.

To make flat-color areas Web safe:

1. Open the image and optimize it in the GIF format using the File menu > Save for Web dialog box.

2. Choose the Eyedropper tool.

3. Click on a flat-color area to be made Web safe.

4. Click the Color Table tab, if necessary. The color you just clicked on will now be the highlighted swatch **2**.

5. Click the Web Shift button at the bottom of the palette. A diamond will display on the selected swatch to signify that the color was shifted to a Web-safe equivalent.

6. *Optional:* Click the Lock Selected Color button to preserve the currently selected

(Continued on the following page)

swatch even if the number of colors in the GIF palette is reduced.

➤ Shift-click with the Eyedropper tool on other areas in the image to select more than one color, then Web-shift all the selected colors at once.

➤ Click a Web-shifted color swatch, then click the Web Shift button again to unshift the color from being Web safe.

To optimize to file size:

1. You have Illustrator pick your optimization settings based on the desired file size.

2. Open the Save for Web dialog box, then choose Optimize to File Size from the Optimize menu **1**.

3. Choose a Start With option. Current Settings uses your current optimization settings; Auto Select GIF/JPEG tells Illustrator to choose either GIF or JPEG depending on the program's analysis of your image **2**.

4. Enter a value for the desired file size.

5. Click OK.

You can resize your image directly in the Save for Web dialog box. *Note:* To make best use of this option, size your artboard first before opening the Save for Web dialog box.

To resize your image:

1. Open the File menu > Save for Web dialog box, then click the Image Size tab **3**.

2. Click Constrain Proportions if you want to maintain the relative width and height of your image.

3. Enter a percent value if you want to make the new image a specific percentage of the original size.
   or
   Enter specific width and/or height values. If you clicked Constrain Proportions, the height will change as you change the width, and vice-versa.

4. To clip the exported illustration to the size of the document's current Artboard size, choose Clip to Artboard. This can

1 *Choose* **Optimize To File Size** *from the* **Optimize** *menu.*

2 *The* **Optimize To File Size** *dialog box.*

3 *Click the* **Image Size** *tab to display its panel of settings.*

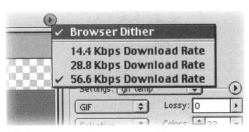

1 *Choosing* **Browser Dither** *from the* **Preview** *menu.*

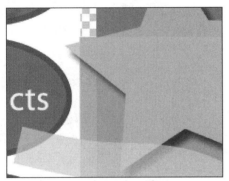

2 *Optimized image with* **Browser Dither** *unchecked.*

3 *Optimized image with* **Browser Dither** *checked. Soft edges and transparent areas become dithered.*

be useful for clipping artwork to an artboard that's the size of a banner ad.

5. Click Apply to preview the clipping effect on the image. (If you need to Undo Clip to Artboard, uncheck the option, then click Apply again.)

Controlling dithering

Using various preview methods in Illustrator, you can get a pretty reliable idea of how optimized images will look when they're viewed online. This will help you choose appropriate settings as you optimize them.

Most Web viewers use an 8-bit monitor, which displays a maximum of 256 colors. Mac OS and Windows browsers, on the other hand, use a color palette of 216 colors. Dithering is used to recreate any colors in an image that are not on the browser's palette. Follow the steps on this page to preview browser dithering on an image.

To preview potential browser dither in an optimized image:

1. With the illustration open, choose File menu > Save for Web, then click the 2-Up or 4-Up tab.

2. Choose Preview menu > Browser Dither *1*–*3*.

When you use Illustrator to optimize an image, the application applies dithering to simulate gradients, gradient meshes, and semi-transparent colors that were in the original image but won't appear on the color palette of the optimized image. You can control the amount of dithering via the Dither field in the Save for Web dialog box. If you raise the Dither value, the optimized image will more closely color match the original— but at the expense of a slightly larger file size.

The Web Snap value in the Save for Web dialog box also affects the amount of browser dithering in an image. The higher the Web Snap, the less the optimized image will be dithered, and the smaller will be its file size. Some degree of dithering is acceptable in continuous-tone imagery, though, and it may be more pleasing than the color banding that a high Web Snap value can cause.

Image maps can be created in Illustrator 9. In fact, any object you create can be linked to a URL.

To create an image map:

1. Select the object to which you want to attach a URL 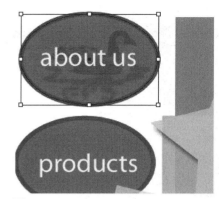.

2. Choose Window menu > Show Attributes.

3. From the Image Map pop-up menu, choose one of the following: None, if you don't want to create an image map; Rectangular to create a rectangular image map around the object (the image map boundaries will be similar to the object's bounding box); or Polygon to create a map that follows an object's irregular contour.

4. Type a URL into the URL field ▪, or choose an URL from the drop-down menu. If you want more URL entries to display on the list, choose Palette Options from the Attributes palette menu, then enter a value between 1 and 30.

5. You can check the URL location by clicking the Browser button on the palette to launch a browser (assuming you have one loaded on your system and your computer is currently connected to the Web).

6. When you're ready to export, use the Save for Web dialog box to optimize your image. Click OK when you're done, and in the Save Optimized As dialog box, check Save HTML File (if it's not already checked) to save the necessary HTML file, complete with the image map and URL links. The HTML-generated file and the optimized file containing the image map must be kept in the same folder when the image map is imported into your Web-page design application.

The HTML file contains the URLs, image name, dimensions, and necessary code in order for the image to display on a Web page.

▪ *Select the object to which you want to assign a URL.*

▪ *The **Attributes** palette with the URL for the selected object entered in the URL field.*

KEYBOARD SHORTCUTS

To assign custom shortcuts, see page 467.

	Mac OS	Windows
Files		
New Document dialog box	Command-N	Ctrl-N
Open dialog box	Command-O	Ctrl-O
Close	Command-W	Ctrl-W
Save	Command-S	Ctrl-S
Save As dialog box	Command-Shift-S	Ctrl-Shift-S
Save a Copy dialog box	Command-Option-S	Ctrl-Alt-S
Document Setup dialog box	Command-Option-P	Ctrl-Alt-P
Quit/Exit Illustrator	Command-Q	Ctrl-Q
Tools		
Selection	V	V
Direct-selection	A	A
Lasso	Y	Y
Direct-select Lasso	Q	Q
Pen	P	P
Type	T	T
Ellipse	L	L
Rectangle	M	M
Paintbrush	B	B
Pencil	N	N
Rotate	R	R
Scale	S	S
Reflect	O	O
Free Transform	E	E
Blend	W	W
Column Graph	J	J
Gradient Mesh	U	U
Gradient	G	G
Eyedropper	I	I
Scissors	C	C
Hand	H	H

	Mac OS	Windows
Zoom	Z	Z
Add-anchor-point	+	+
Delete-anchor-point	-	-
Convert-anchor-point	Shift-C	Shift-C

Dialog boxes

Highlight next field/option	Tab	Tab
Highlight previous field/option	Shift-Tab	Shift-Tab
Cancel	Command . (period key) or Esc	Esc
OK	Return	Enter

Open/Save dialog boxes

Desktop	Command-D	
Up one folder level	Command-up arrow	

Palettes

Show/hide all palettes	Tab	Tab
Show/hide all palettes except Toolbox	Shift-Tab	Shift-Tab
Apply value in palette field	Return	Enter
Apply value in field, keep field selected	Shift-Return	Shift-Enter
Highlight next field (pointer in palette)	Tab	Tab
Highlight previous field (pointer in palette)	Shift-Tab	Shift-Tab

Views

Preview/Outline view toggle	Command-Y	Ctrl-Y
Pixel Preview view on/off	Command-Option-Y	Ctrl-Alt-Y
Overprint Preview view on/off	Command-Option-Shift-Y	Ctrl-Alt-Shift-Y
Use crosshair pointer (drawing tools)	Caps lock	Caps lock
Show/Hide Edges	Command-H	Ctrl-H
Display entire artboard	Double-click Hand tool	Double-click Hand tool
Fit In Window	Command-0	Ctrl-0
100% view size	Double-click Zoom tool or Command-1	Double-click Zoom tool or Ctrl-1
Zoom out (Zoom tool selected)	Option-click	Alt-click
Zoom in (any tool selected)	Command-Spacebar-click or Command-+	Ctrl-Spacebar-click or Ctrl-+
Zoom out (any tool selected)	Command-Option-Spacebar-click or Command- – (minus)	Ctrl-Alt-Spacebar-click or Ctrl- – (minus)
Adjust Zoom marquee position	Drag with Zoom tool, then Spacebar-drag	Drag with Zoom tool, then Spacebar-drag

	Mac OS	**Windows**
Zoom in on specific area of artboard	Drag Zoom tool or Command-drag in Navigator palette	Drag Zoom tool or Ctrl-drag in Navigator palette
Use Hand tool (any tool selected)	Spacebar	Spacebar
Hide all unselected objects	Command-Option-Shift-3	Ctrl-Alt-Shift-3
Show All	Command-Option-3	Ctrl-Alt-3
Show/Hide Template(s)	Command-Shift-W	Ctrl-Shift-W
Show/Hide Bounding Box	Command-Shift-B	Ctrl-Shift-B
Show/Hide Transparency Grid	Command-Shift-D	Ctrl-Shift-D
Standard screen mode/Full screen mode with menu bar/Full screen mode	F	F

Undo/redo

Undo last operation	Command-Z	Ctrl-Z
Redo last undone operation	Command-Shift-Z	Ctrl-Shift-Z

Create objects

Draw object from center using Rectangle, Rounded Rectangle, or Ellipse tool	Option-drag	Alt-drag
Draw circle with Rectangle or Rounded Rectangle tool; square with Ellipse tool	Shift-drag	Shift-drag

Polygon, Star, Spiral tools

Move object as you draw with Polygon, Star, or Spiral tool	Spacebar	Spacebar
Constrain orientation as you draw with Polygon, Star, or Spiral tool	Shift	Shift
Add or subtract sides as you draw with the Polygon tool, points as you draw with the Star tool, or segments as you draw with the Spiral tool	Up or down arrow	Up or down arrow
Align shoulders as you draw with Star tool	Option	Alt
Increase or decrease outer radius as you draw with Star tool or decay as you draw with Spiral tool	Command	Ctrl

Select/Copy

Select Again (last used command on Edit menu > Select submenu)	Command-6	Ctrl-6
Use last-used selection tool (any non-selection tool chosen)	Command	Ctrl
Toggle between Selection tool and Direct-selection tool or Group-selection tool	Command-Ctrl-Tab	Ctrl-Tab
Toggle between Group-selection and Direct-selection tools	Option	Alt

Keyboard Shortcuts

	Mac OS	Windows
Select All	Command-A	Ctrl-A
Deselect All	Command-Shift-A	Ctrl-Shift-A
Select an object hidden behind another object	Command-Option-[-click	Ctrl-Alt-[-click
Add to selection with either lasso tool	Shift-drag	Shift-drag
Subtract from selection with either lasso tool	Option-drag	Alt-drag

Move

	Mac OS	Windows
Move dialog box	Double-click Selection tool	Double-click Selection tool
Drag copy of object	Option-drag	Alt-drag
Move selected object the current Keyboard Increment (Preferences > General)	Any arrow key	Any arrow key
Move selection 10x Keyboard Increment	Shift-arrow key	Shift-arrow key
Constrain movement to multiple of 45°	Shift	Shift

Clipboard

	Mac OS	Windows
Cut	Command-X	Ctrl-X
Copy	Command-C	Ctrl-C
Paste	Command-V	Ctrl-V
Paste In Front	Command-F	Ctrl-F
Paste In Back	Command-B	Ctrl-B

Transform

	Mac OS	Windows
Transform tool dialog/set origin (any transform tool except Free Transform)	Option-click	Alt-click
Transform object along multiple of 45° (Shear, Reflect, Rotate tool)	Shift-drag	Shift-drag
Scale object uniformly (Scale, Free Transform tools)	Shift-drag	Shift-drag
Show/Hide Attributes palette	F-11	F-11
Transform Again	Command-D	Ctrl-D
Transform pattern fill, not object (any transform tool)	~ drag	~ drag
Transform copy of object (any transform tool)	Start dragging, then Option-drag	Start dragging, then Alt-drag
Transform copy of object (Transform palette)	Modify value, then press Option-Return	Modify value, then press Alt-Enter
Scale object uniformly (Transform palette)	Modify W or H value, then press Command-Return	Modify W or H value, then press Ctrl-Enter
Transform Each dialog box	Command-Option-D	Ctrl-Alt-D

	Mac OS	**Windows**
Bounding box		
Scale object uniformly using bounding box (Free Transform or Selection tool)	Shift-drag handle	Shift-drag handle
Resize object from center using bounding box	Option-drag handle	Alt-drag handle
Blends		
Blend > Make	Command-Option-B	Ctrl-Alt-B
Blend > Release	Command-Option-Shift-B	Ctrl-Alt-Shift-B
Free Transform tool		
Transform from center	Option-drag a handle	Alt-drag a handle
Distort	Start dragging corner handle, then Command-drag	Start dragging corner handle, then Ctrl-drag
Skew	Start dragging side handle, then Command-drag	Start dragging side handle, then Ctrl-drag
Make Perspective	Start dragging corner handle, then Command-Option-Shift-drag	Start dragging corner handle, then Ctrl-Alt-Shift-drag
Pen/Reshape		
Add-anchor-point and Delete-anchor-point tool toggle (either selected)	Option	Alt
Use Add-anchor-point tool (Scissors tool selected)	Option	Alt
Use Convert-anchor-point tool (Pen tool selected)	Option	Alt
Smooth and Pencil tools toggle	Option	Alt
Constrain direction line angle to multiple of 45° with Direct-selection or Convert-anchor-point tool	Shift-drag	Shift-drag
Join two selected endpoints	Command-J	Ctrl-J
Average two selected endpoints	Command-Option-J	Ctrl-Alt-J
Average and Join two selected endpoints	Command-Option-Shift-J	Ctrl-Alt-Shift-J
Close path while drawing with Pencil or Paintbrush tool	Drag, then Option-release	Drag, then Alt-release
Cut in a straight line with Knife tool	Option-drag tool	Alt-drag tool
Cut in 45° increment with Knife tool	Option-Shift	Alt-Shift
Fill & Stroke		
Show/Hide Stroke palette	F-10	F-10
Default fill/stroke	D	D

	Mac OS	Windows
Eyedropper and Paint Bucket tool toggle (either one selected)	Option	Alt
Fill/Stroke box toggle (Toolbox and Color palette)	X	X
Apply last-used solid color	< (comma)	< (comma)
Apply fill/stroke of None	/	/

Color palette

	Mac OS	Windows
Show/Hide Color palette	Command-I or F-6	Ctrl-I or F-6
Change fill color if Stroke box on Toolbox is selected, or vice versa	Option-click or drag color spectrum bar on Color palette	Alt-click or drag color spectrum bar on Color palette
Cycle through color models	Shift-click color spectrum bar	Shift-click color spectrum bar
Swap fill/stroke	Shift-X	Shift-X

Swatches palette

	Mac OS	Windows
Select a swatch name	Command-Option-click list, start typing name	Ctrl-Alt-click list, start typing name

Layers

	Mac OS	Windows
Show/Hide Layers palette	F-7	F-7

Grouping

	Mac OS	Windows
Group	Command-G	Ctrl-G
Ungroup	Command-Shift-G	Ctrl-Shift-G

Restacking (keyboard)

	Mac OS	Windows
Bring To Front	Command-Shift-]	Ctrl-Shift-]
Send To Back	Command-Shift-[	Ctrl-Shift-[
Bring Forward	Command-]	Ctrl-]
Send Backward	Command-[	Ctrl-[

Select

	Mac OS	Windows
Select layer, sublayer, group, or object	Click selection square or Option-click name	Click selection square or Alt-click name
Add to selection	Shift-click square	Shift-click square
Copy selection to new layer, sublayer, group	Option-drag square	Alt-drag-square

Views

	Mac OS	Windows
Hide/show all other layers	Option-click eye icon	Alt-click eye icon
View a layer in Outline/Preview view	Command-click eye icon	Ctrl-click eye icon
View all other layers in Outline/Preview view	Command-Option-click eye icon	Ctrl-Alt-click eye icon
Lock/unlock all other layers	Option-click blank in second column	Alt-click blank box in second column

	Mac OS	Windows
Create top-level layers		
Create layer above currently selected layer	Command-L	Ctrl-L
Create layer at top of list	Command-click New Layer button	Ctrl-click New Layer button
Create layer below currently selected layer	Command-Option-click New Layer button	Ctrl-Alt-click New Layer button
Lock/unlock (keyboard)		
Lock (selected object)	Command-2	Ctrl-2
Lock all unselected objects	Command-Option-Shift-2	Ctrl-Alt-Shift-2
Unlock All	Command-Option-2	Ctrl-Alt-2

Type

	Mac OS	Windows
Show/Hide Character palette	Command-T	Ctrl-T
Show/Hide Paragraph palette	Command-M	Ctrl-M
Hard Return	Return	Enter
Soft Return	Shift-Return	Shift-Enter
Highlight font field on Character palette	Command-Option-Shift-M	Ctrl-Alt-Shift-M
Show/hide Tab Ruler palette	Command-Shift-T	Ctrl-Shift-T
Force hyphenate a word	Command-Shift – (hyphen key)	Ctrl-Shift – (hyphen key)
Create Outlines	Command-Shift-O	Ctrl-Shift-O
Type tools		
Use Area Type tool (Type tool selected, over open path)	Option	Alt
Use Path Type tool (Type tool selected, over closed path)	Option	Alt
Switch to vertical/horizontal type tool equivalent as you create type	Shift with any type tool	Shift with any type tool
Switch to Type tool when selecting type block	Double-click with any selection tool	Double-click with any selection tool
Selecting type		
Select a word	Double-click	Double-click
Select a paragraph	Triple-click	Triple-click
Select all the type in a block	Command-A	Ctrl-A
Move insertion pointer left/right one word	Command-left/right arrow	Ctrl-left/right arrow
Move insertion pointer up/down one line	Up/Down arrow	Up/Down arrow
Alignment		
Align left	Command-Shift-L	Ctrl-Shift-L

Keyboard Shortcuts

Keyboard Shortcuts

	Mac OS	**Windows**
Align center	Command-Shift-C	Ctrl-Shift-C
Align right	Command-Shift-R	Ctrl-Shift-R
Justify	Command-Shift-J	Ctrl-Shift-J
Justify last line	Command-Shift-F	Ctrl-Shift-F
Point size		
Increase point size	Command-Shift->	Ctrl-Shift->
Decrease point size	Command-Shift-<	Ctrl-Shift-<
Leading		
Increase leading	Option-down arrow	Alt-down arrow
Decrease leading	Option-up arrow	Alt-up arrow
Set leading to the current font size	Double-click leading button on Character palette	Double-click leading button on Character palette
Horizontal scale		
Reset horizontal scale to 100%	Command-Shift-X	Ctrl-Shift-X
Kerning/tracking		
Increase kerning/tracking	Option-right arrow	Alt-right arrow
Decrease kerning/tracking	Option-left arrow	Alt-left arrow
Increase kerning/tracking 5x	Command-Option right arrow	Ctrl-Alt right arrow
Decrease kerning/tracking 5x	Command-Option left arrow	Ctrl-Alt left arrow
Reset kerning/tracking to 0	Command-Shift-Q	Ctrl-Shift-Q
Baseline shift		
Increase baseline shift	Option-Shift up arrow	Alt-Shift up arrow
Decrease baseline shift	Option-Shift down arrow	Alt-Shift down arrow
Increase baseline shift 5x	Command-Option-Shift up arrow	Ctrl-Alt-Shift up arrow
Decrease baseline shift 5x	Command-Option-Shift down arrow	Ctrl-Alt-Shift down arrow
Curly quotes		
'	Option Shift-]	Alt-0146
'	Option-]	Alt-0145
"	Option Shift-[	Alt-0148
"	Option-[	Alt-0147

Numeric keypad only

Brushes

Show/Hide Brushes palette	F-5	F-5

Combine Paths

Compound Path > Make	Command-8	Ctrl-8

	Mac OS	Windows
Compound Path > Release	Command-Option-8	Ctrl-Alt-8
Repeat last-used Pathfinder command	Command-4	Ctrl-4

Masks/Transparency

Gradients

	Mac OS	Windows
Show/Hide Gradient palette	F-9	F-9
Reapply last-used gradient	> (period)	> (period)
Reset gradient palette to black and white	Command-click thumbnail	Ctrl-click thumbnail
Duplicate color stop	Option-drag	Alt-drag
Apply swatch color to active color stop	Option-click swatch	Alt-click swatch
Move mesh point along one of its lines	Shift-drag with Gradient Mesh tool	Shift-drag with Gradient Mesh tool
Add mesh point using adjacent mesh color	Shift-click with Gradient Mesh tool	Shift-click with Gradient Mesh tool
Remove mesh point	Option-click with Gradient Mesh tool	Alt-click with Gradient Mesh tool

Clipping masks

	Mac OS	Windows
Clipping Mask > Make	Command-7	Ctrl-7
Clipping Mask > Release	Command-Option-7	Ctrl-Alt-7

Transparency palette

	Mac OS	Windows
View only opacity mask in mask edit mode	Option-click mask thumbnail	Alt-click mask thumbnail
Disable opacity mask	Shift-click mask thumbnail	Shift-click mask thumbnail

Effects

	Mac OS	Windows
Apply Last Effect	Command-Shift-E	Ctrl-Shift-E
Last Effect (reopen last effect dialog box)	Command-Option-Shift-E	Ctrl-Alt-Shift-E

Appearances

	Mac OS	Windows
Add new fill	Command-/	Ctrl-/
Add new stroke	Command-Option-/	Ctrl-Alt-/
Sample style and append appearance of selected object	Option-Shift-click with Eyedropper	Alt-Shift-click with Eyedropper

Filters

	Mac OS	Windows
Apply Last Filter	Command-E	Ctrl-E
Last Filter (reopen last filter dialog box)	Command-Option-E	Ctrl-Alt-E

Precision Tools

	Mac OS	Windows
Show/Hide Rulers	Command-R	Ctrl-R
Show/Hide Guides	Command- ;	Ctrl- ;
Make Guides	Command-5	Ctrl-5

Keyboard Shortcuts

Keyboard Shortcuts

	Mac OS	Windows
Release Guides	Click selection square on Layers palette, then Command-Option-5	Click selection square on Layers palette, then Ctrl-Alt-5
Release a guide	Command-Shift-double-click guide	Ctrl-Shift-double-click guide
Convert guide between horizontal/vertical orientation	Option-drag new guide	Alt-drag new guide
Lock/Unlock Guides	Command-Option-;	Ctrl-Alt-;
Show/Hide Grid	Command-"	Ctrl-"
Snap To Grid	Command-Shift-"	Ctrl-Shift-"
Snap To Point (Pixel Preview off); Snap To Pixel (Pixel Preview on)	Command-Option-"	Ctrl-Alt-"
Smart Guides	Command-U	Ctrl-U
Constrain Measure tool to multiple of 45°	Shift-drag with tool	Shift-drag with tool

Preferences

	Mac OS	Windows
General Preferences dialog box	Command-K	Ctrl-K

Export/Print

	Mac OS	Windows
Save for Web	Command-Option-Shift-S	Ctrl-Alt-Shift-S
Page Setup/Print Setup dialog box	Command-Shift-P	Ctrl-Shift-P
Print dialog box	Command-P	Ctrl-P
Show/Hide Info	F-8	F-8

Shortcuts/Help

	Mac OS	Windows
Keyboard Shortcuts dialog box	Command-Option-Shift-K	Ctrl-Alt-Shift-K
Illustrator Help (online)	Command-Shift-?	F1

Reset keyset

To **reset** the keyboard shortcuts in the Keyboard Shortcuts dialog box at any time, Option-click/ Alt-click the Cancel (Reset) button.

Customizing shortcuts *new*

Illustrator 9 introduces the capability to assign your own shortcuts to commands and tools. Shortcuts are organized into keysets. You can create your own keysets in addition to the Illustrator Factory Defaults keyset.

To assign your own shortcuts:

1. Choose Edit menu > Keyboard Shortcuts (Command-Option-Shift-K/ Ctrl-Alt-Shift-K).

2. To edit an existing keyset (set of short-cuts), choose a keyset name from the Set pop-up menu (■, next page). To create a new keyset, ignore this step (you'll create one later).

3. Choose Menu Commands or Tools from the next pop-up menu.

4. Click the command or tool name to which you want to assign a shortcut.

5. Press the shortcut key, then click on a blank area of the dialog box.

   If that key is already assigned to another command or tool, an alert message will appear in the dialog box, and the short-cut will be removed from the previous command or tool. To assign a new short-cut to the command or tool from which you just removed a shortcut, click Go To, then press a shortcut.
   or
   If you change your mind, click Undo in the dialog box. The shortcut will be reas-signed to its original command or tool. To clear a shortcut altogether, click Clear.

6. *Optional:* In the Symbol column, enter the keyboard symbol you want to appear on the menu or tool tip for the command or tool.

7. Repeat steps 4–6 for any other shortcuts you want to assign.

8. As soon as one user-defined shortcut is entered in the dialog box, the word "Custom" appears on the Set pop-up menu. To create a new keyset to include your new shortcuts, click Save, type a

(Continued on the following page)

Customizing Shortcuts

name for the new keyset, click OK, then click OK again to exit the dialog box. The new keyset name will appear on the Set pop-up menu.
or
To save your changes to the currently chosen keyset, click OK.

To choose, delete, or print a keyset:

1. Choose Edit menu > Keyboard Shortcuts (Command-Option-Shift-K/ Ctrl-Alt-Shift-K).

2. Choose a keyset from the Set pop-up menu.

3. To use the chosen keyset, click OK.
   or
   To delete the chosen keyset, click Delete, then click OK.
   or
   To print the chosen keyset, click Export Text, type a name for the keyset, click Save, then click OK to exit the dialog box. Open the new SimpleText (Mac OS)/ Notepad (Win) file and print it.

		Shortcut	Symbol
▶	Selection	V	V
▷	Direct Selection	A	A
▷⁺	Group Selection		
⊕	Lasso	Y	Y
⊕	Direct Lasso	Q	Q
✎	Pen	P	P
✎⁺	Add Anchor Point	=	+
✎⁻	Delete Anchor Point	-	-
⌐	Convert Anchor Point	⇧C	C
T	Type	T	T
⤳	Path Type		
⊞	Area Type		
IT	Vertical Type		
⤳	Vertical Path Type		

OK

Cancel

Save...

Delete...

Export Text...

Set: [Custom]

Tools

Keyboard Shortcuts

Redo

Clear

Go To

INDEX

Index

Index

L

M

Mac OS
 dialog boxes, 12
 and file exporting, 403
 Files & Clipboard preferences, 390, 403
 Illustrator screen, 4–5
 keyboard shortcuts, 457–466
 monitor calibration, 421–423
 and printing, 393, 399
 Save dialog box, 42
 starting program on, 35
 Startup file, 381
Mac OS Finder, 238
macro. *See* action; Actions palette.
Macromedia Flash, 187, 409–410
Macromedia FreeHand, 27
magnification. *See* Zoom tool.
Make Blend command, 95, 96. *See also*
 Blend tool.
Make Clipping Mask button, 316
Make Compound Path command, 267
Make Crop Marks command, 394
Make Guides command, 361
Make Opacity Mask command, 329, 330
marquee selection, 72
mask, 316–320. *See also* opacity mask.
 adding object to, 317
 arranging objects for, 316
 locking, 318
 and printing problems, 398
 purpose of, 316
 recoloring, 320
 releasing, 319
 removing object from, 320
 restacking objects in, 318
 selecting clipping path for, 317
masking object, 73, 316. *See also* opacity mask.
Masks command, 73
Matchprint proof, 432
Measure tool, 370
measurement, units of, 25, 385
memory, 56, 389
menus, 10–11, 26. *See also* specific menus.
Merge command, 273
Merge Selected command, 189
Merge Styles command, 305
Merge Swatches command, 144
merging layers, 190
mesh line, 282, 286, 287
mesh object, 282, 283
mesh patch, 282, 285
mesh point, 282, 285, 286–287
metafile formats, 411

Microsoft Word, importing type from, 200
millimeters, 25
mini-glossary, 8–9
Minimum Undo Levels setting, Units & Undo
 preferences, 385
Minus Back command, 272
Minus Front command, 268, 271, 272, 398
mirror image, 93. *See also* Reflect tool.
Misspelled Words list, 222
mistakes, undoing, 26, 31, 385
Miter Join button, Stroke palette, 138
Miter Limit setting, for stroke, 138
Miter style, Offset Path, 82
Mix commands, 147, 335–336, 336
mixing colors, 127, 129, 130, 131. *See also* Color
 palette.
MM Design palette, 16, 210
MM fonts. *See* Multiple Master fonts.
monitor
 calibrating, 125, 421–423
 color considerations, 129
Monitor RGB work space setting, 424
Move dialog box, 365
moving
 actions commands, 377–378
 anchor points, 77, 104
 appearance attributes, 291, 301
 brushes, 254
 endpoints, 120
 illustrations, 57–58
 layers, 186
 objects, 75–77, 174, 188, 365–367
 opacity mask, 332
 ruler origin guides, 359–360
 swatches, 143
 type, 203
Multiple Master fonts
 and Find Font command, 224
 and Horizontal/Vertical Scale commands, 216
 and MM Design palette, 210
Multiple Masters Design palette. *See* MM Design
 palette.
multiple undos, 26, 31
Multiply blending mode, 323

N

naming
 actions, 379
 brushes, 254, 258, 261
 gradients, 278
 layers, 165, 166, 180
 objects, 164

Index

Index

Index